FIRE IN THE
CRUCIBLE

D1530816

FIRE IN THE CRUCIBLE

CRUCIBLE

The Self-Creation
of Creativity
and Genius

JOHN BRIGGS

JEREMY P. TARCHER, INC.
Los Angeles

The publisher gratefully acknowledges the following sources for permission to reprint. Figure 1 is here reprinted by permission of Lillian Schwartz. Figures 2 and 3 are here reprinted by permission of the Syndics of Cambridge University Library. Figure 4 is here reprinted by permission of the U.S. Department of the Interior. Figure 5 is here reprinted by permission of Monica McGoldrick and Randy Gerson. Figures 6, 7, and 8 are here reprinted by permission of the Museo Nationale del Prado and the Artists' Rights Society of New York. Figures 9 and 10 are here reprinted by permission of Pilobolus Dance Theatre.

Library of Congress Cataloging in Publication Data

Briggs, John.
  Fire in the crucible: the self-creation of creativity and genius/John Briggs.
    p.   cm.
  Reprint. Originally published: New York: St. Martin's Press, 1988
  1. Genius.   2. Creative ability.   I. Title.
BF412.B824   1990   89-38314
153.3'5—dc20   CIP
ISBN 0-87477-547-7

Copyright © 1990 by John Briggs

All rights reserved. No part of this work may be reproduced or transmitted in any form by any means, electronic or mechanical, including photocopying and recording, or by any information storage or retrieval system, except as may be expressly permitted by the 1976 Copyright Act or in writing by the publisher.
Requests for such permissions should be addressed to:

Jeremy P. Tarcher, Inc.
5858 Wilshire Blvd., Suite 200
Los Angeles, CA 90036

Distributed by St. Martin's Press, New York

Design by Karin Batten

Manufactured in the United States of America
10 9 8 7 6 5 4 3 2 1

First Edition

For my mother and father

CONTENTS

ACKNOWLEDGMENTS

A heartfelt thanks to all those I interviewed for this book. I'm grateful not only for the time and enlightenment they offered but especially for their extending themselves to help me explore my particular angle on creativity. Many also extended themselves further to review the text for misperceptions and errors.

Deep thanks as well to the following: Muriel Briggs for her penetrating review of the psychological aspects of the Emily Dickinson literature; Mark Hussey of Pace University for his trenchant general critique of the manuscript and for his special critique of its Virginia Woolf material; Joe McLaren of Mercy College for his reading of the Ellington, Toomer, and Hughes material; Lynn Goldsmith of the MIT Career Development Project, and giftedness teacher Tonia Grote for the challenging and extremely useful comments they made of the draft text; Frank McClusky of Mercy College for his close, honest, incisive, and humorous readings; Joseph Lauinger of Mercy College for his ever-alert eye and sympathetic mind during his review of the text; Signe Hammer of the late *Science Digest* for incentive to make initial contact with several of the creativity researchers reported on here; Peter Senge of the Sloan School, MIT, for his help in clarifying several issues about systems thinking, an approach that as I wrote this book became increasingly formative; composer Stephen Dydo for his always keen observations about the process of composition; Jerry Monaco for his help on Orson Welles; Hal Bowser for his sage editorial advice; Debbie Posner for her heroic job of copyediting; Judy Willington for her generous help in the process of proofreading; St. Martin's executive editor Tom Dunne for waiting patiently while the scope of this book expanded frighteningly beyond its deadline; my agent Adele Leone for her continuous encouragement during dark months; my wife

Joanna for much more than I can say, and last but not least, the members of my classes at the New School for Social Research who over the years have provided an unending source of inspiration through their insights and enthusiasms about the subject of creativity.

A NOTE ON GENDER

The historical development of the English language has yet to produce a gender-neutral third-person singular pronoun. This poses a problem for an author. I have addressed it in three ways: by trying to write sentences so as to avoid the use of the singular third-person pronoun; by using the neologism "(s)he" in the nominative case; and by occasionally using the technically incorrect plural "their" in place of "his" and "him."

PROLOGUE

This book about the roots of genius is essentially a book about the roots of creativity. In researching the one, we research the other. More important, in researching genius, we are researching ourselves. In the pages that follow the reader will scrutinize the workings of some of history's most remarkable minds. The question is: Are these minds like our own or are they in some respects so vastly different they should qualify as another species?

The question is far from academic. In asking about creativity we are really asking about what is best, what is deepest in life. Perhaps most of us would say we do as well as anybody at living deeply. But we see the genius seems to do it better. Through a science or an artform—through creativity—the individual genius seems to live at the exhilarating edge of what it means to have our human mind. How did the genius come to that edge? Are geniuses born or made?

It would be easy to think that they're born. If so, we could excuse our own failures of creativity. On the other hand, it would be more comfortingly egalitarian to think that geniuses are made, and that with the right kind of effort or environment anyone can be a genius.

In the pages that follow we will discover the curious fact that geniuses are not born, nor are they made. We may all have in us intuitions and perceptions that could take us to the deepest place that genius inhabits. But can we access these intuitions? And how? The study of genius may tell us.

Confrontation with genius thus forces us to acknowledge the originative power of life, which we may and commonly do neglect. . . .

—MICHAEL POLANYI, *Personal Knowledge*

The way in which Leonardo or Newton were unlike other people is precisely what they are known and remembered for.

—DORIS WALLACE, "Giftedness and the Construction of a Creative Life"

INTRODUCTION

Smoke from the Fire

A PARABLE

Picture the medieval alchemist in a flickering chamber of arches and icons. Retorts bubble an intoxicating, noxious steam. Beakers swirl with strange colored fluids and precipitating crystals. In the center of a table littered with pipets, measuring weights, and brass plates of herbs is an ovoid vessel, the alembic or "philosopher's egg." This sealed crucible is the focus of his work. There is the air of the wizard about him but also that of the scientist. Reason inhabits the room and something other than reason—a vast mystery which he is trying to draw down into his alembic.

We are told that this adept is not, as has been popularly supposed, devoting his energies to the untenable commercial fantasy of transforming lead into gold. His project is much more incredible. He is trying to fabricate the *prima materia*, the First Matter, that ethereal protoplasmic substance out of which all other substances are born.

By some ancient accounts, this substance will precipitate in the alembic as a red stone, called variously the Bird of Hermes, the elixir of life, the philosopher's stone, the sophic fire and a score of other names. It is this fire in the crucible the adept seeks. With it, the ancients have told him, he may perform miraculous transmutations. The cold red stone of infinite energy has been likened to a cornucopia, to a seed crystal for matter, and to the powers by which Christ produced the loaves

3

and fishes for the multitudes. Not the least of its powers is its ability to bestow immortality on its possessor.

Perhaps this last power is the reason certain esoteric accounts suggest that the real, the ultimate, object of the alchemist is to transform *himself* into the philosopher's stone. These ancient texts insist that the adept is simultaneously the crucible and the fire, the lead and its resulting gold, and they stress that his process, too, is riddled with paradox. For example, his alchemistry involves an expansion yet negation of his knowledge. Also, virtually all reports agree that while the apprentice alchemist should consider himself as a part of a long tradition of brethren, he must puzzle out the Hermetic secret for himself. In order to do that he requires (another paradox) both daring and patience.

As the following chapters will illustrate, the above description of the alchemist could also apply to the creative genius. The possibly mythical quest of the alchemist to find the root of matter is a metaphor for the literal quest of a Darwin, Einstein, Bohr or Watson to disclose the essence of natural law; of a Picasso, da Vinci or van Gogh to express the essences of form and color; of a Shakespeare, Dickinson, or Woolf to name the secrets of the human spirit. Like the alchemist seeking to turn himself into an immortal philosopher's stone, the genius seeks to become the immortal source of creativity.

The alchemy metaphor has several appeals. For example, alchemy is generally credited as early chemistry. Newton dabbled in alchemy, as did Francis Bacon, the reputed founder of the scientific method. At the same time, alchemy was magic. Indeed, the science and magic of alchemy are inextricable. For example, a number of creditable scholars contend that Newton's belief in the alchemical principle of sympathetic forces led directly to his formulation of the law of gravity.

Thus, in its duality as science and magic, the alchemy metaphor can illustrate what might be called the "lucid" and "opaque" sides of contemporary creativity research, the research that sheds the most light on the extraordinary powers of genius. On the lucid side, there is the fact that a surprising amount of creative process has become accessible to the instruments of science and reason—and perhaps in the future, no aspect of it will remain totally beyond their reach. On the opaque side is not so much a fact as an observation: that every probe into the creative realm seems to become infused with a magic and mystery which seem to infuse the probe with a glow. The scientists interviewed for this book are, for example, probably as lucid as any human beings can be about creativity, yet inevitably in their words and gestures a glimmer of the opacity appears.

The Hermetic ideal that the alchemist, his devices, his process and his product are all inseparable, dynamic and interwovenly circular also makes the alchemy metaphor a particularly apt one for creative genius. How great creators work, why they work as they do, the way creative techniques and talents appear, and the flowering of a particular creation—all are one movement, not a matter of stages and elements. It's not a smooth movement by any means; indeed it's often extremely turbulent and turbid, but it has wholeness. The alchemistry metaphor serves nicely as a reminder of this wholeness. One particularly delightful instance of the reminder lies in the felicitous phrase *magnum opus*. So often applied to superior creative productions, the term originally was alchemic, referring both to the final product of the hierophant's activity, the philosopher's stone, and to the ongoing alchemical activity that created the stone.

Felicities and Newton's alchemy notwithstanding, however, by using this metaphor I am neither affirming nor denying any of the claims of alchemy as such. Also, in an actual (as opposed to a metaphorical) sense it should be kept in mind that geniuses are quite unlike alchemists. For one thing, the esoteric tradition asserts that any alchemist who had succeeded in concocting or discovering the *prima materia* would be totally enlightened, a kind of bodhisattva or saint. Very few geniuses have exhibited anything close to spiritual enlightenment, aside from their work. Another difference is more germane. Unlike the alchemists who vanished historically into their enlightenment or their ashes, the great geniuses have left their philosopher's stones, the fruits of their alchemic process, behind them. These treasures are hoarded in museums and recorded in history books. They are the discoveries and the works we consider the high points of our civilization.

SOME PREJUDICES AND PREMISES

Every author has them. Most of mine probably stem from a career-long devotion to aesthetics. W. H. Auden used to say that when he didn't want to talk to people near him on an airplane, he simply told them he was a medievalist. Telling someone you're an aesthetician can elicit a similar reaction. Simply stated, my interest as an aesthetician has been on the way creative things like paintings, poems and scientific theories are put together and how and why they affect people. How do certain works—the works of genius—embody "truth," "beauty" and "universality"? It is an interest that has naturally formed a bias to this book's approach to the quite different set of issues: What, in fact, makes for a creative genius? What are the roots of the creative enterprise? How does genius evolve?

The volume of literature on creativity and genius is mind-boggling, evidencing the great scholarly and popular fascination with the topic. Even a modest hometown library is likely to contain a shelf or two on creativity, ranging from self-help books on harnessing one's own creative powers to the standard tomes on creative process like Rollo May's *The Courage to Create* and Arthur Koestler's *The Act of Creation.* In addition, there are hundreds of biographies on geniuses in every field. Because of my bias, in reading this literature and in interviewing researchers I inclined toward information and insights that could illuminate the motivations, talents and processes that lead a creator to the creation of a truthful, beautiful and universal object. My bias was also spurred by a desire to make sense of a tangle of contradictions that have plagued the traditional explorations of genius. To mention a few:

- Some geniuses have brilliant childhoods. At six German prodigy Karl Friedrich Gauss raised his hand almost at once when his teacher asked the class to add up all the numbers from one to ten. He explained that he had immediately seen the answer and discovered a formula that would solve all similar problems. Stories of geniuses who started out as prodigies abound. But genius is not always quick to emerge. Einstein didn't talk until he was three, and he failed his admissions exams in science at the Zurich Polytechnic. Joseph Conrad didn't begin writing fiction until he was thirty-one. Jazz musician Duke Ellington showed little promise until he was nearly thirty and didn't start doing his best work until he was forty. Balzac, Darwin, Mendel, Tolstoy, Rembrandt, Titian, Turgenev, Faulkner—all were relatively undistinguished in their youth.

- Some geniuses seem able to create extremely quickly. Mozart spilled the overture to *Don Giovanni* straight from his brain onto the page in the few hours before the premiere. Tiepolo painted the *Twelve Apostles* in ten hours; the great twentieth-century mathematician John Von Neumann could sometimes puzzle out an abstruse problem in a matter of seconds. Opposing this picture is Beethoven, who literally worked on some of his compositions for years; Darwin, who took almost two decades to write *On the Origin of Species;* and Flaubert, who was wont to spend an entire exhausting day on a single sentence.

- The image of genius as full of conceit and megalomania has plenty of support in cases like Hemingway, who seemed to tout his masculinity and writing skills at every opportunity; great scientists like Newton or Watson can be fantastically ambitious and concerned with their reputations. Yet Einstein's humble nature was legendary, and virtually everybody who ever met the writer Jorge Luis Borges was impressed by his genuine humility and self-effacement.

- Some geniuses are "omnibus," to borrow a term employed by Tufts psychologist David Feldman, that is, multitalented or multiperceptive. William Herschel, discoverer of Uranus, was by profession an orchestra conductor; da Vinci, prototype of the Renaissance man, was as proficient in science and architecture as he was at art. But most creators are brilliant in only one field.

- Some geniuses have distinguished forebears, lending credence to the idea of inherited traits or, at the least, of the mighty influence of their intellectual environment. Darwin's grandfather, Erasmus, was a famous biologist; Margaret Mead's parents were both distinguished academics. Other geniuses, however, have sprung from the genetic and cultural shadows. Shakespeare (unless you believe the chauvinist claims for Francis Bacon), Newton and Einstein all set forth from unprominent backgrounds.
- The popular romantic image of the genius as neurotic, even psychopathic, is not without foundation. There are plenty of examples of mental illness in genius to point to: van Gogh and Virginia Woolf driven by their interior demons to suicide; inventor Nikola Tesla regularly dining alone and obsessively polishing all the silverware and china on his table at the Waldorf-Astoria. Yet the accounts of Niels Bohr, Einstein and Louise Nevelson show that great creators can also lead mentally balanced and "normal" lives.

Such apparent contradictions cast doubt upon large blocks of the creativity and genius books on the shelves of the library because most of the approaches that have been taken to explain high-level creativity are reductionistic. They are attempts to squeeze the whole of genius down into a simple cluster of traits or mental attributes. A reductionist approach treats the human mind as if it were a computer whose complexity may be explained by the logic of the computer language and the on-and-off status of the electromagnetic switches. But the mind is not a computer and during the past few years a growing number of scientists and philosophers of science have pointed out the serious problems inherent in this view that the universe is fundamentally mechanical and reducible. In the study of genius the drawbacks of reductionism seem especially huge. Saying that creativity is at bottom a compensation for psychological inadequacy, a function of manic depressive illness, dependent on IQ, right hemispheric dominance, a skill at problem solving or the ability to perform a certain kind of thinking is not just to miss something about the process, it is to miss everything. Everything that is important to the creator, everything important to the culture that treasures a creator's work. It is to miss the very smile of Mona Lisa. Creators create in order to find some truth about life and we value them precisely because we see that they have found it and have bequeathed to us their mind-altering vision.

Curiously, the notion that a great genius possesses "vision" is usually slipped into even the most reductionist discussions of creativity—an element assumed but not defined, vital but almost totally ignored. "Truth," however, is a word seldom used by creativity theorists—though it is not uncommonly found in statements by creators. Perhaps modern researchers are a little shy of talking about truth because it reeks of metaphysics, and science presumably left metaphysics behind when it separated itself from philosophy. Indeed, it's a little hard to imagine that you could say much scientifically about a person's intimate sensations of truth.

Nevertheless, the obvious fact is that the lives of great creators are importantly motivated or guided by some quest for truth, some vision, some inner spirit, like the voice of Socrates' daemon, which he consulted when he was worried about going off in the wrong direction. Joseph Conrad called it "the inward voice that decides." Such a view of genius is contained in the Latin origins of the word, *genius,* which meant a god or demon who presided over a person's birth and destiny.

The sense of an "inward voice" seems related to the reverence most creators have for the mysterious and even mystical side of their creative activity. Evelyn Fox Keller, biographer of Nobel prize-winning geneticist Barbara McClintock, says that mysticism "plays an essential role in the process of scientific discovery. Einstein called it 'cosmic religiosity.' "

In the arts, creators frequently speak of a mysticism and mystery that permeate the creative process. A statement by

Hemingway is typical: ". . . There is a mystery in all great writing and that mystery does not dis-sect out. It continues and it is always valid. Each time you re-read you see or learn something new."

Vision and truth are somehow entangled in such amorphous mystical perceptions, but in what way? The question is not about whether there is "truth" to mystical claims—such a question could never be settled—but about the nature of the role of the mystic state of mind in the creative process, its relation to vision. What *is* vision? Is it some single truth held by the creator? A feeling? How are all the complex processes involved in the development of a creator and in the creation of any particular work connected to creative vision and the quest for truth? Has anyone studied these things scientifically?

SOURCES

In looking for answers to these questions I explored the findings and speculations of a diverse cadre of researchers. Several, including Gerald Holton, Monica McGoldrick, David Feldman, Doris Wallace, Howard Gruber, David Perkins, Reese Jenkins, Mihalyi Csikszentmihalyi and Albert Rothenberg are a new breed of investigator using multiple techniques—interviews, self-reports, notebooks, and letters—to peer into the creative mind. Others, like Howard Gardner, William Gray, Paul LaViolette, Matti Bergström, Gerald Edelman and Charles Laughlin are molding observations in neuroanatomy and psychology into new theories of the brain and its extraordinary capacities. Still others, like Maurice Wilkins, a Nobel laureate in biology, and physicist David Bohm are exceptional creators who have themselves become interested in creativity as a subject of study. Together, these and other scientists represent an impressive convergence of fields: psychology, brain science, systems theory, cybernetics, the history of science and technology, historiometry, psychiatry, physics, biology.

Most of the above researchers I was able to meet with

personally. Though often the investigations they were pursuing did not deal directly with the questions I was asking, all I spoke to were kind enough to help me probe the implications of their findings for the puzzle of creative vision and its role in the alchemy of genius. The reader should not, however, hold them responsible for this attempt to make a synthesis of their work. Aside from interviews with researchers, the major sources for *Fire in the Crucible* were biographies, autobiographies and observations about creativity made by creators themselves. Certain problems that are inherent in these sources should be noted.

Geniuses, like other people, tend to load their reflections about their own experience with assumptions that give a distorted or idealized picture. Biographers, too, are caught in assumptions and sometimes in myths about their subjects. Not infrequently they are also tripped up by faulty data. For every interpretation by a biographer there exists a potential counterinterpretation by another biographer; for every fact there may lurk an as yet undiscovered fact that could dramatically change the meaning of a biographical statement or event.

A possible safeguard against such a swarm of uncertainties might be to cross-check several biographies of geniuses against each other. Or, better, to deal only with original sources. Several of the researchers I interviewed use this method, immersing themselves for years in the biographical materials of a single creator. For obvious practical reasons neither the extensive cross-checking nor the in-depth approach was feasible for dealing with the wide range of geniuses I'd chosen to discuss here.

But the disadvantages of a wide-scale approach are negated to some extent by an advantage that comes from sampling the biographies of geniuses representing many time periods and creative professions. Such a sampling allows a cross-checking among statements by and about highly creative persons to see what there is in common.

The organization of this book reflects the sampling approach.

Throughout I've kaleidoscoped together the lives and

thoughts of a broad variety of geniuses in order to emphasize the underlying unities of creative process. To further highlight these unities, the book returns frequently to the processes of two geniuses—Albert Einstein and Virginia Woolf. No doubt my attraction to Woolf and Einstein—particularly to Woolf— has much to do with their wonderful eloquence about the subtle aspects of how creative works unfold.

To catch the different dimensions of that holistic unfolding, this book has been organized into three parts. Part 1 asks, What is creative vision and where does it come from? Part 2 discusses the standard equipment of genius such as talent, the ability to think profitably by means of contradictions, comparisons or images, and the necessity of the creator to interact with the forces of history. This part ends with a chapter considering whether a touch of madness is also a necessary part of the creative equipment. Part 3 traces some of the key movements involved in the lifelong process to create a particular work that shows genius, a *magnum opus.*

GENIUS PRELIMINARILY DEFINED

But at this point the reader may begin to wonder just what is meant by the term "genius." It's often a loosely used word. Here is the starting point.

The geniuses discussed in this book are, for the most part, women and men who have altered in some significant way our perception of a major field of human endeavor. The number of fields they represent, however, is restricted here to those usually covered by the concept of creativity: science, invention, the plastic, musical and literary arts. In the case of the arts, significantly altering a field means leaving an indelible impression of vision. Nearly everyone has a feel for the distinctiveness of Melville, Cézanne, or Brahms. These artists brought new perceptions to the world through their artforms.

The reader will probably accept that most of the illustrious people used as examples here were (or are) geniuses. But there may be a few that the reader will object to. This is fitting because any overall picture of genius must also include the fact that some part of genius lies in the beholder's eye.

There is some interest among creativity scientists these days in the concept of a "moral giftedness" and surely Gandhi, Martin Luther King, Jr., and Krishnamurti would fit a definition of genius in this sense. The problem is that at this point there isn't enough known about these types of creativity to see how they fit or whether they fit what we know about the traditionally recognized fields of creative activity.

Not included here are geniuses in fields like politics and sports. Machiavelli, Queen Elizabeth I and John Kennedy; Wilma Rudolph; Babe Ruth and Bill Russell certainly had profound effects on their respective fields—but was it genius? Possibly, but here, again, we don't know enough at this point about the nature of creativity in these fields to decide.

Another important aspect of definition: psychologist David Perkins, codirector of Harvard's Project Zero and author of *The Mind's Best Work,* has cautioned that creativity shouldn't be defined as a single faculty but as a "combination of ingredients." The warning is sound. Genius is a mix—another reason to favor the alchemical metaphor. Vision is only one of the ingredients.

A major objective of this book is to show how the combination of these ingredients—including such elements as vision, talent, absorption, courage, even history—together form a whole, integral process, a single gem: a fluid gem in this case. A second major objective will be to show why each gem (or genius) is a lens for the universal and yet is necessarily unique.

The book also aims to review the fascinating new research being done into creativity, and to expose a number of myths about creative genius, among them: the myth of inspiration, the myth of the lone creator, the myth that creators are motivated by the desire to make something new, the myth that creativity is primarily an unconscious process, the new myth that it's primarily a conscious one, and, finally, the growing myth that intelligence and creativity may one day be duplicated in a machine.

INTERROGATOR: Pardon me, Mr. Author, this document you're composing, is it a theory about creative genius?

MUSING AUTHOR: Not really. Perkins has also made a good point about that when he notes there are basically two kinds of work in the field of creativity that are useful. The first is research conducted according to scientific protocols. The second is what he calls a "construal" of the data. A construal isn't necessarily testable itself but can give a useful orientation into what is going on. So to answer your question, this book is not a theory but a try for a good construal.

INTER: Humph. Well, construe if you will, but I'll be keeping my eye on you.

I should explain that this curious fellow is either an alter ego or some scalawag fragment of mind left over from the time of the alchemists (actual) whom I discovered while lurking about in the shadows of the alchemists' dens (metaphorical). His ostensible task will be to pop up from time to time to interrogate us on the sticky points.

PART 1

VISION AND THE *PRIMA MATERIA*

The only reality that I recognize is my reality—through the work.

—LOUISE NEVELSON

> There's a certain slant of light
> On winter afternoons
> That oppresses like
> The weight of cathedral tunes
>
> . . . Heavenly hurt it gives us
> We can find no scar,
> But internal difference
> Where the meanings are . . .

—EMILY DICKINSON

And when it is accomplished—behold!—all the truth of life is there: a moment of vision.

—JOSEPH CONRAD

Dadd has painted the vision of the act of vision, the look that looks at space in which the object looked at has been annihilated. The axe which, when it falls, will break the spell that paralyzes them, will never fall. It is an event that is always about to happen and at the same time will never happen.

Between never and always there lies in wait anxiety, with its thousand feet and its single eye.

—OCTAVIO PAZ, *The Monkey Grammarian*

. . . The *Rosarium* says: "At the end of the work the king will go forth for thee, crowned with his diadem, radiant as the sun, shining like a carbuncle . . . constant in the fire." And of the worthless *prima materia* they say: "Despise not the ash for it is the diadem of thy heart, and the ash of things that endure.

—C.G. JUNG, *Alchemical Studies*

OVERVIEW

In a little book called *A Step Ladder to Painting,* Jan Gorden suggests the vital role of vision in creativity.

Looking at any single object the spectator is easily able to decide; "Yes, that is a nice shape" (or ugly shape as the case may be). In selecting another object he can also decide; "This, too, has a nice shape." But here comes the test of artistic vision. In placing the two objects together in a group is he able to decide whether the group-shape is also nice?"

Imagine Picasso, Cézanne, Breughel and Dali contemplating, say, a tin plate and assorted fruit on a kitchen table. Clearly the vision of each artist would arrange and portray such a still life differently and render it in a way that would be immediately recognizable as the work of that creator. Each in his own fashion would make a group-shape not just "nice" but stunning—revealing something unexpectedly profound.

The ability of someone to choose and arrange the details of their creative field guided by a vision is a major hallmark of a genius. In the case of a great painter, the vision directs which features of an object to paint or not to paint, which angles to take things from, which shapes and perspectives and colors to mix. Vision guides a great scientist fatefully toward those problems whose solution will eventually shatter the conventional wisdom of the day. Vision seems to make it possible for the creator to see things freshly and more deeply, not just by some clever permutation of the previous way of looking, but by coming up with a new way of looking. Philosopher Edward von Hartmann observed, "Millions stare at the same phenomenon, and one genius finally grasps the concept." The well-known theoretical chemist and philosopher of science Michael Polanyi said: ". . . The vision of a hidden reality, which guides a scientist in his quest, is a dynamic force. At the end of the quest the vision is becalmed in the contemplation of the reality revealed by a discovery. . . ." And Virginia Woolf says in *A Room of One's Own* that the artist's chief task is to find a hidden reality and communicate it to her readers.

Confronted by the shapes on the kitchen table, most of us would be left flat. We wouldn't know where to start arranging and ordering such details. We would probably conclude we had no vision. Does that mean that only great geniuses have unique and significant visions? Probably not. The word "vision" is a metaphor of seeing, perception—and, as the research in the next chapters will indicate, it's plausible to maintain that because each of us is different, each is endowed by those differences with a special sensitivity to some subtle dimension of reality that others overlook. And why not? After all, the universe itself is infinitely subtle, as a review of the staggering catalogue of discoveries and perceptions recorded in the history of science and the arts would suggest. Probably from time to time nearly everyone has felt the rise of their unique vision into awareness—as nuances, as uncanny moments, as a fleetingly strong sense that a mix of different contours and feelings one has about the world must somehow go together. These instants of vision are extremely tacit. They are sensations we have no words or forms for and which other people don't seem to experience, or at least don't experience in quite the way we do.

But, of course, we're not committed to those elusive perceptions the way the genius is. For the genius such fugitive sensations of what Polanyi called a "hidden reality" are everything. They are—or become at some turning point in the creator's life—more important than family or money or security, even fame. While for the rest of us our unique mix of subtle perceptions, our vision, becomes submerged and fragmented, carried along by the way the consensual world perceives things, the genius is able to make a concrete discovery or history-shaking work because (s)he *develops* the vision within the confines of some creative field. There, as in a secret laboratory, (s)he works like the ancient alchemist to distill and further distill that vision until it condenses, coalesces and emerges in a miraculous and powerful form. As psychologist Howard Gardner observes: "[The creator] must feel compelled to express [his] vision, over and over again, within the symbolic medium of his choice. He must be willing to live with uncertainty, to risk failure and opprobrium, to return time and again to his project until he satisfies his own exacting standards, while speaking with potency to others."

This could equally be a description of the alchemist's quest for the *prima materia.*

According to alchemic tradition, the *prima materia* or true state of matter is produced by taking as raw material some compound of common matter and gradually distilling or "improving" it. In the arcana of the Hermetics, there is a debate about what that proper raw matter is, and some adepts have argued that it could in fact be anything because at the root of all things lies the *prima materia.* For the creator the raw material, the "anything" are the tacit sensations of vision. In themselves those sensations are perhaps no more extraordinary than anyone else's, but creators concentrate their fire on them. Both creators and the alchemists are materialists at heart, but of a special kind. They crave possession of a material or *objective* form (a scientific law, a painting, a concerto—a philosopher's stone) to capture something exquisitely nonmaterial like a truth or subtle perception. Alchemists claimed that the process of distilling the raw material into *prima materia* releases a spark of life. The spark is a return to "inspiration," that is, the vibration breathed into all diverse things at the first creation.

Richard Cavendish, a modern scholar of Hermetic texts, observes that alchemy "is based on the belief that the universe is a unity. The alchemists found a principle of unity and order in a substance called First Matter, which remains unchanged behind all diversity. First Matter is not matter in any normal sense of the term, but the possibility of matter." The First Matter for a creator is the distillation of vision.

Once the crystal gleam of First Matter has been distilled, and its spark of life released, First Matter and spark are then recombined into a philosopher's stone (genius) from which new and amazing properties emerge. The *prima materia* (vision) now possesses the ability to produce new elements, convey immortality and ascend to the power of what alchemists call "multiplication or augmentation," i.e., the ability to produce more of itself. Polanyi says of the scientific genius whose vision of a "hidden reality" has led him to a great discovery: ". . . The vision is renewed and becomes dynamic again in other scientists and guides them to new discoveries." Something similar could be said of the philosopher-stone visions of a Picasso or Brahms.

Creativity, like alchemistry, is perplexing work. There are devilish paradoxes in the process. "Circular paradoxes," they might be called: The distiller is the very thing distilled. The creative *prima materia* (the vision) is both the object sought and its own raw material. Conceit begets humility; uncertainty, a certainty; the individual, the universal . . .

INTER (threatening, stepping out from the shadow of an arch): Hrrumph. Possibly you're not aware that the great Gothic cathedrals of our age were built on alchemic formulas. But those were more serious times. I remember the architect of one of our cathedrals used to say, "God is in the details." What evidence is there for all this expatiation about alchemistry and vision?

MUSING: I was getting to that.

INTER: Yes? You mean you have a plan?

MUSING: We do. In chapters 1, 2, and 3 we'll examine evidence for what vision is, where it comes from and what recent scientific research suggests about these matters. In chapter 4 we'll look at how vision is the creator's attempt to mirror "the whole." Then, finally, in chapters 5 and 6 we'll consider a visionary paradox that connects the everyday experience of ambivalence to the enlightenments of mystics.

1

Qualities of Mind

EINSTEIN'S COMPASS

Say the word "genius" and the name most likely to spring to mind is Albert Einstein. Einstein has become the modern symbol of genius. For good reason. By discovering the limitations or "relativity" of the venerated concepts of Newton and Descartes, he changed our perception of the structure of the universe. At age twenty-six, an obscure technician in the Swiss Patent Office, he wrote a paper that won him a Nobel prize and fired a crucial shot that brought in the quantum revolution and the atomic age. In accomplishments and aura Einstein seems Olympian, supernatural, a man of the future. Curious, then, that he should have said in 1953:

I know quite certainly that I myself have no special talent. Curiosity, obsession, and dogged endurance, combined with self-criticism, have brought me to my ideas. Especially strong thinking powers ("brain muscles") I do not have, or only to a modest degree. Many have far more of those than I without producing anything surprising.

Is this an example of Einstein's famous humility or is he pointing to something significant about the properties of high-level creativity? What lies at the bottom of Einstein's obviously extraordinary mental powers? Consider several biographical facts which demonstrate Einstein's "curiosity, obsession, and dogged endurance." Such data as this has led one creativity researcher to discern a vital secret of genius.

21

• When Einstein was five years old and ill in bed, his father brought him a magnetic compass. It was a momentous gift. Years later he remembered that he had gazed bewitched by the iron needle drawn toward north no matter which way the compass case was turned. It was "a wonder," he declared, referring to the power of this unseen field or force. "Young as I was," he said, "the remembrance of this occurrence never left me." On his seventy-fourth birthday Einstein was asked if he really thought the compass could have so strongly affected him and he replied, "I myself think so, and I believe that these outside influences had a considerable influence on my development." Then he added, "But a man has little insight into what goes on within him. When a young puppy sees a compass for the first time it may have no similar influence, nor on many a child. What does, in fact, determine the particular reaction of an individual?" In his *Autobiographical Notes* written a few years earlier he had said, "I can still remember—or at least I believe I can remember—that this experience made a deep and lasting impression on me. Something deeply hidden had to be behind things."

• When Einstein was sixteen he sent a copy of a paper on ether in the magnetic field to his uncle in Stuttgart. A short time later the boy stumbled upon a rather extraordinary paradox which carried his fascination with magnetic fields into puzzling territory.

  Scientists in the early days of this century believed that electromagnetic waves such as light and radio waves traveled through the vacuum of space in an invisible elastic medium, the ether, something akin to the way sound waves travel through air. It was also assumed that a stationary observer measuring the speed of a passing wave of light would get one value, while an observer in motion would get a different value. For example, an observer moving along in the same direction as the light wave should find the measured speed of light is slower than the speed measured by an observer traveling in the opposite direction from the light ray. What would happen, the sixteen-year-old Einstein wondered, if the observer were going the *same* speed as the light ray and in the same direction? Wouldn't the light appear to this observer as a frozen wave in the ether? The absurdity of this convinced him there was something wrong with the contemporary ideas. Thereafter the problem never left him until he'd solved it—a solution that came to be called the theory of relativity.

- Shortly after he had become a world-famous scientist, Einstein fell into a dispute with the group of physicists, which included Niels Bohr, Werner Heisenberg and Max Born, who were developing the ideas of quantum mechanics. Quantum theorists had figured out that at the microscopic level of existence, particles jump around from energy level to energy level discontinuously, that is, without following continuous paths. Bohr and Heisenberg theorized there is no way to predict exactly when any particular particle will jump; the best that can be done is to devise equations to predict accurately the statistical movement of particles. Though Einstein had contributed mightily to the founding of quantum theory with his 1905 paper on the photoelectric effect, he considered the Bohr-Heisenberg-Born formulation "incomplete" and refused to believe that there weren't some "hidden variables" that would explain away the discontinuous quantum behavior.

Einstein's stubborn resistance to an idea that nearly all other prominent physicists had come to accept as true, turned into one of the most remarkable quarrels in scientific history. Relentlessly, in international meetings of physicists and journal papers, he posed brilliant "thought experiments" to challenge the logic of quantum mechanical tenets. Each time, the opposition, usually led by Bohr, beat Einstein back.

In the late 1920s, when Erwin Schrödinger had proposed an alternative to the quantum-mechanical ideas—an alternative that seemed to give a picture of continuous movement inside the atom—Einstein wrote him enthusiastically "I am

convinced that you have made a decisive advance with your
formulation of the quantum condition, just as I am equally
convinced that the Heisenberg-Born route is off the track."
At this point Heisenberg, who had said he found the
Schrödinger theory "disgusting," made a valiant effort to
persuade Einstein to quantum mechanics. He reported: "It
was a very nice afternoon I spent with Einstein, but still
when it came to the interpretation of quantum mechanics I
could not convince him and he could not convince me. He
always said, 'Well, I agree that any experiment the results
of which can be calculated by means of quantum mechanics
will come out as you say, but such a scheme cannot be a final
description of Nature.'" Heisenberg added, "I doubt
whether the unwillingness of Einstein, Planck, von Laue,
and Schrödinger to accept [quantum-mechanical ideas as
basic] should be reduced simply to prejudices. The word
'prejudice' is too negative in this context and does not cover
the situation." It later turned out that Schrödinger's alternative, apparently continuous view was really a variation of
Heisenberg's quantum mechanics and it left the new discontinuous and statistical conception of atomic activity intact.
Schrödinger was forced to more or less side with the opposition. Einstein continued to hold out.

The debate had unhappy personal consequences for Einstein. When he'd first met Niels Bohr in the 1920s he'd felt
an incredible closeness to the Danish scientist, almost, he
said, as if they were brothers. Bohr had felt it too. But
eventually the two men were no longer speaking. Bohr and
other physicists came to treat Einstein as an eccentric, over
the hill, a man lost in his fantasies and no longer really
practicing physics. For his part, Einstein said bitterly: "The
Heisenberg-Bohr tranquilizing philosophy—or religion?—is so delicately contrived that, for the time being, it
provides a gentle pillow for the true believer from which he
cannot very easily be aroused. So let him lie there." Einstein
told a colleague that as far as the quantum revolution went,
"I may have started it, but I always regarded these ideas as

temporary. I never thought that others would take them so much more seriously than I did."

- In the last decades of his life Einstein retreated from the mainstream scientific scene and while working on refinements of relativity, tried to formulate an answer to those aspects of quantum theory he found repugnant. He called his proposal the "unified field theory." In it he hoped to show that all atomic particles and forces such as electricity and magnetism are embedded in space-time like vortexes in the seamless flowing of a stream. He was not successful in devising the mathematics for his universal field.

What do these biographical facts of one of the world's greatest geniuses tell us about vision? Gerald Holton thinks they tell us a great deal.

HIDDEN THEMES

Holton is a Harvard professor of physics and professor of the history of science. His work is contained in a gradually accumulating collection of scholarly essays in books and journals that document how great historical figures of science have arrived at their discoveries and which portray how scientific creators think. Holton, like several of the researchers I talked to, is at a special advantage in his research because his training as a physicist enables him to move about freely in the details of such historical scientific documents as lab notes, letters to colleagues and early drafts of scientific papers. From that vantage, he can follow the emergence of a particular discovery at great depth. Holton works in the area of overlap between the history of science and the psychology of scientific creativity. Perhaps his greatest contribution has been the unearthing of what seem important signposts of vision, hidden elements in scientists' creative thinking which he calls "thematic ideas."

Holton has discerned that the work of scientific creativity is shaped by clusters of presuppositions and "gut" assumptions which each scientist has about the universe. He calls these gut assumptions "themata": themes. For the most part themata are aesthetic qualities like the assumption that the universe is basically symmetrical, or the opposite assumption that it's asymmetrical. Some other themata: the conviction that the true order of things involves a hierarchy; the conviction that scientific explanations for natural phenomena must be primarily abstract and formally mathematical, or the contrasting presupposition that the explanations must be visualizable; a sense that the universe is basically a plenum (full), or the contrary view that the source of all things must lie in the void.

The cluster of themata differs from scientist to scientist, though most scientists doing what Thomas Kuhn has called "normal" science share basically the same set of underlying assumptions. Scientists who end up revolutionizing their fields appear to have a collection of themata at variance in some significant ways with the theme clusters held by most of their colleagues.

Holton says, "My guess is that there's a focusing of these ideas fairly early, in childhood. What is impressive is the stability they show over many years. Once the scientist has committed himself to one particular set of presuppositions, the set doesn't change very much." The themata are central to scientific process because they are imposed "on your observations and they often tell you which kinds of experiments to try or not to try."

Holton's themata sound like abstractions but they aren't abstractions in the usual sense. They're a concrete feel for the surrounding world. "Quite a few of the themata have a visual component," Holton says, "very often they're not even conscious." Though he terms them thematic *ideas,* they might also be called thematic *perceptions,* for convictions about symmetry or complexity, simplicity, even formalism are convictions about the way things "look" or should look. Themata also seem perceptual in the sense that they act like special sense organs, attuning the scientist to certain subtle facets of nature. Einstein said of his march toward relativity theory: "During all those years there was a feeling of direction, of going straight toward something concrete. It is, of course, very hard to express that feeling in words . . . but I have it in a kind of survey, in a way visually."

Holton believes that that "direction" Einstein felt, his vision, had something to do with the compass story and a very early commitment to the theme of the "continuum," or "field." This sense that the "something deeply hidden" in reality must be a form of continuum, like the magnetic continuum that held the compass needle, guided Einstein in his later work as a physicist. But, that wasn't all. For, as the boy had gazed at the amazing instrument that his father had brought to his sickbed, another primitive presupposition must also have been awakened, Holton believes. Perhaps the constancy of the needle that always points north convinced Einstein that there must be a fundamental "invariance" in nature. Significantly, Einstein first called his theory of special relativity *"Invarianten Theorie."*

WHERE THE NEEDLE POINTED

On his seventy-fourth birthday Einstein wondered what "determine[s] the particular reaction of an individual," why he should have been taken so powerfully with the compass and another child not. It is altogether too easy to impose our interpretations on the childhood memories of great creators. Speculation is possible but certainty remains elusive. For that reason Holton is careful when he offers the speculation that some of Einstein's themata, such as the themes of continuum and invariance, might be connected to an early religious obsession.

Though Einstein's parents were nonreligious, their son became so enthralled by religious sentiments that he managed to compel his reluctant elders to keep a kosher house. His fervor, according to his autobiography, went through an abrupt deflation when he was twelve and realized after reading popular science books that many things in the biblical stories could not be true. "The consequence," Einstein wrote, "was a positively fantastic [orgy of] freethinking coupled with the impression that youth is intentionally being deceived by the state through lies; it was a crushing impression. Suspicion against every kind of authority grew out of this experience. . . . It is quite clear to me that the religious paradise of youth, which was thus lost, was a first attempt to free myself from the chains of the 'merely personal.' " In another context he explained that

. . . one of the strongest motives that lead persons to art and science is flight from everyday life, with its painful harshness and wretched dreariness. . . . With this negative motive there goes a positive one. Man seeks for himself, in whatever manner is suitable for him, a simplified and lucid image of the world, and so to overcome the world of experience by striving to replace it to some extent by this image. This is what the painter does, and the poet, the speculative philosopher, the natural scientist, each in his own way. Into this image and its formation, he places the center of gravity of his emotional life, in order to attain the peace and serenity that he cannot find within the narrow confines of swirling, personal experience.

Escaping a world which you feel is dreadful and trivial may not be the motivation of all creators but it was for Einstein. Holton says in one of his papers that "Einstein's attempt to restructure science, then, seems to me . . . to be a return . . . to the childhood state of innocence by a secularization of the religious childhood paradise."

Biographies have noted Einstein's first years of life were troubled in at least one respect. He had a serious speech problem which some have claimed (probably incorrectly) was dyslexia. He constantly repeated things to himself and seemed headed for the label "retarded." But his mother introduced him to music, which acted as a "psychological safety valve." He began to sing to himself and was much more coherent when he sang than when he spoke. If he was asked what he was singing, he would say, "I'm making up songs for God."

Could it be that the fluidity, the tranquil continuum of sound he felt when singing, was another resonance of what he found so intriguing about the compass?

Holton imagined the moment when young Einstein held the compass: "All through the room, therefore perhaps all through the world is some command implanted in it which tells that needle where to point. The needle is constant, fixed, despite all the turmoil, all the motions you might make."

Holton says Einstein's other important themata included a belief that scientific explanations should be a formalistic mathematical set of ideas rather than involving observable natural phenomena; a belief that whatever laws that are found should be applicable anywhere in the universe; a belief that the best explanation for nature is the one that is simple and shows how the natural events which we observe are a necessary result of the interaction of laws; a conviction that the universe is in its deepest sense unified, symmetrical, simple, and causal; and a need to have descriptions and explanations be "complete."

▪

The psychologist interested in creativity might yearn to trace each of these themes back to its origins in the childhood of the creator and so have an outline of the developing vision, but in fact it's highly unusual to have such a poignant thematic "story" from childhood as the one about the compass. This raises a reservation. The compass story may have been subject to what creativity researchers call "chunking," a kind of lumping together of emotions felt at the time of an incident with later—sometimes much later—feelings about the subject. Einstein himself admitted that memory is tricky, so he could never be absolutely certain that his childhood remembrance wasn't colored. But probably gut feelings about qualities of existence like symmetry and unity, continuum and invariance don't appear all at once in a creator's experience anyway. They develop over time. Holton's point is that themata are guiding visionary elements connected to the creator's emotional life. For that point, chunking or lack of chunking doesn't matter.

The sixteen-year-old Einstein's image of a wave of light frozen in the ether came to him shortly after he had sent a paper to his uncle entitled "On the Examination of the State of the Ether in the Magnetic Field," a clear extension of the budding scientist's fascination with the magnetic compass and the thema of continuum. Another possible—and quite curious—extension came in the special theory of relativity where Einstein elevated the speed of light to a high status as the only constant, or "invariance" (that other thema) in the universe. Light is electromagnetic. It is a concrete, visible form of the kind of invisible field that held the compass needle. Conceivably light had an unconscious biblical significance for Einstein, too, linking him to the themes that were part of his childhood sense of a religious paradise. In relativity theory, light becomes the cornerstone of universal order.

Holton believes that Einstein's emotionally rooted commitment to the theme of the continuum brought him into inevitable conflict with scientists like Bohr and Heisenberg, who were equally convinced that the truth of nature's laws lay in quite different themata. The opposite of continuum is discreteness, the idea that things are made up of parts or points, which the Greek scientist Democritus called atoms. "Most modern physicists are thematically Democriteans," Holton says, "but Einstein, Erwin Schrödinger, and others to whom the fundamental tool of explanation was the continuum, passionately disagreed; if discreteness had to be adopted as basic in atomic processes, one of them asserted, he would prefer giving up being a physicist."

With Bohr and Heisenberg it was not quite so simple as a choice between discreteness and continuum. At least toward the end of his career, Heisenberg himself didn't concur with the atomistic point of view and wanted to found things on another thema: "What then has to replace the concept of a fundamental particle? I think we have to replace this concept by the concept of a fundamental symmetry." Bohr, for his part, introduced an entirely new thema into the scientific debate, the theme of "complementarity," which stipulated that light, for example, was neither a continuous phenomenon nor a discrete one, but somehow *both*. Bohr proposed this idea, as we'll see in a later chapter, as an expression of *his* vision. Heisenberg and Bohr were able to interpret each other's themes so as to incorporate them into their own sense of things—their own visions—though not without an effort which forced each to make new discoveries. But they were not able to integrate Einstein's themes. Holton's point is that the scientists who were trying to master the rules of the cosmic puzzle were passionately committed to different sets of themata, so they had different visions that shaped their orientation. Not surprising that there were quarrels.

In this light it also isn't surprising that Einstein risked the mockery of his colleagues to devote the last years of his scientific life to the development of the unified field theory. It would have been the perfect end of his lifelong effort to make his themata concrete, giving the vision apparently awakened by such experiences as his father's compass and early biblical stories a complete scientific form.

Einstein said, "Adhering to the continuum originates with me not in a prejudice, but arises out of the fact that I have been unable to think up anything organic to take its place." The belief that the universe must be organic—each part seamlessly interconnected to the next—is another version of the continuum. Thus Einstein's statement is really a tautology—and a testimony to the single-minded focus of his vision. Holton thinks the particular constellation of themata of a great scientist is like a fingerprint. "When you have a scientific paper and you take off the names and ask what is this person preoccupied with, you can see the thematic fingerprints on it." Holton calls these obstinately held constituents of the scientist's vision themata because they recur through history and the total number which have thus far appeared in science is really quite small—around one hundred, he believes. At different moments in history, different themes come to the fore. There is an old theme of a universe composed of four elements—air, earth, fire and water. This has recently reemerged in physics as the search to explain all phenomena in terms of four elemental forces: gravity, electromagnetism, the strong and the weak nuclear forces.

Themata are never resolved. Depending on the problems being confronted at any given period of history, some themes may produce real insights into nature and others will not. One could reasonably speculate that great scientists have a much higher commitment to the pursuit of their idiosyncratic ensembles of themes than their less creative colleagues. Colleagues may ignore, even suppress some of their own subliminal thematic perceptions because they are not perceptions that people around them acknowledge. Scientists might also relegate these perceptions to the noncareer parts of their lives; for example, some scientists may give expression to some of their gut assumptions about the universe through the practice of religion and keep these feelings out of the laboratory. Scientists may accept the commonly held themata of their peers, less because they feel such themata to be personally important than because adopting a set of common themes allows them to be part of the great scientific enterprise and to work with other scientists toward a common goal.

Great creators are different in the sense that they feel compelled to show the world that their themata in fact point to a hidden reality that people pursuing the consensual themata of the moment have failed to notice.

The strength of this commitment is so powerful that rather than bend or suppress personal themata in order to carry on a successful career in a scientific field, some scientists have switched fields looking for a place where their themata could attain full expression. John Dalton, for example, started out in science as a meteorologist and then went into chemistry where he made an important breakthrough in the theory of atomic weights. Holton suggests that a scientist who switches fields has the advantage of being free from the tyranny of certain themata shared by the other practitioners of that field; the creator is then free to allow his or her own unique thematic ensemble to operate on the new field's materials and problems.

Donald Hovey, for his 1962 doctoral thesis at the University of Colorado, performed an experiment which dramatizes the tremendous importance of themata (and, consequently, of vision) in creativity. Hovey realized that Benjamin Franklin had figured out how to calculate the beginning of a storm by applying the already-known techniques used to calculate when water in a canal begins to flow. Hovey guided experimental subjects in the solution of the water-in-canal problem. They were then presented with the storm-movement problem. However, despite having all the information they needed, none of the subjects was able to solve that problem. Historically, of course, that is precisely what happened. No one did solve that problem until Franklin came along. Hovey concluded that the solution required more than information; it required a long-standing commitment to what might well be called a vision containing emotionally important ideas. With these ideas in his vision, Franklin was able to "see" the connection between the water-in-canal and storm-movement problems. Hovey identified several recurrent (and apparently emotionally significant) ideas in Franklin's thinking, including atomism, conservation, equilibrium. Though Hovey doesn't call these ideas themata (his research predates Holton's), his approach points in the same direction.

Robert Keegan, whose research was influenced by Holton, examined in detail Charles Darwin's intense, lifelong commitment to certain themes. Keegan calls these themes "thought-forms." He says, "The thought-form can be viewed as the incarnation of a theme *within* an individual." For example, in his books, papers and journals Darwin struggled for twenty years to give expression to the "thought-form" (or theme) of gradualism—just as Einstein had worked all his life to give expression to his personal collection of themes which included continuum and invariance. Keegan discovered that scale, progressionism and materialism were other recurrent thought-forms or themes in Darwin's creative process.

INTER (from a staircase above): You'll pardon a question. I might admit these themes explain something about what your hero Einstein called his curiosity, obsession and dogged en-

durance, but what about this other element, "self-criticism."
How does that fit into this vision picture? It seems mighty
important to me. I mean, in my day we had plenty of bewitched people who saw visions of strange realities they believed were true even though nobody else saw them. But I
gather you moderns wouldn't call them geniuses.

MUSING: Self-criticism is important for two reasons, at least.
First, the creator wants to communicate his or her unique
vision to colleagues. To do that, (s)he has to discover a form
that will be convincing and explicit. And to achieve such a
form (s)he needs self-criticism. Second, the whole thrust of
vision is the creator's belief that his or her elusive feelings—
themata—are *inherently* true. This means that from the outset
truth is of vital importance to the creator. A creator doesn't
want to deceive him- or herself, or anybody else. To avoid
self-deception you need self-criticism.

INTER (arching an eyebrow): You know, in our time we
didn't make a distinction between art and science. They were
both *scientia*. However, I've heard you moderns treat them as
quite different. *Ergo,* all this you're saying about themata in
creative scientists, does it also apply to creative artists?

MUSING: Holton thinks his hundred or so themes may be a
basic toolbox of primitive perceptions we all have available to
us with which to view the world.
  We're all born with the capacity to feel that the environment that surrounds us is complex or simple; ruled by some
smooth continuous invisible flow or basically broken up into
discrete fragments; symmetrical or asymmetrical; orderly or
disorderly. Which among these possible perceptions becomes
emphasized in our experience and with what weight it
becomes imbued is an individual affair. If Holton is right, then
in this sense the artist's vision may be not unlike the scientist's.
Judging from his paintings, impressionist Edgar Degas was
fascinated with the feeling of asymmetry; Bach, with symmetry and recursion; Russian film giant Sergei Eisenstein was

obsessed with cruelty (a form of disorder in a moral and social dimension) and with images of order as complexity. What Holton calls the theme of discreteness seems to have appeared in literary works as the theme of man's psychological or social or cosmic isolation, and as a sense that life occurs in discontinuous bursts of events the way it's portrayed in picaresque fiction. The theme of unity seems to have appeared, for example, in Joseph Conrad's novels, as what he termed the "solidarity" of mankind with itself and with "the visible world."

INTER: Wait! But if Holton is correct there's only a small number of these themes and pairs of themes; I don't see how new things get discovered or expressed. Isn't there a limit to what you can do with different combinations of themata?

MUSING: No, there's never a limit. Even with only a hundred you can get a lot of combinations. It's like the huge variety of instructions possible with the small number of basic nucleotides in DNA. But there's a far more important reason. Themata are limitless because for each creator the themata are riddled with and enveloped by nuance. To borrow a metaphor from Einstein, imagine the themata as a magnet drawing the creator into a hidden reality, into a vision. Nuance is the electromagnetic field surrounding the themata. In this nuance field we can get a glimpse of the true power of the *prima materia*.

2

Subtle Vibrations

THE LIGHT THROUGH THE WINDOW

Late in her career, Virginia Woolf recalled what she described as her "first memory":

> . . . in fact it is the most important of all my memories. If life has a base that it stands upon, if it is a bowl that one fills and fills and fills—then my bowl without a doubt stands upon this memory. It is of lying half asleep, half awake, in bed in the nursery at St. Ives. It is of hearing the waves breaking, one, two, one, two, and sending a splash of water on the beach; and then breaking, one, two, one, two, behind the yellow blind. It is of hearing the blind draw its little acorn across the floor as the wind blew the blind out. It is of lying and hearing this splash and seeing this light, and feeling, it is almost impossible that I should be here; of feeling the purest ecstasy I can conceive.

She went on to say, "I could spend hours trying to write that as it should be written, in order to give the feeling which is even at this moment very strong in me. But I should fail (unless I had some wonderful luck): I dare say I should only succeed in having the luck if I had begun by describing Virginia herself." Woolf's recent literary biographer Lyndall Gorden says of this early memory, "Years later, [Woolf] wanted the waves' rhythm to sound all through her greatest books, *To the Lighthouse* and *The Waves*."

Psychiatrist and creativity researcher Albert Rothenberg cautions that Woolf may be reporting what is called a "screen

36

memory," which is a little different from "chunking." A screen memory is a recollection of an event that may not even have actually occurred. It's an image that has become a personal myth representing some significant early period in one's life and concealing unconscious drives and motivations. Jean Love, author of a psychological study of Woolf, accepts this possibility but thinks Woolf's "early memories were recalled with eidetic vividness that is very convincing, and most of them contain internal signs of their own validity. For example, . . . synesthetic and egocentric thought, typical of young children's thinking."

In any case, as with chunking, it may not matter whether this was a memory of an actual event, or an event cast up out of Woolf's unconscious. The fact remains that in this image of childhood she has captured, in an amazingly concentrated form, a vibration that ripples through all her fiction. A few examples to suggest the range of this resonance:

Not only the title but the entire structure of *The Waves* is based on the metaphor of waves tumbling one after another on a beach. Having eliminated plot and the traditional time-space structure of the novel, Woolf replaced it with sections in which the consciousness of each character speaks. These sections fall one after another in repeating sets, like waves. The early pages, representing the early childhoods of the characters, are filled with what Woolf called elsewhere "moments of being," moments of exquisite, vibratory perception like the one she described having had as a baby in the nursery at St. Ives. From page one of *The Waves:*

"I hear something stamping," said Louis. "A great beast's foot is chained. It stamps, and stamps, and stamps."
"Look at the spider's web on the corner of the balcony," said Bernard. "It has beads of water on it, drops of white light."

Here, obliquely, is the St. Ives light; here are echos of the insistent falling of the St. Ives waves.

The opening page of *Mrs. Dalloway* contains a metaphor

which comes to the main character, Clarissa. "What a morning," she thinks, "fresh as if issued to children on a beach." A few pages later Clarissa's thoughts ring out with quite a different resonance of Woolf's nursery room reverie: "She had a perpetual sense, as she watched the taxi cabs, of being out, out, far out to sea and alone; she always had the feeling that it was very, very dangerous to live even one day."

Jacob's Room begins on a beach where Jacob Flanders is playing as a child and his mother is writing a letter. Mrs. Flanders looks up from her writing, feeling for a moment (from a fresh direction) the kind of impossibility that one "should be here" expressed in Woolf's "first memory": "The entire bay quivered; the lighthouse wobbled; and [Mrs. Flanders] had the illusion that the mast of Mr. Connor's little yacht was bending like a wax candle in the sun. She winked quickly. Accidents were awful things."

It's possible to locate hundreds of passages as resonant as these, or even more so. And the resonances appear at every level of Woolf's work.

For instance, Woolf's typical narrative rhythm might be described as a "mood wave." A character will begin a rumination in a positive frame of mind about her life; this mood will swell to exaltation until, within a few words or sentences or pages, the mood crashes into a discovery of some oppressive aspect of being. Or, if the mood has begun with a depressive insight, the wave rises and swells into ecstasy. Sometimes the mood of a single character rises and collapses in this way for pages.

Thus, from the predominating presence and pulse of waves in *To the Lighthouse* and *The Waves* to the metaphor of the sea as "growing up" in Woolf's first book, *The Voyage Out,* the half-awake, half-asleep moment remembered in the St. Ives nursery evidently contained an ambience, a nuance or subtle reality which was an endless source of inspiration for this genius of the English novel. She could return to it again and again from different angles and never exhaust it.

■

Think of nuance in terms of color. The three primary colors may be mixed to produce a virtually endless number of shades, tones and hues—that is, nuances. Or, more dramatically, think of perfume. The same perfume on one woman smells different on another. The perfume itself is composed of a huge number of odors, some of them not typically associated with pleasant aromas. Roots, mosses, beaver castoreum, even skunk oil are common ingredients in perfume. Together, the different scents fuse to produce a single subtly vivid odor. Probably the nursery memory could be analyzed into various qualities or themata it contains, but the thematic qualities are in fact fused in the nuance.

For Woolf it wasn't one or two qualities of the nursery memory but a whole complex of feeling, the nuance of it all, she was obsessed with. In new sentences, new characters, new books she tried new tacks and gave the reader new glimpses or inhalations of the nuance—new nuances of the nuance, as it were. The nuance represented by the St. Ives memory was only one of many powerfully interrelated nuances that Woolf was trying to express. The vague ghost of her mother, Julia Stephen, and the sight of an "idiot boy" begging for candy are others she emphasized, saying of such nuances that all her life was "built on that, permeated by that: how much so I could never explain."

Again and again in her critical writings Woolf tried to articulate the importance of nuance. Nuances were part of the hidden "reality" which she felt it was the writer's "business to find . . . and collect . . . and communicate to the rest of us."

What is meant by "reality"? It would seem to be something very erratic, very undependable—now to be found in a dusty road, now in a scrap of newspaper in the street, now a daffodil in the sun. It lights up a group in a room and stamps some casual saying. It overwhelms one walking home beneath the stars and makes the silent world more real than the world of speech—and then there it is again in an omnibus in the uproar of Piccadilly. Sometimes, too, it seems to dwell in shapes too far away for us to discern what their nature is.

Robert Frost emphasized the importance of nuance by retorting when someone asked him what one of his poems meant with something like, "What do you want me to do, say it again in worse English?" John Keats said of his favorite passage of Shakespeare, "One's very breath while leaning over these pages is held for fear of blowing these lines away." Cézanne averred he didn't need to take a vacation from painting his famous still lifes of fruit; he got all the excitement he could stand from the nuance of moving his easel a few inches. Nature photographer Ansel Adams asked, "Why is an Edward Weston photograph of a rock vastly more exciting than a very competent informational or technical picture of the same rock? The chances are that the latter might be physically 'sharper,' and may reveal to a geologist certain physical facts in all aspects that the Weston picture cannot do. The difference between the creative approach and the factual approach is one of purpose, sensitivity and the ability to visualize an emotionally and aesthetically exciting image. To further verbalize on this is futile." Why futile? Because an emotionally and aesthetically exciting image can't be verbalized. It's a matter of nuance.

In the arts, a sense of the centrality of nuance is everywhere. Nuance is the raw material whose distillation is the creative act.

OTHER CASES OF NUANCE

Beethoven was asked where his ideas for compositions came from. He replied that they emerged, in effect, from emotional nuance. "They come to me in the silence of the night or in the early morning, stirred into being by moods.

The American painter Georgia O'Keeffe said:

My first memory is of the brightness of light—light all around. I was sitting among pillows on a quilt on the ground—very large white pillows. The quilt was a cotton patchwork of two different kinds of material—white with very small red stars spotted over it quite close

together, and black with a red-and-white flower on it. I was probably
eight or nine months old. The quilt is partially a later memory, but
I know it is the quilt I sat on that day.

Anyone familiar with O'Keeffe's paintings will immediately
recognize the quality of color and light in this description.
Evidently, over the course of her creative life O'Keeffe distilled into a *prima materia* of vision her sensitivity to such light
and color. These nuances constituted a hidden reality that in
time she learned to make accessible to others.

The sculptor Louise Nevelson, famous for creating whole
universes ("cathedrals" as she sometimes calls them) made of
boxes and containers filled with abstract shapes, remembers
her immigration as a child from Russia to Maine.

Well, then we got to Liverpool, and I remember the depot. The
lights, the big spaces, and people going and moving . . . and there
on the shelves I saw every color of hard candies in jars. And then
the lights—it was glass that had reflection. So it looked like heaven.
Young as I was I remember this image, it made such an impression
on me. It was very magical. It still is, because how many times are
you moved to have an insight of that kind? An impact that even now,
seventy years later, still thrills me.

The complexity and sensuousness of shapes inside her collections of containers and boxes makes her work full of movement and energy. Nevelson is also known for painting most
of her huge sculptures a single color, usually black or white.
Perhaps there's a connection between that and her memory of
another scene filled with subtle vibrations. At the least, Nevelson's recollection suggests the artist's acute sensitivity to nuance and its role in vision:

. . . Going to school . . . I saw a black horse. It wasn't a race horse
or a work horse. It might have been pregnant because it had a *big
torso.* The horse was running wild, running alone . . . Because it was
running and running, and this *marvelous* body . . . it seems to me that
the torso was just bigger . . . than most of the horses I'd seen. And
this color of black against nature of green . . . everything was in

foliage, everything was in bloom . . . and this horse was *right* for this environment, because everything was oozing, and the speed of those legs and the hindquarters . . . they were *enormous* . . . it had the *energy* of all of nature and had *symmetry* in its body. It had *movement* no machine could match. I was alone, running to school, when I saw this . . . I couldn't have been more than eleven or twelve, and I never forgot the image . . . Let's not forget this: evidently we can see a million horses, but *that* horse . . . we can have a million lovers, but *one* lover, and have a million dogs, but *one* dog. So it's always a selection. You don't select it and it doesn't select you. But it happens. It's a *marriage* of some sort.

The next case shows that nuance is as important to the vision of a scientist as it is to an artist and illuminates how nuance and themata may be related.

The young Einstein's wonder at the magnetic compass was—though he wouldn't have been aware of it—something of a tradition among great scientists. Early scientific giants like Copernicus and Kepler had also been fascinated by magnetism. They drew from the action of magnets the theme of symmetry, though each felt the pull of this thema in his own way. For Isaac Newton the pull was more complex (or at least, biographers have had the data to say more about the nuances surrounding Newton's thematic perception).

In his acclaimed biography of Newton, Frank Manuel argues convincingly that the physicist's emotional life was preoccupied with feelings about powerful attractions in which one object is drawn irresistibly by an invisible force toward another. Manuel thinks the preoccupation was born in Newton's sense of attraction to his father, who had died before Newton was born, and to his mother, who was "lost" to him when she remarried (Newton was three at the time). Manuel believes that the emotional meaning of attraction for Newton accounted for the physicist's interest in magnetism and in the alchemic notion of sympathetic attraction, and that it gave him "his ardent religious longing for God the Father."

The information necessary to discover the laws of gravitational attraction was available to other scientists in the seventeenth century. Newton, however, was the one to "make the last leap," Manuel says, because nuances of attraction had such broad and passionate personal meaning for him. Indeed, the unrequited emotional attractions Newton experienced seem especially suited to his famous key discovery that the moon is continuously attracted to the earth by gravity but is prevented from having physical contact with it because of celestial mechanics. Celestial mechanics resolved Newton's personal problem with unequal attraction by making such attraction a central part of the universal order. Unequal attraction, Newton was able to show, keeps the very planets in their orbits. Fused into the nuances of attraction were perhaps the themata of symmetry—or more importantly *asymmetry* of the kind that occurs when a larger attracting object exerts its gravitational force over a smaller one. But Manuel's interpretation suggests that it was essentially the complex coloring, the powerful personal perfume enveloping these themata that drove Newton on.

What might this tell us about the case of Albert Einstein? By noticing the themes of continuum and invariance in the compass story, Holton has discovered rather startling signposts in a cloudy landscape. Now we can begin to appreciate the clouds surrounding the signposts. As young Einstein watched the faintly vibrating needle of the instrument his father held out to him, the moment was filled with nuances: his religious longing, his wonder, a sense of destiny and order and much more that can't be teased apart. In the needle's yearning north lay intimations of a hidden reality whose themata Einstein would progressively distill into the *prima materia* of his vision—and eventually transform into the philosopher's stone of his genius.

▪

Howard Gruber offers an insight into one of the nuances that deeply influenced Charles Darwin. Gruber, currently a professor of psychology at the University of Geneva, is a major pioneer in what he calls the "evolving systems" approach to the study of creativity. He spent fifteen years in quest of insights about Darwin's creative process. Studying not only Darwin, but also his contemporaries, steeping himself in the scientific ethos of the mid-nineteenth century, and carefully analyzing the complex movements of thought recorded in Darwin's notebooks, Gruber pieced together a detailed picture of Darwin's thinking as he struggled toward his revolutionary theory of evolution.

Gruber claims Darwin experienced an early, continuing and quite sensuous appreciation of the "wildness of nature," its "irregularity and richness." This sensation of nature, Gruber says, was quite different from that of Darwin's contemporaries, who perceived the biological world as a closed system, rigidly ordered. Certainly "wildness" contains the themata of complexity and asymmetry, but it also contains many dimensions of nuance. As we'll see later on, Darwin's particular sense of "wildness" may have guided him to the major metaphors that helped unlock his new theory.

Nuance also worked something like this for Nikola Tesla. When physicist David Peat was working for Canada's think tank, The National Research Council, he was asked to investigate claims for some of Tesla's still unbuilt futuristic technologies. Tesla is best known for having invented the alternating current system of electrical distribution we now use in our homes. He is credited with having actually beaten Marconi to the invention of the radio; he invented neon and fluorescent lighting and the molecular-bombardment lamp, precursor of the electron microscope. He also invented the first robots.

I asked Peat whether he thought Tesla had been guided by a nuance or themata or a vision of some sort. "Yes. There was one thing. He always believed nature was an infinite energy source and that if you were clever, you could tap into that energy." Dr. Andrew Michrowski, who is president of a scientific research network called The Planetary Association for Clean Energy, Inc. (PACE) and a scholar of Tesla, confirmed Peat's diagnosis. Michrowski wrote in a letter that in regard to nuance, "It might be appropriate to underline Nikola Tesla's personal fascination with potential energy." He listed several experiences in Tesla's life that are indicative of this fascination. The first was when Tesla was only a few years old.

The Croatian village where the future inventor was raised had just bought a new fire engine, and during the festivities to celebrate the purchase, the village fathers decided to demonstrate the new pump. The pump pistons squeezed, but not a drop came from the nozzle. As the elders stood in dismay, young Tesla plunged into the river and found, as he'd suspected, that the hose had collapsed so that all the water which the pump could liberate into useful form was inaccessible. Tesla reinflated the hose, which immediately shot a spray that drenched the whole crowd. Tesla became the hero of the day.

Michrowski says that later on Tesla used his sense that nature contains a vast reserve of available but sometimes difficult-to-access energy (like all that water in the river) as a spur to devise instruments for tapping into the hydroelectric power of Niagara Falls and harnessing the stupendous voltage of Rocky Mountain thunderstorms. But that isn't the end of the story. According to Peat, this feeling of vast, unused natural energy was linked in Tesla's mind with the idea of resonance.

In a book he wrote about his Tesla researches, Peat explained: "All systems in nature have their own particular way of vibrating; for example the swing of the pendulum in a grandfather clock, the notes on a violin, waves on a lake, vibrations of a tuning fork, oscillations of an electric circuit, signals from a pulsar. Resonance describes the way in which large quantities of energy can be exchanged between such systems when their vibrations coincide."

Peat gives the example of a little girl able to pump her brother higher and higher on a swing by timing her pushes to coincide with the natural oscillation of the swing. "If the pushes are 'in resonance,' then each impulse adds progressively." The principle of resonance, Peat says, "lies at the heart of many of Tesla's inventions." He used it, for example, in the Tesla coil, a device that turns ordinary household elec-

tric current into current at very high voltages. Resonance was
the mental plug Tesla used to draw out energy from nature's
outlets.

Tesla's resonance principle is what Howard Gruber calls an
"image of wide scope," that is, an image—often visual—used
repeatedly in the creator's thinking. What is interesting here
is how the image of resonance fits with and extends (resonates,
if you like) with Tesla's nuance-sense that nature contains a
vast and sometimes hidden source of energy.

Perhaps a fatal case of nuance is that of Marie Curie. As an
emigrée in Paris from Poland, poor in French and money and
lacking a scientific background, Curie (then Marie Sklodow-
ska) had to work hard for her degrees at the Sorbonne in
physics and mathematics. When it came to choosing a subject
for a doctoral dissertation, she become intrigued with the
"hidden reality" of radioactivity that had only been recently
discovered. At the time no one knew what radioactivity was
or what it meant. Marie and her husband Pierre discovered
part of the answer. Drawn to expose this subtle reality, she
engaged in years of backbreaking labor in a leaky, under-
heated shed. There she worked purifying huge quantities of
uranium ore in order to reach the new element, radium.
Sometimes at night, during the refinement process, she and
her husband would return to the shed to gaze in wonder at
what they were bringing forth. When their eyes had grown
accustomed to the darkness, they could see the containers on
the shelves around the room emitting a glow, the literal vibrations of this hidden world. Who can say what nuance, what
lovely fragrance was evoked for Marie Curie when she
said that the sight "stirred us with ever new emotion and
enchantment."

The Curies paid for this enchantment with sore and split
fingers, stiff joints and a miscarriage for Marie—symptoms a
physician would now diagnose as signs of radiation poisoning.

▪

What do all these cases show? It appears that for many
geniuses, an obsession with some particular nuance or com-

plex of nuances burns at the core of vision. For other geniuses, a general sensitivity to certain classes of nuances may be significantly at play. Such sensitivity would help a scientific creator, for example, sort out the relevant details from what is called the "noise" in the experimental situation and go straight to the subtle heart of the matter. Nuance and themata are clearly related. Nuance is the aura or nimbus that surrounds a thema or several themata, the energy that infuses thematic convictions. It is the vibrating field around thematic magnets. Over the course of a career a creator works to distill that field into a *prima materia* so powerful that it will draw others into a reality they had not previously realized was there. Of course, in a sense, the creator had not really realized that reality was there either, for at first it was only a nuance.

An important question: Where do these nuance-fields come from? Some new ideas in the neurosciences are suggesting answers.

3

The Open Brain

NUANCE CYCLES

The theory of "feeling tones," first developed by William Gray and later reformulated by Paul LaViolette, is a psychodynamic and neuroanatomical picture of how the brain is organized. Gray, a psychiatrist, tells about the moment the idea occurred to him.

He was listening to a patient who had spent a long time trying to write a novel. The patient said he realized books had been very meaningful to him in his childhood and the most meaningful were those that resonated with things he himself had gone through. However, the man felt now that none of the books had quite captured the feeling tone connected with certain of his personal experiences. He wanted to write a book himself that would do that.

This man's ruminations stimulated Gray to the idea that thoughts and memories may be coded or logged in the brain according to their "emotional nuances or feeling tones." Gray's notion can be related to recent research indicating that it is much more difficult to recall facts you learned if you're not in the same mood as you were when you learned them.

Feelings are basic, Gray says: anger, rejection, fear, loss, joy, astonishment. Between and among these are a huge variety of possible shades and combinations: nuances. Gray hypothesizes that early in our development certain nuances become a kind of filing system for our thoughts and ideas—the so-called cognitive aspect of mind. Gray says:

The emotional coding of cognitions may be understood as follows.
. . . If one has an emotional nuance of fluctuating helplessness colored by gray-green despair with mild flickerings of optimism, such
a nuance might well code a certain ecological concept of the world,
or an adolescent's view of adult society. Or, certain types of feelings
of continuity and wholeness, say, the emotional experience of seeing
how steps form a staircase, might attach themselves to a cognitive
package called integral calculus.

Thoughts containing a similar nuance of feeling are filed
together, even if they aren't logically or chronologically connected. This would account for the mind's sometimes strange
association of ideas. In the ordinary course of thought, however, we don't pay much attention to the underlying nuances
of our ideas but only to the ideas. To explain why this is so,
let's borrow a simple illustration that Gray gives for the cognition $2 + 2 = 4$.

Try to remember what it must have *felt* like to learn that
concept. Something called 2 has a feeling to it. The process of
adding, the process of equaling and something called 4 also
have feelings to them. There must have been a small amaze-
ment, a shock to the brain, at being shown or told that all these
nuances form an order. That order, $2 + 2 = 4$, now has its
own nuance that includes a sense of finality or closure, a sense
that "this is the way it is." Eventually that nuance-with-closure
overshadows the others until $2 + 2 = 4$ seems to be pure
cognition, a rational thought with no emotion at all. That isn't
true, of course. Thoughts always have emotions connected
with them and, in humans, emotions are mostly set in motion
by thoughts.

According to Gray, thought-emotions become associated
together into structures vastly larger and more complex than
$2 + 2 = 4$. The structures include, for example, our knowledge of mathematics as a whole, or our political attitudes.
These "emotional-cognitive structures" become "organizationally closed" when the richness of their nuances are sum-
marized by a simpler emotional response (such as liking

blondes) or turned into thoughts which have a feeling of closure attached to them.

■

"Thoughts are stereotypes or simplifications of emotional themes," Paul LaViolette says. LaViolette is head of the Starburst Foundation, an interdisciplinary research organization based in Portland, Oregon. "Thoughts are feelings, but simplified feelings." Sensations and feelings are constantly pouring into our brains, a tangle coming both from outside ourselves and from our own physiology. When we form a thought, we abstract from this complexity. "Thoughts are sort of like cartoons of reality," LaViolette says. "Once formed they shape the way we perceive the world. When we look at a tree, we're filtering the stream of sense data through a stereotyped thought pattern, the pattern we're accustomed to. As a result, there's a lot of data there that never comes to our consciousness."

LaViolette is a systems scientist and has a rather daunting range of interests, publishing in journals on topics that extend from neuroscience to physical cosmology. He synthesized Gray's hypothesis with the systems approach to develop a new model of how the complexity of an emotional theme becomes reduced to the simplicity of cognition. His model provides a picture of how creators like Woolf, Nevelson and Einstein may be able to make use of nuance as a resource for their creativity.

To understand LaViolette's model, it's helpful to have a rudimentary idea of the geography of the brain. The popular "triune brain" theory of Paul Maclean provides a quick and useful map. Maclean, a neuroanatomist at the National Institutes of Health, has argued that the wrinkled ball of tissue in our skulls is composed of three layers or shells developed at different stages in our evolution from lower forms.

The spinal cord, midbrain and reticular activating system is the innermost shell. Maclean calls this the "reptilian brain." It's the brain that governs such basic elements of consciousness as attention and arousal.

Next up, is the "old mammalian brain" comprising the limbic system, made up of a number of brain "organs" involved in emotion. The limbic system includes, for example, the hypothalamus, which is known to be the seat of pleasure, and its neighbor, the amygdala, the site of rage. Sites for the visceral functions, heart rate, blood pressure, respiration, digestive activity and hormone levels are also located in the limbic system, hence a literal connection between our emotions and our digestion, between the feeling of love and the quickened beating of the heart. The hippocampus, another limbic organ, retrieves long-term memory from storage and turns short-term memories into long-term form. The hippocampus is particularly active during dreaming. The limbic system is also involved in integrating memories from a variety of senses. Thus emotion, which the limbic system controls, includes a complex mix of inner sensations, memories and movements from one state of inner sensation to another.

The third brain is the "new mammalian brain," the great outer shell of cells that has evolved above the other two brains. The neocortex is responsible for the kind of abstraction we associate with high-level (human) thought and perception. Abstracting is our ability to formulate categories, to know that the maple and birch in our backyard, though vastly different entities, are both "trees." The prefrontal part of the cortex is also involved in the emotional responsiveness we associate with intentionality. People who have had connections between the frontal lobes of the cortex and the limbic system severed—a frontal lobotomy—lose creativity and emotional affect; their personalities become flat.

LaViolette views the fate of nuance as depending on a series of interlocking loops of electrical activity circulating among the reptilian, old mammalian and new mammalian brains.

Imagine young Virginia Woolf (née Stephen) lying in the nursery at St. Ives. The movement of the blind and the sound of its cord weight scraping on the floor activate her arousal system, the reptilian brain. Feedback loops coming from the auditory canal to the reptilian brain pass up through the cortex and down into the old mammalian limbic areas, stimulating the release of neurotransmitters that increase her heart rate. The emotional centers of her limbic system are in full swing, drenched with information about her momentary sense of pleasure and pain, the state of her internal chemistry.

New mammalian cortical areas are also quite active. A famous series of experiments by Hubel and Weisel has established that the visual cortex located at the top back of the brain is designed to recognize or abstract certain patterns, like straight lines and circles. Other research suggests that the rest of the cortex is similarly designed. Thus in Virginia's cortex, the angle of the blind, the rhythmic patterns of the waves are being abstracted out and transmitted through the brain as sensory information.

In *The Interpersonal World of the Infant,* Daniel Stern reports recent evidence that "affective and cognitive processes cannot be readily separated" in an infant, so that even these abstractions originating in the sensory processing parts of the cortex are entirely infused with the electrical activity of the feelings originating in the limbic system. Stern also says that "information is probably not experienced as belonging to any one particular sensory mode. More likely it transcends mode or channel and exists in some unknown supramodal form." In other words, the categories of thought—even such basic sensory distinctions as whether something is being seen or heard—have not yet been etched in the brain as they will be later on in the child's development.

Woolf herself confirms this. She said of her early memories, that if she could depict them, "Everything would be large and dim; and what was seen would at the same time be heard; sounds would come through this petal or leaf—sounds indistinguishable from sights."

According to LaViolette, raw sense data passes through the thalamus into the limbic system where it circulates around and around in what is called the Papez circuit, a closed-loop network of neurons connecting the limbic organs of the mammalian brain. There they trigger feeling-tone responses and generate what Gray and LaViolette call an emotional 'theme.' Similar to a musical theme, which is composed of an organized pattern of musical notes, an emotional 'theme' is composed of an organized pattern of feeling tones.

Coincidentally, the Gray-LaViolette use of the term 'theme' has something essential in common with Holton's idea of themes or themata: In both cases the term refers to the qualitative and emotional elements underlying thought. However, as there are differences, I'll leave the neurophysiological 'theme' in single quotes to avoid confusion.

The evolving collection of nuances or 'themes' circulating in the Papez circuit of young Virginia Stephen's unconscious would have included many nuance-laden sense impressions from other days: for example, her relationship to her mother, associations with the smell of the room, memories of feelings of security or insecurity evoked by the sights and sounds and sensations around and inside her. In "A Sketch of the Past," Woolf said, for example, that the nursery had a balcony which connected to her mother's and father's bedroom and that her mother would come out onto her balcony in a white dressing gown.

LaViolette proposes that sense data and emotional nuances (feeling tones) physically manifest as neuroelectric waveforms. As these waveforms circulate through the Papez circuit and pass through the hippocampus, they evoke long-term memories having waveforms with similar nuance characteristics. These memories, in turn, become part of the evolving 'theme.' In Woolf's case, the angle of light, the sound of the waves would have activated memories with similar tags or waveforms, like the sound of her mother's footsteps or the ghostly sight of her dressing gown in the wind. Together these would circulate and build as a rich 'theme' of nuance-laced sense data. Gray says of 'themes,' "Wondering is an essential aspect of emotional nuances [and] emotional themes . . . as they seek out cognitions to organize. There is always a questioning, a wondering, an incompleteness. . . ." In the normal course of events, however, this wondering and incompleteness is obscured by the transformation of the 'theme' into an organization of thought, an emotional-cognitive structure.

Woolf wrote that her feeling in the nursery was "due partly

to the many months we spent in London. The change of nursery was a great change. And there was the long train journey; and the excitement. I remember the dark; the lights; the stir of going up to bed."

Suppose that the nursery room nuance had activated in Virginia Stephen a set of nuances that were part of the large 'theme' of nuances having to do with her feeling about her St. Ives summers. This 'theme,' circulating mostly below the level of awareness, would contain hundreds of sensory fragments, each impregnated with emotional nuances. Over time these nuances would constantly be modified by other nuances, so that the 'theme' would vary in a complex way—shifting like sand in an undertow. (Interestingly, this movement of the 'theme' is just the kind of thing Virginia Woolf would later depict in her "mood waves.")

LaViolette suggests that the 'theme' circulating in the Papez circuit of the limbic system enters a second loop communicating between a portion of the thalamus and the prefrontal regions of the cortex in the new mammalian brain. This "prefrontal-cortex-dorsomedial-thalamic loop" (PCDT loop, for short) abstracts or filters out certain nuances and amplifies them, and reintroduces them into the Papez circuit: Woolf's feeling of happiness at the sound of the waves would be an example of an abstracted set of nuances. Happiness was only one aspect of all she felt that day and only a small aspect of the larger 'theme' of things she felt and experienced about her summers at St. Ives. But in the brain a small movement can become rapidly amplified.

LaViolette is among a number of scientists who see the brain as a nonlinear system. In nonlinear systems relatively small events can have immense consequences. Nonlinearity operates like the straw that breaks the camel's back. A system goes along in a random, fairly stable way until some relatively insignificant element coming at just the right time transforms it. With each cycling through the prefrontal cortex, the idea of happiness at St. Ives might be abstracted and amplified "to the point where it would massively transform the content of the theme and become a major organizing focus." The result would be the thought, "I was happy at St. Ives." This thought, or emotional-cognitive structure, would be made up of a series of feeling tones abstracted from the various memories and sensory fragments in the circulating 'theme' together with the accompanying organizing feeling (thought), "I was happy then." The nuances, the complex of emotion and perception, are still there, but they now lie in the shadow of this abstraction.

Although the newly emergent thought dominates the content of the 'theme', as the 'theme' continues to circulate the possibility remains that another nuance might become amplified and reorganize the whole complex into another thought such as, "I wasn't so happy then." However, this emerging feeling-tone pattern would have to become sufficiently intense to dominate the original "I was happy" emotional-cognitive structure.

The birth of a thought that she was happy or not happy at St. Ives is, as we know, not what happened to Virginia Woolf. Woolf apparently didn't simplify her experience into a definite thought. So what she remembered was not a cognition, but the 'theme' itself with all its nuances. She said the memory supported something you could fill and refill, a bottomless bowl. The memory had for her, in Gray's terms, a "wonder" and "incompleteness." The exact emotion she felt could not be defined in thoughts: It was an emotion that contained wonder, fragility, happiness, vastness, security, insecurity—and more. Nuance in the sense that Woolf experienced it was, therefore, a brain state that was not mainly thought but also not mainly feeling, and not mainly perception. It was a state in which feelings, thoughts, memories and perceptions flowed vividly into each other and were inseparable. The words "emotion," "nuance" and "feeling-tone theme" do not imply that the state is emotional in the ordinary sense of the word emotion, nor should we conclude that nuances do not importantly contain thoughts.

Thoughts are obviously an immense and indispensable fea-

ture of a creator's mental activity in all phases of creative
process. It's only when a child begins to formulate cognitions
that creativity as we recognize it becomes possible. However,
creators seem inclined to keep their thoughts pulsating in a
field of nuance rather than having them dominate the field.
Why are creators inclined to do that?

No one knows. Child psychiatrist and long-time creativity
watcher Phyllis Greenacre thinks that great creators have an
inborn special sensitivity to nuance. She says it gives the creator a capacity to detect "deeper resonances and more overtones than . . . the less gifted child." However, such a
"capacity" could conceivably derive from a developmental
impairment, a delay in the ability to use abstract thought as
we'll see could have been the case with Einstein.

Perhaps there are as many reasons for a creator to begin to
give attention to nuance as there are creators. It's likely that
everyone is alert to nuances in some areas at some times.
However, creators move to make a profession out of their
nuance sensitivity, a move which undoubtedly heightens and
fosters their sensitivity.

Woolf's career-long sensitivity to the St. Ives nuance theme
again highlights a point made earlier. It doesn't much matter
if Woolf's memory of the nursery scene was of one event, an
imaginal event or a composite of real and imaginary experience from many days or years formed into a nuance-filled
image. The important thing was that she found the rich nuances of the feeling-tone 'theme' which were represented by
the event more vital than any simplified thoughts or feelings.
She said that she saw the past "as an avenue lying behind; a
long ribbon of scenes, emotions." This statement speaks of her
commitment to nuance as a movement and continuum rather
than as a series of discrete moments and feelings.

LaViolette says, "It is good to tune into feelings before they
get abstracted into a thought. People who can do this are able
to directly tune into data of far greater complexity. Such sensitivity fosters creativity and the ability to see things in new
ways."

Psychiatrist Erich Fromm's description of "the creative attitude" captures the difference between a nuance approach to reality and the approach most of us take. Fromm calls a sensitivity to nuance "full awareness" and argues that it makes possible a more intimate connection between the observer and the observed. He wrote:

If we are fully aware of a tree at which we look . . . then we have a kind of experience which is the premise for painting the tree. . . . In conceptual knowledge the tree we see has no individuality; it stands there only as an example of the genus "tree"; it is only the representative of an abstraction. In full awareness there is no abstraction; the tree retains its full concreteness, and that means also its uniqueness. There is only this one tree in the world, and to this tree I relate myself. I see it. I respond to it. The tree becomes my own creation.

This emphasizes a circular paradox. Language, Woolf's chosen medium, is high-level abstraction-cognition. One would expect that employing language to think and write about the feeling tone infusing a tree or a childhood memory would tend to convert nuance into an emotional-cognitive structure. Yet in Woolf's case, language and thought seemed actually to enrich her thematic nuances. For example, Woolf claimed that she often pictured the nursery scene to herself as "lying in a grape and seeing through a film of semitransparent yellow"—a linguistic abstraction that ramifies the nuances of the scene rather than simplifying them. Jean Love's psychobiography of Woolf offers insight into why Woolf used language and thought in this way:

Woolf, like Einstein, was late in learning to speak. She admitted that even as an adult she sometimes had difficulty with language, and words sometimes seemed like meaningless sounds to her. But she observed that words which seemed at one moment "opaque" could also suddenly come together in her mind and, when they did, they would become "transparent," as if the objects of experience shone through them.

For most of us language is a means of arranging and simplifying experience. It is like a flexible, hugely cross-indexed
Rolodex to manage the world's complexity. For Woolf, however, language was a means to grasp what she said was a
painful and shocking "nonreality"—a world of nuances—
which she felt lay hidden behind the appearance of the scenes
around her. By using language she believed she could make
that nonreality a reality and so take away its power to hurt. In
other words, by giving the nuance a voice, publicizing it
through language that others could share—not by simplifying
it or categorizing it—she could find some solace from her
thematic feeling that she was, as Love puts it, "the result of
some mere protoplasmic accident."

Thus, in her work Woolf pits the abstractive power of language against itself, using massive amounts of metaphor,
irony, paradox and rhetorical ellipsis to do exactly the opposite of what language usually does.

The reasons Woolf and Einstein both had childhood problems with language may have stemmed from the kind of experience Simone de Beauvior expressed when she said:

The world around me was harmoniously based on fixing coordinates
and divided into clear compartments. . . . From the moment of my
first stumbling words and thoughts all my experience belied this
absolute position. White was only rarely totally white; and the black-
ness of evil was relieved by lighter touches; I saw grays and half tones
everywhere. Only as soon as I tried to define their muted shades, I
had to use words, and then I found myself back in a world of
inflexible concepts.

The tendency to constant repetition of words and phrases
that reportedly afflicted young Einstein is similar to a condition known medically as "perseveration," commonly associated with impairment of the frontal lobe and the ability
to abstract. Not that anyone would suggest actual brain damage in this case, but it is enticing to think that for some reason—perhaps because his sensations of the world were too

complex or because of a delay in his cerebral development—
young Einstein found it difficult to abstract his experience
and so lived more closely with the nuances of his perceptions. When he did develop his powers of abstraction, he
may have found them more balanced than is usual by habits
of mind alert to the "incompleteness" and "wonder" of
nuance.

Einstein himself said when asked why he thought he was the
one who developed the theory of relativity:

The reason, I think, is that a normal adult never stops to think about
problems of space and time. These are things which he has thought
of as a child. But my intellectual development was retarded, as a
result of which I began to wonder about space and time only when
I had already grown up. Naturally, I could go deeper into the
problem than a child with normal abilities.

Keeping a set of nuances in one's mind is what LaViolette
calls "priming." He says, "Just as a primed water pump is able
to draw water, so too when the mind is 'primed' with feeling
tones, these nuances tend to 'draw' out relevant data." The
compass Einstein's father showed him may have acted as a
primer, as had Woolf's St. Ives memory. When I told him
about that memory, LaViolette commented: "Probably she
kept the memory alive and kept thinking about it a lot so its
feeling tones often circulated in her mind. In that kind of
situation a set of feeling tones can act as an organizing focus
that allows relevant data to continually link up. So she might
have found this memory resonating in all kinds of ways in her
work."

Priming keeps the nuances circulating in the limbic-cortical
loop where they can resonate with data coming both from
internal activity of the brain—dreams, memories, reveries,
visual sensations, thoughts—and from outside the brain—perception and information. Woolf apparently allowed the nuance of St. Ives and its larger 'theme' to resonate with all sorts
of material and strategies that she could use in her stories.

LaViolette says, "It's possible to keep a number of different feeling-tone themes primed and looping at the same time." He believes that a person can focus the mind on nuances, "selectively attending to themes evolving at a subliminal level." Such attention increases the level of arousal given to the PCDT loop by the reptilian brain.

Since the level of a person's mental arousal determines whether feeling tones became amplified or attenuated in intensity, by controlling arousal, LaViolette believes, a creator would be able to magnify sets of cycling feeling-tone themes. That magnification would, in turn, increase arousal. It is known that watching TV stimulates the visual cortex and strengthens the connections to that part of the brain. In a similar way, LaViolette is saying, attention to nuance would power up the brain's loops that attend to nuance.

The feeling-tone model of mind throws new spotlights on the traditional idea that a genius is someone who is able to dwell continually on a single problem. Newton said when asked how he was able to make his discoveries that it was because "I keep the subject constantly before me, and wait until the first dawnings open slowly little and little into the full and clear light."

I asked LaViolette about this directly.

QUESTION: In effect, you're saying the issue of gravity which Newton was working on permeated his mind, first as the nuance of attraction. Would that nuance also have helped him with choosing the right problem to work on, what the creativity people call "problem finding"?

LAVIOLETTE: Yes. Then in solving it. He's got the problem of gravity and a nuance attached to it [attraction]. As soon as data with the right feeling tone comes up, that's going to make things click; it will congeal. If he didn't have the feeling-tone theme and its nuances circulating beforehand, he wouldn't have found the answer. It takes a lot of energy to be creative. It's like giving birth to something. It's like keeping something alive and caring for it. In fact, the PCDT loop in the brain concerned with creativity is also concerned with caring.

THE POSSIBILITY CLOUD

A complementary but quite different view of how a creator keeps open to nuances comes from neuroscientist Matti Bergström, director of the Institute of Physiology at the University of Helsinki, Finland.

Bergström's more than thirty years of primary research on brains and neuroanatomy have led him to believe that creativity lives at a threshold between neuroelectrical order and chaos. His model divides up our mental tissues a little differently from that of Gray and LaViolette. He pictures the brain as a "bipolar generator."

According to Bergström, at the "information end" of the generator is the cortex with its powerful ability to abstract and categorize. A stimulus on the retina of the eye goes to the visual cortex where it is abstracted or sorted out by the system as bars and circles, shadow and light and other sorts of information. But the stimulus also takes another path. It travels to the "random end" of the generator.

This end is located in the brain stem (reptilian brain) and in the hypothalamic part of the limbic system (old mammalian brain) controlling digestion and normal heart rate—the so-called vegetative activities. Bergström says this pole of the generator receives "nonspecific" input from all over the body and from the senses. This input stimulates the reticular activating formation, that organ of the reptilian brain which keeps us conscious and directs our attention. What does "nonspecific" mean? In the cortex input is abstracted and turned into information. However, in the brain stem, input is added together, mixed up and sent through the reticular activating formation as a random, chaotic or "nonspecific" stream of electrical activity. The effect of this random activity is what Bergström terms a sense of "pure existence, pure consciousness without information, without time and space."

We are all familiar with this state, Bergström says, in those first instants of waking in the morning. Lying there we don't know who we are, what we are, or where we are. We are only aware of existence. Then a fraction of an instant later the informational pole of the brain generator kicks in and our coordinates begin to come back. Bergström has done experiments where people were exposed to extremely short bursts of light or touch or sound. Not enough stimulus was given to activate the cortical system, but the reticular activating system responded by "knowing something had happened but not what or where or when it was."

When the random fields of neuroelectric impulses from the brain stem end of the generator meet the information-packed impulses from the cortex end, a selection process takes place, Bergström argues. The random bursts from the brain stem mix up some of the information coming from the cortex and from the memory-retrieving limbic areas. The result is new information, new angles of seeing, new thoughts, the possibility of new behavior—depending on the situation. Old information, previous thoughts, habits of behavior also are mixed in—all of these creating what Bergström calls a "possibility cloud" of electrical activity.

He compares what happens in this neuroelectric possibility cloud to the Darwinian struggle for survival. The possibility cloud, he says, contains "mutations" or variants or "errors" produced by the random generator's impact on the structured cortical firing patterns and these mutations struggle with the old firing patterns for "synaptic space." The strongest signals in relation to the whole context of signals at that instant will survive. A signal's survival is like the survival of the variant animal most suited to the environment at that moment.

The key to nuance in Bergström's model is the strength of the electrical field coming from the brain-stem end of the generator. If the nonspecific input—that state of pure being without time or space—is high enough, then the brain will generate a cloud of new information and new angles of seeing that will survive the "neuro-Darwinian" selection. If the brain stem input is too high, the result is confusion.

Bergström thinks that an illustration of this is the effect of alcohol on the brain. Alcohol depresses the information-generating capacity of the cortex. The random-generating capacity is therefore relatively higher. At low levels of alcohol intake people feel looser and more alive, wittier, more in touch with others, more open. Above a minimal level, however, the information capacity becomes so depressed that nonspecific, chaotic input dominates and produces the reeling distortions and mental chaos of drunkenness. Alcohol is hardly recommended as a method for instant openness, however, because its effects are impossible to regulate. Staying open to the possibility cloud (what Gray and LaViolette call nuance and feeling tones) while not allowing all those possibilities to overwhelm the brain's orderly function is a high wire act. Creators perform this act by self-regulating, giving constantly modulating weight to both the cognitive and the "nonspecific" sides of their mental activity. An interesting example of this is Michael Faraday.

Faraday, who made several major chemical and electrical discoveries, called the two sides of his creative mental activity "imagination" and "judgment." One biographer reports that, in essays, "Faraday described imagination as akin to idle woolgathering yielding pleasure but little else. Judgment, on the other hand, was what forced the mind to attend to its business and unravel twisted skeins of events [emphasizing the importance of the pattern-perceiving sensory parts of the cortex]. But, Faraday insisted, there is really no opposition between these two faculties." Extolling the "nonspecific" (nuance) side of thinking, Faraday wrote:

A sensitive mind will always acknowledge the pleasures it receives from a luxuriant prospect of nature; the beautiful mingling and gradations of colour, the delicate perspective, the ravishing effect of light and shade, and the fascinating variety and grace of the outline, must be seen to be felt; for expressions can never convey the ecstatic joy they give to the imagination, or the benevolent feeling they create in the mind. There is no boundary, there is no restraint 'til reason draws the rein.

Thus Faraday depicts a world without boundary, interacting harmoniously with the boundary-making processes of cognition.

▪

There are other recent neuroscientific theories portraying nuance in the brain. Nobel laureate Gerald Edelman, for instance, has hypothesized that even the abstract, information-generating cortex is built on mechanisms that produce and then—by a process of selection—eliminate nuance. His model may coincide with research that has found that young children have many more neuronal connections in their brains than adults do. Some scientists have linked children's daydreaming to this plethora of connections, which begin to thin out by the time the child reaches adolescence. Edelman believes that in the young, cortex cell groups have overlapping responses to a stimulus. The effect is like having several brands of radios responding to the same signal and exhibiting subtle differences in the reception. One brand of receiver might pick up more treble than bass; another brand might have a louder volume; another, a tendency to drift away into nearby stations. These cell groups or "receivers" engage in a Darwinian competition with each other. Eventually the number of overlapping signals is reduced because the receivers best suited to that particular incoming signal are listened to more often, thus forcing the other cell groups out of the competition. Could it be that creators are able to retain some of that original overlapping reception present in a young child's cortex, causing a persistence of nuance? Anyway, Edelman's work suggests how uniquely responsive each brain can be to nuance. Nuances, according to his idea, could shape the brain because, after all, the cell groups which survive the "neuro-Darwinian" competition are nuances of the cell groups that don't.

It's far too early to tell if any neurophysiological theory is right. The surprising thing is to find coherent theories proposing that qualities as elusive as nuance and as subtle as themata may be central to the structure and processes of the brain, and may even be the *prima materia* of thought. Is neuroscience beginning to tell us that the creators who articulate nuances are articulating a fundamental feature of our brain and so a fundamental feature of our connection to reality? Composer Roger Sessions indicated something like this when he described nuance in music by associating it "with those primitive movements which are among the very conditions of our existence. . . . Is not this the key both to the content of music and to its extraordinary power? These bars from the prelude to *Tristan* do not express for us love or frustration or even longing but they reproduce for us both qualitatively and dynamically, certain gestures of the spirit which are to be sure less specifically definable than any of these emotions but which energize them and make them vital to us."

A CAVEAT: EDISON'S GAME

Themata, nuances, feeling tones, possibility clouds—all seem useful ways to get a handle on some of the elusive elements of creative vision. The examples posed thus far have been relatively straightforward. The data has fallen reasonably into place.

But it's only fair to admit that sometimes there's not such a neat fit.

I'm thinking of an insight into vision given me by a scientist doing research into one of the world's greatest inventors.

Reese Jenkins, professor of the history of technology at Rutgers University, is at the head of a mammoth effort to catalogue the more than three million pages of Thomas Alva Edison's papers. Along the way, Jenkins has come upon fascinating glimpses into the crannies of Edison's creative process. I asked Jenkins if he had run across anything in the Edison story that might give a clue to the inventor's guiding vision.

He nodded and began to explain how Edison was a "systems thinker." For example, Edison didn't just invent an electric light bulb—other people had invented electrified lamps—he invented a whole practical system for electric lighting, including dynamos, conduits and a means for dividing up current that could illuminate large numbers of bulbs.

Jenkins said, "I think Edison was playing a game with nature, having a contest. I don't mean to suggest that he'd personify nature that way, but there's a kind of technological game in which he's trying to outsmart nature." In order to outsmart nature Edison had to use similar rules. Nature doesn't just make leaves; it makes branches and trees and roots to go with them; it makes whole systems.

Jenkins's portrayal of Edison's vision suggests a preoccupation with certain themata: wholeness, causality, organicity, to name a few. But an unconscious game with nature is not exactly a collection of themata. Nor is it exactly an obsession with a nuance, at least not a nuance that Jenkins could name.

So Edison is an example that doesn't quite fit our themata-nuance model of vision. But that's all right. In fact, it emphasizes the point that this model, like any model, can go only so far. On the other hand, while Edison's "game" is not the same as themata or nuance, both nuance and themata are there. I trust the reader can see that.

INTER: Wouldn't you moderns call that faith?

MUSING: Yes, but maybe all fruitful thinking requires a little faith.

In any case, nuance and themata are only two of a number of features we'll discriminate in the *prima materia* of creative vision. We next turn to a quite dynamic feature summed up in an old astrologer's dictum.

4

As Above, So Below

PART PROLOGUE TO THE WHOLE

Today if you go to an astrologer, (s)he may use a computer but (s)he will still cast your chart in the ancient belief that the exact pattern of stars and planets above the place of your birth contains an imprint of your destiny. Palm readers insist the whole of your life is encoded in the lines of your hand. The Chinese oracle book, the *I Ching,* embodies a similar conviction. Tossing coins or yarrow stalks to obtain one of the *Ching*'s sixty-four hexagrams presumably yields the questioner a window into the total movement of the whole as it can be seen from the angle of the question. The ancient Greek practice of casting entrails or telling the future from the flight patterns of birds, the reading of tea leaves and tarot cards—all assume that it is possible, as the poet William Blake put it, "to see a World in a Grain of Sand."

The followers of the Hermetic science subscribed to their own brands of this as-above, so-below assumption. For example, the first chapter of Genesis was said by the hierophants to contain all the secrets of the work of alchemy so that "some adepts devised processes which were intended to be a copy of the seven days of creation." Another as-above, so-below mirror was the alchemist's belief that he was the actual *prima materia* that he sought; thus he equated himself with the very origins of the universe. The philosopher's stone, that ultimate object of the hierophant's work, was also infused with the as-above, so-below assumption. The stone was the quintessen-ial grain of sand, a seed or microcosm of creation.

For the creative genius, the ancient perception that it is possible to invoke an identity between the universal and particular, between the personal and the vast impersonal, the part and the whole, is also pervasive. It burgeons at all levels of creative process and dominates creative vision. We've already seen it in Einstein's desire to escape from the "merely personal" and in his attempt to derive the physical law of the whole cosmos in his unified field theory. We've seen it in Edison's drive to create whole systems, little organic cosmoses of technologies. We've seen it in the way Woolf portrayed her St. Ives memory as a moment of life that somehow was also the whole of life, "a bowl that one fills and fills and fills . . . Virginia herself," and in the way that memory infused the whole of her fiction. Woolf, Jean Love says, "tried much of her adult life, by means of her writing, to compose the perfect whole of her own experience."

In this chapter we'll ponder some of the many moods and meanings which a search for wholeness and a personal/universal identity can have for a creator. We'll discover that the creations produced are the very places where the search is rewarded. And we'll see that between search and reward lies a swarm of those circular paradoxes of creativity.

THE WHOLE TRUTH

The desire to achieve wholeness (or, to put it more precisely, the desire to reach the meeting place between the nuances of personal themata and universal laws) is synonymous, in the creator's mind, with a journey across the terrain of truth. "My country is truth," Emily Dickinson declared. The journey is also an attempt to reach the *prima materia.* In order to see how *prima materia,* wholeness and truth, are aspects of each other, it's necessary to circulate a little around the question of what is meant by "truth."

It's commonly accepted that an idea or statement is "true" if there is a correspondence between the statement or idea and "that which is" in reality. This is sometimes called the "correspondence theory" of truth. As one dictionary puts it, truth means "conforming to fact and reality to the utmost extent that these are discernible by the human mind . . . conforming to fact in statement."

In the past it was recognized that you can make ideas and statements correspond with reality in two distinct ways, so there are two kinds of truths: conditional and absolute. Conditional truths include those of logic or mathematics. Here a conclusion statement is true if it corresponds with (follows from) the premises. Of course, premises can be wrong, leading to conclusions which are faulty, which is why logical truths are called conditional; they're conditional on the truth of the premise.

What about the absolute? For a long time Western culture considered God an absolute truth. With the rise of science, the laws of Newton were considered absolute. Absolute truths are whole truths, fixed and eternal. They are statements and ideas that are believed to correspond completely to an unchanging or basic reality.

From the eighteenth century through the twentieth century intellectual history records a growing uneasiness over absolute truths. There were several reasons. The growing skepticism about universally accepted metaphysical systems such as Christianity made it harder to agree upon the underlying source for absolute truth. Even in science, Newton's laws were found to be limited and philosophers began speculating that it might not be possible for the human mind to grasp absolute truths, even should such truths exist. The paradoxical discoveries of quantum theory seemed to confirm this problem. Science had stumbled into a position that made it like the juror in a law court who hears witnesses warned to tell "the truth, the whole truth and nothing but the truth"—and then learns that some of what the witnesses would like to say will be inadmissible. The concept of absolute truth became quite confused.

The existentialists tried to escape the problem by asserting that there is no such thing as an absolute, whole and unconditional truth; all truth is man-made and relative to cultural context and human choice. The escape didn't succeed, however, because the statement that all truth is relative is clearly an absolute truth.

INTER (stepping out of a closet): I take it the question is, which of these truths is the creative genius seeking, conditional or absolute? From your earlier declarations about genius and wholeness, I gather it must be some kind of absolute truth. But wouldn't that depend on the individual? Aren't some creators just looking for relative truths? And even if they are all looking for the absolute, didn't you just say you moderns have proved that it's impossible either to let go of absolute truths or to have them. In short, it seems to me you've gotten yourself into a terrible pickle when you talk about the genius searching for truth.

MUSING: Yes, but the way out of the jam, if I may mix a metaphor, is this: The truth creators are searching for is an exotic animal, a circular and paradoxical one, a round one at least. For it's a truth that is *both* conditional and absolute.

The great Russian abstract expressionist painter Wassily Kandinsky had this to say about truth:

As time went on I very gradually recognized that "truth" in general and in art specifically is not an X, not an always imperfectly known but immovable quantity, but that this quantity is constantly moving in slow motion. It suddenly looked to me like a slowly moving snail that scarcely seems to leave the spot, and draws behind it a slimy trail to which shortsighted souls remain glued. . . . This movement of truth is very complicated: the untrue becomes true, the true untrue, some parts fall away like the shell of a nut, time smoothes this shell; for this reason some people mistake the shell for the nut and bestow on the shell the life of the nut; many wrestle over this shell, and the nut rolls on. . . .

In one of his essays, philosopher Martin Heidegger describes truth in a similar manner, one that in fact seems quite consistent with the creative point of view. Truth, Heidegger says, is the freedom of letting things reveal themselves as they are—but, he points out, when anything is revealed, other things are concealed. Thus truth also includes the possible (actually inevitable) transformation of itself into untruth and illusion. Think of an urn, like the famous one John Keats said was the essence of beauty and truth. If you hold up such an urn and turn it, the motion will reveal new aspects of it to your eye, but at the same time will conceal aspects previously seen. Seeing the truth is the act of seeing both the relative detail and the movement that implies the whole (the whole urn). If you stop turning the urn, you'll be transforming the truth into untruth because you might fall victim to the deluded perception that the urn is the same on all its sides as it is on the side you're looking at. However, put the urn into rotation, and perception has a sense of the unknown and of the transience of what is known, thus a feeling for the whole. Indeed, Heidegger thought the best place to get a good glimpse of the truth is not in what we know but on the edge of what we know. Dickinson said, "Tell all the Truth but tell it slant—/Success in Circuit lies." In other words, truth lies in nuance.

What is creative truth, then? Neither absolute nor relative, it is less a statement or idea than an act of perception. William Faulkner was expressing this when he responded to a question about which of the characters in his novel *Absalom, Absalom!* had the true view of the central situation: "You look at it and you see one phase of it. Someone else looks at it and sees a slightly awry phase of it. But taken all together, the truth is *in* what they saw though nobody saw the truth intact" (emphasis added).

In the preface to his novella *The Nigger of the Narcissus,* Joseph Conrad offers a provocative glimpse into what truth means to a creator.

Conrad begins his essay by identifying creative truth with wholeness, for the primary purpose of art, he says, is to do "justice to the visible universe by bringing to light the truth, manifold and one, underlying its every aspect."

Conrad then links truth to nuance by insisting that the artist's "appeal is made to our less obvious capabilities: to that part of our nature which, because of the warlike conditions of existence, is necessarily kept out of sight within the more resisting and hard qualities—like the vulnerable body within a steel armor."

Next, while spelling out the amalgam of emotions contained in nuance, Conrad draws together the threads of nuance, truth and wholeness. The artist speaks, he says, "to our capacity for delight and wonder, to the sense of mystery surrounding our lives; to our sense of pity, and beauty, and pain; to the latent feeling of fellowship with all creation—and to the subtle but invincible conviction of solidarity that knits together the loneliness of innumerable hearts."

Throughout the preface Conrad insists that the universal creative truth he speaks of can be reached through the "sincere" examination of some momentary part. Any part will do, he says, because this truth is everywhere. It is therefore in the tale he is about to tell of "an unrestful episode in the obscure lives of a few individuals out of all the disregarded multitude of the bewildered, the simple and the voiceless." In the nuance of the part lies the whole—and that is truth. It is not an *idea* of truth Conrad is talking about but something that takes place in perception. "My task . . . is by the power of the written word to make you hear, to make you feel—it is, before all, to make you see." If he succeeds in this, he believes, his readers will then have "that glimpse of truth."

In this statement about his "task" of making the reader see, Conrad reveals yet another feature of the meaning of truth for the creator: It is something which must be shared. Indeed, the drive to share the truth that (s)he sees is the heart's blood of every creator's vision. Why else would creators engage in the lifelong, often arduous struggle to mold a language for expressing creative insights that others can understand?

Ansel Adams said after explaining the care and attention that must go into what he calls "visualizing" a photograph: "The picture we make is never for us alone."

Even Emily Dickinson, who evolved an idiosyncratic style and actually resisted suggestions to publish her poems, shared drafts of work in her letters to relatives, friends and literary advisors, considering her poetry her "letter to the world." The poems were even written in letterlike style. She also bound up and carefully arranged collections, stitching the sheets together by hand (after she died they were found in her dresser drawer). Her revisions show she worked carefully to refine her images in a way that would make them more effective to a reader. Though someone might argue that the audience Dickinson wrote to was ultimately only herself, the undeniable fact remains that the language she chose was a public one.

Phyllis Greenacre calls the artist's inclination to share "a love affair with the world." She says, "The artistic product has rather universally the character of a love gift, to be brought as near perfection as possible and to be presented with pride and misgiving."

The circle of sharing, wholeness, truth and nuance is evidently a tight one in the creative mind. Indication comes, again, from Conrad, who said that if a creator is "deserving and fortunate" he may achieve a "clearness of sincerity" in his work so that "the presented vision . . . shall awaken in the hearts of the beholders that feeling of unavoidable solidarity; of the solidarity in mysterious origin, in toil, in joy, in hope, in uncertain fate, which binds men to each other and all mankind to the visible world."

Isadora Duncan expressed her appreciation of the circle in a more personal way. "My art," she wrote in her autobiography, "is just an effort to express the truth of my Being in gesture and movement. It has taken me long years to find even one absolutely true movement. . . . Before the public which has thronged my representations I have had no hesitation. I have given them the most secret impulses of my soul."

Duncan appears to be describing an effort to reach what psychoanalysts call "authenticity"—a gesture and movement that is whole, without fragmentation, in which the as-above, so-below dictum might be rewritten to "as inside, so outside." Judging from comments by those who saw her dance, Duncan's public found that the movement which was intimately "true" for her was also true for others.

To sum up: For the creator, truth is a correspondence, but not a correspondence between "statements or ideas" and "reality." Instead, creative truth is correspondence between a part and the whole, between the creator's apprehension of nuance (or the creator *as* nuance) and the whole of what is. The truth is "in" the work itself which, like the completed philosopher's stone, expresses this conjunction between vision and universe. As French director François Truffaut said, he wanted to make films to prove to his viewers that his truth was the only truth. The creator experiences the truth (s)he seeks as neither absolute nor relative but active, like a perception.

INTER (closing the door of the closet behind him): I see a problem with that last bit of your statement. Maybe it applies to artists. But don't your scientists think of their laws as absolute, not "neither absolute nor relative" as you say?

MUSING: Yes, that's one of the differences between artistic and scientific creativity. In early stages of the process—particularly in the formation of vision—the two are quite similar, but then their paths diverge. Einstein thought of relativity as an absolute law which he had discovered—if Holton is right—from the nuances of his personal themata. Artists try to capture the truth of personally detected nuance by creating a context (a painting, poem, symphony) in which someone else may experience the truth, "see" it as Conrad says. Appreciators of works of art usually find that "truth" quite elusive when they try to restate it, indicating that the very structure of a work of art is designed so as to preserve the nuance ("slant") quality of truth. Great scientists, on the other hand, work to convert the nuance to something hard and fixed: a law, "experimental evidence," an invention. The nuance becomes a "reality" and doesn't seem to be nuance any more. Such truths seem absolute. But are they really?

In the last twenty years, historians of science and technology have put their fingers on a problem with the notion of absolute scientific truth, a problem that suggests, in fact, that scientific discoveries and poems may have something unexpected in common.

While making his now famous survey of the history of science, MIT professor Thomas Kuhn discovered that science doesn't actually progress closer and closer to the truth of how nature works. Instead, Kuhn concluded, there are long periods when a certain way of looking at nature is explored. Then a revolution comes (science historians dispute Kuhn's contention of how quickly these revolutions happen) and a new way of looking at nature is explored. Kuhn calls these revolutions "paradigm shifts."

One of the curious things about paradigm shifts, Kuhn says, is that conclusive truths that were discovered in the prior paradigm may, in the new paradigm, become open questions. Some things are revealed, previously revealed things are concealed.

Philosopher Max Black has said worldview shifts occur when one metaphor or scientific model becomes exhausted. An example is the Newtonian metaphor of the universe as a celestial machine. When scientists had stretched that metaphor of nature about as far as it would go (and in the process had seen many aspects of nature they wouldn't have seen otherwise), Einstein's relativity metaphor came along and opened a whole new way of looking.

Reese Jenkins says something similar happens in technology. We're used to thinking of new inventions and technology as "progress." But Jenkins says that technology is really very much a matter of a culture's way of relating to the physical world, its angle or nuance of relating, if you will. Native Americans didn't lack technology prior to the arrival of the Europeans, Jenkins says. Nor did they have a "primitive" technology; they simply had a different sort of technology. And it served them perfectly well for what they wanted to do in their environment. A great deal of that native technology and way of looking at the world was lost when America was overrun by European technology.

INTER: *Ergo?*

MUSING: The point is, individual scientific creators might believe they are discovering truths in the absolute sense—that there is one absolute way of looking at things which we inch closer and closer to (or that technological "progress" is being made)—but it's not entirely clear that that is what's happening. In the long run, scientific truths may prove no more absolute than the human truths discovered by Homer in *The Iliad.* Homer's truths are both universal and bound by the culture of the ancient Greeks. They are both absolute and relative, or—if you like—they are neither. As Faulkner said, the truth is "in" what is seen. It is wound into the perception.

Nobel prize-winning geneticist Barbara McClintock put it this way. "Basically," she said, "everything is one. There is no way in which you draw a line between things. What we [normally] do is make these subdivisions, but they're not real. I think maybe poets—although I don't read poetry—have some understanding of this."

The urn turns. The paradox circulates. The nut rolls on. In its movement the truth reveals itself as the *prima materia* or alchemist's eternal substance. In the creator's vision, (s)he sees a glimpse of that movement. If (s)he is successful in distilling the vision and fabricating it into a philosopher's stone—then we will see it too.

AT THE CENTER OF THINGS

The creator's vision that there is truth hidden in nuance and that such truth gives access to the the whole is identical with the creator's feeling that (s)he must be at the center of things, at the place where "above" and "below" coalesce. This feeling is expressed in many ways in creators' lives and behavior.

Einstein said his desire was simply to be able to "experience the universe as a single significant whole."

Darwin wrote: "From earliest childhood on I have had the

strongest desire to understand and to comprehend whatever I observed."

Gruber calls this hunger the "cosmicality" of the creator's aspirations. He gives several examples of it from Darwin's notebooks. It was typical for Darwin to think of his work in universal terms: "The grand question which every naturalist ought to have before him when dissecting a whale, or classifying a mite, a fungus or an infusorian is, What are the Laws of Life?"

Similarly, Freud thought of himself as the new Copernicus or Darwin, showing that man's rational mind was not in control of his life, just as his predecessors had shown man was not at the center of the universe nor the human species at the apex of the earthly chain of being. In the dethroning process, however, Freud felt that he himself was at the center of truth.

Louise Nevelson spoke of her drive for cosmic centrality somewhat differently. "Some of us, even when we were little children, wanted something else—what life really gives. Something that would justify our being here. And I meant it. And I would take nothing less."

Wordsworth believed he had been given the power to "see into the life of things."

Holton speculates that an important aspect of a creator's psychology is a sense that (s)he is "chosen," a special person assigned the task of unifying and revealing. Young Albert Einstein sang his "songs to God," a sign of his chosenness. Isaac Newton had survived a difficult birth and a plague, and so came to consider himself divinely selected. At the bottom of a folio listing some alchemical writings Newton inscribed in Latin an anagram for his name that identified him as the son of God. Niels Bohr believed he was chosen to create a scientific renaissance in Denmark. Werner Heisenberg felt himself to be the scientific conscience of the German people.

A sense of chosenness goes hand in hand with a certain ambition, creative ambition it might be called because it focuses not so much on the attainment of money or fame as on achieving the "cosmical" task.

Virginia Woolf's literary biographer says, "She was vastly

ambitious. Her aim was no less than to 're-form' the traditional novel, the traditional biography, and the traditional treatment of character so as to capture . . . 'multitudes of things at present fugitive' [i.e., nuance].''

James Watson's frank account of the discovery of the double helix structure of DNA seems at one level to be a tale of vaunting ambition. A talented but relatively unknown young geneticist, Watson knew his fame and fortune would be made if he was among the first to decipher the molecule. What is curious about Watson's position, however, is that unlike Linus Pauling and others who were in the race to crack the genetic code, Watson lacked many of the special scientific skills necessary for the enterprise and was not a particularly likely candidate to succeed. He reports numerous opportunities to do productive work on other scientific problems but kept being drawn back to the puzzle of the genetic code, a puzzle that first attracted him during his senior year in college. It was only this central biological question about the structure and origins of life itself that could hold his interest—so much so that his obsession probably put his career at risk. Of course, the risk paid off.

The obverse of the feeling of chosenness-as-ambition-and-conceit is a sentiment quite common among creators: the sentiment that since they have been selected as vehicles for the transmission of a higher or deeper order of things, they deserve little personal credit. Painter Paul Klee put it most succinctly. The artist's "position is humble. . . . He is merely a channel.''

Faulkner said, "If I had not existed, someone else would have written me, Hemingway, Dostoyevsky, all of us. Proof of that is that there are about three candidates for the authorship of Shakespeare's plays. But what is important is *Hamlet* and *Midsummer Night's Dream,* not who wrote them, but that somebody did.''

Marcel Proust spelled out another good reason for creators to feel humility. The self that is ambitious for success and takes credit for a great work is not in fact, the same self that created it. Proust wrote:

A book is the product of a different *self* from the self we manifest in our habits, in our social life, in our vices. . . . In fact, it is the secretion of one's innermost life, written in solitude and for oneself alone, that one gives to the public. What one bestows on private life—in conversation, however refined it may be . . . is the product of a quite superficial self, not of the innermost self which one can only recover by putting aside the world and the self that frequents the world.

Perhaps Einstein's need to escape the "merely personal" was recognition of a need to put aside conceits and torments of the "superficial self" and take on the humility required to achieve that greatest possible conceit implied by the cosmical task. All this suggests humility and conceit are in circular paradox.

Witness Emily Dickinson.

During her lifetime Dickinson preferred to remain anonymous; of the handful of poems published while she was alive, none bore her name, and she indicated unhappiness with the editing they were subjected to. Her correspondence with an *Atlantic* magazine editor, Thomas Wentworth Higginson, and with poet Helen Hunt Jackson, indicated a desire to publish, but she bridled at yielding to even the simplest poetic customs of her day, like putting titles on her pieces. It was as if a self-imposed humility or anonymity— even to the point of having her work lost to the world completely—was preferable to compromising the egocentricity of her vision.

Darwin delayed publishing his theory for years, fearing the theological uproar it would cause, humbly and conceitedly wanting to perfect his evidence, finally rushing into the open with it at the last minute when it looked like Alfred Russel Wallace would get the credit for advancing the idea of evolution through natural selection. Darwin's struggle on the cross of the humility-conceit paradox indicates its connection to creators' perfectionism and their desire for "more" (discussed in chapter 6).

Noting the humility-conceit paradox in great scientists,

Arthur Koestler observed that scientific geniuses possess a dichotomy between "self-asserting" and "self-transcending."

John Keats seemed to take a giant step toward explaining the circular humanity-conceit paradox when he pointed out a basic requirement for creativity: empathy, openness, the ability to take in or become the whole world. "Men of Genius . . . have not any individuality, any determined character. They have a receptivity to all experience, sorrow, joy, the commonplace, the heroic." To illustrate this receptivity Keats said, " . . . If a sparrow come before my Window I take part in its existence and pick about the Gravel."

Erich Fromm echoes Keats's approach. Fromm says the creator

. . . has to give up holding on to himself as a thing and begin to experience himself only in the process of creative response; paradoxically enough, if he can experience himself in this process, he loses himself. He transcends the boundaries of his own person, and at the very moment when he feels "I am" he also feels "I am you," I am one with the whole world.

Becoming the whole world is conceited. It is also humble. It is also cosmical.

Virtuoso pianist Lorin Hollander recalls the very feeling Fromm describes: "By the time I was three, I was spending every waking minute at the keyboard, standing, placing my hands on the keyboard and pushing notes. And I would choose very carefully what tones I would choose because I knew that when I would play a note I would become that note. . . . I knew I had to work at the keyboard. That was where I became most fully myself." Conceit, humility and cosmicality circle back to self-identity, to what Jean-Paul Sartre expressed when he said that as a child of nine he felt keenly that "by writing I was existing."

For Nikola Tesla, who was seeking in his inventions a power to unite the earth, creating was "a sacred vow, a question of life and death. I knew that I would perish if I failed."

Tesla meant it literally. Acutely sensitive to even the sound of a fly landing on the table or the vibrations of a locomotive thirty miles away, Tesla believed he would go mad if he didn't continue inventing.

Van Gogh, who grandiosely identified himself with Christ, wrote his brother Theo that he humbly didn't deem himself worthy of survival unless he could grandiosely produce a body of work of universal import. Beethoven also grandiosely and humbly saw his art as a matter of life and death. Recalling his suicidal depression over his deafness, he wrote, "I would have ended my life—it was only *my art* that held me back. Ah, it seemed to me impossible to leave the world until I had brought forth all that I felt was within me."

Holton agrees that for high-level creators, doing their work is at least figuratively "a matter of life and death." Put another way, creators feel that they are *not* alive unless they can find their way into the cosmic center.

THE WORK AS A WHOLE: THE INDIVIDUAL-UNIVERSAL EQUATION

Of course, the goal of a creator—the way to the center—is his or her "work," whether it's teasing the solution to an important scientific problem like the structure of DNA or composing symphonies. The work—like the philosopher's stone—is the actual interface between the creator and the cosmos. Wholeness and truth must be manifest in the work for the creator to have accomplished the task. Consequently, creators tend to view their creative products and the process of making them in holistic and cosmical terms.

Toward the end of his career Faulkner reflected on the body of his work, spanning generations of characters and more than a score of books about the doings in his fabled Yoknapatawpha County. "I like the idea of the world I created being a kind of keystone in the universe. Feel [sic] that if I ever took it away the universe around that keystone would crumble away. If they believed in my world in America the way they do abroad, I could probably run one of my characters for President."

Faulkner's literary biographer says:

From very early on, Faulkner spoke of his kingdom [Yoknapatawpha] as though it had presented itself to his mind as a given locality with a history and processes of its own. Since each of its parts implied all the rest, it always included characters and adventures he had not recorded, corners he had not fully explored. If on one side it constituted a world of which he was the only adequate master, on the other it contained multitudes even he could not exhaust.

Writer Eudora Welty also experienced her work as a preexisting whole which unfolded from each part:

From story to story, connections between the characters' lives already existed: there to be found. Now the whole assembly—some of it still in the future—fell, by stages, into place in one location already evoked.

Mozart said that a piece would grow in him until "the whole, though it be long, stands almost complete and finished in my mind, so that I can survey it, like a fine picture or a beautiful statue, at a glance. Nor do I hear in my imagination the parts *successively,* but I hear them, as it were, all at once."

René Descartes saw his work in the fields of geometry, optics, anatomy, theology, developing a universal language and perfecting the scientific method as a single creative endeavor. "He became less desirous of solving a particular problem than of finding the universal principle which lay behind all such problems," says one Descartes scholar.

Howard Gruber has shown that a common feature of the highly creative life is the development of what he calls a "network of enterprises," projects and lines of thought that to the outsider might seem unrelated. However, in most cases these disparate projects appear to be aspects of an underlying unity, the *prima materia* the creator is trying to distill.

In her provocative book, *Notebooks of the Mind,* Vera John-Steiner compares the creative life to the noncreative one.

Work in the marketplace is discontinuous; one is given a task, which once completed leads to another, a discrete assignment. . . . Once we close the door behind our paid work, we also tend to close our mind to it. Indeed, ordinary, repetitive work needs to be extrinsically rewarded because it lacks the intrinsic rewards of sustained, continuous mental labor.

The tools and skills used for solving daily problems may not be so different from the tools and skills used by individuals engaged in creative endeavors. But their sustained commitment to their queries transforms the power of the tools and the magnitude of their achievement.

As Ivan Turgenev put it, "A man wishing to create something integral must devote to it his whole integral self."

Paul LaViolette described the devotion wryly in terms of his theory of cycling emotional 'themes.' "It has to do with the interests of the person. If you're interested in what is the nature of reality in the universe, these thoughts will be circulating more than in someone else's mind who's just concerned with lunch."

The creator's perception that his or her work is a whole leads inevitably back to the creator's desire to be at the center of things, to the effort to use the products of creative activity to identify the self with the whole, to complete the circle and reveal that as above, so below.

■

From all of this it is evident that the creator's task is very large. It is nothing less than the re-creation of the universe or, more precisely, finding or constructing a whole, integrated microcosm in order to reflect the whole macrocosm. To do this requires the creator's conviction (spurred by nuances such as Woolf's St. Ives memory) that a microcosm of the whole can be made to reveal itself in some part: in a mathematical problem or field, in the story of a white whale, the harmonies of the tonic scale, the possibilities of primary colors, or the movements of the human body across a stage.

As Louise Nevelson explained, "I always wanted to show the world that art is everywhere." She said that even the smallest thing can become the microcosm that instantiates the universe in its essence.

Now you go to the hardware store and buy a dowel. You buy it for a few pennies. Yet that dowel has the same importance in the ultimate scheme of things as a diamond ever did. Oh, the greatest diamond is beautiful and it comes out of the same aliveness and livingness but it doesn't have the same function, it doesn't have a use for me. I tell you when I use that dowel and *place* it, then that order has a rightness in the universe.

Koestler believed that an essential of a great work of art and science is that it discovers an intersection between what he called the "trivial" and the "absolute" planes: "The scientist discovers the working of eternal laws in the ephemeral grain of sand, or in the contractions of a dead frog's leg hanging on a washing-line. The artist carves out the image of the god which he saw hidden in a piece of wood. . . . The interlacing of the two planes is found in all great works of art, and at the origin of all great discoveries of science. The artist and scientist are condemned—or privileged—to walk on the intersection as on a tightrope."

So a dowel, providing it is placed to evoke nuance, can become a keystone of the universe just as a whole body of work can.

▪

Painter Piet Mondrian said that "art has shown that universal expression can only be created by a real equation of the universal and the individual." The creator's task is to formulate that equation.

The great scientist or mathematician does it by tuning into the nuances of his or her themata and developing them into a form of expression that fits with the whole body of scientific/mathematical laws. (In the process the creator may be compelled to reject or change some of the existing laws, or give them a new context.)

For the theoretical scientist, the goal is to develop a "complete theory." All great scientists seem to share the thema that the completeness or wholeness of the theory is crucial. During the great debates between Einstein and Bohr, Einstein accused Bohr's quantum theory of being "incomplete" because it couldn't explain how particles jump from one place to another. Bohr was deeply stung. Incompleteness is the theoretical scientist's ultimate malediction. A "complete" theory is both an individual piece of the whole scientific puzzle and a universal expression of nature's laws. The theory of DNA structure, relativity, Newtonian mechanics—all are microcosms of the whole of how matter behaves.

For the genius inventor, the task involves making new objects which demonstrate the inventor's grasp of the whole. Nikola Tesla's sense that nature is an infinite energy resource and that resonance is the key to tapping into it led to inventions like the radio and the AC motor. Each of these individual inventions was a microcosm of Tesla's universal belief about the whole.

The great artist formulates the individual-universal equation by constructing a sort of nuance generator. Consider da Vinci's painting of the Mona Lisa. There is no one like her. She is unique and individual and her smile is the epitome of nuance. The landscape behind her contributes to this nuance. In its filminess da Vinci suggests, as one critical text puts it, "how the earth 'grew' from rocks and water." A wall separates her from the landscape. "The figure, the low wall behind her, and the distant landscape are no longer set off against each other as separate things; the picture as a whole has now become more important than any of its parts." There is an embryonic sense to the painting, as if the viewer were present at the birth of the world. By various techniques and impressions, da Vinci transformed a commonplace woman into a universal image; he found a way to formulate his equation.

That formulation exists at several levels. A fascinating level

Figure 1 Bell Labs researcher Lillian Schwartz was able to match Mona Lisa's face to the only known self-portrait by Leonardo da Vinci. Using the computer, Schwartz flopped da Vinci's face and resized it. Computer examination of the proportion of the faces revealed they were the same but with some elements like the mouth and angle of the sitter reversed. Reprinted by permission of Lillian Schwartz.

has been detected recently by a Bell Labs consultant who discovered through computer analysis that the mysterious subject for the Mona Lisa was a feminized version of da Vinci's own face.

An equally unusual claim has been made for van Gogh's universal-individual image of stars and flowers, landscapes and interiors. One art scholar thinks they are images of the physical qualities of van Gogh himself. His rough and shaggy appearance is manifest in the texture of the paint; his unusual orange hair and blue eyes show up as unique coloristic effects, and the swirling lines of his composition depict the vertigo from which he suffered.

Hamlet, The Brothers Karamazov, Debussy's *Claire de Lune* and Bach's B Minor Mass—all contain elements of style and structure that are unique and individual and yet each as a whole creates an impression of the universal, as if each were in some way a microcosm reflecting essential elements of the whole of the universe. The impression created by a great work of art is a little like the impact of peering through a microscope into a drop of pond water teaming with a life and structure that seems in a startling and thoroughly alien way to mirror the life and structure that we ourselves are immersed in at the other end of the eyepiece.

Formulating an individual-universal equation, the great artist reinvents the universe with each creation. Mondrian started out as a realistic landscape painter, but eventually developed a style which minimalized the viewer's perceptions by presenting only highly abstract tensions among lines, forms and colors. Mondrian sought in his abstractions to go down to the very ground from which our perception of forms like landscapes arises. It was an effort, in modernist terms, to go to the center, to the origin of things—analogous to the alchemist's effort to mirror in his Hermetic process the first days of Creation. One irony of Mondrian's universal, impersonal pattern of lines is that his individual, very personal effort to create them is evident in each piece. Animating the abstract pattern, the personal touch of the individual artist appears prominently as uneven thicknesses of paint, waviness of line, the cracking of the painting's surface.

Within the structure of artworks themselves exist other complex equations between individual and universal. Such equations involve how the individual "parts" of the piece mirror the piece as a whole. Igor Stravinsky said that his purpose in composing music was to create a "unity which is a harmony of varieties." The unity is achieved, he said, by revealing to the listener the bonds of similarity that exist between different things. Leonard Bernstein illustrates Stravinsky's point in his concept of "intrinsic metaphor." In a musical composition phrases and melodies repeat with slight variations; a line of music played by the brasses is echoed in the strings in a different key—there is a constant tension of similarities and differences. Arnold Schönberg insisted, "Whatever happens in a piece of music is nothing but the endless reshaping of a basic shape." It is nothing, he asserted, "but what comes from the theme, springs from it, and can be traced back to it." "Dissonances," he also said, "are the remote of consonances." The listener's sense of the whole is therefore evoked in each part, which is like a haunting echo of what is past and yet to come in the music.

In fiction, great works are also built on elements that reflect each other and therefore reflect the whole work from various angles. Polonius is a windy reflection of Hamlet's tendency to talk rather than act; Jim Wait in Conrad's novella *The Nigger of the Narcissus* is poised at the threshold of death, unable to cross over; his dilemma is mirrored by a paralyzing calm that besets his ship on her homeward course. Hemingway insisted that in fiction writing, "any part you make will represent the whole if it is made truly."

In the visual arts, the Mona Lisa's embryonic, enigmatic smile is mirrored by the embryonic, enigmatic landscape behind her. Da Vinci was evidently aware of such mirrors in his own work, and saw his paintings as an attempt to capture a mirroring property of reality itself, which he described in visionary terms: "Every body placed in the luminous air spreads out in circles and fills the surrounding space with infinite likenesses of itself and appears all in all and all in every part." He also said, "This is the real miracle, that all shapes, all colors, all images of every part of the universe are concentrated in a single point."

In engendering works which (s)he feels are microcosms of the universe, in constructing a work so that its parts reflect the whole, in formulating the equation of the individual and the universal, the creative genius appears to be following the old alchemist's maxim: "The most natural and most perfect work is to create that which is like itself."

▪

But I'm afraid we've gotten ahead of our story because a creator's finished work is the perfected vision; it is the philosopher's stone or sophic fire of genius. However, our story of the creative alchemist has a transmutation or two to go before it can show the birth of that stone. Just now we've a bit more chemical analysis to do on the creator's vision.

5

Contraries

SOME POLAR CHEMISTRY

It's rare to pick up a biography about a creative genius without somewhere running into the biographer's list of the creator's paradoxes or polarities.

Biographer Jean Love cites a number of contradictions in Virginia Woolf's personality. She "was brave and tough . . . in spite of being frightened, depressed and fragile. She was as fascinated with life as she was preoccupied with death."

Margaret Mead's biographer lists Mead as: "loving, scolding, ebullient, irksome, heroic, and at times vindictive. Like most great characters she was inconsistent."

A typical class of polarity stressed by biographers seems related to the creator's circular paradox of humility and conceit. One writer said of Charlie Chaplin: "He shrinks from the limelight, but misses it if it isn't turned upon him. He is intensely shy, yet loves to be the center of attention. A born solitary, he knows the fascination of the crowd." Duke Ellington has been described as an intensely private man who could be remarkably broad and gregarious on stage. Barbara Lemming says of filmmaker Orson Welles that all the ego petting he received as a child prodigy left Welles "supremely confident," yet he "never really overcame his innate shyness." Edison's biographer notes his "simultaneous brashness and introversion." William Faulkner is described as "driven by conflicting urges: the urge to avoid life and the urge to explore it; the urge to disguise his thoughts and feelings in a thousand ways and the urge to disclose them in a single sentence."

Perhaps we all have polarities in our personalities and if we were famous enough to have need of a biographer, we might find these polarities trotted out as proof of our genius. The idea that genius involves polarities is surely an old one. In the Latin origins of the word genius, the genii said to preside over a person's birth and destiny were believed to come in a polar pair—one white, the other black.

In the last chapter we saw polarities connected with the as-above, so-below element of creative vision. Polarity is a key part of Matti Bergström's claim that from the perspective of neurophysiology, creativity results from a dynamic interaction between two poles of the brain. Classic studies of creative people have shown that male creators have more "feminine" interests even though they are "of normal masculinity" and vice versa. Researchers think that creators may be more "androgynous," that is, possessed of a greater balance of the polar characteristics which a culture labels as male and female. Recently another kind of polarity-creativity link has been reported in the scientific press. Several studies have found that artists as a group show a much higher than average tendency to manic-depressive illness and sharp mood swings.

Gerald Holton thinks polarities are an important aspect of creativity. In an essay entitled "On Trying to Understand Scientific Genius," he enumerates a number of polarities in Einstein's "style and life's work."

Einstein, Holton says, appeared as both a wise old man and a "childlike person"; he had an "iron ability to concentrate, often for years, on a single basic problem in physics," yet there was also "his ever-ready openness to deal after all with the 'merely personal' from which he so longed to flee—to deal with the barrage of requests for help and personal involvements." Like many other creators, he was both charismatic and solitary. He was both aloof and accessible. He said of himself, "My passionate sense of social justice and social responsibility has always contrasted oddly with my pronounced lack of need for direct contact with other human beings and human communities." Einstein was the "apostle of rationality," yet insisted that to do serious work it was necessary to make unlogical (intuitive) leaps from experience to theory. He was simultaneously agnostic and deeply religious. Einstein himself said in an essay that he felt being in the thick of polarities was important for doing high-level research.

Holton believes there were also polarities in Einstein's themata. So as it turns out, although Einstein had a gut conviction that the universe is a continuum, he also felt discreteness must be involved in the continuum. These opposing themata drove Einstein, Holton thinks. Einstein's seminal work on Brownian motion and his 1905 paper on the photoelectric effect were based on discreteness. His 1905 paper on relativity was based on continuum.

Physicist David Bohm has argued that at a subtler level the relativity paper itself involves Einstein's merging of the opposing themes. The idea of a "signal" figures prominently in relativity and implies that this essentially discrete element is a feature of the continuum. Later, in his work on the unified field theory, Einstein was trying to unite discreteness and continuum in an even more all-encompassing way. Had he been successful, the theory would presumably have explained the discreteness of quantum theory as a part of the continuum.

Metaphorically one might say that throughout his scientific career Einstein was trying to show that these contraries are poles of the same magnet.

Howard Gruber thinks Darwin also might have been trying to unite polar themata in his theory of evolution. Gruber says that it wasn't only an attraction to nature's "wildness" that drove Darwin on. He had another thema, a contrary or at least contrasting one, which he also felt to be inherently true. He believed that the wildness must have some "simple" explanation. Eventually Darwin's evolution theory showed how the complexity or wildness of nature's forms comes out of the relatively simple rules of adaptation and variation.

Artists could also be said to have polarities in the major themes that obsess them. In Conrad's stories for instance, the theme of solidarity is almost always allied with the theme of isolation and aloneness; passages depicting great passivity and stillness in nature or in a character are usually concurrent with elements of explosiveness and high drama.

Could contraries be at the root of creative vision? The possibility would not have surprised the ancient alchemists. The entire process of the alchemy they practiced was wreathed in contraries. The *prima materia* itself was reputedly describable only in contradictory terms. For instance, it was said to have "no qualities or properties, but at the same time it has all qualities and properties, because it contains the possibility of all things latent within it." In a further contradiction, the ancient alchemists held that the distillation of the *prima materia* into the philosopher's stone depended upon the raw material being something "found everywhere and universally regarded as valueless." The process of finding in this "valueless" raw material the invaluable sophic fire was reportedly a continual process of confronting and unifying contraries.

Certainly contraries are prominent in creative process. For example, we've already considered Koestler's idea that creativity involves a bringing together of the "trivial" and "absolute" planes. It may even be that one of the things that distinguishes the vision of a genius is its curious relationship to contraries.

AMBIVALENCE

In the 1970s, psychiatrist Albert Rothenberg logged over seventeen hundred hours of interview time with Pulitzer and other literary prize-winning writers, Nobel laureates in science and prominent visual artists, trying to figure out how high-level creators think. He followed their worksheets, sketchbooks and journals and asked them about life events and thoughts going on in their minds while actually in the throes of creating particular pieces of art or undertaking scientific projects. His research left Rothenberg convinced that polarities and oppositional elements are pervasive in creative thinking. As a result, he proposes that in a great many cases (not in all) the oppositional tendencies of creators are related to deep psychological contraries which take the form of ambivalence. He says, "There's a high level of ambivalence in the personalities of creative people which fuels the creative process."

A review of the biographies of great creators offers support for Rothenberg's conjecture.

■

The life of Leonardo da Vinci, for example, was shot through with ambivalence. According to de Vinci's biographer, Antonina Vallentin, the great Renaissance artist-scientist had an "ambition to leave a lasting memory of his activities on earth," which lived "side by side with his keen interest in research for its own sake. These two motives pulled him to and fro," leading to perhaps the most glorious string of half-finished projects ever amassed by one individual in history.

Typical was da Vinci's work on a colossal equestrian monument to Milan's ruler, Francesco Sforza. Contemporary accounts extol the magnificence of the twenty-six-foot-high model, for which da Vinci had employed both his engineering and his artistic genius, creating what could well have been one of the greatest statues of its day. When it came to the job of casting the bronze, however, he got caught up in technical details, then was distracted by other projects until a war came along, consuming all the available bronze and leaving the model to be ruined by time and weather.

Vallentin explains that da Vinci's desire for perfection continually ran counter to his desire to immediately carry out a task; his ability to become totally absorbed in a project continually ran counter to his tendency to become deflected into other trains of thought by some detail. During his life he asked himself repeatedly in his diaries: "Has anything been done?" In his last days, he made a valiant but unsuccessful effort to finish some of his works and collect them. But sickness and old age overtook him and he died "full of distress and torturing self-accusation" for a misspent life.

Other ambivalences displayed by da Vinci: He admired luxury but preferred an abstemious, austere life and surroundings. He repudiated violence, was a vegetarian and had a legendary habit of buying up birds caught by peasants for sale in the market so that he could free them from their cages. However, his tenderheartedness toward life was opposed by an aggressive streak that made him ever eager to engage in scientific research requiring him to cut up corpses in the local mortuary. He also filled sketchbooks with designs for machines of destruction and war which he energetically offered to his patrons. In one drawing, he shows a car resembling a modern mowing machine slicing through human bodies.

Designer of ideal cities, admirer of the order of nature, da Vinci was bedeviled by dreams of horrible cataclysms of fire and flood—his sympathy for things counterposed by his misanthropy.

His fascination with the simple, classic beauty of a Mona Lisa or the Virgin of the Rocks was countered by his fascination with deformity. It was not uncommon for da Vinci to wander through the streets of Milan following women with corroded noses, misshapen breasts, goiter or warts in order to return to his rooms to reconstruct these features into pieced-together monsters, vivid as creatures of hell but unmistakably human.

Da Vinci's sexual ambivalence has been the topic of much discussion among biographers, psychoanalysts and critics, including no less prestigious a commentator than Freud. It's not clear that da Vinci was homosexual but at age twenty-one he was accused, and then acquitted, of homosexual acts with a male model. He was mortified by the incident. Nevertheless, at age thirty-eight he took into his care a ten-year-old boy named Salai whom he described as a thief, liar and "little rogue." He lavished on Salai many gifts and patiently put up with the boy's unruliness. Many commentators believe they were lovers, but the evidence is inconclusive. Other commentators have observed the hermaphroditic quality of da Vinci's paintings (such as his John the Baptist) and have noted his intuitive ability in drawing the female figure—though at least in one case da Vinci portrays the female genitalia as a yawning abyss. In his diary he wonders how anyone could find the feel or sight of the sexual organs attractive.

The contention that da Vinci portrayed himself as the Mona Lisa should add fuel to the debate over the exact nature of the great master's sexual ambivalence. But whatever the psychodynamics, no one doubts that he was indeed under the influence of that ambivalence.

To describe the whole range of da Vinci's ambivalences would take many pages. But perhaps his overall situation is symbolized by an incident in his early childhood.

The incident is a vision or dream or memory, or some combination. Da Vinci remembered lying in the cradle when he was about two or three years old. He said that as he looked at the blue sky above, he saw a black spot come toward him, growing quickly until it revealed itself as two powerful wings and a bird's sharp beak. The bird's tail swished through the air and the shadow of wings hovered above the cradle. Then the creature opened young Leonardo's mouth with its tail and "struck me with it several times between my lips."

Was the bird anointing him or attacking him? A sign of humiliation or of greatness? Many interpretations are possible, but clearly da Vinci's first memory is as rife with ambivalence as his ultimate life was. After becoming both intuitive artist and rational scientist, da Vinci tried several times to formulate his sense that masterpieces are born of ambivalence: "That painter who has no doubts will achieve little."

▪

Another creator manifestly riddled with ambivalence was Ludwig van Beethoven. The contraries in Beethoven's psychology ranged from his desire to conform and his rebelliousness to an oscillating altruism and violence.

According to biographer Maynard Solomon, the great composer's ambivalence toward both his parents was profound. His father, a mediocre musician and an alcoholic, brutalized his son to keep the boy at his musical studies, beating him and sometimes shutting him in the cellar. Solomon thinks young Beethoven reacted to this by creating a fantasy of an ideal father that eventually led him to believe that he was really the illegitimate son of an aristocrat. Later in life this fantasy caused the composer considerable embarrassment when he was unable to prove the claim. The text of Beethoven's first known composition was a song entitled "To an Infant" centering on the theme, "who is my real father?"

Beethoven also had strong mixed feelings about his mother, despising her for entangling him in his father's fall into profligacy and alcoholism yet continuing to idealize her throughout his life, calling her "goodhearted" and "my best friend." Beethoven's negative feelings toward her were in fact embodied in his fantasy of his illegitimate birth. As Solomon points out, by portraying his mother as having had a child out of wedlock, the fantasy degraded her into a "fallen woman." Beethoven's powerful love-hate feelings toward his parents were probably also bound up with his contradictory feelings of inadequacy and specialness (the discovery, for example, that he was a far better musician than his father, who was more powerful).

This ambivalence no doubt influenced Beethoven's strong contrary emotions about women and marriage. Throughout his life he managed to fall in love with women who were either already married, didn't want him, or were of the wrong class. His love affairs were repeatedly torn by his desire to be possessed and the opposing fear that he would lose what he called, somewhat ambiguously, his "vital powers" in the relationship.

In the one instance where a woman fully reciprocated his affections, Beethoven panicked. The woman has become known to history as the "immortal beloved," after the form of address Beethoven used for her in the single letter that survives as a reference to their romance. His letter to her indicates that this unknown woman was ready to leave her husband and live with him, an offer that left Beethoven reeling with ambivalence. " . . . Your love makes me at once the happiest and the unhappiest of men," he declared, and then added, "at my age I need a steady, quiet life—can that be so in our connection?" Nothing further came of the affair.

Beethoven also frequently talked of suicide, keeping himself in the midst of primal ambivalence—desire for both life and death.

According to Solomon, Beethoven's storms of contraries over the women he fell in love with, or relatives, or over life itself were associated with periods of high creativity. Beethoven was aware of the connection. Writing in his daybook after the immortal-beloved affair, he concluded that his inability to find a female companion signified a destiny to taste life only through his art. *"Thou mayest no longer be a man,* not for thyself, only for others," he wrote. (The italics are his.)

It's fair to say Beethoven's works are in important ways musical representations of the torrents of ambivalence he experienced. Solomon describes the opera *Fidelio* as "a seething compound of contradictory and ambivalent psychological themes and fantasies, lightly disguised by an ethical content and a *Singspiel* surface." In the *Eroica,* Beethoven's personal ambivalence hooks up with the ambivalence many others of his day felt toward the heroic figure of Napoleon Bonaparte. Solomon says, "Striving to free himself from his lifelong pattern of submission to the domination of authority figures, Beethoven was drawn to the conqueror who had confounded the venerable leaders of Europe and set himself in their place. If homage is on the surface, the underlying themes are patricide and fratricide." In the flow and counterflow of his musical themes and phrases Beethoven's ambivalence is mirrored everywhere in his work.

▪

Psychobiographer Mary Gedo argues that the giant of modern art, Pablo Picasso, was driven by strongly ambivalent feelings about females, stemming in part from his admiration for his mother's tenacity and his anger at her tyrannical domination of his childhood household. Gedo says, "As an aged man, he would describe himself as one who had suffered greatly at the hands of women, a statement borne out by the stormy history of his heterosexual relationships. Perhaps at a deeper level he regarded his suffering, including his venereal infection, as a just punishment for his underlying ambivalence toward women."

Picasso's ambivalence about women fed directly into his art—becoming infused in a seemingly endless stream of paintings of females where the monstrous and harsh aspects of his emotions were integrated dynamically with their opposite.

Françoise Gilot, mother of two of Picasso's children, writes that it regularly took her four hours to get Picasso out of bed in the morning, most of the time spent convincing him that his life was worthwhile. Getting him to make a decision to go anywhere was next to impossible. In the context of such extraordinary ambivalence surrounding even the most ordinary activities, it is interesting to hear Picasso describe his working process—an echo of da Vinci:

I start with a head and wind up with an egg. Or even if I start with an egg and wind up with a head, I'm always on the way between the two and I'm never happy with either one or the other. What interests me is to set up what you might call the *rapports de grand écart*—the most unexpected relationship possible between things I want to speak about. . . . There's a certain tension and for me that tension is a lot more important than the stable equilibrium of harmony, which doesn't interest me at all. Reality must be torn apart in every sense of the word.

■

Isaac Newton's central ambivalence has been alluded to in his sense of chosenness. Newton was born prematurely on Christmas Day 1642 and was not expected to live. His biographer, Manuel says, "There was something miraculous about Isaac's survival, a feeling that was communicated to him early in life and would be reinforced when he escaped the bubonic plague; like the biblical Isaac whom he knew so well, Isaac Newton too had been saved at the last moment by divine intervention."

On the other hand, Newton was so weak he had to wear a "bolster around his neck to keep his head upon his shoulders" and had difficulty breathing. "The shakiness of Newton's self-esteem throughout his life may have one of its origins in an infantile failure to be satiated at the breast and in his littleness."

Manuel thinks Newton felt passionate ambivalence toward his mother for remarrying after his father died—furious, yet longing to possess her. The biographer cites a free-associated list of words Newton set down in a notebook as evidence of this unconscious ambivalence spilling out. Newton's list was written under the rubric "Of Kindred, & Titles." Manuel reports on its contents:

M starts with *Marriage,* moves on to *Mother* . . . ; it is followed by a word of idealization, *Marquesse,* and then by *Manslayer. Wife, Wedlock, Wooer, Widdow, Widdower* . . . completed by *Whoore.* The letter F begins with *Father* . . . followed by *Fornicator, Flatterer,* and then two geographic proper nouns with overtones of sin and sensuality to a young puritan, *Frenchman* and *Florentine.* At the end, under *Y, Yeoman* stands alone—the status of his true father, who died before he was born. Ambivalence toward his mother would color Newton's whole style of life.

Manuel goes on to speculate that Newton's relationship with his mother was "a great source of power, strength, and energy." It was in his mother's garden that he reputedly noticed the apple drawn ("attracted") to the earth and conceived of the principles of gravity, and he referred to his knowledge and inventions as his "Garden." Thus Newton's ambivalent attraction to his mother was linked directly to his vision.

■

An ambivalence seems contained in Georgia O'Keeffe's early "memory" of the nuance of "the brightness of light" and the color of the flowered quilt. O'Keeffe said she could recall that her first months of life were shrouded by the dark rooms of the farmhouse where she was born and kept during the long Wisconsin winter. Being set out in the bright sunlight on the multicolored quilt was a delicious contrast. However, there with her that day, she remembered, was her older brother and another child who was receiving all the attention from the adults. She said that as she crawled around the quilt she felt, "Why doesn't anyone think *I'm* beautiful?" She squirmed off the quilt, she recalled, and was thrust back onto it. O'Keeffe clearly intended to convey that these early impressions of her ambivalent delight and jealousy played an important role in her later vision.

▪

Ernest Hemingway's obsession with suicide places him with Beethoven and Woolf in having a central ambivalence about living itself. He accused his father of cowardice for shooting himself and yet chose that method for his own death. As a young man, Hemingway confided in letters to the woman who would become his first wife that it required an effort to convince himself not to take his own life. Hemingway was strongly ambivalent about many things, including his mother and father; homosexuals; his own courage and hunting.

These last two may be a surprise to readers familiar with the accounts of Hemingway's heroism and of the almost sadistic blood lust that would sometimes lead him to kill hundreds of animals on a single hunting trip.

Hemingway's heroism is counterposed by his preoccupation with fear and cowardice. For example, a large number of the heroic characters in his stories are afraid of the dark. This ambivalence is also suggested by the report of biographers that when he was five years old, young Hemingway boasted fearfully that he was " 'fraid of nothing."

Hemingway's ambivalence toward hunting, which he glorified, comes through most strongly in his story of the young boy hunting elephants in *Garden of Eden* and in the old fisherman's dialogue with the marlin he has caught in *The Old Man and the Sea.* But it is also present in almost all of his fictional descriptions of hunting and fishing, where his use of sensual detail conveys a poignant sense of the life and death struggle of—and an implicit identification with—the animal being killed.

It is significant that Hemingway consciously appreciated the value of doubt and uncertainty, as did da Vinci and Picasso.

Like many other great male creators in history, Hemingway also exhibited heavily ambivalent feelings toward women (and toward his own sexual identity, as has been recently claimed in new Hemingway biographies). The result of the ambivalence in this case was not one beneficial to the artist's creative vision. In an effort to suppress negative emotions, Hemingway tended to unconvincingly idealize the women in his fiction or make them "bitches." John Gedo, who has worked with high-level creators in his psychoanalytic practice, supports the hypothesis of Conrad psychobiographer Bernard Meyer that "the artist has to avoid subject matter too close to his active conflicts in order to do his best work." Hemingway was generally unable to do this with women. In contrast, Beethoven's choice of Napoleon as the image for the *Eroica* was probably successful because, while activating his ambivalence, the subject was far enough removed from it.

▪

Poet Langston Hughes was also able to get distance on his ambivalence. Though his parents were both black, Hughes wrote frequently on the theme of the "tragic mulatto." Hughes's biographer, Arnold Rampersad, says that in the poet's portrayal of this theme, "typically, a young man of mixed race is caught disastrously between the black and white worlds, but especially between longing for acknowledgment by his white father and being disowned by him." When a scholar friend pointed the tragic mulatto theme out, Hughes indicated that he identified with such a doomed young man and that the theme had to do with what he called his "own parental situation." Rampersad believes that Hughes was referring to his ambivalence toward his mother and a deep hatred (necessarily also ambivalent) toward his father. The mulatto theme evidently allowed Hughes to achieve the distance he needed on these feelings so he could transform them into universal drama.

▪

Does all this indicate that ambivalence is a core feature of creative vision?

Rothenberg, for one, believes that biographers stressing ambivalence are responding to more than just an old implicit theory that creators are full of polarities and ambivalences. He adds, however, "It's the human condition to be ambivalent. It's the way creators use ambivalence that makes the difference."

NEGATIVE CAPABILITY

The term ambivalence was coined by psychotherapist Eugen Bleuler in 1910. Freud elaborated on Bleuler's idea of mixed thoughts or feelings, postulating that there are opposing pairs of instinctual tendencies such as activity-passivity, masculinity-femininity, sadism-masochism, life-death. These develop into emotional ambivalence toward people and objects.

People usually handle their ambivalence in a couple of ways. If you're ambivalent about which TV to purchase, for example, you can compare brands and resolve the ambivalence by making a choice. If you're angry with someone you love, you can determine the real, underlying reason you've been angry and do something about it—"work through" the anger, as the therapeutic professionals say. Such mature resolutions of psychological ambivalences are rather rare, however. It's more usual for people *not* to "work through" the ambivalence. Instead, one side of the feeling becomes denied or suppressed, only to pop out somewhere else. An example is the way Hemingway's ambivalence seemed to pop out in his fiction. The denied disappointment and anger side of his ambivalent feelings toward real-life women apparently reemerged as his fictional female "bitches," while the denied idealizing side resulted in fictional women who are romanticized cartoonlike subordinates to males.

A strong ambivalence that is not resolved can manifest in this sort of displacement behavior, or show itself as paralysis, an inability to act or think at all on matters touched by the ambivalence.

How could such an unfortunate mental state have a positive role in creative vision?

We might start to answer that question by considering an interesting piece of research. A few years ago scientists found that when they presented people with conflicting or incongruous information, dyssynchronous brain waves, indicating alertness, appeared. The investigators concluded that conflict can be a source of drive which causes increased learning and attention. Ambivalence is derived from conflict and it arouses the brain. If the ambivalence in some area or context is not denied, suppressed or resolved but instead is "tolerated" it leads individuals to experience a state which Desy Safán-Gerard, a UCLA psychologist who is also a painter, described as "an enrichment in our appreciation of reality and ourselves."

The creator's ability to *tolerate* ambivalence may be what romantic poet John Keats called a "Negative Capability," that is, when a person "is capable of being in uncertainties, mysteries, doubts, without any irritable reaching after fact and reason." Keats's idea is an echo of da Vinci's belief that a painter needs to doubt, and of Picasso's interest in the "tension" between things. Famed physiologist Claude Bernard said doubt is crucial because "those who have an excessive faith in their ideas are not well fitted to make discoveries." Margaret Mead insisted, "The only people who can get a thing done well are those who think they can't do it." Sculptor Jean Arp described something like negative capability in terms that tie it to the circular paradoxes we discussed in the last chapter. Arp said that the creator must maintain a state in "the fire of balance," in a movement "between Above and Below, light and darkness, eternity and transitoriness."

Such sustained uncertainty probably involves some discomfort. In fact, LaViolette points out that the loop between the limbic system and the prefrontal cortex—the loop that amplifies emotional nuances—is also concerned with psychological pain. When the connections of that loop are severed, there's a reduction in the intensity of pain. Thus a type of psychological pain may be the price required for adhering to nuances with all their doubts and uncertainties.

Erich Fromm wrote that a "condition for creativeness is the *ability to accept conflict* and *tension* resulting from polarity, rather than to avoid them. This idea is very much in contrast to the current climate of opinion, in which one attempts to avoid conflict as much as possible" (italics Fromm's).

So, resisting the brain's tendency to seek after certainties and experiencing the pain and the arousal that go with the uncertainty, produces what Keats called "the wakeful anguish of the soul." The depth to which creators experience this wakeful anguish as a function of their vision seems illustrated by a comment O'Keeffe made in a PBS interview given just before her death. On the surface it would appear that O'Keeffe lived a life essentially free from want and the kind of dramatic personal tragedy that often haunts modern artists. Yet in the interview she readily agreed with the statement that she had in fact lived all her life on a "knife's edge." She said, "I'd walk it again. So what if you do fall off?"

Negative capability may well be linked to many aspects of creativity, including the creative scientist's ability to stay with a problem long after colleagues would have gone on to apparently more fruitful research, and to the oft-quoted finding that creators have a much higher tolerance than the rest of us for ambiguity. In the case of Hemingway, evidently he could achieve a negative capability for his doubts and uncertainties (ambivalence) about hunting, but not for his feelings about women. He was unable to get enough distance so that those uncertainties could enrich his work.

INTER (a vague shape in a chair): Hold on. Earlier you said these geniuses were so sure of themselves because they had this "nuance" and "sense of truth" to guide them. Now you're saying the important thing is doubt and uncertainty. Caught in a bit of ambivalence yourself, aren't you?

MUSING: Maybe not. Because I suspect there's an inherent ambivalence to nuance and creative truth. They are a perception of a reality which is not exactly this and it's not exactly that.

David Bohm illuminates this point. Bohm, coauthor of a recent book analyzing creativity and science, argues that ambivalence is a fundamental but generally unrecognized aspect of thought. "Any particular thought," Bohm says, "will arouse the notion of its opposite by simply adding 'not.'" Bohm believes that by "tolerating" ambivalence in some area creators are zeroing their visions in on the very ground out of which thought arises: for instance, the polarity in Einstein's themata mentioned by Holton. Bohm explains, "See, one moment you may favor continuity, then the next moment you may favor the opposite. You can see continuity and discontinuity are related because any continuous system can be thought of as made up of a large number of discontinuous elements. Any discontinuous element is formed from a continuous background and this can go on indefinitely. This ambivalence could never be resolved." He postulates that staying with that ambivalent movement (exercising negative capability) gives a creator access to great energy and insight into nuances usually obscured by our polarized patterns of thought.

INTER (leaning forward): Now, before you go any further, let me ask you something. Do geniuses all have some big ambivalences motivating them which they do something with?

MUSING: Heavens, no! No one is trying to imply that psychological ambivalence is an explanation for creativity. That would be ridiculous. Think of all the people in the world who are profoundly ambivalent about one thing or another and don't produce any creative work.

INTER: Hrumph. It's clear you're no logician. Might one not argue that powerful ambivalence is a necessary condition but not a sufficient one for creativity?

MUSING: That won't work either if we consider the exceptions.

Let's consider, for example, the case of Niels Bohr.

▪

Bohr was undoubtedly one of the towering geniuses of twentieth-century physics. He worked in the paradoxical realm of the atom where he was the first to propose that electrons appear in one place, then in another without any traveling in between. He embraced the startling quantum idea that the subatomic building blocks are both particles and waves. In the 1920s, while at the epicenter of the activity to formulate quantum theory, he promulgated his principle of complementarity. It says that no language will be sufficient for giving a picture of what goes on at the smallest and most basic levels of reality; we can only describe this reality from opposing or complementary directions. We are condemned, Bohr insisted, to a kind of permanent ambivalence with regard to the subatomic world. Nothing like this notion had ever been introduced into science. The actual formulation of complementarity is so subtle that it's still not understood by most scientists.

Bohr's fascination with the elusive, contrary dimensions of reality can be traced to his childhood. Bohr's son, Hans, said: "One of the favorite maxims of my father was the distinction between the two sorts of truths, profound truths recognized by the fact that the opposite is also a profound truth, in contrast to trivialities where opposites are obviously absurd."

Bohr's biographer, Ruth Moore, says that in college the young scientist was attracted by the twists and paradoxes of Kierkegaard and by a curious little book called *Tale of a Danish*

Student. Moore believes one of the characters reflected Bohr's own state of mind:

> Certainly I have seen before thoughts put on paper; but since I have come distinctly to perceive the contradiction implied in such an action, I feel completely incapable of forming a single written sentence. . . . . The mind cannot proceed without moving along a certain line; but before following this line, it must already have thought it. Therefore one has already thought every thought before one thinks it. . . . . The insight into the impossibility of thinking contains itself an impossibility, the recognition of which again implies an inexplicable contradiction.

Later, during the heated debates in Copenhagen over the ultimate interpretation of quantum theory Bohr reportedly beamed when they reached an impasse: "How wonderful that we have met with a paradox. Now we have some hope of making progress." Colleagues observed that writing a paper was an excruciating experience for the Danish physicist because he felt it necessary to accompany every statement with its opposite.

It would be reasonable to expect from the above that Bohr was afflicted by a high degree of psychological ambivalence. However, it would be difficult to show that in fact this was the case. By all accounts Bohr was an exceptionally well-adjusted individual. He had an apparently unambivalent relationship with his father, who was an eminent physiologist, and with his mother, brother and sister. His childhood was a happy one. He played national team soccer with his brother, and did well in school. His marriage lasted over fifty years and was an extremely congenial one. He was a doting father to his five sons. Brilliant, sane, compassionate, energetic—such attributes are easily applied to Bohr. There are reports that he could seem bullying and stubborn in pursuit of a scientific idea, but that hardly qualifies as conflict or ambivalence.

In fact it seems quite wrong to view Bohr's creative productions and theoretical preoccupations in terms of ambivalence or characterological polarities. It may turn out that future biographers will reveal that Bohr suffered from some deep emotional conflicts, but it seems safer to assume that Bohr's complementarity idea and his lifelong interest in paradox have another source.

INTER (exasperated): Another source! But you've forgotten my question!

MUSING: No, because to some degree there's always ambivalence. It is, as Rothenberg reminds us, the human condition. So Bohr must have experienced it, too, at least in the usual doses. But I think your real question was about the role of ambivalence in creative vision and how it is connected to what Keats called negative capability. In order to answer that we'll need to look into this other "source."

6

Omnivalence

THE HUNGER OF 'MORE'

Addressing a group of her Bloomsbury friends who met regularly to take turns entertaining each other with their memoirs, Virginia Woolf said:

Am I speaking for myself only when I say that though nothing worth calling an adventure has befallen me since I last occupied this thorny and prominent chair I still seem to myself a subject of inexhaustible and fascinating anxiety?—a volcano in perpetual eruption? Am I alone in my egotism when I say that never does the pale light of dawn filter through the blinds of 52 Tavistock Square but I open my eyes and exclaim, "Good God! Here I am again!"—not always with pleasure, often with pain; sometimes with a spasm of acute disgust—but always, always with interest?

There is something more in this last statement than simple ambivalence about life. There is an experimental attitude. In her disgust and interest Woolf was like an alchemist contemplating the contrary meanings of the *prima materia*. Robert Frost called this state "a lover's quarrel with the world." Contradictory feelings are experienced not as mere conflict or ambivalence, but as possibilities, potentials, mystery, openness. *Omni*valence might be a better term.

As we'll see, omnivalence is similar to ambivalence in some ways and yet quite unlike it. The relationship between the two is complex. Omnivalence is a dusky sea of uncertainties and nuance. Powerful ambivalences and polarities in the creator's life and personality may be used as a vehicle to reach or remain

110

in that sea. The reverse may also be the case. Immersion in omnivalence may foster as a side effect heightened degrees of ambivalence or polarities in the creator. In both cases, omnivalence and psychological ambivalence (either the powerful conflictual ambivalences that beset Picasso and Newton or the perfectly ordinary ones that undoubtedly attended Bohr) blur into each other. Perhaps the two crosscatalyze each other like two chemicals which both need to be present in order for a new product (a creative vision) to form. If so, then my guess is that omnivalence can be catalyzed by a rather moderate, even normal, degree of ambivalence, whereas ambivalence requires a high concentration of omnivalence to achieve creative function.

But what is omnivalence? Let's back up a minute and try to get a feel for it.

A wonderful capsule expression of omnivalence infuses the opening sentence of Hemingway's short story "In Another Country." The narrator, a wounded soldier, says, "In the fall the war was always there, but we did not go to it any more." Consider the depth of the line. It contains a host of contraries: relief, loss, wistfulness, despair—and more. The sense that there is "more to it" is a characteristic of omnivalence. Hemingway also captures this 'more'ness poignantly in *A Moveable Feast*, where he writes about the years he and his first wife lived in Paris. He remembers spending a splendid day at the races and having a picnic, then a meal at a good restaurant.

It was a wonderful meal . . . but when we had finished and there was no question of hunger any more, the feeling that had been like hunger . . . was still there and was still there when we caught the bus home. It was there when we came in the room and after we had gone to bed and made love in the dark, it was there. When I woke with the windows open and the moonlight on the roofs of the tall houses, it was there. I put my face away from the moonlight into the shadow but I could not sleep and lay awake thinking about it.

Mathematician-philosopher Bertrand Russell detected a keen sense of omnivalence containing quite a different mood in his friend Joseph Conrad. Russell, who had come to know Conrad in later years, said it was evident that the great novelist experienced "civilized and morally tolerable human life as a dangerous walk on a thin crust of barely cooled lava which at any moment might break and let the unwary sink into fiery depths." Russell's impression of Conrad's sense of life is confirmed by Conrad's novels, which consistently convey that there is more to things than meets the eye or mind and that at any moment one may simply fall through the world into a hidden reality.

The sense that there is something 'more' or 'other' is probably inherent in the nuances and themata that comprise a creator's vision. The 'more'ness probably derives from the action of contraries in the nuance. Recall our earlier metaphor: A nuance is like a vivid but subtle perfume. Ironically, good perfume is made of such contrary-smelling substances as skunk oil and flowers. Because of the way the contraries interact with one another, the elements that make up the scent of a nuance remain elusive; it is neither one thing nor another. It is 'more'. A creative artist tries to make the audience feel the pressure of the 'more' in the artwork—which seems to be what short story writer Jorge Luis Borges meant when he said, "the aesthetic act is the imminence of a revelation which is never fulfilled."

That something like this can occur in the sciences as well is illustrated by Russell who, as it turned out, had reason to be sympathetic to Conrad's sense of omnivalence. In 1902 Russell discovered a hidden paradox in the new approach then being employed by mathematicians seeking to prove that the hundreds of theorems of arithmetic could be derived from a few assumptions using Aristotelian logic. To everyone's dismay, Russell detected a twist in the new mathematical argument that meant that as far as any totally systematic logical approach went "each alternative leads to its opposite," a state of omnivalence. After introducing such a dramatic deep uncertainty into mathematical systems, however, Russell spent the next twenty years trying to prove that systematic certainty could exist, nonetheless. "I wanted certainty in the kind of way in which people want religious faith." *Wanting* religious faith, however, is not the same as having it. Such wanting is an imminence never fulfilled. Thus Russell was describing his own walk along the crust of lava, his own omnivalent acrobatics over the certainty/uncertainty precipice.

Omnivalent contraries or contrasts in a nuance create a movement that can be described as the activity of revealing *and* concealing, the turning of the urn—making omnivalence the movement of 'more'ness in creative truth. Federico García Lorca called perceiving the truth of a great work of art perceiving its *duende.* His account suggests that *duende* is also omnivalence. Lorca wrote, *"Duende* likes the edge of things, the wound, and . . . it is drawn to where [contrasting yet similar] forms fuse themselves in a longing greater than their visible expressions."

Think of the Mona Lisa's smile. Rothenberg points out that the nuance of that smile has been described throughout history in contrary ways, as "both 'good and wicked,' as well as both 'cruel' and 'compassionate;' 'smile of the Saints at Rheims' and 'worldly, watchful and self-satisfied;' showing both 'modesty and a secret sensuous joy.' " This integration of contraries creates in the viewer a perception of omnivalence or something 'more' which includes the viewer's sense that the smile conveys some elusive and universal truth.

Creators have sometimes attempted to analyze their feeling that their work represents an embodiment of omnivalence in which contraries fuse and move. Woolf said she was able to "achieve a symmetry by means of infinite discords." Stravinsky claimed he accomplished unity in his compositions by a "harmony of varieties." "Variety," he said, "is valid only as a means of attaining similarity. . . . Similarity is hidden; it must be sought out. . . ."

But the language of omnivalence is tricky. The words opposite, contrary, contrast, variety and similarity, symmetry and discord—all are attempts to convey the movement of omnivalence which is not in fact adequately conveyed by any of these terms.

The same limitation applies to the term ambivalence. Omnivalence is superficially like ambivalence because in both cases a mind is stretched between things that are pulling at and away from each other. But there the similarity ends. For in ambivalence the stretch involves merely conflict, while in omnivalence the mind is moved to unfold itself in what Bohm calls "the space between." In the space between, there is a richness of meanings. "If you say north and south are opposites," Bohm says, "you then have to recognize there's a whole range in between. Therefore you have to tremendously enrich the field to another level in order to resolve the opposites."

The chief instruments of creative writers—metaphor and irony—are cunningly designed to produce this space between. John Donne's famous metaphor comparing two lovers to the two legs of a drawing compass depends upon compelling the reader's mind to explore the gap between items that are held in such different categories of thought that they are contraries in effect if not in fact.

Irony also explores the gap by making a statement mean both what it says and something opposite (or something sharply contrasting). Oedipus proclaims that he's going to get the murderer of his father. His statement is ironical because the murderer turns out to have been Oedipus himself. Irony is a perfect instrument for nuance. Philosopher of art Suzanne Langer said, "The very structure of human feeling is ironical." In the normal course of thinking and feeling, the omnivalent aspects of the world, which irony and metaphor so wonderfully express, are flattened out or shaped into the simplified categories of our literal and fairly certain reality. A great creative work like *Oedipus Rex* plunges our awareness into a richness and fundamental uncertainty (the 'more') that lies around us and in our feeling and thought.

According to the theories of Koestler and French philosopher Henri Bergson, humor should be fitted into this picture, too. The regal cultured doyenne who gets a pie in her face has something in common with irony and metaphor. For irony, metaphor, humor—all undercut our fixed meanings, suddenly springing upon us the revelation that things which we have categorized emotionally as contraries and contrasts (grandes dames and slung food) are *not* so contrasting and contrary after all. And yet they are. So round and round they go in "the space between" of omnivalence. Creative vision contains a playful quality. The Hemingway line, ". . . the war was always there, but we did not go to it any more" has a kind of cosmic humor. Picasso's paintings, even Einstein's relativity, are playful. For example, consider the subtle humor in the fact that *"Invarianten Theorie"* becomes "relativity theory" and in Einstein's thought experiment where he imagined himself riding on a light wave.

Bohm believes that since thought itself is normally polarized—asserting one opposite or another—omnivalence can be considered the result of a momentary suspension of thought. It is the terrain that lies on the other side of exercising a negative capability. "If you hold these opposites together, then you suspend thought and your mind must move to a new level. The suspension of thought allows an intelligence beyond thought to act. Then you can create a new form."

David Shainberg offers a similar idea. Author of *The Transforming Self,* Shainberg is a psychotherapist who gave up his practice in order to pursue a career as a painter. He has written extensively about the structure of consciousness. "Consciousness itself is a polar phenomenon," he says. "Given that, one capacity of the creator is to make clear that we're in polarity and not in it at the same time."

The semiotician Alfred Korzybski proclaims, "Whatever you say a thing is, it isn't" and "the map is not the territory." A sense of omnivalence makes the mind aware of that.

The sense of omnivalence—with its suspension and tension and movement of contraries and contrasts in the space between, and with its longing for 'more'—is probably related to the dynamics of the opposing themata geniuses become obsessed with. It is probably involved in the "questioning," "wondering" and "incompleteness" mentioned by Gray as the characteristics of nuances and in what LaViolette calls the activity of keeping the brain "open." It is the brain's negative capability.

And omnivalence is also surely related to all that ambivalence that wreathes the lives of so many great creators. If feelings of a simultaneous love/hate toward a parent or an uneasiness over one's sexual identity do nothing else, they acquaint the future creator with the inadequacy and uncertainty of what are presumably the most basic categories we use to define our lives. Ambivalence about life, sexuality, authority, money or anything else can undermine or cripple (as it usually does) or it can link to a wider questioning, sensitivity and exploration at the boundaries of the contraries that schematize our existence. Ambivalence can help sustain a commitment to the omnivalent outlook, or the omnivalent outlook can give birth to the ability to tolerate ambivalences (negative capability) and transmute them in the sphere of creative activity. Or perhaps all these factors revolve together in a circular paradox.

Look at how many of the aspects of omnivalence we've discussed are evident in this passage from Darwin's journal, written shortly after he arrived in Brazil on the *Beagle*.

The delight one experiences in such times bewilders the mind; if the eye attempts to follow the flight of a gaudy butter-fly, it is arrested by some strange tree or fruit; if watching an insect one forgets it in the strange flower it is crawling over; if turning to admire the splendour of the scenery, the individual character of the foreground fixes the attention. The mind is a chaos of delight, out of which a world of future & more quiet pleasure will arise.

Note the last sentence: The nuance-veiled themata of complexity and simplicity. It appears Darwin is near the core of what compels him to do his creative work. His emotional state and his cognitive quest for a simple explanation to nature's wildness have merged. The 'more'ness of it all surrounds him and wells up in him, filling even his sense of time, where something 'more' will happen. His state is almost ambivalence about this chaos, but it is much more than that because it includes mystery and wonder—and negative capability. This capability is evident in his willingness to let the swarming wildness and his desire for simplicity remain suspended together until the "future."

Another example illustrates the transformation and mutual catalyzing of ambivalence and omnivalence.

Russian filmmaker Sergei Eisenstein became known for his cinematic depictions of cruelty. Eisenstein grew up in an abusive household and cruelty became part of his vision. He claimed that this aspect of vision was catalyzed by an image in a French film he saw when he was very young. The image seems to have had a focusing effect on Eisenstein somewhat like that which the compass had on young Einstein and the memory of St. Ives had on Virginia Woolf. The film was about a farmer who had some prisoners working on his farm. One of them was a sergeant who fell in love with the farmer's wife. In retribution the farmer had the man branded on the shoulder. Eisenstein said:

In my childhood it gave me nightmares. It used to come to me at night. Sometimes I became the sergeant, sometimes the branding iron. I would grab hold of his shoulder. Sometimes it seemed to be my own shoulder. At other times it was someone else's. I no longer knew who was branding whom. For years on end, blond side-whiskers (the sergeant was fair) or black ones . . . evoked this scene from me. Until the time came when . . . the ocean of cruelty in my own films swamped the impressions produced by this "fateful" film. . . .

Every time Eisenstein visualized some scene of cruelty to put in a film, he would see in his mind the smoke rising from the prisoner's flesh.

Probably the branding image reflects Eisenstein's ambivalence about the cruelty he was subjected to by his parents—his anger at them, his guilt that he may have somehow deserved such treatment. But there is 'more.' In his mind he doesn't know who is being cruel to whom. The film image has become turned into an image of total omnivalence. This omnivalent impression becomes reflected in Eisenstein's own films as a profound ambiguity between cruel acts (disorder) and the aesthetic order of the film itself.

Shainberg thinks the dynamic contraries and the space between of omnivalence help the creator see the truth without judging or excusing it. When the creator is beyond categorizing judgments, (s)he is beyond what (s)he knows. "It's the willingness to be *aware* of that. Then one sees the truth exists beyond even the creative form one makes. It might be embedded in that form, and the creator tries to convey that, but it is also beyond it."

Such a sense spreads out across creative process. Praised for one of his poems, Shelley said that the words conveyed only a shadow of what he saw. Beethoven wrote of being inspired by the contemplation of the night sky, but that "when from time to time I try to give shape and form in sound to the feelings roused within me, alas! I meet with cruel disappointment. In disgust I throw away the sheet of paper I have soiled, and am almost convinced that no earthborn being can ever hope to set down by means of sounds, words, colour, or in sculpture, the heavenly pictures that rise before his awakened imagination!" He then links the effort to capture this omnivalence, or 'more'ness of his insight, to his drive to formulate the individual-universal equation. "For only by hard, persistent labour through such powers as are bestowed on a man can the work of art be made worthy of the Creator and Preserver of everlasting Nature."

Newton said:

I do not know what I may appear to the world; but to myself I seem to have been only like a boy playing on the seashore and diverting himself and then finding a smoother pebble or a prettier shell than ordinary, while the greater ocean of truth lay all undiscovered before me.

In the 'more'ness of omnivalence also lurks the circular paradox that the act of expressing one's vision is an act of discovering what it is. Flannery O'Connor articulated this when she said:

It is what is left over when everything explainable has been explained that makes a story worth writing and reading. The writer's gaze has to extend beyond the surface, beyond mere problems, until it touches that realm of mystery which is the concern of prophets. True prophecy in the novelist's case is a matter of seeing near things with their extensions of meanings and thus of seeing far things close up. If a writer believes that the life of a man is and will remain essentially mysterious, what he sees on the surface, or what he understands, will be of interest to him only as it leads him into the experience of mystery itself.

The pervasiveness of omnivalent 'more'ness for creators is implied in experimental evidence gathered in a University of Chicago study that showed that the higher level the creator, the more likely (s)he is to feel that more could be done to improve the work.

Koestler calls the 'more'ness aspect of omnivalence in scientists an "oceanic sense of wonder" that occurs in the vision of great scientists no matter what their religious persuasion or lack of persuasion. Koestler links it closely with the drives of "self-asserting" and "self-transcending"—that is, with the great scientist's urge toward formulating an individual-universal equation. Koestler's list of exemplars for this oceanic wonder includes Galileo, Kepler, Newton, Franklin, Faraday, Maxwell, Darwin and Pasteur. Galileo, for example, "was the first of a race of . . . scientists convinced of the infallibility of their 'exact empirical methods,' in fact he created the type. It comes as a surprise to hear him talk about things 'not only unknown but unimaginable.' But this ultimate modesty, derived from a sense of wonder close to mysticism, is found in all great scientists."

CREATORS AND MYSTICS

The step is not a long one between the omnivalence in a creator's vision, and the mystical and quasireligious pronouncements dotted here and there like exotic flowers in the biographies of most creative geniuses.

The drive to wholeness alone might incline creators to a literal interest in mysticism or a tendency to sound like mystics, but there are other reasons too. For example, traditionally mystics have insisted on the *coincidentia oppositorum* (coincidence of opposites) of their mystical experience. The creator's immersion in nuances fraught with the contraries and 'more'-ness of omnivalence suggests a similar experience.

Isadora Duncan wrote of her omnivalence in terms of her propensity to perform in "a state of complete suspense." It was a state that, as creativity scholar Brewster Ghiselin has pointed out, was very close to a religious one.

René Descartes built his rational system on a kind of ongoing negative capability that he called "methodological doubt." This omnivalence was related to his project to unify all the sciences and mathematics and reveal the secret mind of God.

Mystical religious experience is traditionally characterized by awe, an emotion composed of wonder and dread. The implicit contraries in awe make it quite similar to the emotion (or perception) of omnivalence: that is, a stunning richness of meanings suspended and pointing beyond our customary understandings of reality.

Creativity and mysticism are not merely similar; for some creators mystical religious feeling is literally a part of their vision. Van Gogh's early desire to become a prophet and evangelist was frustrated. He then came to believe that his painting could be his prophecy. He wrote his brother Theo: "To try to understand the real significance of what the great artists, the serious masters, tell us in their masterpieces, *that* leads to God." Emily Dickinson set out to recapture the omnivalence of the Bible by writing a new kind of spiritual text with her own poems.

Modern creators, born into secular times, have turned to creative activity as an apparent substitute for omnivalent religious experience. Kurt Badt claims Cézanne underwent a conversion in which the loneliness of his loss of God was transformed into an ascetic determination to use his art to "reunite man with the transcendental." The statement is an interesting one to think about next time you look at Cézanne's bowls of fruit on a wrinkled tablecloth.

When Einstein's early religious feelings turned sour with the discovery that biblical stories are not literally true, he devoted himself to science as the outlet for what he called "cosmic religious feeling." He wrote:

The religious geniuses of all ages have been distinguished by this kind of religious feeling, which knows no dogma and no God conceived in man's image; so that there can be no church whose central teachings are based on it. . . . How can cosmic religious feeling be communicated from one person to another, if it can give rise to no definite notion of God and no theology? In my view, it is the most important function of art and science to awaken this feeling and keep it alive in those who are receptive to it.

Einstein's pronouncement is quintessential mysticism. Mystics have always found themselves outside the orbit of organized religion, though organized religion depends upon mystical experience for its revelations. Mysticism involves a direct apprehension of the truth of the divine not mediated by theology. Theologies exist by keeping contraries contrary— dividing those who will achieve salvation from those who won't, for instance. The mystic sees contraries fused or suspended, contacting a hidden reality beyond the polarities of thought.

The cases of van Gogh, Cézanne, Einstein and Dickinson indicate that for some creators mystical omnivalence is linked with the desire to formulate the individual-universal equation. This includes an evangelical need to share the omnivalent experience by creating works that will—to use Einstein's word—"awaken" a mystical feeling in others.

For other creators, mystical beliefs or interests seem largely a spillover from the omnivalence in creative activity rather than a primary preoccupation informing the activity.

One of Edison's biographers says, "Through much of his life Edison was attracted by mysticism. After the phonograph came into existence, he could almost sense a mystic force moving about in the universe." Edison reportedly developed an interest in Theosophy, an amalgam of spiritualism and Eastern mysticism.

Two of the fathers of quantum theory became fascinated by oriental mystical thought. Erwin Schrödinger believed our scientific view needed to be "amended, perhaps by a bit of blood transfusion from Eastern thought." Niels Bohr adopted the ancient Chinese mystical symbol of yin and yang for his family crest. Geneticist Barbara McClintock, intrigued by the paradoxes of Buddhism and Taoism, has declared she is proud to think of herself as a mystic.

■

Creators seem similar to mystics and sometimes have an affinity for mystical, religious-style perceptions. But are they truly mystics? Undoubtedly not. Or, they are so only metaphorically. Metaphorically we might say that their mysticism is like that heretical variety practiced by the ancient alchemists. Like the alchemists, who believed that the whirlpool of contraries was manifest in the *prima materia* wherein lay wholeness, truth and the powers of creation, creators find these attributes in the movement of omnivalence. Like the alchemists, who believed that the physical distillation of the *prima materia* was identical with the spiritual distillation of the soul, creators believe that transcendental experience can be manifested in a physical form—in an artwork or scientific discovery.

However, unlike the alchemists, creators don't seek by their labors to ultimately transcend the physical world and achieve a purely spiritual good. Instead, their goal is to burrow themselves more essentially in the sensory realm.

In his fascinating study of Virginia Woolf, Mark Hussey captures this idea nicely when he says, "In all [Woolf's] novels there is a sense of yearning, a tending toward the numinous and some revelation of mystery, and this conceptual background often shares the contours of a theology." But, then he adds, "Woolf . . . attested to . . . a 'reality' apart from actual life and yet rooted in it; not mysticism."

It is appropriate that even a definition of the creator's mystical bent loses itself, in the end, in the folds of omnivalence: that is, the creator's mysticism is always "more" than our defining terms.

A MYTH OF CREATIVITY

But recognizing the mystical, religious, sacred side of omnivalence prepares the way for dispelling a long-standing myth about creativity: the myth that the creator's drive is to make something new.

The newness myth was brought to a head a number of years ago by the eminent anthropologist, Claude Lévi-Strauss, who made the provocative charge that the centuries-old Western belief in creativity is an illusion. In a discussion of masks, Lévi-Strauss asserted that those "primitive" artforms so admired and imitated by modern artists like Picasso are not, in fact, examples of individual creative expression. Rather, the whole point of the mask for the mask-maker was to carry out the tradition of his tribe. Howard Gardner emphasizes this point: "In some tribes an artist trying to make something new could get himself killed." If this is the case, the argument goes—if the tribal creator's purpose is not to make something new and if creativity has been defined as the creator's desire to make something new—then what we call creativity must be a Western cultural invention.

The problem with the argument is that the idea of creativity as essentially the act of making something new, as "originality," is not an idea even modern creators would necessarily agree with. In fact, many would explicitly deny that this is what their creative activity is all about. Remember Faulkner said that only what a person "creates is important since there is nothing new to be said."

But what did he mean by this?

In other writings and in his Nobel acceptance speech, he expressed his belief that truth is "that which touches the heart." Such truth is eternal but must be constantly recreated by each "heart" that perceives it. Faulkner believed that Homer and Shakespeare created devices that stimulate this perception of truth and omnivalence in the hearts of their audience. Such stimulation is the aim of creative activity, according to Faulkner.

Faulkner's convictions are a clue that Western creativity with its emphasis on originality and "tribal" creativity with its emphasis on conformity are not really so different as they seem.

Anthropologists have observed that in many cultures masks are worn to stimulate what is called a "transpersonal experience." The phrase means that in some way the mask-wearer becomes the god or animal portrayed on the mask, or recognizes that god or animal nature within himself. For example, the Pacific Northwest Coast Indian transformation masks studied by Lévi-Strauss are transpersonal metaphors. One well-known long-beaked eagle mask pops open on hinges to reveal inside a carved painted human face; the mask itself is, of course, being worn by another "mask"—the human face beneath.

Marjorie Halpin, an anthropologist at the University of British Columbia and curator of ethnology at the university museum, which houses many of the finest examples of West Coast masks, has said that "in these masks you continually find beings transforming into other beings. A man is a bear, bear is a killer whale. The artist is showing a shared spirit—that all beings are in some way the same."

The mask-wearer, who is often also the mask-maker, is said to have a direct experience of this omnivalent state. Anthropologist Charles Laughlin calls it the "polyphasic" state (the *duende* "where forms fuse," as Lorca described it). Laughlin, who teaches at Carleton University in Ottawa and is coauthor of *Biogenetic Structuralism* and *The Spectrum of Ritual*, is trained in neurology. He believes masks like the Pacific Coast transformation masks serve to harmonize or "entrain" the reptilian, old mammalian and new mammalian brains. The masks are tools of a mental hygiene and are necessary because these three brains get out of sync with each other. Laughlin says, "One of the characteristics of human development is a process where the conscious part of the cortex is involved in establishing an organization for the brain. It assigns certain processes to different levels of brain function then loses track of them. They are then carried out more or less unconsciously." He believes the mask serves to entrain these unconscious personalities with more conscious ones so that the mask-maker, mask-wearer and the audience of masking rituals can recognize themselves as a spectrum of consciousness, a multiplicity of realities—a 'more'ness—rather than as conflicted or isolated islands of self.

The mask bestows on its maker, wearer and audience direct experience that a human being shades off into other animals, into the gods and into the unknown. He is everything and nothing. At the same time, according to Halpin, the masker and the audience are also aware that it is "just Uncle Harry behind the mask. That only deepens the mystery."

Laughlin thinks that our symbol-laden Western art serves the same neurological function as such ritual art—to provide an integrating omnivalent experience for both the maker and the audience. There are also crucial differences. One is this: The Seneca shaman cuts a "false face" mask from a tree and then waits to see if the tree will survive and prove the mask "good." The Bali performer receives the mask of an archetypal character from a mask-maker and then "lives" with it until he molds to it. Both the Seneca and the Bali inhabit cultures that value nuance, accept the simultaneity of contradictions, and appreciate the 'more'ness and mystery of existence more readily than our Western culture. Tribal cultures routinely accept the world around them as omnivalent, full of subtleties and hidden realities, whereas we have turned the universe into categorical knowledge.

But perhaps our Western geniuses retain the old spirit—

though they don't always realize it. Bohm mentions, for example, that contemporary physicists who strongly reject a mystical point of view and insist on the rational, in fact betray an omnivalent attitude in their reverence for mathematics, their quintessential rational tool. They treat mathematics, Bohm says, "as pure spirit," as "the truth about matter." Yet they admit they "don't know what the source of their mathematics is, they call it 'mysterious.' Poincaré called it mysterious as did Einstein."

The importance to creators of themata, nuance, omnivalence, truth, wholeness and the individual-universal equation strongly suggests that their motivation is not so much an urge to create something new as it is to find what anthropologist Mircea Eliade in a religious context called "sacred space" and "sacred time." Like their Seneca and Bali counterparts, the Western creator desires to put the self at the *axis mundi* (center of the world) and in *ab origine* (when the world began). The creator attempts to find for him- or herself and for others with whom (s)he shares the creation, the center of existence— however the creator defines that center, whether religiously, mystically, skeptically, scientifically, artistically, ritualistically. Whatever strikes us as "new" or "original" (even in a piece of conforming ritual art) is an inevitable by-product of this motivation. Creations *are* new because every nuance contains a hidden reality that is different from the reality hidden in every other nuance. But the perception of omnivalence in nuances is as old as the human mind. Perhaps that is why not a few great Western creators like Faulkner have been of the opinion that their genius rests not on creating something new but on rediscovering something very old. Thus, in the sense that they "awaken" the mind to the mysterious omnivalent order of things, to the continual freshness of reality, conforming creators like the Seneca mask-maker and the Bali performer and original creators like Einstein, Cézanne, Edison, McClintock and Woolf have much in common.

David Bohm has proposed that the reason creators from different eras, cultures and belief systems have ultimately so much in common with regard to omnivalence is that omnivalence is built into the very structure of nature. Bohm calls the 'more'ness or omnivalence of the universe its implicit or "implicate" order. He defines this order as the movement of the whole, which is implicit in everything but also always beyond reach. Because nature is an implicit wholeness, science keeps coming up with new paradigms, new inventions, new sides to reality, Bohm says. He points out that new theories and new inventions never serve to make our grasp of reality less ambiguous or more true; rather, "they make the ambiguity subtler." Astrophysicist Edward Harrison has argued that the universe is essentially unknowable and we put various masks on it, the animistic mask, the Newtonian mask, the Einsteinian mask. Presumably the idea that the universe is unknowable is also a mask.

The biological physicist Maurice Wilkins believes Bohm's general thrust may be right. But Wilkins adds his own slant to the story. To put it in the terms we're using here, Wilkins thinks that omnivalence in human creativity is a direct mirror of the omnivalence in nature's creativity. He pegs Bohr's idea of the "complementarity" of atomic processes as a key image for how the material universe works. If particles are also waves, then matter and energy exist in a self-contradictory state, a state of 'more'ness. It is the complementarity in nature, Wilkins argues, which gives rise to nature's creativity.

He cites DNA as a prime example. Wilkins himself, along with James Watson and Francis Crick, discovered that the DNA molecule is a helix like a spiral ladder. The atoms on the outside of the ladder are in a regular arrangement. Yet the rungs are irregular. "Thus DNA would be like a cine film which has regularly spaced holes on its sides (which engage the sprockets) and yet carries on it a complex sequence of pictures." The net result is that four chemical groups which make up the genetic molecule create a complementary or omnivalent structure, both regular and irregular at the same time.

Wilkins says many other complementary properties of

DNA have also been detected. For instance, "It has also been found that the irregular sequence of groups inside the double helix produces slight irregularities on the outside. These are not so great that they hinder the processes which depend on the outside being regular, but they seem to provide a guide to protein molecules which need to find particular sequences inside the double helix." The complementary or omnivalent structure of DNA—both regular and irregular—expresses a creative possibility: the evolution of organisms able to both replace themselves and generate continuous variations.

Wilkins sees complementarity everywhere in nature, for instance in the surprising fact that crystals build symmetrically by forming their attachments at the subtle asymmetrical parts of their own structure.

Since nature in its creativity is complementary, it seems logical to Wilkins that creativity in the human mind—which is after all an artifact of nature—should also be complementary, or omnivalent.

Through ideas such as Bohr's, Wilkins's and Bohm's, modern science seems moving toward an ancient perception. No one knows for sure if these ideas are right or if they will be fruitful. If they are, then creativity might not be such a mystery after all since it's inherent in nature.

INTER (wiping his brow): A little attempt at irony, eh? My dear fellow, you know this whole story seems rather complicated. It reminds me of a certain theologian. . . . But now you must tell me, these things you've talked about like truth and omnivalence, are they all separate parts of a creator's vision or just different words for the same thing?

MUSING: They're all the *prima materia* of the creator's vision, attributes of it. You could think of these elements of vision as becoming linked to each other in the creator's mind by feedback loops flowing into one another. For instance, an individual perception of a nuance or 'theme' might lead—as was the case for Woolf—to a heightened sense of wholeness and the wholeness and nuance together might amplify the perception of omnivalence, leading back to the nuance 'theme.' That brings up an important point about these elements of creative vision. Looked at from some perspectives a vision is quite personal and unique to the individual. From other perspectives the elements that make it up appear general and impersonal. Throughout the vision the personal and impersonal interact with each other in circular paradox. Perhaps this circular paradox is the one that generates what Conrad called "the inward voice that decides"—the vision's voice, which is both personal and impersonal: the voice calling from a hidden reality.

▪

But now the caveat at the end of chapter 3 needs to be strengthened, too, because vision is surely more subtle than all I've said about it. In fact, the whole point here is that vision is the essence of subtlety. It's also affected by feedback loops and paradoxical loops we'll take up in later chapters (loops involving the creator's talents and skills or lack of them), by the other creators and works (s)he admires in the field, by the forces and issues of the time period in which (s)he lives, by the life events that befall the creator and by the reception given the creative work. All these ingredients are both *part* of the vision and help *distill* the vision.

But having tried here to say what vision is, we should also say something about what it isn't.

It isn't static; it evolves. The vision may stabilize after a while as the creator begins to realize it through successful creations, but each creation adds to the creator's 'theme' of omnivalent nuances by extending the nuances into new areas, enriching the 'theme' with new material. We saw Einstein unfolding and enriching his vision as he moved from special relativity toward the unified field theory and Virginia Woolf expanding her initial nuance from *The Voyage Out* through her last works. As Woolf said, "The vision must be perpetually remade."

Vision is also not the creator's belief system. Sometimes the vision may even be quite contrary to the creator's opinions. Ernest Hemingway's daily belief system included the imperative to be tough and stoical at all times. Nevertheless, in his writing Hemingway dwelt repeatedly on the ironies of the tough guy's inner fragility and self-deception. Flannery O'Connor's devotion to Catholicism didn't prevent her from writing scathing satires about the violence and perversion produced by belief in religion. Max Planck was fervently convinced of Newtonian mechanics yet his vision led him to the discovery of the quantum of energy, and that idea eventually overturned Newtonianism. However, Planck himself rejected the implications of his discovery.

▪

During my interview with him, Shainberg observed that in his struggles as a painter to articulate his vision he repeatedly found himself fighting the temptation to resolve the forms on his canvas into closed ideas, visual tricks, the habits of his daily convictions and perceptions. He said he had to fight to stay in touch with his sense of nuance and omnivalence "so the viewer can constantly have the sense that this omnivalence is constantly going on." Anyone who has seriously tried to create anything expressing a nuance must understand how immensely difficult that struggle is. It is undoubtedly why most of us don't give our whole lives to such an implausible and tenuous pursuit.

Of course we're also aware that even a powerful commitment to nuance is not enough. In nuance and omnivalence are the seeds of vision. But the vision must be distilled.

PART 2

THE DISTILLING AGENTS

We're all infant prodigies. . . .

—THOMAS MANN

My theory is that when we come on this earth, many of us are ready-made.
. . . Some of us—most of us—have genes that are ready for certain perfor-
mances. Nature gives you these gifts. . . . There's nobody that's common.
I think that in every human being there is greatness.

—LOUISE NEVELSON

Doing easily what others find difficult is talent; doing what is impossible for
talent is genius.

—HENRI-FRÉDÉRIC AMIEL

A man of genius must have talents, but talents are possessed by many
without [genius]. . . . Genius is inventive, a creation of something not before
existing; to which talents make no pretence. . . .

—WILLIAM JACKSON (1798)

... It is the one thing that cannot be learnt from others; and it is also a sign of genius, since a good metaphor implies an intuitive perspective of the similarity of dissimilars.

—ARISTOTLE

Godlike genius, Godlike nothing! Sticking to it is the genius!

—THOMAS EDISON

I can imagine myself being a much better painter and nobody paying any attention to me at all. But it happens that things I've been doing were in touch with their time.

—GEORGIA O'KEEFFE

There is no genius without a deal of madness.

—SENECA

OVERVIEW

Consider a moment another metaphor for creative genius.

A few years ago IBM researcher Benoit Mandelbrot invented a new form of mathematics that applies to such complicated natural objects as trees, seacoasts, snowflakes and crashing waves. Using the "fractal" geometry he developed, Mandelbrot has revealed that these objects in nature possess "self-similarity." Perhaps you have noticed that a twig has the shape of the branch it sprouts from, the branch has the shape of the tree; a tiny bit of rock has the form of the mountain it litters. According to Mandelbrot, that's only the start of the surprise.

Imagine the jagged coastline of Maine from a satellite view. Now picture zooming in on a bay. At this smaller scale the jaggedness reappears. Zoom in further to a stretch along one side of the bay and jagged subbays appear. Mandelbrot says we can continue to zoom all the way down to the scales of the grains of rock and sand and the self-similarity will continually reappear. Each deeper crank of the zoom into the landscape descries something different, but also an eerie identity with the previous scale. It's as if the world has been continually folded in on itself and now unfolds before one's eyes.

In its various scales, the creative process is like a fractal. In the first chapters we saw the whole creative fractal from the large scale we called vision. Now we'll zoom in to another scale and encounter a new landscape that will reiterate in unexpected ways the terrain we just left.

The scale in the next few chapters will be the special capacities of mind and motivation that are possessed by creative genius. In alchemy these capacities were symbolized by the two chemical agents, mercury and sulphur, used to distill the raw material into *prima materia*. Alchemic texts say that volatile sulphur (symbolized by chemists as S) is the "hot fire" of the distilling process and signifies the adept's passions. While mercury (Hg), the "cold fire," signifies the spirit or mind. Though mercury and sulphur are opposites, the lore insists they are also mirror images of each other, two sides of the same reactant. More than that—to combine our metaphors—fractallike, the alchemist's Hg and S fold in upon themselves, for alchemists affirm that they are distilled out of the very raw material they distill.

In creativity, the correlates for the distilling agents mercury and sulphur are such traditionally recognized characteristics of genius as talent, insight, playfulness, flexibility, drive, and even psychopathology. Since in creativity, as in alchemy, opposites must be reconciled, our landscape at this scale will remind us of the larger scale of vision—that is, it will contain plenty of paradoxes, both regular ones and the circular kind.

One, for example, is contained in the fact that Benoit Mandelbrot, the inventor of fractals and, possibly, the Euclid of the twentieth century, claims not to know the alphabet. Having to use a telephone book, he says, reduces him to near helplessness. Because of a spotty educational history, Mandelbrot is also untrained in basic mathematics and is unable to do solutions "the straight way." What is it that lies behind such a paradox of genius?

The plan for exploring that paradox and the other interesting fauna that inhabit this scale is as follows:

In chapters 7 and 8 we will try to discern the psychology and biology of talent by looking at science's attempts to measure it and at the scientific studies being made of the extraordinary talent of prodigies. We'll also speculate about how talent is "mapped" in the brain. Chapter 9 will examine evidence for some unusual talents or turns of mind that geniuses seem to favor. Chapter 10 investigates a piece of the creative engine called the powers of concentration or absorption—a hallmark of genius. Chapter 11 suggests that the collision of a creator's talents and a vision with the forces of history may also be a faculty of genius. Finally, in chapter 12 we'll find out if the old cliché is true, that there is madness in genius.

In all of the chapters of this next section we'll see that elements of genius such as talent, absorption and history are neither the products of nature nor of nurture, neither genetics nor environment. Rather, they are the creative "feedback structures," unique in every case.

7

Quicksilver

HG → WHAT MEASURE OF GENIUS: THE SEARCH FOR THE BRAINPOWER SECRET

Alchemists sometimes identified mercury, or quicksilver, as the divine spark itself and called gold or other precious objects produced by the philosopher's stone "the projections of mercury." Similarly, a creator's talent is the quicksilver by which (s)he transforms the raw material of vision into its *prima materia.*

In the alchemy of creativity the mercurial agent of talent is implicated in many of the paradoxes of genius, like those exhibited by Mandelbrot. Clearly, in order to make sense of such paradoxes we will need to understand what place talent has in the economy of genius.

For many people, however, such an inquiry would be confusing because they believe talent and genius are synonymous; talent is assumed to be the "given" of genius—the gift of God or heredity.

In 1869 Francis Galton published a landmark book entitled *Hereditary Genius,* in which he set out to show that talent runs in the family. Galton's collection of the geneologies of great men was one of the first scientific attempts to identify the source and mechanism of extraordinary brainpower. When genetics came along, it was considered proof that Galton must have been right, talent is inherited.

But is it?

When people hear that something is genetically inherited, they often assume that means "inevitable," says biologist Stephen Jay Gould. But in fact that's not how genes work. "Genes do not make specific bits and pieces of a body; they code for a range of forms under an array of environmental conditions." How the complex genetic code expresses itself is variable, depending upon the interaction of a great many genes and the way the genes are pushed and pulled into expressing themselves by the environment. Even if the purely genetic explanation for genius were correct, the uncertainties of genetic expression would explain why it's extremely rare for the children of geniuses to be geniuses themselves. Environment and genetic interaction transform the delicate dance of the genes in a Joseph Conrad genome into a different dance in the next generation. The relationship of genes to each other and the environment is so complex and interactive that to say genius and talent is governed by genetics is really to make an almost meaningless statement.

The popular notion that brainpower is inherited has been paralleled by the widespread belief that science possesses the means to measure that genetically inherited brainpower and quantify genius.

By far the best known of the brainpower measures is the Intelligence Quotient or IQ. But here, too, actuality falls far short of the popular idea. In his scathing book *The Mismeasure of Man,* Gould assails the standardized IQ test, pointing to problems that were present since its inception in the early 1900s and that continue today. One problem involves the test's narrowness. Gould cites as an example a question which appeared in Lewis M. Terman's American version of the Frenchman Alfred Binet's original test:

An Indian who had come to town for the first time in his life saw a white man riding along the street. As the white man rode by, the Indian said—"The white man is lazy; he walks sitting down." What was the white man riding on that caused the Indian to say, "He walks sitting down."

In scoring the test Terman chose to accept "bicycle" as the only correct response to this question. He did not accept cars or other vehicles because a rider's legs wouldn't go up and down as when walking. He also rejected horses because an Indian would know what a horse is. Gould says that horse was the answer he himself gave to the question "because I saw the Indian as a clever ironist, criticizing an effete city relative." Responses such as "a person riding on someone's back" and "a cripple in a wheelchair" were also marked wrong. It looks like what was really being tested was not so much brainpower as the answerer's ability to guess at the mentality of the tester. Perhaps it was a problem such as this that caused the brilliant mathematician Henri Poincaré to give such a miserable performance on the Binet version of the IQ that if he'd been judged as a child instead of a celebrity, he would have been rated an imbecile.

But exposing the problematical features of IQ testing has not been enough to dissuade a very large number of people including many scientists from the impression that IQ is a snapshot of general intellectual talent or innate brainpower. A more effective critique of IQ (at least among some educators and psychologists) has been its inability to predict very much about how well people do with their brains when they go out into the world and actually use them.

After following 1528 IQ "geniuses" (IQ over 135) for six decades researchers in a study that had been initiated by Lewis Terman himself were forced to conclude that the attempt to quantify intelligence was not a smashing success because high IQ does not presage extraordinary achievement. Psychologist David Perkins sums up the verdict: "Contrary to its popular image, IQ simply does not predict effectiveness within a professional field that well, although IQ relates somewhat more closely to academic success as a student." The correlation of IQ to schoolwork may even be suspect since the teaching procedures and information structure of modern education have been shaped in no small measure by the belief that the IQ test and tests like it are valid.

Howard Gardner suggests one of the many reasons why IQ has turned out to be such a poor indicator of talent even in mathematical fields where the test seems most suited: "I think what's missed by the IQ and by all short-answer kinds of instruments is that to do anything significant in culture takes a long time. Almost all problems of significance are problems people have been working on a long time. Someone might appear to solve them in a flash but that's only because he's been thinking about it for years. The IQ test is just the opposite. It favors somebody who can glibly shift from one kind of question to the other. And the more you know people who achieve things, the more you know that's not what distinguishes them. What distinguishes them is determination to work something through to completion no matter how long it takes."

In the 1950s, psychologists recognized that the capacity for real mental achievement was slipping through the net of the IQ test, and so they began to measure talent and brainpower from another direction, using "creativity tests." An example of such a measure is the "divergent thinking" test, which requires its subjects to perform tasks like "list as many white, edible things as you can in three minutes," and "list all the uses that you can think of for a brick in three minutes." Most creativity tests aim to quantify the subject's "fluency" and imagination on the assumption that these are the keys to creative talent. Yale psychology professor Robert Sternberg, an expert in test theory, says succinctly that he thinks this type of test, too, contains a flaw that makes it a poor gauge: "The things that matter in creativity are a very few *good* ideas, not a lot of so-so ideas." And David Feldman observes that "after thirty years of research . . . the ability of these tests to predict actual creativity is almost nil."

Both the attempt to tie brainpower to genetic inheritability and to measure it with tests take for granted the idea that genius and talent have a basically physical explanation. There must be, according to this assumption, some physical difference in the brain that could account for the difference in functioning. In the past two decades scientists have been able to pursue this idea directly into the physical brain where, in some respects, the assumption has been verified and in other respects, called into question.

In the 1970s neuroscientist Roger Sperry's work on "split brain" patients stirred considerable excitement among creativity researchers who believed the experimental results showed there must be a partitioning of brainpower anatomically, with creativity located in the right cerebral hemisphere and intelligence in the left. The belief turned out to be naive. In the past ten years scientists have learned that there is in fact a surprising variability to the physical location of brain activities.

One neuroscientist in search of the physical key to brainpower has gone so far as to take the search into the literal cells of the most celebrated brain in history: Einstein's. Marian Diamond, a neuroanatomist at the University of California at Berkeley examined the embalmed remains of some of Einstein's frontal cortex and the inferior parietal regions, which she obtained thirty years after Einstein's death. Diamond compared these regions with tissue taken from eleven men who had died between the ages of forty-nine and eighty and were known to have had no brain damage. She learned that the seventy-six-year-old physicist who said he had no brain muscles did have statistically more glial cells in his parietal lobe.

The glia support and nourish neurons. Studies have shown that laboratory animals raised in enriched environments with toys and companions to challenge their brains had more glia than animals raised in an impoverished environment with few companions and toys. In an educated person, damage to the parietal lobe results in a loss of the capacity to do complex thinking and to generate mental imagery. The frontal cortex is involved with will and the ability to do abstract thinking. Presumably if an area is enriched, so would be the capacities "located" there.

There's no way of telling, of course, whether Einstein was born with extra glia or developed them, as the lab animals did, by exercising his brain. Diamond has cautioned that the sample of brains used for comparison with Einstein's was too small to allow her to say anything definitive. Stevan Harnad, editor of a scientific journal on the brain, notes: "You can make an infinite number of inferences from this one sample. Would there have been a difference between Einstein's brain and those of ordinary 'gifted' academics? If you had a population of Einstein brains and a population of normal brains, the data generated still would not say much about intellectual giftedness until we better understand normal brain functions."

Perhaps the premier sleuth on the trail of a link between the physical brain and giftedness was the late Norman Geschwind, a neurologist at Harvard Medical School. Geschwind and his colleague, neurologist Albert Galaburda, proposed that the level of the male hormone testosterone in the developing fetus is a key factor in determining how the brain is organized. Hormone levels can be affected by things like stress on the mother during pregnancy and chemicals from the environment. Variations in the hormone level in boys, Geschwind hypothesized, would result in a less developed left hemisphere and such brain activities as speech and handedness—normally located in the left side of the brain—would be sited in the right side of the brain. This would lead to left-handedness. It has been found that left-handed people have a much higher incidence of dyslexia, migraines, allergies, autoimmune disorders like arthritis—and talent in math. Left-handers have also been discovered to have a larger corpus callosum, the area that joins the two halves of the brain.

Geschwind was a member of an informal group which gathered in the Boston area from time to time to talk over questions of creativity. The group includes Holton, Feldman, Gardner, University of Chicago psychologist Mihaly Csikszentmihalyi and occasionally Howard Gruber. Feldman says that before Geschwind's death, the neuroscientist was speculating to the group about a number of possible connections between hormone levels, anatomical differences in the brain and the development of talents. The loss of Geschwind was surely unfortunate for this line of research. His theory moved away from a purely genetic explanation for talent and added to other research indicating how flexible the brain is about the way it can organize its capacities and the ways variant organizations produce different deficits and talents.

▪

Many people would not look at this research in that way, however. Some people's excitement about this work may be driven by the ultimate lure of a mechanical explanation for genius—and the possibility of a mechanical way to produce it. Imagine a twenty-first-century brave new world where alpha (genius) individuals are produced by a fetal injection of artificial hormones or genetic implants in embryo; where intelligence is beefed up by brain steroids as simply as a mechanic can attach a supercharger to a car. All this might conceivably happen if talent and genius turns out to have a basically physical explanation. One of the strongest reasons to think that such an explanation must in the long run exist is the occasional appearance of prodigies.

IN THE PRODIGY LAB

There is no disputing that prodigies are truly amazing instances of talent.

Young Wolfgang Amadeus Mozart, history's best-known prodigy, was composing symphonies at age eight, and years before that was playing piano with his prodigy sister Nannerl for the crowned heads of Europe. By the time of his death at thirty-six, Mozart had compiled an opus of enduring compositions.

Christian Heinrich Heinekin, the Infant of Lubec, was less fortunate. According to contemporary accounts, young Heinekin talked within a few hours of birth, learned Latin, French, history and geography by age three and predicted his own death at the age of four, possibly from exhaustion. In 1885 another young four-year-old, Daisy Ashford, showed her talents by writing a comic novel about a Jesuit priest. Her second novel, written when she was nine, sold hundreds of thousands of copies. Ashford stopped writing in her teens and lived until age ninety.

On April Fool's Day 1898, American prodigy William James Sidis was born to ambitious parents who believed they could create a genius. The Sidises were an unusual couple. Russian émigrés who had been deprived of educational opportunities in their homeland, they worked their way through the American school system with honors. Boris became an eminent psychologist; Sarah was one of the few women at the turn of the century to graduate from medical school. When their son was born, they named him after their close friend psychologist William James and supplied him with an incredibly rich home environment. Within six months the boy was speaking; by age six he had mastered seven languages and had written a treatise on anatomy. At eight he delivered a lecture at Harvard on four-dimensional bodies. But it was the beginning of the end. In his teens Sidis lost direction, floundering amid notoriety. He spent the rest of his life as a recluse, taking menial jobs and pursuing his hobby of collecting streetcar transfers.

In 1970, a three-and-a-half-year-old English girl born to Ukrainian émigré parents began to show a talent for drawing. Surprisingly, Nadia didn't pass through any of the usual stages by which children learn to represent figures. For example, from the start she could move around the paper drawing separate parts of the figure until the scattered lines would knit perfectly to form the picture. Nadia's drawing ability was dramatized by the fact that she was autistic. In areas other than that of her extraordinary talent she was lethargic, exhibited slowed motor development and was unable to understand words or communicate through language or gesture.

Thomas Fuller was born in Africa about 1710 and when he was fourteen was brought to Virginia as a slave. In 1788 two Pennsylvanians interviewed Fuller and asked him how many seconds there are in a year and a half, to which Fuller thought for about two minutes and then replied: "Forty-seven million, three hundred and four thousand." Fuller was a calculating prodigy and he could reckon with perfect accuracy the number of grains of corn necessary to sow a certain area of ground or the number of posts and rails necessary to enclose a yard.

■

These examples illustrate many points, but one should be noted immediately. While prodigies are amazing, they are not creative geniuses, though occasionally a prodigy, like Mozart, may grow into one. "You are not a genius," the tutor of British mathematics prodigy Ruth Lawrence recently cautioned, "until you have left your personal mark on your subject." A study of the frequency of early Mozart recordings and the opinions of critics argues that even Mozart didn't produce works of genius until he'd been in the business a few years. David Feldman says, "There has never been a child genius in the sense that there has never been a child who has fundamentally reorganized a highly demanding domain of knowledge and skill. Nor by any means have individuals who have produced works of genius all been prodigies." Not genius itself, David Feldman believes, prodigy is an instance of pure and specialized talent; as such, prodigy provides a laboratory for studying what talent is, whether it is a purely physical property of the brain and how it arises.

Feldman is director of the Tufts University's Eliot-Pearson Department of Child Study. He and his wife Lynn Goldsmith recently completed a decade-long project following six prodigies, including a boy who could speak nine languages and write Egyptian hieroglyphics by the time he was four; two child chess masters; a musical prodigy who was composing symphonies before he was eight; a seven-year-old who spent his days exploring higher mathematics and reading about quarks; and a boy who taught himself to type at two and a half because he felt compelled to fill blank sheets with stories and poems.

Despite the awe, envy, titillation and sometimes fear prodigies have evoked over the ages, little has been done to study them scientifically and Feldman's was the first attempt to observe them closely over a long period of time. He did it by interviewing them, going to class with them, scrutinizing their productions, and talking at length to their parents, teachers and peers. One result was an important book, *Nature's Gambit,* stocked with new insights and hypotheses.

Feldman believes most prodigies are "special-purpose," one-talent phenomena, like Mozart, Ashford, Nadia and Thomas Fuller. Rarer are what he calls "omnibus" prodigies like Sidis, children extraordinarily talented in a number of fields. Omnibus prodigies may be examples of an extreme compression of developmental time frames or of a discontinuous jump, skipping over intermediate developmental stages, almost as if the prodigy had the fully formed schema of an adult brain in an infant's body.

Amazing as omnibus prodigies are, they fit the old notion that intelligence or brainpower is unitary. The omnibus prodigy is an apparently high-wattage generator that goes from zero to full bore so quickly that some people have suggested that such prodigies must be the result of a reincarnation. In fact omnibus prodigies like Sidis or John Stuart Mill were provided by their parents with such obsessively enriched learning environments that it is difficult to separate the effects of environmental effects from natural talent.

Special-purposes prodigies present the same problem but in a more dramatic form. And some special-purpose prodigies are particularly amazing because they violate the unitary brainpower picture. How is it that an infant can possess a remarkable, seemingly inborn affinity for an activity as peculiarly specialized as chess playing, violin playing or map-making, and exhibit no remarkable talent for anything else?

Feldman's answer is a concept he calls "co-incidence." Think of co-incidence as the first slide we'll place under the microscope in the prodigy lab. We see the following swim into view.

According to Feldman's concept, the prodigy's specialized ability is like an ember that must land in just the right environment in order to burst into flame. A computer prodigy born

into a culture where there are no computers or a musical
prodigy born into a family where music is forbidden would be
like sparks falling into the desert. Nature strikes off these
strange sparks as part of its continuous gamble for adaptation.
Individuals able to quickly master complex and specialized
cultural fields create an evolutionary advantage, Feldman believes. Though the particular talent would probably not be
transmitted directly to the prodigy's offspring (due to the
complexity of a talent's genetic dance), a culture's cultivation
of its prodigies and emphasis on certain domains of knowledge
might fuel a general genetic drift in a direction favoring those
talents. Most often, however, the prodigy's special spark is
"lost" because it finds no tinder.

Feldman is certainly not the first to notice the role of co-
incidence in the development of talent, but his clear formulation of it creates a useful conceptual tool for seeing how
important it is that talent and environment co-incide.

In fact, psychologists Csikszentmihalyi and Rick Robinson
offer a co-incidence "thought experiment" as a way to settle
the long-standing dispute between a purely physical explanation for the appearance of talent or an environmental explanation; between "nature or nurture." Imagine a new game is
invented called "mo." To play a good game of mo you must
be able to recognize fine spatial and color distinctions and
remain agile while drinking titanic quantities of alcohol.
Could one find prodigies for mo? Undoubtedly there must be
a small number of individuals who are outstanding in all these
skills. The psychologists write: "Should we conclude that talent in 'mo' was caused by physiological factors? Certainly,
because all the component skills depend on demonstrably
neurological processes. Or should we say that talent in 'mo'
is culturally constituted? Certainly, because the combination
of physiological skills was meaningless before the game was
invented."

Talent, it seems, is another circular paradox, one which is
rather complicated, as we'll see.

Feldman notes that one of the most important co-incidences

of the many which must occur for a specialized talent to emerge, is the co-incidence between the prodigies and their home life. The parents of the prodigies Feldman and Goldsmith studied were all sensitive to what he calls "child-initiated changes"—the child's own interests—letting those dictate the course of study. To underscore his belief in the importance of this element of co-incidence and talent, Feldman compares the parental care given his prodigies with that given to a profoundly retarded child, Leslie Lemke.

As the story goes, Leslie was afflicted with cerebral palsy which left him unresponsive to touch and sound. His eyes had been surgically removed shortly after birth. His parents relinquished him to institutional care and he was eventually taken in by May and Joe Lemke. A deeply religious couple, the Lemkes spent over fifteen years providing Leslie with attentive sensory and emotional stimulation despite the fact that he remained unresponsive. When the boy plucked at a string tied around a package, May decided he wanted to make music and began to sing to him, play records and show him how a piano worked. He began to make some progress but it was slow until one night May and her husband awoke to the sound of Tchaikovsky's Piano Concerto no. 1 coming from Leslie's room. The boy had gotten up and for the first time seated himself on his own at the piano where he was flawlessly playing a piece he had heard on record. As Feldman sees it, the Lemkes and the families of his prodigies have something in common. Both were "flexible in their curricular plans, readily incorporating what they perceived to be child-initiated changes and additions into the types of activities offered. They both possessed an unusual willingness to act immediately on requests or other signs of interest, virtually regardless of time or place, and both sets of parents possessed an incredibly strong conviction— transmitted with great love, physical affection, and even vehemence—that their child was extraordinarily special and wonderful." These qualities, he believes, allowed the children's special talents to emerge.

Sidis shows how co-incidence can fail. William spontaneously demonstrated extraordinary talent for languages and science but actively disliked mathematics. Boris and Sarah Sidis pressured their son into math, however, with apparently dire results. A few years after his Harvard lecture on four-dimensional bodies he started his spiral away from his prodigiousness. When Sidis's cousin Clifton Fadiman tried to discuss mathematics with him years later, William replied furiously, "I don't ever want to talk about that kind of thing." He said the subject made him physically ill.

Feldman's logic suggests that as each of us has potentially a unique vision, each of us may have unique talent(s). This implication of co-incidence has its humorous side. Feldman tells about a father who discovered that his six-year-old son was gifted with the uncanny ability to open combination locks. Perhaps for some of us the activity for which we have special talent(s) hasn't yet been invented, like the game of mo.

Feldman believes that the way co-incidence brings out talent applies to all prodigies, including the omnibus prodigy. The omnibus prodigy Feldman studied he calls Adam. Adam's parents scrambled continually to find tutors who could keep up with their son's voracious appetite for learning. When Adam was five he drew up a curriculum and asked his mother and father to obtain instruction for him in physics, philosophy, karate, astronomy, computer science, English literature and creative writing, Latin, archeology and anthropology, the history of the Middle Ages, violin, piano, composition and ballet. Feldman counts the willingness of Adam's parents to endure the financial, emotional and physical strain of making these arrangements and supervising them as an important facet in Adam's talent, a key co-incidence.

So co-incidence works to produce prodigies, according to Feldman, except in certain fields. For example, there has never been a literary prodigy, that is, someone who has produced a major literary work before the age of ten. There have been "writing prodigies" (Feldman's term) like Daisy Ashford and one of Feldman's subjects, Randy, who wrote voluminously and skillfully a series of conventional stories about Dracula and Dr. Who. The prodigy was able to handle plot and character but, as Feldman says, "Randy's writing is by and large more stylistic than substantive, more a technical tour de force for his age than a source of expression of his most significant emotions and thoughts about his experience."

Feldman observes that prodigies seem only to occur in fields where there are well-defined steps for achieving mastery. In fields like literature and philosophy the steps are not clear, nor are the criteria for judging performance clear, as they are in, say, mathematics or chess. Attaining mastery in the field of literature or philosophy also requires a complex vision, which takes time to evolve. Or as novelist V. S. Naipaul observes, "There are no prodigies in writing. [That is, literature.] The knowledge a writer seeks to transmit is social and sentimental; it takes time, it can take much of a man's life, to process that experience, to understand what he has been through; and it takes care and tact, then, for the nature of the experience not to be lost, not to be diluted by the wrong forms. The other man's forms served the other man's thoughts."

■

Now it's time to change the slide in the microscope and look at another view of what makes a prodigy: hard work.

Perhaps what is really the most extraordinary thing about prodigies is their ability to concentrate. Feldman says, "They all seem to have tremendous energy that they can focus on the task at hand. They simply cannot be prevented from doing what it is they want to do. One chess player I watched sat at a chess board for eight hours at a stretch, almost without moving. The intensity of concentration is truly remarkable."

For example, he writes about the intensity of his omnibus prodigy, Adam, at age three. One day Adam's mother felt compelled to explain to him that he was literally wearing her out with his nineteen-hour-a-day study schedule. Adam looked startled and asked why she hadn't told him before. He promptly began going to bed earlier, a few days later inquiring solicitously if his mother wasn't feeling more rested.

Why do prodigies concentrate so hard?

One explanation might be their engagement in a phenomenon Csikszentmihalyi calls "flow." By doing studies of rock climbers, musicians, chess players and dancers, Csikszentmihalyi discovered that people enter an almost addicting state when they can "concentrate their attention on a limited stimulus field, forget personal problems, lose their sense of time and of themselves, feel competent and in control and have a sense of harmony and union with their surroundings." Flow occurs when there is a proper alignment of skill and challenge. Flow is experienced as a loss of ego boundaries. It may involve, as is the case with long-distance running, a buildup of the brain's opiates, endorphins. Some research has suggested a link between flow and hypnosis.

Csikszentmihalyi's subjects were teenagers and adults and the application of his finding to prodigies is uncertain. However at least one study indicates that the ability to achieve flow is genetically influenced. So perhaps flow ability is a "given" feature of the prodigy's makeup, an inborn talent or potential talent brought into play by co-incidence. Another possible explanation for the prodigy's powers of concentration is that youngsters have more loosely formed ego boundaries in the first place, which would facilitate their entry into a state of flow when working in a field such as music or chess that challenges and stimulates them.

But Feldman is sure there's more to it. "Flow is the best of life and that's part of it. But prodigies also keep going when things aren't working well, when it isn't flowing. And for them what they're doing is not just the best of life, it's all of life."

■

Another slide. We focus the microscope down for a moment on pianist Lorin Hollander's memory of putting his hands on the keyboard when he was three and feeling that he would become the note he'd play. The prodigy's concentration also seems to come out of a unique physiological relationship with the materials of his field. As Feldman points out,

Hollander "feels that way about the notes on a piano but he wouldn't feel that way about a saxophone. It can be that specific."

MIT psychologist Jeanne Bamberger has done innovative studies of young musical performers which speak to this observation. Bamberger notes that gifted child performers have amazing capacities for imitating other players, including making the same body gestures. This ability is holistic and intuitive, and the youngsters don't want to think about it for fear of losing it. In a clever experiment using bells of different notes which she asked gifted youngsters to arrange so as to play a simple tune, Bamberger found that the children had extremely flexible and fluid ways of representing musical structure to themselves. The older players arranged the bells in the conventional structure found on musical scores.

Bamberger also discovered that young performers respond sensually to their musical instruments. They don't think abstractly about the structure of the music they are playing but experience instead a kinesthetic, emotional relationship between the instrument and their body.

Investigation of very different kinds of prodigies have yielded parallel insights. In his wonderful account of a pair of calendar calculator twins, neurologist Oliver Sacks reports that the prodigious talent of the two remarkable brothers involved the ability to directly "see" and sensually experience mathematical relationships which the rest of us would find utterly abstract.

The twins were *idiots savants* who had been institutionalized since they were seven and variously diagnosed as autistic or severely retarded. However, despite their deficits, they possessed the amazing ability to tell the day of the week on which any date would fall within a period of eighty thousand years, including the date of Easter, which is notoriously difficult to compute. Working out the algorithm for Easter is difficult because it involves phases of the moon, a problem that gave even the mathematical genius and lightning calculator Karl Friedrich Gauss some pause. Yet the twins were capable of arriving at a correct date apparently without knowing how to add or subtract accurately, and with no comprehension of multiplication or division. The twins could also recall with exact detail the weather and events of any day in their lives from about the time they were four.

Sacks reports the twins also possessed other abilities that he thinks were part of their remarkable talent. One day a box of matches fell on the floor, spilling its contents and Sacks heard the twins cry simultaneously "one hundred eleven" and then "thirty-seven." They had not only ascertained the number of matches, instantaneously (and correctly—Sacks counted) but had factored them (37×3), again apparently not having the slightest idea what factoring is. Sacks mused:

> Is it possible, I said to myself, that they can somehow "see" the properties of numbers, not as formal properties, in a conceptual, abstract way, but as *qualities,* felt, sensuous, in some immediate, concrete way? And not simply isolated qualities—like "111-ness"— but qualities of relationship [like the factors 37]? Perhaps in somewhat the same way as the young Mozart might have said "a third," or "a fifth."

Sacks conjectures that the twins saw numbers and the events associated with them as a "vast (or possibly infinite) landscape in which everything could be seen, either isolated or in relation." In their minds they explored that landscape with all the joy of a pair of seagulls, and with the seagull's perfect inability to communicate abstractly what they saw.

Feldman believes that the prodigies he studied are "pure talent with adjunct capabilities" like the ability to communicate abstractly, while *"idiots savants* are pure talent without adjunct capabilities." Does the similarity in the two types of thinking imply that pure talent involves a strong sensory component?

Steven Smith's recent survey of the calculating prodigy literature adds plausibility to the idea that there is a strong sensory component to talented thought process. There are

auditory calculators who hear the numbers they are comput-
ing as rhythms and visual calculators who see the numbers
moving in their mind. One calculator, Périclès Diamandi is
reported to have "visualized numbers and other objects (as
in, horses, dogs) in an empty space surrounded by grayish
masses (apparently something like clouds)." There have
been tactile calculators like Louis Fleury, who could feel
"the outlines of imaginary cubarithms passing beneath his
fingers." A physician who studied Fleury at the asylum
where he was housed reported that the calculator's "fingers
moved with extreme rapidity. With the right hand he
grasped the fingers of the left hand one after another; one
represented hundreds, another tens, a third units. He moved
his fingers feverishly over the lapel of his jacket and it was
curious to watch him using these tactile images to obtain sensations corresponding to those he would have had in touch-
ing cubarithms."

Smith notes that "numbers sometimes have for prodigies
something akin to connotations. [Salo] Finkelstein, for example, reacted emotionally to numbers, just as everyone does to
words. . . . He thought 214 a 'beautiful' number, while 8337
he described as 'very nice' (though not, I suppose, the sort of
number you'd like your sister to marry). Zero was his 'pet
aversion.' " George Parker Bidder, a nineteenth-century civil
engineer and famous mental calculator said that as a child
when he learned to count by ones and then by tens, the numbers "became as it were my friends, and I knew all their
relations and acquaintances." Numbers become corporeal.

The sensory aspect of talent may be one reason why child
prodigies sometimes don't carry their prodigiousness forward
into adult life. Bamberger speculates that musical prodigies
often suffer a "mid-life" crisis when the developmental processes that occur during adolescence force them to analyze and
conceptualize musical structure. Apparently many are unable
to make this transition without a fatal loss of the sensory,
perceptual, emotional contact with their instrument and the
music.

LAB LESSONS

INTER: Now, pray tell me, Professor, what have we learned about talent from this prodigy lab?

MUSING: One thing for sure, the results are preliminary.

INTER: *Non disputandum.* The professorial response! You types could never be alchemists. You have all the courage of flies.

MUSING: All right. Consider these:
1) Our prodigy lab indicates that talent requires co-incidence. Talent doesn't just primarily depend upon possessing a high wattage of brainpower. In fact it's probably impossible to separate out brainpower from co-incidence. Neither exists without the other. As we'll see in chapter 11, this is true for creative geniuses as well as for prodigies, with the added factor that for creators co-incidence has what I call "a twist."
Co-incidence has a corollary, too, because what was said about vision also seems true of talent. Talents aren't static. They evolve. As Csikszentmihalyi and Robinson put it, "talent should be thought of not as a stable characteristic but as a dynamic quality dependent on changes within the individual and within the environment." This doesn't just mean that the skills learned with talent get better or grow rusty. Rather, as circumstances change new talents emerge; old ones may grow dim. So some prodigies fade out. Feldman's chess prodigies stopped competing in their teens; his writing prodigy, Randy, turned his enthusiasms to music; the autistic artist Nadia started talking and quit drawing; Oliver Sacks's twins were separated, put in halfway houses and given menial jobs. "They seem to have lost their strange numerical power," Sacks reports. So talent may not be just something you're born with, a potential that gets developed or doesn't. It seems to be a dynamic phenomenon that may appear or dissipate at any time, depending on circumstances.
2) The prodigy's amazing talent appears to have a highly sensory, perceptual and emotional quality, distinguishing it

from the ordinary forms of abstract mental operations. This seems similar to the sensory thinking reported by great creators like Einstein and Woolf—and perhaps such thinking is a strong feature of the secret life of a talent. Even creators who achieve a high degree of abstraction in their work seem to retain a concrete "feel" for their subject.

3) The prodigy's talent is usually highly specialized. The notion that talent is a quite specialized capacity rather than a general capacity (like IQ) will come up in the next chapter in our investigation of talent in creative genius.

4) The prodigy's talent includes an intense commitment to that talent. This is similar to the life or death commitment genius creators make, but it's not the same. And the difference is worth noting. In the literature on prodigies, there is little indication that themata, nuance-laden 'themes', truth, omnivalence or the individual-universal equation are key elements in a prodigy's experience. Chances are it takes time for these elements of vision to evolve to the place where they become matters of overriding importance, infusing virtually all dimensions of the individual's consciousness. Hollander's memory of becoming the notes of the music he was playing and Sartre's memory of discovering that in "writing I was existing," might be an early step in that evolution. Both these prodigies went on to mature creative work. Most prodigies don't. We might put the difference this way: Prodigies commit themselves intensely to their talent; geniuses commit their talents intensely to their vision. As Feldman says, with the prodigy "the early fit between talent and field is too good. For prodigies everything goes too well, in a way. For creativity things can't go that well. If this goes too well, then the person's going to be satisfied with things the way they are."

So, a prodigy's sensory-based thinking and intense commitment may set him or her on the road to creative genius or, ironically, the very facility for mastering the field with phenomenal speed may overpower the development of the vision necessary to achieve genius. This in turn highlights the last point.

5) Talent is not the same as genius. For genius to occur, at

some moment vision and the person's unique talent(s) must come together like the merging of *prima materia* and mercury to make the philosopher's stone. The feedback dynamics of genius includes high doses of omnivalence and nuance, themata and the capacity of uncertainty; and these in turn take part in the dynamics of talent.

INTER: One question. What about the physical basis of talent? You know you haven't really answered that question.

MUSING: I suppose the reason I haven't is that there isn't really an answer yet, and there may never be a definite one. The failure of intelligence tests and creativity tests to pin down talent, the slipperiness of the genetic explanation and yet the extraordinary seemingly "inborn" talent of prodigies indicate that the question of the physical basis of talent should probably be viewed as a circular paradox. It's clear that a physical basis for talent exists—genes, hormones, perhaps the glia in Einstein's brain, and so on—but it's also clear that talent (particularly as it appears in genius) requires a much subtler and more dynamic explanation. And that's what we'll try to suggest next.

8

Mercurial Maps

HG^N → THE MANY-INTELLIGENCES APPROACH

Howard Gardner has taken an important step in clarifying the link between the physical basis of talent and its dynamical nature. For one thing, Gardner's work suggests how prodigies could be born with such specialized talents.

In 1983, Gardner published a theory which argues that the mind is composed of a number of semiautonomous intelligences, each with its own separate capacities and developmental trajectory. The linguistic and the mathematical-logical intelligences are the two assessed by the IQ test, though the test doesn't gauge even these two intelligences completely. Besides the linguistic and logical-mathematical, Gardner believes there are at least five other intelligences that have been almost totally ignored by mainstream psychologists: musical intelligence, spatial intelligence, bodily-kinesthetic intelligence, and what he calls the interpersonal and intrapersonal intelligences.

At the time I interviewed him, Gardner was using part of the five-year fellowship grant he had received from the MacArthur Foundation (a so-called "genius" grant given to especially creative professionals) to fund continued neuropsychological research at the Boston Veteran's Administration. It was here that he gathered evidence for his theory. On neurological rounds at the VA Gardner regularly observed patients with many different kinds of brain impairment, for example, persons with damage to their right hemisphere who had difficulties in reading a map or finding their way around an unfamiliar space but who had undamaged linguistic abilities. He correlated these observations with historical neurological tidbits he had unearthed, such as the fact that the Russian composer Schebalin had been able to compose competently despite severe aphasia and that Stravinsky and Randall Thompson went on writing music after strokes. His observations and the medical literature encouraged Gardner to his conclusion that music, linguistic, spatial and other abilities must each function in a relatively independent way. This, he believes, explains how somebody can be good at math and bad at art, and how it is that prodigies come in such specialized packages. According to Gardner the seven intelligences are directly related to talent. We all possess all seven, and a manifestation of any one intelligence in a high degree is what we mean when we say that someone "has talent."

But why just seven? As we've seen, a prodigy may show an affinity for the piano but not the saxophone, for cracking a safe but not for fixing a clock. Why not a separate intelligence for each of these potential talents? Gardner's first reason is anatomical. His seven intelligences correspond to the known data showing that brain damage can impair certain functions while leaving others intact. The second reason is political.

Feldman confides that his friend Gardner chose the mystical seven as the maximum number of intelligences (potential talents) he thought his psychology colleagues could stomach at one dose. "It worked brilliantly, I think," Feldman says, "because the theory is being taken seriously."

In his book *Frames of Mind,* however, Gardner hints that there may in fact be a multitude of intelligences and potential talents. He lists other past theorists who believed there are a great many more. One suggested thirty-seven intelligences; another claimed to have detected one hundred and twenty. Even in Gardner's scheme a larger number of intelligences is implied because each of the seven contains "core" elements. Musical intelligence, for example, includes as core elements (subtalents) the ability to grapple with pitch, rhythm and timbre. In addition, there's the ability to remember pieces of music or improvise on them, indicating that some abilities may be a crossover of elements from one intelligence with elements of others, and some of these crossovers may turn out to be neurophysiologically discrete.

Bear in mind, too, that when we're talking about an intelligence and talent which develops so that it has a neurophysiological place in someone's brain, we're also talking about how an environment has made demands and offered opportunities for that talent to exist. The two are inseparable. A talent doesn't exist without a culture that demands it; the culture doesn't exist without talent. Consequently, in the long run it may not be possible to actually determine the total number of human talents or to precisely locate the lines distinguishing one from another.

According to Gardner's hypothesis, talents or intelligences, however many there turn out to be, have their control offices in the cortex. Since that's the case, it will be useful to appropriate one of the new neurophysiological theories about cortical development in order to get a better feel for how the physical basis of talent and its dynamics may go together.

OF TALENTS AND FEEDBACK

In chapter 3 we noted that a theory by Gerald Edelman may shed light on the existence of nuance in the brain. Actually, as a theory of cortical formation, Edelman's hypothesis is better suited to illuminating talent (and perhaps the theory works for both because in creators, at least, nuance and talent are closely related).

Edelman, who conducts his research at the prestigious Rockefeller University in Manhattan, is both an M.D. and Ph.D.; he won his 1972 Nobel prize for work on the immune system. Edelman demonstrated his theory that animals are born with a complete repertoire of antibodies and that invading antigens such as bacteria act to select from the repertoire those antibodies best able to best cope with the bacteria's presence. Which antibodies are selected is unique for each individual. This strategy is advantageous because it provides the immune system with great flexibility in responding to all the new antigens invented by nature and man. In recent years, Edelman has used these insights to help formulate his model of how the structure of the cortex unfolds.

Edelman is convinced that the brain's physical structuring is not strictly under genetic control. Instead, there is a dynamic of interacting feedback loops formed between genes and randomly migrating neurons. That interaction results in the laying down of a significantly different cell landscape even in identical twins.

What kind of landscape is it?

In the late 1950s, neuroanatomist Vernon Mountcastle discovered that cortical tissue is composed of neurons grouped together into columns. Each columnar group, containing perhaps one hundred neurons, is thought to function as a unit, something like a transistor packed in among a host of other transistors in an electrical device. However, in the case of the brain's transistors, each group or column of neurons has a unique wiring diagram. It's also connected up in a unique way with the other groups of neurons around it. Edelman theorizes that early in life a selection process takes place in which the pressure from environmental and internal brain stimuli selects some of the cell groups over the others because their wiring diagrams are more efficient for responding to a particular configuration of stimuli.

Edelman proposes that the things we learn about the world we perceive—the shape of familiar faces, the different textures of objects—are not fixed at certain cortical sites, not etched onto a "grandmother cell" that fires every time we see our grandmother's face. Rather, a familiar face and or any perception, is implicit in a pattern of relationships (firing patterns) among many neuronal groups.

Support for this part of Edelman's idea comes from the discovery of the plasticity of the brain's sensory maps. In one piece of research, scientists at the University of California found that individual monkeys of the same species showed significant variation in the sites on their cortex where sensations and motor reflexes are mapped. (The sites have been located by stimulating the brain with electrodes to find which areas cause which parts of the body to respond.) The site that represented the monkey's hand, for instance, was not in exactly the same place (though it was in the same general area) as that hand's site in another monkey. The sites also changed slightly over time. The scientists noted that when a nerve to a monkey's hand was injured, the maps of the other fingers drifted over to fill in where the damaged finger's map had been.

Edelman thinks that the patterns or context of relationships among neuron groups are, in effect, the brain's perceptual maps. These maps in turn make feedback relationships with other maps, and so create maps of maps. The maps, and maps of maps, are flexible and dynamical entities formed out of the neurons' firing patterns. The maps are subject to constant slight modification so, for example, the map of grandmother's face is changed over time by changes in the whole context of other maps which the map of her face is embedded in.

As it stands now, Edelman's theory describes only the ways in which visual, auditory and tactile stimulation are formed into perceptual categories (maps) by the brain. Nobody knows if or how feedback-constructed neuronal maps may form the various "intelligences" (talents) such as language and music, so an attempt to carry the model beyond this point must be considered metaphor.

INTER: *Speculation ad infinitum,* eh?

MUSING: Perhaps, but remember all these theories are just that, still theories. Neurophysiology is a virtually uncharted frontier and there's a very long way to go before anyone will have a good picture of the physical elements of creativity, or even a good explanation of our ordinary consciousness. In the meantime, extending Edelman's model metaphorically can help convey a picture of talent establishing itself physically in the brain by means of dynamical feedback. In a general sense, such a picture is quite plausible because in recent years there has been a growing appreciation among scientists from many fields that nature makes and maintains its structures out of feedback. My bet is that feedback is involved at many scales in the appearance of talent: there is feedback between the genes and randomly migrating neurons as they lay down a unique brain for each individual; there is feedback between that brain and the home, cultural and historical environment that the individual is born into (co-incidence); and, conceivably, there is feedback in the formation of the maps and maps of maps that make up a particular talent. In short, talent doesn't originate in a given physical attribute of the brain; it evolves as an immensely subtle dynamical feedback structure. This talent-structure certainly includes the brain's physical elements, but the feedback links them in ways that are strikingly different for each creator and are therefore not predetermined or predictable. It could even be that over time, the activity of creativity may have the effect of physically altering the brain's anatomy, enriching the depth and efficiency of the physical components of an intelligence: that is, physically mutating the brain and increasing the talent(s). Scientists are aware of a few of the loops that go to make up the talent-structure. Many remain to be explored.

▪

In the past, the evolution of the prodigy Mozart into the exquisite composer of the *Jupiter* Symphony and *Marriage of Figaro* was viewed as the inevitable destiny of a man given talents by God. Later Mozart's talents were viewed as the attributes of a rare genetic endowment. The dynamical feedback approach yields another perspective.

Mozart's father Leopold, a capable violinist, composer and assistant conductor in Salzburg seems to have been a suitable progenitor for the future musical genius. However, Leopold was himself the descendant of an undistinguished line of book-binders in Augsburg. Mozart's mother was the daughter of a lay official at court and was, in the words of a Mozart biographer, "quite devoid of any talents"—none that had surfaced in her culture and time at any rate. The role of genetic inheritance in Mozart's talent was undoubtedly important, but, in the end, it was a role that is elusive.

Also uncertain—though surely vital—was the role of the uniquely wired terrain laid down by the interplay of genes and randomly migrating neurons in the areas of Mozart's brain devoted to musical intelligence. More certain is the influence that his home environment must have had on mapping this terrain.

Gardner says that the musical intelligence is developmentally the first to mature. That means that we are fully equipped with all the rudiments of this intelligence long before we are equipped with all the rudiments of our spatial abilities or bodily-kinesthetic ones. Perhaps the early maturity of musical talent has something to do with its highly sensuous nature. A very young child may find it relatively easy to imitate and to feel in the physical body transformations of the core elements of the musical intelligence: rhythm, pitch and timbre. According to accounts, young Mozart's sensual contact with these elements was almost immediate.

Mozart was surrounded by music and responded to it with the sensual imitative capacity that researcher Bamberger described as characteristic of prodigy. Biographer Marcia Davenport novelistically depicts Mozart's childhood. When his older sister Nannerl was having lessons, young Wolferl couldn't stay away. After she had left the piano he "would reach up and tentatively, delicately touch the keys. His midget fingers found a third; ah! He gurgled, cooed and touched the next two keys in order; another third! Ecstatic delight. Then the fingers moved on, but missed the lower note, struck two together, a discord. The baby stopped, gasped, began to bawl with disappointment. Next day he could remedy the mistake; a little later, try to pick out what he had heard Nannerl playing."

When he was five, Mozart stood watching his father and two colleagues preparing to play violin trios. He begged to play second fiddle with his little violin. Leopold reproved him, pointing out that Wolferl hadn't yet had a violin lesson. *"Aber Papa,"* the boy said, "One need not have learnt in order to play second fiddle." Father refused, tears fell and in the end the prodigy was indulged. He followed the first fiddle perfectly.

Perhaps it was Mozart's uncanny capacity for imitation that initially inspired him to emulate his father in composing music as well as playing it. Perhaps composing stretched Mozart's musical talent maps into the areas of his logical-mathematical intelligence, thus helping him across the usually difficult transition between prodigy and active creator. Probably his intentions to pursue composing as a career expanded as a result of feedback from the eighteenth-century musical world he moved through and the exposure to music and adulation it provided him. His growing intentionality in turn extended his talent maps into areas of musical architecture. For example, his intention to compose could have spurred him to draw on his facility for imitation in order to analyze the musical structures employed by other composers. Acquiring by this means a large repertoire of musical structures could have helped him develop his fabled talent for holding an entire composition in his head until it was finished. As Gardner has pointed out, this talent was probably the ability to visualize in his mind the overall structure of a piece he was working on rather than an ability to literally know all the details before writing them down.

The point is, what we know and admire as Mozart's phenomenal and apparently magical musical talents didn't preexist in the pram. They grew into being as a matrix of interlocking feedback loops formed through his genes, his brain's unique anatomy, his home life, eighteenth-century culture and the prodigy's own circling intentions and attentions in the area of musical structure.

Creative intentions obviously have a great deal to do with

the creator's vision and Mozart clearly developed vision. Perhaps he did it by elaborating the kind of visceral feeling prodigy Lorin Hollander experienced when he put his hands on the piano and felt his identity in the notes. If Mozart was able to integrate such feelings (the embryonic desire to formulate an individual-universal equation) with thematic and nuance-driven perceptions about the nature of the world and with the conceptual demands of musical structure, then talent and vision would have evolved together, as evidently they did. Later, talent, nuance, themata, negative capability, omnivalence, creative intention must all circulate in feedback, for unless talent always changes through its feedback, it dies.

Csikszentmihalyi and Robinson say:

To maintain her or his talent over the life-span, a person has to integrate more and more complex experiences in consciousness and behavior. A child prodigy who fails to grow . . . becomes an increasingly pathetic example of unfulfilled promise. At what age does the unfolding of giftedness stop? There does not seem to be a definite end to its growth. Verdi, who was considered to have talent early in life, composed *Falstaff* when he was nearly eighty years old, and the joy and beauty in that work is like nothing he had ever written before.

The dynamical view of talent has explanatory power. For instance, it provides a way to contemplate a nagging riddle of creativity that might be called, "Are mathematicians really butterflies?"

Butterflies glory in the sunshine and air for only a brief season. Such, it has been claimed, is the fate of great mathematicians. Talent for mathematics seems to have an early developmental profile, though not quite so early as that for music. Late in life the eminent mathematician G. H. Hardy lamented, "Like any other mathematician who has passed sixty, I have no longer the freshness of mind, the energy, or the patience to carry on effectively with my proper job." Conventional wisdom has it that a mathematician's active creative life is pretty much over by the time (s)he's twenty-five or thirty.

However, a statistical examination of the important contributions made by some four hundred mathematicians does not entirely validate this wisdom. There are numerous instances of creators who didn't make a significant contribution till they were past seventy.

According to the dynamical view of talent, such creators could have mapped their talent in ways that would enable them to continue to do significant work or even begin significant work well past the time when the edge of mathematical deftness should have otherwise dulled. In fact, the dynamic approach suggests it's possible that some creators may require a very long time to bring their full talent into being.

THREE FUNNY THINGS ABOUT TALENT

The dynamical view of talent also allows a glance with fresh eyes into the murky corridors of three rather odd things about creative talent: 1) talent as sense-mixing, 2) the uniqueness of talent, 3) some mysterious ligatures between talent and deficit. Actually, as we'll see, the three corridors are probably connected.

The Sensory Mixing of Talents

The sensory, perceptual quality that Bamberger noted as a feature of musical prodigies' thought process also shows up in creative genius. Here it presents itself as a synesthesia. As a process, synesthesia is not well understood. It is commonly defined as a perceptual experience of sense mixing, hearing colors or smelling sounds for example, or associating a combination of sensory impressions with an idea or concept.

For purposes of clarifying the first odd phenomenon of talent, we'll expand this synesthesia definition by adding to it Gardner's notion of intelligences. Sense mixing, sense and concept mixing, and intelligence mixing do seem to have something in common since some of the intelligences as Gardner defines them have a high degree of sensory content (i.e., the spatial and bodily-kinesthetic intelligences) while others are high in conceptual content (i.e., the logical-mathematical and linguistic intelligences). All seven intelligences, in turn, are mixtures of core intelligences which are also sensory and conceptual. Synesthesia goes beyond the ordinary mixing of senses that takes place in consciousness. It is sense and intelligence mixing in unusual combinations, leading to unusual patterns of perception and thought.

It's possible that mature creators retain the ability to mix senses or types of intelligence in unusual ways from early childhood (when the differences between the senses and intelligences were not yet discriminated), or they learn, later, through feedback, to map one intelligence onto another.

Synesthesia probably keeps the creator in touch with the nuance level of perception. Nuance may even be the actual source of synesthetic thought, or vice versa. Certainly synesthesia and creative vision are closely connected. Jean Love says of Woolf:

. . . highly pleasant emotions came with synesthetic sensation. That is, she was enormously and pleasurably excited when sights, sounds, and other sensations seemed unified with each other. She was elated when her inner sensations seemed to be fused with sensations coming from the world around her. She remembered being intensely aware of the diffusion and unity of all her sensations and emphasized that a sense of unity and wholeness was essential to her feeling of pleasure. . . . She associated the sense of wholeness with her writing.

Einstein's synesthetic thinking was pronounced. He reported that his thought processes when working on a problem were accompanied by muscular contractions and visual images and that he could sense when he was on the right track by a tingling at the end of his fingers. Evidently for Einstein the logical-mathematical talent he needed to solve scientific problems was mapped into the visual and bodily-kinesthetic intelligences so the three functioned as one—appropriate for a physicist whose task is to make mathematical sense of the physical world.

Inventor Nikola Tesla came to the idea of the self-starting motor one evening as he was reciting a poem by Goethe and watching a sunset. Suddenly he imagined a magnetic field rapidly rotating inside a circle of electromagnets. The energized-circle imagery apparently was suggested by the disk of the sun and the pulse of rotation by the poem's rhythm. The incident indicates that Tesla's logical-mathematical, spatial, linguistic and musical talents were, at least in that moment, synesthetically merged.

In a treatise entitled "On Sensorial Vision," astronomer Sir John Herschel described how he experienced "the involuntary production of visual impressions" accompanying his abstract thinking.

Biology is dominated by visualization that moves back and forth between the physical and abstract. Watson and Crick's work on the structure of the DNA molecule was given an incalculable boost (spatially) by Maurice Wilkin's crystallographic pictures of the large DNA molecule, which suggested that it was in the shape of a helix. Against the advice of their colleagues, Watson and Crick attempted to resolve the details of molecular structure by manipulating (bodily-kinesthetically) wire models of molecules and their atomic bonds.

In his delightful memoir, Nobel prize-winning physicist Richard Feynman describes the way he thinks synesthetically when presented with an abstract mathematical problem.

I had a scheme, which I still use today, when somebody is explaining something that I'm trying to understand: I keep making up examples. For instance, the mathematicians would come in with a terrific theorem, and they're all excited. As they're telling me the conditions of the theorem, I construct something [in my mind] which fits all the conditions. You know, you have a set (one ball)—disjoint (two balls). Then the balls turn colors, grow hairs, or whatever, in my head as they [the mathematicians] put more conditions on. Finally they state the theorem, which is some dumb thing about the ball which isn't true for my hairy green ball thing, so I say, "False!" . . . I guessed right most of the time. . . .

According to mathematician Jacques Hadamard, many of the greatest mathematicians would probably be making up their own funny pictures right along with Feynman. Hadamard remembered how he had conceptualized one particular problem he was working on. He said he saw "not the formula itself, but the place it would take if written: a kind of ribbon, which is thicker or darker at the place corresponding to the possibly important terms." Benoit Mandelbrot proclaims that for him, "Geometry is sensual, one touches things. I see things before I formulate them."

He also indicates that his talent for working with the geometry of irregular shapes did not just come about through some synesthetic tendencies he was born with. He consciously trained himself to combine abstract mathematical abilities and spatial abilities in order to "see" the geometry of irregular forms. It's a good example of how a creator's creative intentions are also part of the mapping of talents. "Intuition is not something that is given," Mandelbrot says, "I've trained my intuition to accept as obvious shapes which were initially rejected as absurd, and I find everyone else can do the same. These shapes provide a handle to representing nature, and intuition can be changed and refined and modified to include them."

In the arts, synesthetic talent is the *sine qua non* of creative thinking. John-Steiner reports that many authors rely heavily on the musical sound, the cadences of words and sentences to guide the conceptual content of their language. It might be added that they sometimes have the cadences before they even have the words. There is evidence that Emily Dickinson—possibly unconsciously—wrote many of her poems to church hymns. For example, her poem "This is My Letter to the World" can be sung to the hymn "O God Our Help in Ages

Past." In Dickinson's case the synesthesia was linked directly to her visionary attempt to re-create religious text through her poems.

Isadora Duncan said she experienced orchestra music as dance movement (musical and bodily-kinesthetic talents mapped) leading to nuance. The conductor, she says,

raises his baton—I watch it, and, at the first stroke there surges within me the combined symphonic chord of all the instruments in one. . . . I feel the presence of a mighty power within me which listens to the music and then reaches out through all my body, trying to find an outlet for this listening. . . .

Architect Frank Lloyd Wright synesthized music and mathematics with the spatial forms of architecture, a combination which he said was influenced by his father having played Bach to him on the organ for hours. Wright said:

Music and architecture blossom on the same stem—sublimated mathematics. . . . Instead of the musician's systematic staff and intervals, the architect has a modular system as the framework of design. My father, a preacher and music-teacher, taught me to see—to listen—to a symphony as an edifice of sound. . . . I am grateful to music and to him for genuine refreshment in architecture—my field of creative endeavor. . . . I wish more life to more creative music revealing the cosmic rhythms of great Nature, nature spelled with a capital N as we spell God with a capital G. Why? Because Nature is all the body of God we mortals will ever see.

Again, a creator expresses a synesthetic experience in tones that connect it to vision.

Uniqueness

So the creator experiences a synesthetic mix of intelligences that chemically alters the intelligence or talent that governs their creative field (mathematics and music, for example, altering the spatial talent for architecture). By itself this would tend to make each creator's central talent unique. But the uniqueness of a talent goes beyond the synesthesia of intelligences. Consider these two expressions of spatial talent:

Sculptor Auguste Rodin said he was able to represent different parts of the body by visualizing the interior volumes: "I forced myself to express in each swelling of the torso or the limbs the efflorescence of a muscle or of a bone which lay deep beneath the skin." Sculptor Henry Moore exercised a quite different facet of spatial talent. According to one commentator, Moore imagined the sculpture, "whatever its size, as if he were holding it completely enclosed in the hollow of his hand; he mentally visualizes a complex form *from all round itself;* he knows while he looks at one side what the other side is like; he identifies himself with its center of gravity, its mass, its weight; he realizes its volume, as the space that the shape displaces in the air."

So each individual talent has its special cast. There's also a unique fit between the kind of talent or collection of talents that a creator possesses and the talents required for participation in the creator's field. A developing creator must both find a field which accommodates their set of talents (and vision) and then, where necessary, accommodate the field to the talents. The uniqueness of the fit between creator and field can end up altering the field, just as the field helps shape the creator's vision and talents.

For example, in the creative field of literature, the talents required for writing lyric poetry or short stories are not the same as those required for writing novels. In novel writing dramatizing characters demands a high degree of what Gardner calls the interpersonal and intrapersonal intelligences. That doesn't mean the creator needs to be good at getting along with people or at living a well-balanced intrapsychic life—but a novelist does need a capacity for insights in these areas. Gardner and a colleague, psychologist Joseph Walters, have argued that Virginia Woolf's strong intrapersonal intelligence was manifest in what she called her "shock-receiving capacity," that is, her ability to be jolted into making insight out of the moment-by-moment cruelties and joys of daily life. Woolf said that this capacity was "what makes me a writer. I hazard the explanation that a shock is at once in my case followed by the desire to explain it."

Woolf brought other unique talents to her writing. Poet Stephen Spender has said that the lyric poet needs a sense memory for experiences:

Memory exercised in a particular way is the natural gift of poetic genius. The poet, above all else, is a person who never forgets certain sense impressions which he has experienced and which he can relive again and again as though with all their original freshness. . . . It therefore is not surprising that although I have no memory for telephone numbers, addresses, faces, and where I have put this morning's correspondence, I have a perfect memory for the sensation of certain experiences which are crystallized for me around certain associations.

Woolf in fact possessed the kind of eidetic sense memory referred to by Spender. When she applied it to her work in fiction, it became one of the qualities that made her novels so highly "poetic" and original that she forever changed the definition of the novel itself.

Modern-day science requires the ability to exercise a strong interpersonal intelligence. Without the intelligence for working with colleagues and benefactors, a contemporary creative scientist would be at a fatal disadvantage for distilling vision.

This illustrates another facet of the uniqueness of talents: Each creator embodies a unique constellation of ancillary intelligences which (s)he brings to bear on the field in which the principal creative talent is exercised.

The Deficit Connection

This may be the oddest thing about talent. It seems that the uniqueness of a creator's talents and the changes these talents bring to a field have something to do with the creator's deficits. In his 1939–40 lectures at Harvard, composer Igor Stravinsky made this point:

The example of Beethoven would suffice to convince us that, of all the elements of music, melody is the most accessible to the ear and the least capable of acquisition. Here we have one of the greatest creators of music who spent his whole life imploring the aid of this gift which he lacked. So that this admirable deaf man developed his extraordinary faculties in direct proportion to the resistance offered him by the one he lacked, just the way a blind man in his eternal night develops the sharpness of his auditive sense.

Melody, Stravinsky insisted, is the "most essential" of the elements of music and yet, there is Beethoven, "whose greatness derives from a stubborn battle with rebellious melody. If melody were all of music, what could we prize in the various forces that make up the immense work of Beethoven, in which melody is assuredly the least?"

Stravinsky then compared Beethoven to Italian opera composer Vincenzo Bellini who "scattered to the winds with indefatigable profusion magnificent melodies of the rarest quality. . . . Bellini inherited melody without having even so much as asked for it, as if Heaven had said to him, 'I shall give you the one thing Beethoven lacks.' "

Great creators on the whole are "very conscious of the special skills they have and their special way of looking at things," Gardner says. "But if they lack something they need, they will study to get it or look for somebody to collaborate with. They will look for artful dodges, for ways to solve the problem or fashion the product where they don't have to use that particular talent they don't have."

"No poet, musician or scientist has the same profile of talent as any other," says David Perkins. "Each capitalizes on what he has." But that also means capitalizing on what they don't have.

An example is anthropologist Lévi-Strauss, who claimed that because of his inability to compose music (his initial creative interest), he was driven to study myths, which he believes exploit the same principles of mental life as does music. Interestingly, Lévi-Strauss told Hadamard that when working through ethnographic problems he would see three-dimensional schematic pictures in his mind, evidence of a strong spatial intelligence mapped onto the logical-mathematical. It appears that Lévi-Strauss's sense of lack about his musical abilities combined in a curious way with his spatial and logical-mathematical talents to create a significantly new slant on the study of mythology.

I should point out that in talking about a creator's sense of deficit, I'm not referring to that old nostrum that appeals to our desire for cosmic justice—the idea that a creator must pay for genius by being psychically or physiologically damaged in some way. This romantic notion might seem applicable to tragic artists like Mozart, Beethoven and Keats but is clearly not true of creators in general, or of those in the arts. In any case, the deficits referred to here are actually in some way a *part* of the talents.

A number of geniuses showed early deficit in developing their linguistic intelligence—a curious fact, since language is the most ubiquitously exercised talent of our species. Nietzsche, Edison, Einstein, da Vinci, Woolf and Dickinson were all late in speaking.

Holton thinks Einstein's late use of language and difficulty in learning foreign languages "may indicate a polarization or displacement in some of the skill from the verbal to another area." The explanation is plausible in light of research showing that a delay in left brain development (housing language) will cause the right brain (housing spatial intelligence) to grow correspondingly in mass and function. Phyllis Greenacre proposes another explanation for the deficit. She thinks "a potentially gifted infant with oversensitivity in sensory responsiveness either in general or in some special sense, may be at first more than usually overwhelmed by the onrush of stimulation and in the extreme react less rather than more." Love thinks this was the case for Woolf. The other angle has already been discussed: Since language is so pervasively entwined in our thinking, it has the effect of quickly leaching nuance out of perception. Delay in using language might allow nuance to become more deeply ingrained in the brain organization of the young creator-to-be. It might give nuance a foothold against the oncoming development of a child's indoctrination into "consensual reality," which language more than any other intelligence brings.

W. B. Yeats had a striking but definitely not unprecedented deficit for a writer. He was dyslexic. He wrote that at nine years of age he had come to think "that I had not all my faculties." Recent neuroanatomical research has suggested that dyslexics have larger right hemispheres with more cells than nondyslexics, and the theory is that the two hemispheres compete in the area of language, causing mixups and confusions in signals. Bernard Sklar at UCLA's Brain Research Institute says that in dyslexic brains there is less synchronization between the two hemispheres than in nondyslexic brains and that the dyslexic brains produce more theta waves. Theta waves are produced by people in new and novel environments and Sklar speculates that part of the dyslexic's problem is that the world never seems quite familiar. If so, that may have been quite a useful deficit for a poet—whose task it is to capture the freshness and uncanniness of the world.

Gustave Flaubert was also dyslexic and throughout his life remained very ashamed of this deficit. His first novel depicts a half-man, half-monkey who can't understand that the signs on a page stand for words. Nevertheless this freakish creature is more sensitive than ordinary literate people. One wonders if there isn't some connection between Flaubert's early dyslexia and his habitual agonies over finding *le mot juste.* Robert Sternberg says, "Dyslexia might not be helpful per se but it might make you have certain understandings. Sometimes you can make your weakness a strength that way."

The individual's attention to words in struggling with dyslexia and the feeling of uncanniness might lead to an emphasis on the verbal intelligence and a heightened sense that language is full of nuance.

From childhood Nikola Tesla was tormented by sense images that were like hallucinations. "When a word was spoken to me the image of the object it designated would present itself vividly to my vision and sometimes I was quite unable to distinguish whether what I saw was tangible or not." To obtain some relief from these hallucinatory images, Tesla made up imaginary worlds and took make-believe journeys. He seemed to be journeying, in fact, toward madness. Then at age seventeen Tesla discovered inventing and the potentially disastrous deficit turned into a talent. He found he could visualize in perfect detail all the parts of his inventions, even testing them in his mind. He said the mental image was so real he could even note if the machine was out of balance. He claimed that if he could get an invention to run in his mind, it always ran on the workbench.

Talent or deficit? Which is which? Where does one begin and the other end?

HG^N → WHAT GOES AROUND COMES AROUND

INTER: You love these circular paradoxes.

MUSING: I admit I do. But they're handy things for discussing creativity. And here we've met some good ones. In fact, I've just been marveling how they're a lot like the alchemical paradox which says that the mercury used to distill the *prima materia* itself must be distilled *from* the *prima materia.* In the creative context, mercurial talent distills the *prima materia* of vision, vision distills talent, and the two keep each other dynamic. In the creative context a deficit can become a talent or can fuel a talent. Now, if you don't think those are good paradoxes, bear in mind Stravinsky's observation about Beethoven and Bellini. Or listen to what Howard Gruber has to say about Darwin:

It has always seemed to me that Thomas Huxley was more brilliant and versatile than Darwin. Certainly, any fellowship awards committee comparing young Huxley's plans when setting out on the voyage of the *Rattlesnake* with young Darwin's plans when setting out on the voyage of the *Beagle*—both wrote them down in a page or so—

would have given first place to Huxley and put Darwin on the waiting list. . . . When Huxley finally heard about the theory of evolution through natural selection, he exclaimed, "Why didn't I think of that?" He might well ask, and so might we. Even if our answers can be only speculative, of one thing we can be reasonably sure, it was not Darwin's greater brilliance that made the difference.

Or consider what art historian John Rewald has to say about van Gogh: "In his early years van Gogh exhibited really no promise. Vincent forced himself to draw against all his own awkwardness and lack of talent."

You can see why scientists have had such a difficult time devising tests that would predict who's going to turn out to be a genius and why they haven't been able to find the origins of talent in the physical brain. The problem, as we can now see, is the way that talent is entwined into the whole creative process.

Talent is the ability to rapidly or finely process information in some domain such as music or art. A person may be born with this ability implied in the way the neurons are laid down or in the way the early environment organized the brain's processing. Or a talent may emerge through a concentration of energies and a feedback linking up and mapping different intelligences onto each other. A few years ago a young woman in Chicago was injured in a car accident that left her partially paralyzed and unable to speak. Though she had previously displayed no talent for painting, in a few months she learned to paint brilliantly. The woman's concentration of energies and motivation to communicate gave birth to her talent. Couldn't the same be said of genius creators?

Synesthesias, the brain's individually wired terrain, genetics, deficits—all the elements discussed here—conspire to create a special mercury. The fact that talent is especially distilled in each individual repeats at another scale the fact of that special hidden reality which is the creator's unique vision. Bringing the talent scale and the vision scale into a fractal harmony with each other becomes one all-important step in the long distillation of genius.

9

Insight Architecture

Hg → BUTTRESSES OF LIGHT

According to one alchemic guide, the distilling agent mercury, representing spirit or mind, slithers in many disguises. Mercury, true insight, is "many-sided, changeable," said C. G. Jung. The mercurial distilling agent of genius also takes many forms. One is talent. Others might be called the creator's "insight strategies."

Though researchers believe creators use these strategies extensively in their work, it is still not certain whether such capacities are inborn, inclinations of mind learned early, later mental distillations, the dynamical effects of talent or even talents themselves. Whatever the case, it's clear that at some point in the creator's development they become part of the permanent architecture of creative thought. Like the columns, windows, vaulted arches and flying buttresses of the Gothic cathedrals that were designed to be images of heaven and were so much admired by medieval alchemists for that reason, these insight strategies help the mind's great cathedral let in light. Soaring, supporting, refracting, they give important structure to the creator's earthly and mystical quest to form an individual-universal equation.

THINKING LIKE A MIRROR

Imagine, if you will, that metaphorical and mercurial structure, a cathedral of insight. Shafts of light filter through the great rosette window above the main portal. The rosette, like the cathedral itself, is devised as a mirror of the sacred universe. As its name implies, the rosette is a glazed flower with numerous petals; it sheds into the dusky nave a tincture of its mercurial light. The petals of the window are symmetrical and opposite each other; it is an appropriate symbol of a special type of creative insight strategy discovered by Albert Rothenberg. Rothenberg defines this strategy simply: It is "the creator's ability to actively conceive of multiple opposites or antitheses *simultaneously.*" He calls this ability "janusian thinking" after the Roman god Janus who could look in many directions at the same time.

Since he identified janusian thinking in creators back in the 1960s, Rothenberg has performed a number of experiments that illustrate how deeply it is a part of the creator's mental repertoire.

The first experiment was done with those ubiquitous experimental subjects, a group of undergraduate students. Rothenberg and his associates had the subjects fill out a questionnaire so that the experimenters would be able to evaluate which of the students were engaged in creative activities of some kind. The subjects were then asked to respond to each word on a standard list with the very first word that came to mind.

The experimental results showed that the students who did creative things tended more often than the other students to respond to the words on the list with opposite words. They also tended to respond faster with an opposite word than they did when they were giving a nonopposite association, and they were faster at giving an opposite word than were the less creative students who made opposite associations. For the creatively inclined students, opposites seemed to come almost instantaneously to mind.

Rothenberg later gave the same test to the group of genius-level professional creators he was following—his Nobel laureates—and an odd result he had noticed with the "creative" students became even more pronounced.

For a large number of the words on the test—words like "dark" and "hot"—an opposite is the standard, popular association. "The paradox is," Rothenberg says, "that these guys who thought the most brilliant thoughts were so turned toward opposition that they'd even give a popular response and then would be embarrassed by it, apologize for it." The creators apparently couldn't help themselves; their minds worked janusianly.

Some of the "creative" subjects did manage to come up with some unusual opposites that were *not* obvious, however. For example, one of them responded to the test word "eagle" with "St. Bernard"; to "memory" a response was "alive"; to "butterfly" the association was "egg" and to "comfort" the reply was "dis-ease." Unfortunately, the way the standard test was scored, responses like these were not counted as opposite. If they had been, the creators' oppositional rating would have been even higher.

A similar result has been obtained by researchers using other tests. In one experiment, Texas A & M psychologists found that students in creative fields like architecture were able to reverse gestalt figures more rapidly and more frequently than students in fields like business.

Rothenberg has concluded from his own experiments that the tendency to think in opposites—in fact to think in opposites so rapidly that both sides occur in the mind simultaneously—is an important property of creative talent. Simultaneous opposition is used quite consciously, albeit automatically, by creators, Rothenberg believes. Samuel Taylor Coleridge apparently thought so too, for he once insisted that the power of the poet "reveals itself in the balance or reconciliation of opposite or discordant qualities."

Rothenberg's early research involved trying to keep tabs on the thought patterns of a number of high-level creators, at first limited to a group of prominent writers. He also studied the manuscripts of past literary geniuses, focusing particularly on elements of the pieces that had received the most extensive revision. During his examination of Eugene O'Neill's *The Iceman Cometh* Rothenberg realized how oppositional thinking works. The evidence came from the complete set of play versions in the archives at Yale and from a series of independent interviews he conducted with Carlotta Monterrey O'Neill, the playwright's last wife. Rothenberg realized that the symbol of the iceman received disproportionately more revision than other elements of the play, and that this fit with what he learned was the origin of the iceman story.

The story "was based on an actual event in O'Neill's youth—that is, before he started writing. His roommate committed suicide, supposedly because his wife was having an affair; all his life O'Neill really believed that, until his maturity when he became aware that it was because of the affair but it was also that the guy wanted his wife to have an affair and had done a good deal to stimulate that. . . . He both wanted and not wanted her to have an affair. It was that that stimulated the play and is implicit in its structure." The strong effect that his roommate's ambivalence toward the wife's affair had on O'Neill suggests why Rothenberg believes that amibivalence in a creator can "fuel" the janusian process.

An equally eminent example of the key role of simultaneous opposition is the story of Einstein's discovery of the general relativity theory.

Einstein told the story in an unpublished essay that was uncovered in the Princeton archives. In the letter, Einstein explains that one day in 1907 while working on a journal article, he was desperately trying to understand why the law of gravitation, alone of all the natural phenomena in the universe, could not be discussed in terms of his special relativity theory. Prior to this he had been pondering a problem involving electromagnetic induction. That problem was a seeming paradox. It had been shown that if a magnet moves relative to a conductor or a conductor moves relative to a magnet, there is no difference in terms of the electricity produced—but the standard theoretical treatment of the two situations was quite different. Einstein admitted this theoretical paradox "was for me, unbearable."

In the context of this electromagnetic problem and his struggle to understand gravity's relation to special relativity,

Einstein had what he called "the happiest thought of my life."
He suddenly imagined a person falling freely from the roof of
a house and realized that this observer would not experience
a gravitational field in his immediate vicinity. "If the observer
releases any objects," he wrote, "they will remain relative to
him in a state of rest, or in a state of uniform motion." That
thought led him to realize that gravitation and acceleration
must be equivalent. In the simultaneous opposition where a
falling observer is paradoxically both in motion and at rest,
Einstein had found the key to his general theory.

And then there are all those simultaneous oppositions embedded in Mona Lisa's smile.

Lillian Schwartz's computerized discovery that the down-
turned glower of da Vinci's self-portrait is the mirror of the
upturned smile of the Gioconda adds weight to Rothenberg's
thesis that oppositional thinking must have been a vital part of
da Vinci's mental process. Rothenberg's thesis, in turn, poses
an interesting dilemma for Schwartz's interpretation that da
Vinci used himself as the model for the Mona Lisa. For it could
equally well be that he used the Mona Lisa painting as a model
for his later portrait of himself. The drawing Schwartz analyzed
is the only extant self-portrait of da Vinci and it dates from a
time when he was looking back on his life as a failure. Perhaps
the self-portrait is the bitter joke of a man who now saw himself
as the antithesis of the sensuous, innocent, enigmatic promise
he felt at the time he painted the Gioconda. Or perhaps he had
molded the Mona Lisa to himself and later molded himself to
the Mona Lisa. From the point of view of thinking in simultaneous oppositions, the state of mind is the same.

Rothenberg has also detected the activity of simultaneous
opposites in James Watson's thought process leading to the
discovery of DNA; in Picasso's conceptualization of *Guernica;*
in Bohr's complementarity; and in Virginia Woolf's early
thought processes about her most ambitious novel, *The Waves.*

It is fairly easy to add examples to Rothenberg's list, for
example:

In different places in her autobiographical conversation

Louise Nevelson reveals the movement of janusian thinking when she calls herself "the architect of shadow," "an architect of light" and "an architect of reflection."

Engineer and creativity theorist Belvin Ellis thinks Thomas Edison's invention of a practical system of electric lighting involved thinking in simultaneous opposites. Edison conceived of wiring his circuits in parallel and of using high-resistance filaments in his bulbs, two things that were not considered possible, in fact were not considered at all because they were assumed incompatible until Edison came along. Edison put these oppositions together.

Neuroscientist Karen Bulloch began to think janusianly while doing work on the thymus, a major organ of the immune system. Until her discovery, the immune system was thought to operate as a system independent of the influence of the brain other than through the nerves regulating blood flow. During an experiment, Bulloch noticed that a line of thymus cells she was examining had neuronal properties and that some neurons exhibited immunelike properties. "That was the turning point," she says. "It never left me." Thinking simultaneously about the opposing properties of the two types of cells drew Bulloch into a nearly ten-year research odyssey during which "people thought I was a little screwy." Nevertheless, she has now been able to show that there are in fact neuronal connections between the immune system and the brain.

▪

Rothenberg certainly isn't the first to make theory based on the notion of opposition. The list of others who have done it is long and distinguished. It includes Nicholas of Cusa who thought that God is a *coincidentia oppositorum;* the pre-Socratics like Heraclitus and Parmenides; Aristotle; the authors of the *I Ching;* Hegel, Kant, Bohr and Lévi-Strauss, to name a few. This list is so long and distinguished that the concept of opposition runs the risk of dissolving into the mist. Fortunately, in identifying the role of opposition in creative thought process

Rothenberg brings several important clarifications to the idea that give it substance.

Perhaps the most significant clarification is the *simultaneity* of the oppositions in the creative mind. When creators conceive of simultaneous opposites, they're not flipping from one opposition to another or even resolving the opposites into a synthesis such as Hegel described. "The Hegelian formulation of synthesis is quite specific and clear: elements of the thesis and anthesis are *combined* to form another, presumably more valid, position. Such a combination brings about a reconciliation of opposites . . . because conflicting aspects are resolved." Janusian thinking is quite different from synthesis because it may "consist of a paradox which is *intrinsically* unresolvable, unreconcilable, unsusceptible to synthesis." Think, for example, of Mona Lisa's smile or the dilemma of the iceman.

A second clarification is Rothenberg's realization that opposition depends on context. For example, in the context of an argument, many people would consider anger and love to be opposites; a psychiatrist would never think they were.

The effect of context is one of the most intriguing aspects of oppositions and creativity, for conceiving of a simultaneous opposition sometimes requires recognizing that the terms *are* opposite as much as it involves seeing, as Einstein did, how the opposition makes sense.

Edison's insight combining the parallel circuit with high-resistance bulb filaments resolved an opposition but had to first reveal that the opposition existed. Contemporary scientific opinion was that low-resistance filaments (presumed to be the only ones that would not burn up) were "opposite" to parallel circuits. "Opposite" in this context meant scientists knew that putting these two terms together would bring into play a law of physics (Ohm's law) imposing a physical requirement on the size of conduits and effectively ruling out practical lighting systems altogether. So, for practical purposes the two were opposite. Edison got around the problem by recognizing that there was another unstated opposition going on between high-resistance filaments and parallel circuits. High-resistance filaments were "opposite" because they would burn up. Discovering that hitherto unrecognized opposition transformed the whole context of the problem. It then remained for Edison to bring the oppositions together simultaneously by finding a high-resistance filament that would not burn up—which he did (carbonized thread).

A third important clarification is Rothenberg's insistence that janusian thinking doesn't just mean the creator entertains the simultaneity of a *pair* of opposites. It can mean conceiving of a number of oppositions in one. For this point, too, think of Mona Lisa's smile.

■

As a mirror reflects an opposing world, which is the same world that we stand in, creators think "mirror-wise" in order to gain new perspective. The ability and inclination of creators to use janusian thinking may be linked to the synesthesia of intelligences, to the creator's psychological ambivalences (if any), to the oppositions in the themata and nuances of the creator's vision or to the creator's visionary omnivalence. The nature of connections between janusian thinking and these dimensions of creativity remains to be explored.

THE CREATIVE MIND'S SORTING PROCESSES

Between the dazzling arched windows, along one side of the nave of our mercurial cathedral, rise three elegantly chiseled columns representing, metaphorically, three more creative insight processes identified by Robert Sternberg.

Sternberg is a leading proponent of what is called the information-processing school of developmental psychology. That means that he likes to put his concepts in computer terms. He has identified the following insight strategies as active in the psychology of creators:

1) Selective encoding: Here the creator sifts the relevant information from the irrelevant. Significant artistic and scientific problems have considerable information or "noise" and the creator has to be able to "recognize what is important." Sternberg and his collaborator, Janet Davidson, say, "The lesser scientists seem almost compelled to evaluate their findings with a uniform distribution of weights. They are unable to distinguish what matters more in their data from what matters less." Alexander Fleming's discovery of penicillin is a famous example of a selective encoding insight. Fleming came back from a holiday and noticed that the bacteria he was growing in one of his petri dishes had been killed by a mold. Where most scientists might have ignored this observation, disgusted that their experiment had been spoiled, Fleming realized that the experiment had yielded something important he hadn't intended. What set the stage for Fleming to recognize this fact was the whole context of his previous work looking for a treatment against sepsis. Selective encoding might be described as a selective alertness related to the person's whole creative enterprise.

2) Selective combination: This insight process involves seeing how to blend together the pieces of relevant information once you have detected them. A novelist, for example, might have the sense of a main character, a setting and a plot. Selective combination is the insight process that enables the creator to put all these together. The facts that formed the basis for the theory of evolution had been available for some time. Darwin's ability at selective combination enabled him to articulate them into a complete theory. "Mathematicians," Sternberg says, "tend to be selective combiners." This insight strategy, too, is entwined with the whole creative enterprise. Darwin's ability to put it all together certainly had much to do with elements such as his themata of wildness and simplicity, and a commitment to his project that was long-term enough to enable him to try out different combinations and select among them.

3) *Selective comparison:* Solving a problem by analogy is an instance of this type of insight strategy. Here the creator "realizes that new information is similar to old in certain ways and uses this observation to illuminate the new information." An example Sternberg gives is Friedrich Kekule's discovery of the structure of benzine. Kekule fell into a sleeping dream or reverie (interpretations of his exact state of mind vary) and saw a snake dancing around and biting its tail. He came out of a hypnagogic state to make the association that the snake biting its tail was a visual image for the structure of the benzine ring.

"Selective comparison is like Koestler's concept of 'bisociation,'" Sternberg points out. Arthur Koestler believed that the central act of creation is the mind bringing together two "habitually incompatible frames of reference." The ancient Greek Archimedes, for example, was set a problem by Hiero, tyrant of Syracuse, to determine whether the royal crown was pure gold or adulterated with silver. Archimedes knew the specific weight of gold by volume but was stumped over how to determine the irregularly shaped crown's volume without melting it down. One day while getting into his bath, Archimedes "watched absentmindedly the familiar sight of the water level rising from one smudge on the basin to the next as a result of the immersion of his body." He shouted *"Eureka"* ("I have it") so the story goes. Archimedes had seen he could determine the crown's volume by its displacement of water. Koestler wrote, "Neither to Archimedes nor to anybody else before him had it ever occurred to connect the sensuous and trivial occupation of taking a hot bath with the scholarly pursuit of the measurement of solids."

Koestler developed numerous examples of bisociation—all of which led him to conclude that the essential act of creation must be a "eureka" or creative flash joining two different reference frames. Long before Koestler, of course, the concept of eureka—the flash—had been enshrined in the legends of creative theory. This idea has recently come under vigorous attack by creativity theorists. Gruber, for one, takes strenuous issue with the creative flash approach and instead views creativity as a long pull punctuated by small insights that result in (and form) a constant shifting of frames of reference. Gruber thinks this gradual movement of thought can sometimes lead to an intense moment when weeks or years of work culminate suddenly. But he's convinced that when the flash occurs it is the result of an evolutionary process, not an accidental, discontinuous or primarily unconscious one. He challenges Koestler's insistence that bisociation involves the conjunction of only two frames of reference. He thinks that usually many frames are involved.

Sternberg's reformulation of the bisociation concept, however, avoids cramping the whole significance of creativity into a flash. He portrays selective comparison as part of the ongoing process of insight employed by a creator.

Jazz genius Duke Ellington seemed to be using selective comparison (bisociation) on a regular basis when he conceived of the melody lines of his compositions as having real-life correlatives. In his monumental "Black, Brown, and Beige," for example, Ellington composed a "tone parallel to the history of the American Negro." In one line, a horn parallels the grunts of the black work song. It was Ellington's regular practice to make parallels of this sort.

Sternberg's categories are convenient because they help classify related varieties of thinking that take place in a wide range of creative situations. He says, "Everyone uses all of these sorting processes to some extent, but usually emphasizes one." He is himself, he confesses, primarily a selective comparer.

INTER: Pardon me, but a couple of these categories of insight sound like that oppositional thinking of Rothenberg's. Are you sure they're not?

MUSING: It's likely they're related but not the same. Let me illustrate. Remember Einstein had been working on a problem in electromagnetism when he hit upon general relativity. We could say that he made a bisociation (selective comparison) by bringing electromagnetism together with relativity. We could say that that bisociation is what gave birth to the subsequent janusian image of a man falling from the rooftop simultaneously at rest and in motion.

However, at this point it's probably a good idea to stop a moment and remember that categories like bisociation, janusian thinking, selective comparison, synesthesia and omnivalence are for our convenience, not the creator's.

Over the many centuries that creativity has been pondered, theorists have used a number of different terms to describe the production of creative insight and many of the terms seem to overlap. For example, many writers, including Aristotle, have insisted that metaphor is an essential insight strategy, though definitions have varied widely as to what metaphoric thinking is and how it works. A good part of what different theorists have meant by metaphoric insight seems to me covered in janusian thinking, selective comparison and in the "image of wide scope" strategy we'll take up in the next section.

An important aspect of metaphoric thinking that is not much included in any of these terms has already been mentioned in the chapter 6 discussion of metaphor and irony in art: Artistic creators use techniques like metaphor or Stravinsky's harmony of varieties to evoke omnivalence because these metaphoric techniques rely on creating an irreducible tension or a "space between" the similarities and differences of their terms. Another important aspect of metaphoric thinking not included here will be discussed in chapter 14 and chapter 15 under the term "reflectaphor."

I suspect the reason creative insight strategies have been historically defined with so much variety and overlap is that the way creators produce insight is subject to the same kinds of dynamic differences in individuals as talent is. Certainly there is no clear line marking where a creator is using one strategy or another. The categories describing them are, at best, an *aide pensée* to get a glimpse into the mercurial movement of the creative mind.

PANORAMIC IMAGES

The light floods the choir of the cathedral and the visitor is surrounded by a fan of vaulted stained-glass windows into which huge sacred images are woven. More images loom as gargoyles on buttresses and columns. The images are emblematic of another strategy, or rather another important glimpse of the mercurial movement.

▪

In July of 1837 Charles Darwin, only a few months back from his five-year voyage on the *Beagle,* started what he called his *First Notebook on Transmutation of Species.* Twenty-one pages into the notebook the young naturalist penned the comment, "Organized beings represent a tree, *irregularly branched,* some branches far more branched,—hence Genera.—As many terminal buds dying, as new one [sic] generated./ There is nothing stranger in death of species."

After exploring the idea of the tree of life for several pages, Darwin wrote on page twenty-five of the notebook, "The tree of life should perhaps be called the coral of life, base of branches dead; so that passages cannot be seen."

On the next page Darwin drew a fragmentary sketch of a tree and on the bottom of that page another tree representing a different aspect of the huge evolutionary problem he was working on. On page thirty-six a third tree diagram appears, this time with more detail and thicker comments.

Within fifteen months of these diagrams, Darwin had solved the major problems of his theory.

According to Howard Gruber, Darwin's discovery of the irregularly branched tree of life image was a pivotal factor in the process leading to that solution. Darwin used the tree image to work through many points. He used it, Gruber writes, as a way of classifying the relation of different species to each other, as a way to represent "the fortuitousness of life, the irregularity of the panorama of nature, the explosiveness of growth and the necessity to bridle it 'so as to keep number

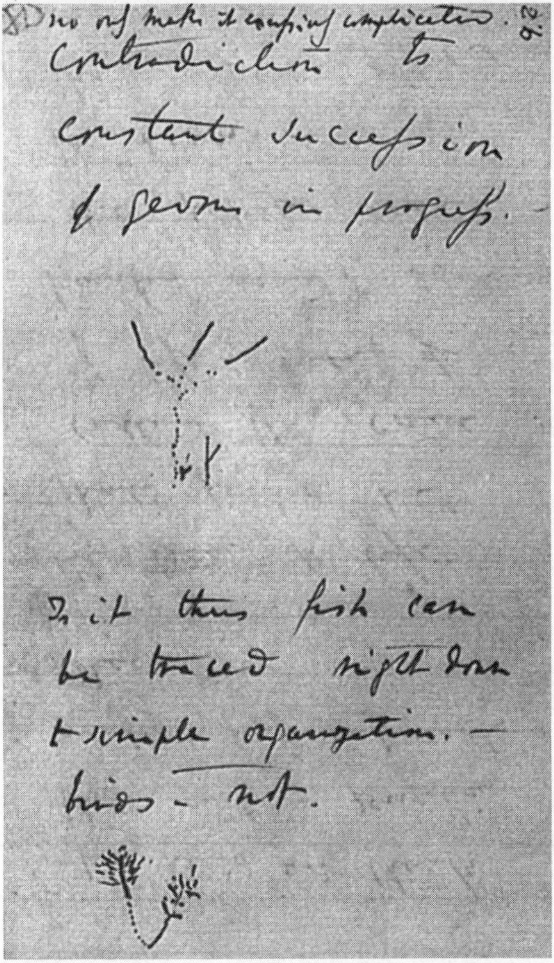

Figure 2 On page twenty-six of his Transmutation Notebook
Darwin drew two versions of his important image of wide
scope—the tree of life. The words above the tree start on the
previous page. "The tree of life should perhaps be called the
coral of life, base of branches dead; so that passages cannot be
seen;—this again offers ((no only makes it excessively
complicated)) contradiction to constant succession of germs in
progress." Between the first tree and the second, he wrote: "Is it
thus fish can be traced right down to simple organization—
birds—not." Darwin was using his diagram to test an idea that
the land, sea, and air creatures had different origins. Courtesy of
the Syndics of Cambridge University Library.

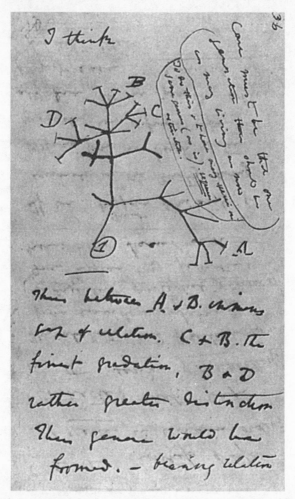

Figure 3 Darwin's third tree diagram appears on page thirty-six of his notebook. He writes, "I think" followed by the sketch. He then says, "Thus between A & B immense gap of relation. C & B, the finest gradation, B & D rather greater distinction. Thus genera would be formed,—bearing relation to ancient types." The last three words are on the next page. Darwin inserted a marginal note, "Case must be that one generation then should have as many living as now. To do this is to have many species in same genus (as is) *requires* extinction." Courtesy of the Syndics of Cambridge University Library.

of species constant.' " Most importantly, he used it to express "the fundamental duality that at any time some [species] must live and others die."

Over the twenty years until he wrote *On the Origin of Species,* Darwin's thought changed in many ways but the image of living nature as a tree remained constant. A tree diagram is the only one in the *Origin* and it is referred to throughout. In his notes during those twenty years, Darwin drew and redrew this image as an accompaniment to his ideas.

Gruber calls such central images or metaphors in a creative life "images of wide scope." He says that an image is wide if it can accommodate "a wide range of perceptions, actions, ideas. This width depends in part on . . . the intensity of the emotion which has been invested in it, that is its *value* to the person."

In one of his essays, Gruber makes an indirect association between the tree of life and the powerful image Darwin uses at the end of the *Origin*—the image of nature's immense complexity and interconnectedness as a "tangled bank." In the same essay Gruber associates Darwin's tangled bank image to the journal entry where he describes the vine-festooned Brazilian jungle and his mind as a "chaos of delight." "Here then," Gruber writes, "is the 'tangled bank' in its early form."

When I asked Gruber if he thought the image of the tree of life might have been implicit in Darwin's nuance 'theme' of nature's wildness, he agreed that he thought it was, and added, "And it's interesting. The first scientific lecture Darwin gave after he came home on the *Beagle* was his study of coral reefs." So the irregular branching was implicit in Darwin's interest in coral, too.

In retrospect, the sequence of Darwin's insight into evolution looks almost predestined. The progression begins with his early fascination with the wildness of nature and his omnivalent wonder at it, moves to his scientific interest in coral reefs; these lead to the discovery of an explicit image that has the shape of both wildness and coral—the irregularly branching tree of life; then finally the progression flows to the emotion-laden image of the "tangled bank"—an image that could be said to have returned Darwin full circle to the "wildness" and "simplicity" themata of his youth, but now having united and concretized them in a completed creation, the theory of evolution. But in truth there was nothing predestined about this progress. The tree of life and companion "tangled bank" images were, as Gruber says, "the product of hard, imaginative and reflective work": the distillation of Darwin's vision.

Images of wide scope are an important discovery in the study of creativity. They seem often to mark the first surfacing into a concrete form of the inchoate, emotional and sensory qualities of a creator's vision; the first materializations of vision into the consensual world where creative products must ultimately be made. Once deposited into reality, images of wide scope serve as levers and scaffolds for building the actual creative products.

The wide scope images are usually visual—though they may be images from the other senses. Gruber identifies several images of wide scope which Darwin used besides the tree of life and "tangled bank." One was the image of nature covered with sharp wedges "packed close together and driven inwards by incessant blows" (an image of the effect of the multitude of small forces acting on any organism in nature. This image was introduced into the first edition of the *Origin* and later abandoned). Another was the image of the struggle for existence as like human warfare; another, the comparison and contrast of natural selection with artificial selection.

Gruber believes that the total number of images of wide scope developed by any individual creator is very small, perhaps four or five over a lifetime. In addition there may be between fifty and a hundred subsidiary images "that are used in the elaboration of these thematic organizers."

Gruber didn't intend his phrase "thematic organizers" as an allusion to Holton's concept of themata or LaViolette and Gray's notion of a circulating nuance 'theme,' but it seems to fortuitously fit with these ideas nonetheless.

Images of wide scope change and evolve as vision evolves.

Jeffrey Osowski, one of Gruber's doctoral students at Rutgers, has tracked several shifting images of wide scope that William James used to probe the question of what consciousness is. Osowski says that James started with "the image of a stream—that became the standard term 'stream of consciousness'—to express the idea of change and continuity. But when he wanted to indicate the way that the consciousness has unity and selectivity, the image of the stream became less useful. So he introduced the image of a sculptor 'selecting' out of a piece of stone the single intended figure." Note here that the image of wide scope allows the creator to explore the limitations of a line of thought as well as its richness. Later James wrote of consciousness as a herdsman herding his sheep; as the flight and perching of a bird; and as a fringe of felt relations.

While on duty in the Civil War, Russian film director Sergei Eisenstein saw a pontoon bridge being built across the Neva River by recruits "like a throng of ants swarming along symmetrically laid-out paths." Their precision "fused into an amazing contrapuntal orchestration in all its varied harmonies." Film historian Ted Perry says, "The building of the pontoon bridge became a seminal image in Eisenstein's aesthetic." The swarming precision appears in many of his films. Moreover, it lies behind his sense of how films are made, by the swarming, precise cooperative efforts of many.

Examples of other images of wide scope developed by creators: W. B. Yeats "gyre" and "tower"; Picasso's image of the bull or Minotaur, which recurred in countless paintings (sometimes revised out of later sketches for a work); Mondrian's image of a finely branched tree, which over time evolved into the rectilinear networks that made him famous; Tesla's idea of resonance, which acted as a lever into his vision of nature as a vast untapped energy resource; Woolf's image of the wave and her idea that she was to be the biographer of the untold history of small acts; Mozart's musical image of pacing, which became a kind of flexible template for his pieces (this image has been called Mozart's "law of growing animation"); Isadora Duncan's attraction to the image of the Greek temple, which she said gave her much inspiration for her dance.

David Bohm recalls that as a young physicist he had done work on electron plasmas and had discovered that while the behavior of individual electrons appeared to be random, the electrons together acted in astonishingly orderly ways. "I saw that as like the relation of the individual and society. I said that to the other scientists and they didn't know what I was talking about. What interested them was that you should make calculations." Bohm confides that all his life he felt he has been "following that image" of the electrons as like both the individual and society. An image with an apparently janusian form and strong omnivalent overtones, it helped him develop a theory of how electrons and other particles unfold out of the whole background of subatomic movement.

▪

As head of the Edison project, Reese Jenkins has examined thousands of pages of the genius inventor's notebooks, sketches and patent drawings. He has teased out of this mass of material threads of several images of wide scope that run through Edison's work.

Two threads that turn up repeatedly are what Jenkins calls the "drum-cylinder" and "stylus" forms. These forms first appeared in an 1868 sketch for a proposed fascimile telegraph, later in Edison's plans for an electrochemical copying machine; in some telegraphic inventions; in a chalk-drum telephone (1877); in a dynamo (1880); a stock ticker (1889) and in his kinetoscope or movie camera where the drum became the rolling film and the stylus the camera eyepiece.

Jenkins traces Edison's acquaintance with these forms back to the telegraph offices and machine shops where the inventor worked as a young man. There, Jenkins says, lay "the repeated appearance in Edison's experience of electromagnets and battery jars, both of which are in fat cylindrical form." There were also "truncated cylinders in the form of wide wheels for carrying paper tape, not unlike those in the shafts and pulleys

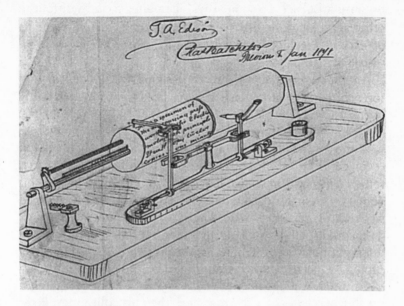

Figure 4 Two images of wide scope—the drum-cylinder and stylus—are prominent features of Edison's idea for an electrochemical copying machine. Courtesy of the U.S. Department of the Interior, National Park Service, Edison National Historic Site.

of the nineteenth-century belted-machine shop. . . . Finally, Edison's experience in machine shops such as that of Charles Williams, Jr., in Boston acquainted him most intimately with the lathe, which closely resembled the drum-cylinder-stylus form in Edison's work, with the stylus analogous to the cutting tool positioned on the tool rest."

Jenkins believes Edison also made use of tactile images of wide scope, carbon, for example. Edison tried to get some form of carbon—which he would have seen ubiquitously in telegraph rooms in the form of lampblack—into many of his inventions, for example, the rubber and carbon button for the speaker of the telephone. Ironically, in developing the practical electric light, Edison initially rejected carbon as a solution because it burned up too easily. Then after months of testing other substances, he discovered that charring silken filaments of carbon produced the very thing he needed for a high-resistance lamp.

Another image of wide scope Jenkins has noticed in Edison's thinking is particularly curious because it was apparently born of an Edison deficit.

Edison began to go deaf as a young man, a definite handicap to someone who had ambition to be a top-notch telegraph receiver. Because of the handicap, Edison was liable to miss some of the transmissions, leaving gaps. Edison overcame his deficit by an artful dodge that yielded an insight. He avoided working on the stock wire where a receiver's missed dot or dash could spell disaster for investors. He worked, instead, on the night news wire. The transmissions were occasionally disrupted by electrical storms, adding to Edison's reception problems, and yet Edison obtained a reputation for receiving a greater percentage of the messages than his colleagues. How did he do it?

His secret, he later admitted, was that at night when he went home from work, he took with him the exchange newspapers. These papers contained the most current national information of the day. By thoroughly familiarizing himself with the names of the newsmakers and issues of the moment, Edison was able to "fill in the gaps"—those created by the storms and those created by his hearing deficit.

In his later inventions Edison applied the idea—or mental image—of filling in the gaps to great success. The most impressive example of this was the movie camera, which exploits the mind's ability to fill the gaps in a sequence of still pictures so the figures in the pictures appear to move.

Jenkins, you may remember, suspects that a central feature of Edison's vision was the inventor's sense that he was playing a game with nature. From his statements and his behavior it seems clear Edison felt that a wonderful previous winner of that game was the telegraph. Clearly Edison greatly admired the telegraph because it had changed the face of the world.

Possibly he saw in the technology of that invention, essential forms—the drum-cylinder and stylus, carbon, gaps that could be filled in by the mind—which were like the cell wall, mitochondria and nucleus to the evolution of organisms. Out of these essential forms, Edison learned, many different technological organisms could evolve.

Jenkins found the images of wide scope prominently delineated in Edison's early sketches for his inventions but less evident or absent in the completed inventions. It appears the inventor was able to use the images as fulcrums in his creative thinking but didn't get carried away by his visionary images so that he imposed them willy-nilly on the inventions he was formulating. He was able to find the line between where his essential forms would work and where they wouldn't—an exercise in negative capability.

INTER (standing on a ladder to change a light bulb): Is that negative capability or stubbornness? Didn't your Mr. Edison say that genius is ninety-nine percent perspiration?

MUSING: Actually, he borrowed the sentiment from Emerson, who put the percentage at fifty–fifty. But it's fortuitous you should mention that. The next distilling agent we're about to look at involves perspiration.

10

The Absorbing Flame

S → ON THE HOT SIDE OF MERCURY

The alchemical symbol is S, which stands for sulphur, meaning passion, the heat of the spirit, the flame of absorption—sweat. In the lore of the alchemists, mercury is said to be outwardly mercury but inwardly sulphur, and sulphur the reverse. The alchemic symbolism is once again especially apt, for in creation, the ability to be absorbed in the creative activity is the mirror if not the essence of talent. Recall Gruber's remark about Darwin and Thomas Huxley; it was apparently Darwin's ability to stick with the problem that brought him his insights.

Psychiatrist Rollo May claims that "absorption, being caught up in, wholly involved" in a work is the hallmark of the artist. Of the scientist, too. While Edison was working on inventing the phonograph, a blizzard swept across the east but the inventor spent days in his laboratory and didn't even know it was snowing until his wife sent a sleigh for him. William Hogarth, like Edison, insisted that "genius is nothing but labour and diligence." Even the miraculous Bach said, "ceaseless work. . . analysis, reflection, writing much, endless self-correction, that is my secret." Newton believed the successful solution to a problem lay in "thinking on it continually." H. G. Wells said of Joseph Conrad, "He had set himself to be a great writer, an artist in words. . . . He had gone literary with

200

a singleness and intensity of purpose that made the kindred concentration of Henry James seem lax and large and pale." Louise Nevelson notes, "You have to be with the work and the work has to be with you. It absorbs you totally and you absorb it totally. Everything must fall by the wayside by comparison." Gruber proposes that creativity is "a magic that comes out of hard work. Like the magician himself is a hard worker, who practices, practices, practices, and then it looks like magic." Absorption may even enable someone to turn a deficit into a talent.

It should not be surprising that classic psychological studies of creativity have confirmed the obvious, that talent is at some levels indistinguishable from intensity and passion. In one revered piece of research, a scientist compared the thinking processes of chess grandmasters with chess "experts" and found that the grandmasters possessed no special abilities like photographic memory. The difference was they were more passionate about the game and spent more hours at it, which made them faster and more powerful players.

Absorption: Einstein's dogged endurance, painters becoming absorbed in their canvases, writers absorbed in their characters. Flaubert claimed, "When I wrote about Emma Bovary's poisoning I had the *taste of arsenic so strongly in my mouth,* I was so thoroughly poisoned myself, that I gave myself two bouts of indigestion, one after another, two very real bouts since I vomited up my entire dinner."

Notebooks, journals and the patterns of creative lives testify to a creator's absorption in work that is so overwhelming that it comes to direct the creator's whole existence. Picasso one day informed his mistress, Françoise Gilot, "Everybody has the same energy potential. The average person wastes his in a dozen little ways. I bring mine to bear in one thing only: my painting, and everything is sacrificed to it—you and everyone else, myself included."

At age twenty-nine Darwin was teasing out the theory of evolution and at the same time pondering the future of his domestic life: "This is the Question," he wrote:

If *not* marry TRAVEL? Europe—yes? America????? If marry—means limited—Feel duty to work for money. London life, nothing but society, no country, no tours, no large Zoology; collect., no books. . . .

His mind reached out to contemplate the common joys of life but spiraled back as if ineluctably attracted to the question of how it will affect his work. If he married, then:

Children—(if it please God)—constant companion (friend in old age) who will feel interested in one, object to be beloved and played with . . . Forced to visit and receive relations *but terrible loss of time*. . . .

Joseph Conrad first took up the almost monastic life of the sea. It left long hours between watches to read the authors who would serve as models for his second career as a novelist. When he made the transition to the writing life, he did it by marrying a woman willing to devote herself to eliminating any distractions that might affect her husband's work. Perhaps not coincidentally, Jesse Conrad had been a professional "type-writer" when Joseph married her and he quickly incorporated her skills at the machine into his arduous creative process. Making himself and his stories the sole support of his family, Conrad imposed crisis deadlines on his writing, a tactic that was clearly his way of enforcing an absorption in the work and wrenching himself from what he felt was his congenital "indolence."

TWO APPARENT PARADOXES OF ABSORPTION

Paradox number one: Curiously, for Conrad, indolence was an essential element of his creative activity. He said that his entry into his literary career in the first place proceeded from a moment of indolence when he was on shore leave and had nothing else to do but start his first novel, *Almayer's Folly*.

Conrad was like many creators who complain of their own

laziness, which they paradoxically associate with their absorption. In a moment of pique over the poor reception of his novels by the public, Faulkner wrote to his publisher, "I think now that I'll sell my typewriter and go to work—though God knows, it's a sacrilege to waste that talent for idleness which I possess."

Perhaps Conrad was explaining the peculiar link between creative laziness and absorption necessary to distill vision when he lamented: "I begrudge each minute I spend away from paper. I do not say from the pen, for I have written very little, but inspiration comes to me while looking at the paper. Then there are flights out of sight; my thought goes wandering through great spaces filled with vague forms."

Could it be that a creator experiences idleness or indolence so keenly because the creative state of mind *seems* indolent compared to the aggressive concentration of purposeful thought? When a specific creative problem is being wrestled with, the solution or truth of vision must lie partly in the spaces *between* thoughts—the spaces of nuance and omnivalence. Looking back on it, creators may have the sense of not doing much of anything because their minds have been in those "great spaces filled with vague forms."

By imagining themselves as basically lazy creators could also be spurring themselves to creative absorption. Feeling a constant need to jar themselves from their sulphuric laziness could be a way of forcing themselves to return again and again and again to the creative enterprise they are working on, keeping it always before them.

That great creators are in fact far from lazy, despite their protestations, has been proved by studies which find that geniuses not only produce high-quality work, they produce a high quantity of work. The great scientist publishes more papers than his peers, the great painter paints more pictures. Geniuses as a group are not the most prolific in their fields, but they are very highly prolific. Such continuous output has obvious consequences. One creativity expert notes of great scientists, "The greater the number of researches, the greater the likelihood of making an important discovery that will make the finder famous." However, the other face of this coin is the one turned over by W. H. Auden, who observed that since major poets are so prolific, "The chances are that, in the course of his lifetime, the major poet will write more bad poems than the minor."

Conrad, who could spend days looking at a blank page, didn't start writing fiction until his thirties. Nevertheless, he averaged a book or play a year until his death at age sixty-six. His wife claimed he died of exhaustion from all his years of work. Only a few of Conrad's pieces are masterpieces, but the ones that are didn't come from a mere few years' inspiration; they came from Conrad's ability and willingness to dedicate nearly his whole existence to his creative activity.

Clearly, the conditions of absorption include having the sheer time to be absorbed. This requires constructing a life-style to provide for the idleness of sustained effort. Time is an oxygen that feeds the flames of absorbing fires. To gain such time men who desired to work in creative fields have needed independent incomes, a commission such as a research fellow-ship, a patron, or supportive domestic arrangements, as in the case of Conrad. If the creator isn't from circumstances that will carry him through during the long years it generally takes for the evolution of vision and its public acceptance and financial rewards (if they ever come), he must be prepared to live in poverty.

If the situation is difficult for creative men, for creative women it has been well-nigh impossible. Historically women who wished to do creative work have found it very hard to carve out conditions necessary for absorption and creative indolence. For example, a life-style of poverty imposed by creativity was never a socially plausible option for a woman, as it was for a man.

Where a male creator could appear to lead a relatively normal life (Conrad, for instance, had two children) because of the traditional support system society made available to his sex (Jesse Conrad did most of the child raising), female crea-tors who wanted to carry on their lifelong work have had to be constitutionally prepared to lead unconventional lives.

Isadora Duncan had children out of wedlock and lived a flamboyant, bohemian life-style supported by her unconventional family who were willing to follow her across Europe. Creativity researcher Doris Wallace points out that four of the greatest women novelists of the nineteenth century—Jane Austen, Emily and Charlotte Brontë and George Eliot—did not have children. Virginia Woolf and Georgia O'Keeffe were also childless and had unusual husbands who strongly supported their work. Emily Dickinson and Barbara McClintock never married. Let's consider McClintock's situation.

McClintock has claimed that in her psychology, "there was not that strong necessity for a personal attachment to anybody. I just didn't feel it. And I could never understand marriage." Her biographer notes, "As a child McClintock had a striking capacity for autonomy, self-determination, and total absorption." McClintock's sole continuing attachment has been to her creative activity as a research biologist. A condition for her work is her sense that it is "just happening," not forced or directed. The phrase "just happening" expresses her sense of having the space and time for her creative absorption to act in. To get that space and time McClintock was psychologically prepared to live a largely hermetic life. But it's also true that the society she was born into made little provision for accommodating the normal life-style of a woman to an intensely dedicated creative absorption.

Some creators—perhaps many—justify the vast amounts of idle time necessary for absorption by focusing on the creating activity as an escape from what they feel are the inadequacies and pressures of their everyday life. Echoing Einstein's desire to escape the merely personal, Stanislaw Ulam said, "A mathematician finds his own monastic niche and happiness in pursuits that are disconnected from external affairs. In their unhappiness over the world, mathematicians find a self-sufficiency in mathematics."

So we come to the end of our first paradox with the realization that having the motivation and absorption to chase the wisps of truth and omnivalence and needing a capacity and the circumstances for indolence aren't really paradoxical after all.

■

Paradox number two: A second apparent paradox of absorption has been pinpointed by Nobel prize biochemist Arthur Kornberg. A creator, Kornberg said, "needs intense motivation or focus, but he also needs a certain restlessness. That may sound like a contradiction."

Howard Gruber and several colleagues have shown that Kornberg is right when he says that restlessness and absorption only *sound* like a contradiction.

In his study of Darwin, Gruber found that the founder of evolution theory seemed to move about restlessly among a number of projects. On his *Beagle* trip, he wrote hundreds of pages of notes on geology, zoology and other subjects. These topics eventually took on semiseparate lives in Darwin's thinking. In his *Red Notebook* and *A Notebook* he kept primarily geological notes. In the *B, C* and *D* notebooks he contemplated the transmutation of species; in the *M* and *N* series he dealt with human evolution, the expression of emotions and the continuity between man and other animals.

Gruber calls the creator's wide interests his "network of enterprises" and thinks the network is an important indicator of creative absorption. A network of projects allows creative individuals to explore their visions from a number of different angles. Shifting back and forth among projects, they can pry loose insights that might have been otherwise impossible to obtain. The differing projects which are nonetheless intuitively united, help the creator move elements of data and insight around to create a new context of relationships, leading eventually to the expression of the creative vision.

From the outside, the creator may appear restless, but in fact the creator's movement among different enterprises is a manifestation of the ongoing activity of creative absorption.

William James jumped about among a wide range of enterprises bridging science and philosophy; Sergei Eisenstein was both a teacher and leading theoretician of film as well as a filmmaker; Leonardo da Vinci darted among activities in science, architecture, painting, medicine, city planning and engineering, one project pollinating his energies for others. His career, however, demonstrates the danger of the network of absorption. There is an inherent pretentiousness and over-reaching in starting up all these enterprises. Thus da Vinci discovered to his despair in his last days, that a human lifetime wasn't long enough to bring all the projects of his network together into a coherent creative legacy.

The network of enterprises helps a creator deal with places where (s)he is stumped in the effort to unfold the hidden reality of the vision, for by utilizing the network (s)he can shift to another project, another angle. (S)he can also "bracket" (put aside) part of the problem (s)he is working on and jump to more productive avenues to keep the absorption going. Gruber says Darwin, not having available to him Mendel's work on genetics, was unable to resolve the issue of how variations in species occur. Darwin bracketed this issue and shifted around in his network of enterprises to resolve the several other issues that surrounded the mechanism of mutation.

So paradox number two is not really a paradox either. Creative restlessness goes quite well with the intense focus of absorption. Both are part of the willingness to put one's entire life at the service of the creative activity. But all this raises an obvious question: Do we have any ideas where this sulphuric drive for absorption comes from?

ABSORPTION: ITS NATURE AND NURTURE

Some studies have shown that the capacity to be absorbed is a "special trait" already functioning in individuals at an early age. An investigation of twins raised apart who were tested for traits like "zest for life," "the need to achieve," "risk-seeking" and "absorption" indicates that these traits could have a genetic origin. Be advised that this investigation is subject to the same proviso applied to the studies suggesting that talents are genetic: No single gene would be responsible for such a complex trait; a child who tended to become easily absorbed in an

aesthetic experience would not necessarily come from a parent
with that tendency.

Certain reservations about the study have been voiced. One
researcher cautioned that the study compared twins who came
from a "relatively narrow range of cultures and environments.
If the range had been much greater—say Pygmies and Es-
kimos as well as middle-class Americans—then environment
would certainly contribute more to these results. The results
might have shown environment to be a far more powerful
influence than heredity."

The reservations notwithstanding, it seems useful to enter-
tain the possibility that absorption is a talent and so would
share the dynamics of talent we discussed in chapter 8—a
feedback among genetics, neuroanatomy, environment, conscious mapping and vision.

If sulphuric absorption is a mercurial talent, the talent appears to be one characterized by a unique sensitivity to nuance
and a special power to amplify the various other intelligences
(talents) at the creator's disposal. How would such a special
talent function?

Neuroanthropologist Laughlin has reviewed the neurophysiological literature and thinks that the key brain site for
creative absorption is the prefrontal cortex. That's the place
where those frontal lobotomies used to be performed. As
noted in chapter 3, this lobe is strongly connected to the limbic
system and to the loops that LaViolette has identified as the
prime channels for circulating nuance.

The prefrontal cortex is the only area to receive input from
all the sensory modes, including smell, and from the association
cortices like the parietal lobe where Einstein had the extra glia.
Damage to the prefrontal area can impair the ability to concentrate and plan, and sometimes leaves victims profoundly indif-
ferent to the environment. Laughlin says that in a number of
studies, "EEG theta waves produced by the prefrontal cortex
have been shown to be associated with sustained attention."
This suggests that a good part of absorption and of what we call
our "intention" or "will" is a function of prefrontal activity.

If you would like to learn more about Jeremy P. Tarcher, Inc., simply complete and mail this card to us. We will be happy to send you a catalog.

PLEASE PRINT

NAME_____

ADDRESS_____

CITY & STATE_____

ZIP_____

In which title did you find this card?_____

_____

JEREMY P. TARCHER, INC.

5858 Wilshire Boulevard

Los Angeles, California 90036

Place
stamp
here

Bergström believes that will and attention exist in their most primitive state in the brain stem. But it's a "chaotic" will, an attention that responds randomly to any stimulus; it's close to the random attention of a newborn child. The prefrontal cortex—which is fed this random attention through the nuance loop—eventually develops a selectivity so that some things are attended to and other things relegated to the background. Over time, the organism accumulates a complex set of intentions based on the things it attends to. These intentions fluctuate in response to the overall internal and external input pouring into the prefrontal lobe.

As Virginia Woolf lay in her nursery and heard, saw and felt (or later remembered) the sound of the waves and the slant of the light and the improbability of her existence, that nuance 'theme' circulated intensely from her limbic system through her prefrontal lobe. The sharp strength of the nuance could have aroused her attention, which actively selected her intention to pay attention to that nuance and to keep it cycling. That intention would, in turn, have made her alert to other nuances resonating with this nuance 'theme.'

How could absorption in an experience of nuances lead to the capacity to create works in a specific field like music or physics? Laughlin says the prefrontal intentional process does two things that have the effect of singling out objects such as musical notes or mathematical equations in which intentionality will then become absorbed: 1) The prefrontal lobe amplifies the electrical activity in the sensorial network that represents the object in the brain, and 2) it inhibits awareness of distracting sensations and objects. Translated, this means the prefrontal cortex is closely wired into all the cortical areas and it can select which areas to emphasize.

So, as time went on, Woolf's intentions and capacity for absorption in nuance would have become associated with the cortical areas that could express and extend her absorption in that nuance—the areas involved in language, for example. This would, in turn, have led her to construct a life to facilitate her continued exploitation of those areas—and her continued absorption.

Csikszentmihalyi's research on activities that produce an addictive sense of "flow" indicates that intense absorption has a fascinating quality: It is intrinsically rewarding. That is, activities that stimulate an absorption are carried on for their own sake, for the continued varied arousal they produce, rather than for the sake of some extrinsic pleasurable reward.

In an ingenious set of experiments, Brandeis University psychology professor Teresa Amabile has shown that creativity itself may depend on the intrinsic nature of absorption, that is, it depends on being its own reward.

Amabile tested subjects ranging from elementary school children to undergraduate women, rewarding some of them for creative tasks. Their creative productions were then rated by a panel of judges composed of professional creators. Amabile and her colleagues report that no matter what the reward was or when it was given, if the subjects thought they were working for an external remuneration, they became less creative.

In a different experiment, Amabile tested seventy-two young creative writers, first asking them to each write a brief poem. Dividing her subjects into three groups, she gave one group a questionnaire that stressed "the external things a person can get by writing" such as impressing teachers and getting into graduate school. The second group was given a questionnaire that stressed the idea a person "would write even in the absence of external goals or pressures." The third group was not given a questionnaire. All the subjects were then asked to write a second poem.

This experiment showed that even the suggestion that external reward should be a part of creativity is enough to dampen creative absorption. The group given the intrinsic suggestion or no suggestion maintained about the same creative output. The creative rating of those exposed to the extrinsic questionnaire dropped significantly, according to the judgment of twelve independent poets who read the poems.

Amabile concludes, "The more complex the activity, the more it's hurt by extrinsic reward."

Zoologist Desmond Morris says the same thing happens to our primate cousins. In *The Biology of Art,* Morris describes how chimpanzees given canvas and paint become eagerly absorbed in making aesthetically balanced patterns of color and form which look a little like abstract expressionism. In fact, the monkeys become so absorbed in this activity that they show little interest in food or sex. But as with humans, if experimenters reward the chimps for their paintings, the quality and quantity of the creative engrossment goes down. The monkeys do only enough painting to get the reward.

In terms of the nuance connections between the prefrontal cortex and the limbic system, there's probably a lot in common between chimps and humans. Offering a reward to an ape brain or a human one may form what Gray would call an emotional-cognitive structure that is "organizationally closed." Such a closed thought introduced into the cycling nuances in the limbic-prefrontal loop could shut off or overshadow the movement of nuances and hence stifle the capacity to be absorbed.

▪

Other factors strongly affecting development of a capacity for absorption may be rooted in the early family environment.

Various studies, including Galton's, have suggested that first-born children—especially first-born sons—are more likely to become geniuses than their siblings. The reasons could be social, cultural and psychological. First-born sons have traditionally received more education and attention. But no one knows if this is the reason more of them become geniuses. One thought is that first children or only children don't learn to compromise the way younger children do. They become more self-centered and thereby more single-minded, with a greater capacity to be absorbed. It could also be that spending more time alone—not in a social mode—facilitates absorption.

Other research points to a correlation between the early loss of a parent and genius. Among the geniuses we've followed here, Conrad, Newton, Beethoven and Woolf lost parents early in life. One study found that fully one-third of geniuses lost one parent by age ten, a much higher percentage than normal. Orphanhood may immerse the future genius in an intense uncertainty, which creative absorption could both compensate for and express.

Many geniuses were "replacement" children for siblings who died and were remembered by the parents as gifted. This was the case with Gregory Bateson, Tesla, Salvador Dali, van Gogh and Margaret Mead among others. Such a family situation here might have the effect of causing the replacement children to compensate for a felt lack of natural talent (in comparison to the dead sibling) absorbing themselves, or escaping, into a creative enterprise.

Some of the most intriguing recent research into the effects of family dynamics on the fires of absorption has been done by Rutgers psychology professor Monica McGoldrick.

McGoldrick, who is also a practicing family therapist, immerses herself in the biographical data about a creator until she can transform it into a schematic diagram she calls a "genogram." These diagrams bring to the surface hidden lines of psychological force. One thing she's discovered is that creators sometimes become absorbed by "family themes."

Consider Alexander Graham Bell, for example. For three generations the males in the Bell family specialized in speech and elocution. Both Bell's mother and wife were deaf. McGoldrick and her colleague psychologist Randy Gerson say that Bell's genogram reveals that some members of Bell's family are "compensating for those who learned to speak with difficulty because they could not hear at all." Bell's absorption in the effort to invent the telephone was clearly influenced by this family theme.

In quite a different way with a different effect, Eugene O'Neill's absorption was spurred by the family theme of addiction which may have provided him with incentive to under-

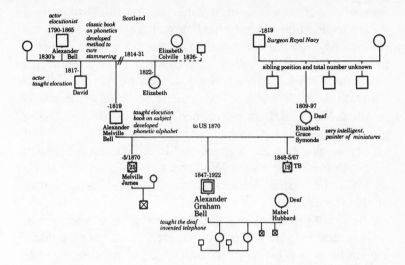

Figure 5 Genogram suggesting how the family theme of hearing and speech communication was bequeathed to the eventual inventor of the telephone. Reprinted by permission of Monica McGoldrick and Randy Gerson.

stand the dramatic tangles of human psychology and certainly provided him with absorbing material.

CHILD'S PLAY, COURAGE AND OTHER CONUNDRUMS

Creators are often known for a type of absorption that takes the form of childlike innocence. When Langston Hughes was an older man he was described by a friend as "like a young person starting out in life. He had such a naive attitude; it was very beautiful to watch." Barbara McClintock said, "One of my friends, a geneticist, said I was a child, because only children can't wait to get up in the morning to get at what they want to do." Emily Dickinson confessed, "I love to be a child."

In his essay on creativity, Erik Erikson associated the absorbed play of children with creativity: "It is striking to see the difference between . . . adult behavior and the attitude of a two-year-old child toward a rolling ball. The child can throw this ball on the floor again and again, seeing it roll a hundred times, and never be bored." Psychiatrist D. W. Winnicott wrote that "it is in playing and only in playing that the individual child or adult is able to be creative and to use the whole personality." Winnicott envisioned play as an activity taking place in the "potential space" between "external reality" and "inner psychic reality," a space that initially existed between the mother and the baby. Winnicott's speculation recalls the notion of the "space between" contraries where there is a play of richness and omnivalence.

The similarity between a child's absorbed play and the absorbed creative play of an adult creator should not be taken too far, however. It's more accurate to say that a creator is *like* a child, and that the intimation of going back to that early state may be one of the attractions for creators of their creative activity. But it's not likely that the child who watches the ball is having the kind of experience described by Guy de Maupassant.

De Maupassant was offering a paraphrase of advice given to him by Flaubert. Formulating (though he didn't know it) an exact equation between mercury and sulphur, Flaubert had said, "Talent is long patience." De Maupassant added:

It involves looking at everything one wants to describe long enough, and attentively enough, to find in it some aspect that no one has yet seen or expressed. Everything contains some element of the unexplored because we are accustomed to use our eyes only with the memory of what other people before us have thought about the object we are looking at. The least thing has a bit of the unknown in it. Let us find this. In order to describe a fire burning or a tree in a field, let us stand in front of that fire and that tree until they no longer look to us like any other fire or any other tree.

Though Schiller believed that we are at our highest only when we play, when we have no conscious purpose (which is the reason creators need all that time for idleness), the problem is that it's impossible to become an adult without accumulating an entire brain full of purposes. Flaubert seems to have been telling the young de Maupassant how to harness his adult creator's purpose to absorption. Yeats described adult creator's play as a "gaiety transfiguring all that grief"—that is, a gaiety or play transformingly aware of grief.

For a young child, purposes have scarcely formed and divisions like consciousness and unconsciousness are barely separated; for an adult creator these are aspects of mind long-since separated and now to be brought together by the creative act. Louise Nevelson says, "You're permitting the whole consciousness and unconsciousness and all things to work for you. So you're tapping everything, like a gold mine."

The distinction between the self and the other, between observer and observed, consciousness and unconsciousness— all sorts of boundaries are overcome in creative absorption, but it's also true that creative absorption exploits and depends on a full appreciation of those boundaries in order to construct its inventions, artworks and scientific discoveries.

■

Willingness to take risks is high on the list psychologists make of characteristics required for creativity. Rollo May devoted an entire book to the subject of creative courage. Faulkner said he agreed with André Gide's remark admiring only those novels whose authors had almost died in order to write them.

Creative courage is typically equated with a daring to go against the grain, the courage to be different, the grit to risk failure by veering from accepted paths. This view is true but its cast is romantic. A harsher side was expressed by Faulkner, employing his customary black humor. He said he saw the creator as driven by demons, a person who would "rob his own mother" in order to create. He argued that Keats's "Ode on a Grecian Urn" "is worth any number of old ladies."

What the world sees as the courage to be different from the norm is for the creator the result of a simple imperative imposed by absorption in vision. Many a creator has avowed that if (s)he could have done anything else—anything "normal" —in life, (s)he would have done it. Barbara McClintock said of her attraction to her creative work. "Whatever the consequences, *I had to go in that direction*" (emphasis hers).

All creators to some extent and some creators to a great extent face—as McClintock, Galileo, Darwin and Joyce did— the prospect that their work will not be accepted or appreciated. This is a particularly painful prospect since having others see the hidden reality the creator sees is a major motivation for doing the work in the first place.

But the life and death commitment to the vision and the creator's faith that (s)he is seeing a true reality is a stronger motivation. Once having felt the sulphuric inflammation, the creator is as fated to undertake a creative life as the victim of a chronic "dis-ease" is fated to adapt to the condition. The true creative courage may be in the daily, yearly living with that peculiar "dis-ease" and the demands it makes: among them, to keep the mind open, to let go of the known and follow the subtle shadows of nuance and omnivalence (vision), and to continue to do this despite the distracting seductions and disappointments of success, flattery, aspersion and neglect.

From everything we've learned about absorption, its connection to the creator's negative capability looks indisputable. The need for idleness, the traits of restlessness and intense focus, long patience, play, creative courage—all seem related to what Keats called the capacity to "exist in doubts and uncertainties," the ability to identify oneself with the sparrow pecking in the gravel, or a beam of light speeding through space. But whether the creator's absorption is brewed from the contraries and omnivalence of vision or vision is amplified by a capacity for absorption is not known. Probably, as with so much else in creativity, the two brew and amplify each other.

But whatever the origins, the courage and effort required to sustain such absorption is huge. The restless focus of absorption in creation allows few of the comforts of mind most of us are used to. Conrad complained, "You know how bad it is when one *feels* one's liver, or lungs. Well I feel my brain. I am distinctly conscious of the contents of my head. My story is there in a fluid—in an evading shape. I can't get hold of it. It is all there—to bursting, yet I can't get hold of it no more than you can grasp a handful of water." When he would finish a novel, he would be exhausted as from a life-threatening experience. At the end of *Under Western Eyes* he lay near death from his effort to bring forth his hidden reality.

In her memoir, Eudora Welty testifies, "I am a writer who came of a sheltered life. A sheltered life can be a daring life as well. For all serious daring starts from within."

What appears to the world as courage or recklessness or egotism or indolence may be for the creator efforts to maintain the absorption which is their condition as a creator: Conrad setting the sword of deadlines swinging above his head so that he could force himself into the abyss of the blank page which he might gaze at for days; Edison brashly announcing to the public that he had achieved an invention long before he had done so, forcing himself into long vigils in his laboratory until he could make good his boast.

I had asked Jenkins why Edison did that.

JENKINS: That may be what he felt he needed to do to screw up the juices. And he does it over and over again. It seems to drive him.

QUESTION: Is it related to his fill-in-the-gaps idea? He says to himself, This is where I am, there is where I want to be. The creativity for him is filling in the gaps between the two.

JENKINS: You mean, if he doesn't set that kind of target, he's not real? Yes, but there's also the historical context of hype, exaggeration, promising what you can't possibly deliver.

INTER (shutting off the tape of the interview with Jenkins): History! That's right, what about history?

MUSING: Yes, it turns out that history is another form of the sulphuric distilling agent.

11

To Burn
with One's Time

S^S → FIRES OF HEAVEN; NO, EARTH

The medieval alchemist depended for his work of transmutation upon more sulphuric fire than that brewed in his alembic. Above him in the heavens beamed the sparks of his circumstance—defined for him on the charts of the astrologers. The "aspects" or relative angles of these sparks (planets and stars) could be auspicious or inauspicious for the process of his alchemy. He was also, himself, astrologers told him, composed of these aspects so that both his desire to be an alchemist and his success at the task were woven into the time and place of his endeavor.

The fire in the soul of a great genius is also indubitably, if not astrologically, woven into the moment and place of his work. For the creator it's not the fiery net of heaven that ensnares him but the earth's net of history. The sulphuric fires of history are a distilling agent which boils the circumstances of creation with what is sometimes called mere accident or fate. But Howard Gruber says that it is the "person-world" connection we must ultimately study in order to understand the creative gift. "The meaning and value of a gift depends on that relationship."

Welcome to another circular paradox. More: a paradox shaped like the mathematical Möbius strip that curls round and round and back around in one curve continuously folding in on itself.

SOME TRIPS AROUND THE SULPHURIC MÖBIUS STRIP

Georg Wilhelm Friedrich Hegel claimed that "the great man of the age is the one who can put into words the will of his age, tell his age what its will is, and accomplish it. . . . He actualizes his age." Thomas Carlyle took the opposite view: "Universal History," Carlyle wrote, "the history of what man has accomplished in this world, is at bottom the History of the Great Men who have worked here." Is the creator mainly affected by history or is it the other way around?

It seems safe to say that no one can entirely escape the context of their times because, as Gertrude Stein put it, "the only thing that is different from one time to another is what is seen and what is seen depends upon how everybody is doing everything."

This point was dramatized ironically by Jorge Luis Borges's fanciful story about a twentieth-century symbolist poet named Pierre Menard who sets out to write the seventeenth-century novel *Don Quixote*. Borges says:

To compose *Don Quixote* at the beginning of the seventeenth century was a reasonable, necessary and perhaps inevitable undertaking; at the beginning of the twentieth century it is almost impossible. It is not in vain that three hundred years have passed, charged with the most complex happenings—among them, to mention only one, that same *Don Quixote*.

Though after an incredible effort Menard succeeds in fabricating a few pages that duplicate exactly pages of Cervantes, he does so as a twentieth-century man engaged in a supreme act of artifice. So though the "truth" or omnivalence for Homer, Cervantes, Balzac or Faulkner may be at some level the same, evidently that truth must be constantly remade through different historical contexts—so it is many different truths as well.

INTER (coming around a corner fast): But what about some-body like da Vinci? Wasn't he a creator who escaped his context? Wasn't he a man "ahead of his time"?

MUSING: If you look closely you'll see that a large part of da Vinci's being "ahead" has to do with our ability to read back into his visions a knowledge that comes from a context da Vinci himself was not a part of. But, of course, that's not entirely true, and indeed you have alerted us that we are on the Möbius strip here: In unfolding a hidden reality, genius is both caught in an historical context and also making its own new context which may later help form, or may coincide with, new historical contexts.

To negotiate these puzzling turns along the historical Möbius strip, let's go back to Feldman's concept of co-incidence.

Co-incidence not only applies to prodigies but also to ge-nius. An individual's home life-support system (or lack there-of), the cultural value and support given to the creative endeavors the individual is interested in pursuing and the historical development of the creative field at that point in time—all have impact on how or whether genius will manifest. For example, Gardner says:

A person with one set of skills may be a tremendous mathematician or scientist in one era, because his skills are just what was needed, while proving relatively useless in succeeding (or prior) historical epochs. For instance, the ability to recall vast strings of numbers or to envision complex relations among forms may prove tremendously important in certain mathematical eras while of little use at other times, where books or computers have taken over such mnemonic functions, or where the notion of spatial concepts as integral to mathematics has not been accepted.

But it's not just talents and history that must co-incide, there is also obvious important co-incidence required between his-tory and vision.

Aesthetician Ernst Gombrich wonders if van Gogh would

have been an impressionist painter if impressionism had already been invented. How would Newton have fared if the laws of motion and attraction had already been formulated? No one can answer these questions, of course. Perhaps it's likely that Newton and van Gogh would have continued to be creators, continued to strive to express their hidden realities. But would their struggles in such different historical contexts have led them to achievements regarded as genius? Don't answer that question too quickly until you've considered the situation of George Washington Carver.

Born about 1864 in Missouri as a slave, and left as an orphan, Carver's supple mind gained him attention and he rose through post-Civil War educational institutions to become the head of agricultural research at the Tuskegee Institute. Carver is generally remembered for his work with the peanut and the host of products he was able to derive from it. His scientific activity is credited with giving a major marketing boost to the peanut industry in the South.

However, it turns out Carver's experiments with the peanut were only a small part of a vision he developed to create a "cookstove chemistry" that would enable the average man—particularly the poor black farmer—to produce products at home for making life healthy, comfortable, economical and aesthetically pleasing.

To that end Carver invented ways to produce high-grade paints and stains from local clays; noncommercial fertilizers by refining local minerals; a laundry bluing agent; a powder for polishing metal; and a bedbug poison. He worked out different methods of dehydrating foods and effective physiotherapy techniques using peanut oil.

At the heart of Carver's activities was a mystical vision he espoused early in his scientific career, "that nature does not expend its forces upon waste material, but that each created thing is an indispensable factor of the great whole, and one in which no other factor will fit exactly as well." One biographer insists that "Carver had preached . . . every action has to be considered within the whole context."

Was Carver a genius? Historically he has not been considered one. He has been judged instead a symbol of black aspirations and a talented scientist who failed in his attempt "to provide a permanent basis for small-scale agriculture." The problem is that none of Carver's natural products led to large-scale manufacturing or "new" technological break-throughs. But that was not his intent. His vision was to put together small-scale technologies harmoniously.

But history foiled Carver. Small farms disappeared and with them the life Carver's vision hoped to revolutionize. Commercial chemical companies supplying fertilizer and large-scale production of household products became the chemistry of the day. Of course, it's not impossible to imagine another scenario. We can imagine a history that would have lifted Carver to genius as the man whose innovative chemistry created a new world where rural families and small communities could be self-sufficient, scientifically sophisticated and harmonious with their environment. Picturing such a history is not impossible but it is difficult—because in fact reality didn't go that way. Carver's science might have worked quite well in the Third World, but he was not born in the Third World. We could imagine that the future will turn us from the giant, highly specialized industrial chemistry that emerged since Carver's day, but we have to wonder. Even if history were to take that unlikely turn toward Carver's vision, would it pass by the same place or by a place close enough to where he had worked to recognize his efforts as creative genius?

While the failure of Carver's vision to co-incide with his times can't be laid solely to the fact he was a black man in a white racist country, that fact was certainly a significant part of his situation. Following Carver's story around the edge of the Möbius strip, we can see how oppressed groups pay a heavy price on all fronts, not the least in their full access to the burning historical fires that make genius possible.

What has happened to women in the last few decades makes this point emphatically. A hundred years ago the idea that women possess inherently less creative potential than men would have seemed valid scientifically, a fact borne out by the relatively few women of genius on record. However, as soon as their historical context changed, the relative numbers of women geniuses jumped dramatically. But one spots a returning bend in the Möbius strip here, too, because it's also true that women geniuses like Virginia Woolf contributed mightily to changing the historical context.

So co-incidence between history and a creator's vision has some bends. It also has some twists.

CO-INCIDENCE TWISTS

While prodigy requires almost perfect co-incidence between talents and circumstance, Gardner thinks genius requires a degree of "dissonance" between the two. He says, "In creative people there are important disjunctions between the creative person and the domain. If things are too far apart, it can't work, but the right kind of tension will push somebody into having a new understanding." We've already seen in chapter 8 how creators stretch their talents to fit the field and the field to fit their talents. That's one way historical dissonance works.

There's also the dissonance between history and *vision*. Here a dissonance in the one mirrors a dissonance in the other. This means that in working out the dissonance of their own visions, creators can resolve the dissonance in the historical context. A case in point follows.

For about two hundred years the "classical" Newtonian paradigm had been embellished by scientists who held in common a collection of important themata. In their deep guts and souls scientists intuitively felt that the way the paradigm expressed all these themes was true. One of the important themes in the classical paradigm was continuity. Another was atomic discreteness. Within the Newtonian worldview these themata were not in opposition. But that began to change. Rothenberg points out, "Scientific knowledge works on a theme until enough information has been gathered that the knowledge becomes polarized and the theme comes into conflict with its opposite." Around the turn of the century, evidence began to emerge showing that energy, which the Newtonian paradigm said was continuous, must be made out of discrete (quantum) bursts. The quantum world also began to suggest that supposedly discrete things like separate atomic particles are somehow connected to each other, perhaps in a continuous fashion. The themes of discreteness and continuum had become polarized within the historical context, creating a "paradigm crisis" that caught most scientists in the middle, choosing one side of those oppositions or the other. For Albert Einstein, the oppositions of the historical paradigm dilemma had quite another meaning.

As we noted earlier, it's possible to discern dynamic contraries in the themata of Einstein's vision, including contraries between the themata of continuum and atomic discreteness. So while most scientists felt mere conflict or confusion over the newly apparent contradictions between continuum and discreteness, Einstein felt these themata must be elements of a single, whole and noncontradictory hidden reality that was his life work to express. In his later years, for example, when he objected to quantum theory, he did so by claiming that there must be a hidden reality composed of what he called "hidden variables" that would resolve the apparent quantum paradoxes and (in effect) show that continuum and discreteness had a unified place. Einstein's burning and quite personal desire to create a new context where his gut perception of the universe as a continuum and his gut perception that there are also discrete parts therefore co-incided with the most burning scientific issues of his time. Bent on making sense of his own internal dissonance (which if he could properly express it would prove a harmony), Einstein mirrored the dissonance-striving-for-harmony of the historical moment. Because his vision and history formed this dissonant twist of co-incidence, Einstein was able to contribute importantly to quantum theory and relativity, revolutionizing the meaning of both the themes of continuum and discreteness, creating new contexts in which previous polarizations made new sense.

Einstein's situation illustrates how a creator's vision helps distill a new shape to history and how the fires of history help distill out the shape of the creator's vision. Here's a stranger case.

▪

The writer Jean Toomer was born in 1894 in Washington, D.C. His mother came from affluent and educated people, his father was "in appearance and mode of living . . . a gentleman." The two divorced when Toomer was four. In his uncompleted autobiography, Toomer said of his early years living alternately in white, then black neighborhoods:

Among the items that came to me were items concerning the racial situation; but they seemed unrelated to my life. Nevertheless, of course, my mind stored them up. I heard of the color line. I heard of segregation. I heard that colored people were barred from white hotels, theaters, and restaurants. I heard of social inequality. I heard of passing. I heard that the white world was the world of opportunity, that the colored world was limited. I heard that if a person was known to have Negro blood, no matter how little, he was called Negro. I was more than curious about these items. Some seemed unfair. Some seemed untrue. But it never occurred to me that this might have some personal bearing on my personal career.

As an adolescent, Toomer developed an intense dislike for the racial label and held to the position that he was "an American neither white or black." According to his recent biographer, Toomer developed an ambivalence toward his racial identity, compounded by many factors. On the one side was an attraction to black American culture and the black historical predicament. On the other was his strong mystical sense of our common humanity. But Toomer's contrary feelings were really much more than ambivalence. They were omnivalence. "He describes high moments when he had visions in which he saw that the ends ordinary men sought did not measure up to the worth and dignity of the lives of human beings, and he longed for the unnamed things that did."

During the first years of apprenticeship as a writer, Toomer was unable to focus this omnivalence. He "linked his inability to capture his own literary voice . . . with a more fundamental problem—a lack of harmony between his mind, his emotions, and his body. . . . He had come to believe firmly that he would have to achieve personal harmony if he were to experience success and happiness." Evidently, Toomer was struggling to both express his vision and find it.

In the fall of 1921, Toomer made a trip to rural Georgia which transformed him, distilled his vision and brought him (momentarily, at least) the harmony he sought. In Georgia, he became intimately involved in what might now be called "the black experience." He wrote to his friend, author Waldo Frank: "My growing need for artistic expression has pulled me deeper and deeper into the Negro group." He described being inspired by "folksongs come from the lips of Negro peasants" and "the rich dusk beauty . . . and a deep part of my nature, a part that I had repressed, sprang suddenly into life and responded to them."

In the months following his return from the South, Toomer began work on a book to crystallize these feelings. His absorption seemed to increase exponentially. "While he worked on the book," his biographer says, "Toomer's deep mysticism and intent search for spiritual connections made the experience [in Georgia] almost supernatural. The essence of black culture enveloped and filled him. He even wrote to Waldo Frank describing times when he felt that he was losing all sense of an identity separate from the materials of his writing."

The result of his writing efforts was *Cane,* a hauntingly beautiful and movingly brilliant collection of poems and stories. In it the contraries of Toomer's vision—his longing for a raceless humanity and his "repressed" longing to make contact with his black experience—came together to form an omnivalent context. It's a context that leaves the reader with a simultaneous sense of the black American's particular history and of our universal human destiny.

Cane was immediately hailed by critics and admired by

other black writers. But Toomer was not pleased with the reception because he sensed it meant his audience was over-looking or minimizing the universal element of the work. "He became upset that everyone around him considered him a 'Negro' writer on the basis of the content of this book." Almost at once the public response caused Toomer to back away from the black experience dimension of his vision and insist again on his belief that he was an American writer, not a Negro one.

But there was a fatal problem for Toomer with this stance; the raceless belief expressed only *part* of his vision, only part of its "truth." The historical response to his work from a racially conscious American society forced Toomer, as a matter of principle, to deny another part of his vision, his personal racial consciousness. It was a denial that cost him dearly.

When his publisher asked him to identify himself as a man of "colored blood," because that was the "real human interest value" of his story, Toomer replied with justifiable anger that he was not a "Negro" and would not feature himself as such even if it meant forfeiting publication.

After *Cane*'s release indelibly marked Toomer as a "black" writer, he became disillusioned with literature as a means for achieving the "wholeness" he was seeking. He spent the rest of his life on a spiritual quest, studying the teachings of Eastern philosopher G. I. Gurdjieff, then joining the Society of Friends, and finally undergoing Jungian psychoanalysis. He wrote at least one other book, but publishers rejected it as mystically propagandistic.

Toomer's creative destiny was a co-incidence with a strange twist. The fire in the contraries or "dissonance" of his vision compelled him to find a context that would express both his black experience and his universal experience. This internal dissonance co-incided with a dissonance or conflict going on at that very moment in American history over the society's acceptance of Afro-Americans as full-fledged human beings. In the context of *Cane*, both writer and readers could come to terms with this conflict, see its "truth." But outside of *Cane*, readers (both white and black) were unable to let go of their historical race consciousness and Toomer was unable to let go of his denial of it. So the very co-incidence of history and vision that made *Cane* possible also prevented Toomer from going on to other creative work. Put another way, Toomer's personal dissonance mirrored the dissonance in historical race relations, but when he rejected that dissonance he could no longer function as a creator.

Compare Toomer's experience with that of poet Langston Hughes, who also took the historical predicament of the American black as his subject matter and universalized it. Hughes experienced the same historical dissonance that Toomer did in terms of society's ambivalent racism. But Hughes's personal vision formed a different co-incidence with this historical situation. The dissonance in Hughes's vision centered around a feeling that though society had left blacks uniquely alienated, they were universal beings. This form of dissonance left Hughes more comfortable than Toomer in accepting his own identity as a black man in a racist world. Hughes expressed his visionary dissonance in terms of the plight of the mulatto, a person who is of no race because (s)he is alienated between the races. The mulatto's dilemma allowed Hughes to bring out both the universal and the historically particular aspects of the American black experience. Thus for Hughes the co-incidence between the dissonance in his personal vision and the historical dissonance of race relations took a form that he was able to explore and exploit for a long creative career.

INTER (making a noise in the half light): Ahem . . .

MUSING: What is it?

INTER: *"Facile,"* my master in logic used to say. Excuse me, but your argument sounds too—simple.

MUSING: You're right, of course. In order to make points about the odd bends of history and vision I've had to greatly oversimplify the visions of both Toomer and Hughes. It seemed a necessary evil.

INTER: Evil? That's what you moderns consider sin, eh? Remarkable. Now what?

HISTORY AND THE INDIVIDUAL: WHICH DISTILLS WHICH?

Let's move a little further round the Möbius strip. Toomer and Hughes, though they both dealt explicitly with the dissonance of the historical race question, formulated it in quite distinct ways because the dissonance of their personal visions were different. That often happens in art. But what about science? In science, the importance of any differences in creators' visions has sometimes been rejected by creativity theorists. The thought is that the progress of history basically makes certain discoveries inevitable. For example, in 1845 English astronomer J. C. Adams used Newtonian astronomy to predict a planet beyond Uranus. A year later, U. J. J. Leverrier made the same prediction, though he was unaware of Adams's work. Elisha Gray and Alexander Graham Bell contacted the U.S. Patent Office on the same day about patents for the telephone; Leibniz and Newton worked out differential calculus at the same time; evolution was discovered at about the same time by Darwin and Wallace.

Simultaneous discoveries in science seem to indicate that the fires of the individual vision are considerably less important to the discovery process than the fires of the zeitgeist. In this view, says University of California psychologist Dean Keith Simonton, "Individual creators must be little more than interchangeable agents."

Simonton examined this possibility using what are called "historiometric" methods and rejects it on several grounds.

First, he notes that simultaneous discoveries aren't actually the same discoveries. "The calculus of Newton was not identical to that of Leibniz, nor did Adams and Leverrier both make the same predictions, in that their calculated orbits for a planet beyond Uranus did not coincide." To infer that multiple simultaneous discoveries actually occur, Simonton says, "requires a high degree of abstraction."

Nor are the discoveries really simultaneous, he points out. "Newton preceded Leibniz by a half-decade or more and Darwin anticipated Wallace by more than a decade." Gruber points out that Wallace also had the advantage of reading Darwin's published *Beagle* journals in which the threads that Darwin would later weave together into evolution lay implicit. Simultaneity turns out to be a rather elusive concept. Using a sophisticated mathematical analysis, Simonton also shows that so-called simultaneous discoveries are so rare that they can't be proof that the zeitgeist is the explanation for them.

Gruber takes a similar view. The zeitgeist surely influences what creators discover, but even presumably simultaneous discoveries reveal significant differences of vision ignored by the scientific community's tendency to homogenize visionary differences into an orthodox idea of reality. Darwin's and Wallace's view of evolution were not the same, Gruber points out. For example, Wallace did not believe human consciousness was the result of the same forces that effected the evolution of the human body. As Arnold Brackman noted some years ago, Wallace saw evolution in a much less hierarchical fashion than Darwin, who envisioned life as rising from "lower" to "higher" forms. Possibly this was related to the fact that Wallace didn't have a hierarchical tree of life image as one of his images of wide scope. Among Wallace's ensemble of visionary metaphors was, instead, a very different kind of image. It shows up in the famous essay he sent Darwin—the essay making Darwin aware that someone else was on to evolution. While Darwin imagined the evolution of life and the struggle it entailed as a branching tree and as analogous to human warfare, Wallace envisioned these aspects of evolution as like a "steam engine, which checks and corrects any irregularities almost before they become evident; and in like manner no unbalanced deficiency in the animal kingdom can ever reach any conspicuous magnitude." Very different images from very different visions, with very different implications for how nature is viewed.

We value the differences in vision between artists pondering the same subject; should we do that with scientists as well? David Bohm thinks so. Bohm has proposed that subtle differences in the creative vision of scientists should be explored rather than ignored or homogenized by the scientific establishment. "We might find all sorts of interesting new things by going into these subtleties," Bohm says. "The differences in views could be brought together creatively and this would lead to new insights." In other words, pay attention to such differences, and in the future development of science individual vision could be even more important than it already is.

INTER: I see you've taken a bend or a twist or a corkscrew somewhere again. These feedback syllogisms are worse than the Minotaur's maze; by gad, our Scholastic philosophers were so much neater. But tell me, Mr. Round-the-Loop, after all this, just what is the answer to the question you started out with? Is the great creator a product of the age or is the age a product of the creator? Was Hegel right or was Carlyle?

MUSING: You remember the story of Oedipus?

INTER: Of course.

MUSING: The question there is, "Was Oedipus the victim of a determinist fate when he killed his father and married his mother exactly as had been predicted by the oracles? Or was he responsible for his fate because of his hubris, his egotistical belief that he could escape from his destiny?" Do you think Sophocles knew the answer to that question?

INTER: No.

MUSING: Well, I don't know the answer to your question.

INTER: You mean your question.

MUSING: The Hegel and Carlyle question. Just to illustrate how irreducible and sulphuric the historical Möbius strip is, I'd like you to meditate on two problems. The first is whether we can call somebody a genius if their great discovery is later proven wrong; the second is a problem that often crops up in science of figuring out just when a discovery is really made. Here's the first.

What if Darwin's theory of evolution turns out to be incorrect? Though it sounds preposterous, many of the central tenets of evolution—adaptation, survival of the fittest, the principle of variations leading to new species—are currently under serious attack by segments of the scientific community. If these ideas should fall and are replaced by other notions of evolution, is Darwin still a genius? Much of the detail in Freud's theory has been discredited. Was he a genius? This is a difficult problem.

Perhaps we can say that whatever the judgment of history, it doesn't change the fact of the creator's omnivalent vision and their success in finding a coherent and persuasive form to express that vision. In science, the "truth" uncovered by the creative process may always be limited and contingent on the way world views shift from era to era, giving emphasis to now one facet of reality, now another. The great scientist helps precipitate these shifts but also may suffer from the effect of future shifts; genius is embedded in this historical process.

The second problem can be illustrated by asking, When was oxygen discovered?

According to Thomas Kuhn, in 1774 Pierre Bayen isolated a gas that would later be called oxygen. But Bayen thought it was an already known substance called "fixed air." A few months after Bayen's work, Joseph Priestley repeated the experiment. Priestley identified the gas as the already known "nitrous air." Antoine Lavoisier, learning of Priestley's results, obtained the gas in 1775 and thought it was "pure common air." For the next two years Lavoisier and Priestly continued to identify the gas with other gases they knew about. It wasn't until 1777 that Priestly realized it was a separate gas. Even then, the way he identified it was mixed up with concepts that were later dropped from chemistry.

So when was oxygen discovered and by whom? Kuhn says: "Discovering a new sort of phenomenon is necessarily a complex process which involves recognizing both *that* something is and *what* it is. Observation and conceptualization, fact and the assimilation of fact to theory, are inseparably linked in the discovery of scientific novelty. Inevitably, that process extends over time and may involve a number of people."

In order for oxygen to be discovered a whole historical context had to shift so that scientists could see they had found something new. Did a moment of history discover oxygen or did individuals discover it? It's a dilemma worthy of Sophocles.

But it's also a dilemma creators embrace. In his essay, "Great Men and Their Environment," William James wrote: "The community stagnates without the impulse of the individual; the impulse dies away without the sympathy of the community." Reese Jenkins tells me that when Edison built a new laboratory in West Orange, New Jersey, with the profits he'd made from his inventions, he was careful to make the front office a top-notch scientific library and to stock his lab shelves with materials from all over the world. "He'd put himself in the center of history," Jenkins says. The Möbius strip of history and creator is a fractal mirror of the creator's desire to create an individual-universal equation. What we call genius is a manifestation at the most intense levels of the basic omnivalent relationship that exists between an individual and the whole community (and its history).

So which distills which? Let me rephrase it.

Philosopher Ortega y Gasset said that a genius is someone who invents an occupation. It has been pointed out that half of all the Nobel laureates in science actually invented their fields. Thus, the action of each creator's vision is singular. In an essay, "Kafka and His Precursors," Borges traces intimations of Kafka's writings in Zeno's paradoxes, Kierkegaard and Browning, and then says, "If I am not mistaken, the heterogeneous selections I have mentioned resemble Kafka's work: if I am not mistaken, not all of them resemble each other, and this fact is the significant one. Kafka's idiosyncrasy, in greater or lesser degree, is present in each of these writings, but if Kafka had not written we would not perceive it; that is to say, it would not exist." Perhaps that's the best statement one could hope to make about the relation of the sulphuric fires of the individual creator to the sulphuric fires of history.

And yet without Zeno, Kierkegaard, Browning and those other writers whom Kafka said he admired (Dickens, von Kleist and Dostoyevsky), without them could the particular and unparalleled vision we know as Kafka have existed?

12

Madness and the Mirror-Maker's Nightmare

HG + S + V → HOW DANGEROUS IS IT?

Sometimes the alchemist went mad. The stress of the long and difficult distillations was blamed, or the alembic. Theoretically, the alchemist's crucible was sealed during the process, but occasionally leaks occurred and toxic vapors from the distilling agents filled the laboratory. The madness was similar to that which befell the medieval mirror-makers who inhaled the fumes of mercury. For alchemists the sulphuric fumes only added to this danger.

■

Critic Edmund Wilson reported that Ernest Hemingway told him of a car trip he had taken with his young son during the 1930s. Wilson says that Hemingway at "one point suddenly became aware that he had entered the state of Mississippi. 'I realized that we were in Faulkner country,'" Hemingway said. In the country hotel where the father and son spent the night, Hemingway "had had the boy go to bed, then had sat up all night himself with his gun on the table in front of him."

"Two ideas I believe were revealed by this story," Wilson says, "The assumption that Mississippi was inhabited by

Faulkner characters, and the assumption that Faulkner was a dangerous rival who would take the same view of Hemingway that Hemingway did of him, and now that he had invaded Faulkner's territory might well send some of these characters to do him violence. I thought this was rather queer, but no queerer perhaps than some other things that came out in drinking conversations."

Years later, the paranoia foreshadowed in this story became full-blown and crippling. In his final days, Hemingway suffered from the delusion that IRS agents were surveilling his every move, waiting for the chance to arrest him on tax evasion. The writer was given shock treatment for his condition. Before ending his life with a shotgun blast to the head, he said the worst part of his mental state was feeling that he would never again be able to write with the confidence he'd once had.

▪

As a young man of twenty-five Nikola Tesla suffered a nervous breakdown in which the acute sensitivity he had displayed since childhood exploded to crisis proportions. He could hear the ticking of a watch three rooms away; he felt the ground under his feet constantly vibrating and rubber cushions had to be placed under his bed so that he could sleep; his pulse fluctuated from subnormal to 260 beats a minute. Eventually, it was his devotion to invention that pulled him from this life-threatening state.

Later on, however, Tesla continued to suffer from nightmares and hallucinations about the death of his gifted brother. He developed a fantastic array of phobias and obsessions, including a violent aversion to earrings on women; he counted his steps when walking; and found it necessary to dine alone because he was compelled to obsessively calculate the cubic contents of the soup plates, coffee cups and pieces of food. He claimed that he could never touch the hair of other people, "except at the point of a revolver."

▪

During her several mental breakdowns, Virginia Woolf heard voices, which her suicide note said dinned in her ear and suggested she was going mad. She had previously described the voices: They "stir the long hairs that grow in the conch of the ear & make strange music, mad music, jangled & broken sounds." The last breakdown was the worst for Woolf, biographers feel, because she had begun to believe that she had lost the urge to write.

▪

Newton fell frequently into paranoias about scientific rivals, a madness that some historians think was caused literally by Newton's having inhaled mercury fumes from his alchemical experiments; the reclusive Dickinson is thought to have experienced psychotic episodes; van Gogh, Kafka, Schumann, Robert Lowell, Dostoyevsky, Nietszche, and Mahler all displayed signs of mental illness. Add in the famous drug-takers and alcoholics like Coleridge, Faulkner, Freud, Baudelaire and the catalogue of great minds who were also apparently pathologically tormented minds becomes an impressive one.

The association of genius with madness is one of the oldest notions we have about the nature of creativity. Seneca quotes Aristotle as saying, "There is no great genius without a deal of madness." English poet John Dryden assured his readers, "Great wits are sure to madness near allied,/ And thin partitions do their bounds divide." Schiller said of the noncreative man, "You are ashamed or afraid of the momentary and passing madness which is found in all creators."

The assumption of pathology and creativity is still strong today. The link seems validated every time we notice that even perfectly sane creators are eccentric. In his autobiography, *Surely You're Joking, Mr. Feynman,* the brilliant Nobel physicist portrays himself as an inveterate prankster, capable of breaking into the safes and file cabinets at Los Alamos that contained atomic bomb secrets in order to leave his colleagues jeering notes about their security systems. Feynman is clearly not a madman, but the partition between his behavior and psychologically abnormal behavior might seem to some fairly thin.

Thus, though creative genius as an expression of sanity seems a perfectly logical position—since much of what we value that is sane in the world has come about through creative insight—there is surprisingly little support for this position.

Yearly, scientific evidence and press reports appear to add weight to the notion that in high-level talent, absorption and vision are a volatile combination which probably derives from a basic unsoundness in the genius mind. In one study of famous poets, 15 percent were deemed psychotic and said to exhibit some pathological symptoms. An article in the *Boston Globe* about the discovery that manic-depressive illness may be tied to a gene said,

From George Frederich Handel, who wrote the "Messiah" oratorio in six weeks, to poets Robert Lowell, John Berryman and Anne Sexton . . . the victims of manic-depression have sometimes been immensely creative and productive. . . .

"I think the relationship [with creativity] is a very real one," said Dr. Kay Jamison, former professor of psychiatry [sic] at the University of California at Los Angeles. . . . "There is an increased rapidity of thinking, a loosening of thought, increased energy, and a range of states experienced, from ecstasy to despair, that is useful to creativity. . . ."

One British psychologist concluded from her study that "intense creative episodes are, in many instances, indistinguishable from hypomania."

Many psychologists and psychiatrists eagerly promote the view that mental illness and creativity are allied, though it's a stance which seems to conflict with other therapeutic definitions. Presumably mental health means the ability to deal with uncertainty, remain open and alert and exhibit empathy—all characteristics of the creative state.

INTER (with a puzzled look): But there's another problem, too, isn't there? Didn't I read a few years ago that your contemporary psychologists, psychiatrists and such realized that what's labeled sane or insane has a lot to do with the culture?

MUSING: Quite right. There's a sociology and politics to madness, and we shouldn't forget that. There have been some eras, for example, when a woman who wanted to devote herself to a creative life would, for that reason alone, have been considered mad. The fact is, the definitions in these areas are so tricky that it would undoubtedly be prudent to introduce a healthy dose of skepticism about all those tests linking creativity and pathology. Such subtle things can happen here that it wouldn't be surprising if scientific testers and evaluators sometimes get fooled by their assumptions about what is creative and what is crazy. Between you and me, I suspect the belief in the connection of creativity and madness is riddled with confused assumptions. At bottom, these assumptions may be rooted in an uneasiness, even an aversion, in the human psyche. Conrad described it as an aversion to anything that seems truly different: ". . . To the negation of the habitual, which is safe, there is added the affirmation of the universal, which is dangerous; a suggestion of things vague, uncontrollable, and repulsive, whose discomposing intrusion excites the imagination and tries the civilized nerves of the foolish and wise alike."

The productions of both disturbed people and creators seem to have these characteristics in common—and so our aversion confounds them.

The psychiatric professions, one could argue, have further compounded this aversion and have perpetuated the old cliché about creativity and madness by concluding that the unconscious is the repository of both pathological impulses and profoundly creative ones. In a *New York Times* article headlined "How Inner Torment Feeds the Creative Spirit" a panelist at an annual conference on "Creativity and Madness" (note the assumption that the two are allied) is quoted as saying, "The material artists use for their art . . . comes from the primitive levels of their inner lives—aggression, sexual fantasy, polymorphous sexuality. . . . We all go through these stages and have these primitive drives within us. As we mature and are 'civilized,' we suppress them. But the artist stays in touch with and struggles to understand them. And to remain so in touch with that primitive self is to be on the fine line between sanity and madness."

■

"I don't agree with that," says Rothenberg, who challenges such facile equations built on the ancient stereotype that creativity and insanity are connected by the untamed wildness of "primitive drives." "I think there's some relationship of those things to creativity, but it depends on the era. For example, in Germany between the wars artists were interested in perverse activity. The nineteenth and twentieth centuries have been interested in psychology which has led us to be interested in artists who have such elements in their art."

In his work, Rothenberg has made a special effort to separate creativity from psychological processes which are "primitive," perverse or pathological. He grants that pathology may sometimes be put to creative use, but insists, "Even if creativity and illness can be shown to coexist in the same person, or in a group of persons, it does not . . . follow that the two factors are . . . interdependent or causally connected."

To prove this point, Rothenberg conducted an experiment comparing psychopathological cognition with creative cognition. The experimental tool was, once again, the word association test. This time, however, he also administered it to a group of eighteen psychiatric patients hospitalized at the Austen Riggs Center where he directs research. The patients in the group represented a number of different diagnostic categories, including schizophrenia, borderline personality disorder, psychosis, clinical depression, anorexia, alcohol and narcotic dependence, and narcissistic personality disorder.

Rothenberg compared results obtained on the test from this group with his results from twelve Nobel laureates and the two groups of undergraduates designated "high creatives" and "low creatives."

Of course, the stereotype is that creative thinking and crazy thinking are akin because disturbed people and creative people both sometimes make bizarre associations. Disturbed people such as schizophrenics also tend to say contradictory things such as "I am a human being like yourself even though I am not a human being"—just the kind of contradictory things creative people sometimes say. In one important respect, Rothenberg's test showed the stereotype is wrong. Though the stereotype would lead us to expect that schizophrenics and other disturbed people would think in opposites just as creative people would, as it turned out, the group that responded with the least number of opposites and took the longest time to give them was the group of psychiatric patients.

Rothenberg, we've seen, thinks that fast oppositional response indicates that janusian creative thought process is at work. He concludes that while schizophrenics often say contradictory things, their pathological thinking is very different from thinking in janusian opposites. He says that when creators think oppositionally, they're fully aware of it as a process that leads to insight. When schizophrenics think in opposites, they're confused; in effect they're thinking back and forth between two or more parts of their personality split off from each other. Schizophrenics are not aware that any contradiction results from this fragmentation, though they are acutely aware of the pain of being fragmented. When given the opportunity to respond oppositionally to the words in the test, the schizophrenics in Rothenberg's study showed no tendency to do so, indicating that "at the very least . . . psychopathology in itself does not confer creative abilities."

The Nobel laureates and psychiatric patients did have in common the fact that when their responses were not opposite ones, they also weren't the responses commonly given to the test words. Rothenberg did not measure whether the patients' uncommon responses to the test words made as much sense as the Nobel laureates' uncommon responses, but presumably they didn't.

The conclusion: Creative and pathological thinking might look similar on the surface but they are definitely not the same.

ON THE EDGE OF REALITY

David Shainberg's professional interest before he became a full-time artist was in delineating how mental pathologies are forms of human consciousness that avoid change. He offered another angle on the pathology/creativity question. Like Rothenberg, he also sees them as very different.

SHAINBERG: Let's take psychosis as an extreme example of pathology, one that's often associated with creativity. One of the basic things that distinguishes psychotic perceptions and creative ones is the ability to test reality. The psychotic organizes his anxiety around one interpretation. He says, "They're poisoning me." He reads every aspect of reality to fit that.

QUESTION: The creator, on the other hand, knows to expect places where his creative interpretation doesn't work.

S: More than that, in a state of omnivalence, you see that *nothing* works. There are things that *imply* working, that's all. I think omnivalence is the basic human state, a condition which we usually try to ignore. But if you're a creator, you don't ignore it. Your desire is to organize that omnivalence. But when you organize one part, you immediately have a relationship between that part and the whole rest of the universe. It draws you on. Compare that movement with the psychotic person who says, there's nothing else but this part. He refuses to see there's more, because anything else makes him anxious.

Q: So the creative vision is a way of evolving the whole in the part, not a way of reducing the whole to the part and excluding uncertainty.

S: I think we're all somewhat psychotic to the degree that we believe our world is complete.

Q: So you're saying that psychosis wasn't the case for Robert

Millikan? You're saying that even though it doesn't look like it, Millikan had a strong ability to test reality?

[We were talking, at this point, about a story Gerald Holton had told us describing the physicist who first discovered the value of the charge on electrons. Holton said that during experiments leading up to his discovery, Millikan had encountered evidence that contradicted a theory he had derived from his themata and vision. Millikan deliberately suppressed this evidence. "In his notebook," Holton reported, "Millikan says, 'Do not use.' He did what we tell all of our students never, never to do—cross out data without any explanation at all." On the face of it, Millikan's reaction to countervailing evidence in his notebooks bore some resemblance to the behavior of a psychotic possessed of a systematic delusion. But what happened later suggested quite a different process was at work. Millikan's intuition had proved right on the electron charge theory. He sensed which of his data were too complex to analyze quickly; and so he did not acknowledge them as disproof of his theory. He engaged in a "suspension of disbelief." Holton said, "Millikan's next project was on the photoelectric effect. There he was betting on the wrong theory, betting on it for six years, until finally he saw it wasn't right and let it go."]

SHAINBERG: The psychotic denies the data. Creators because of their vision, suspend the data; they put it on hold.

Q: Then what's the difference in the objective of the psychotic and the creator in proposing their new versions of reality?

S: The psychotic wants to contain and solve his anxiety. The paranoid delusion, for example, organizes him: "They're against me." The psychotic is trying to make all the uncertainty into certainty. The creator integrates certainty and uncertainty. Creative work makes us aware of mysteries beyond mysteries, what you term omnivalence. Creativity is to desire to live and act from the omnivalent state.

244 ■ John Briggs

Shainberg's description recalls an ancient one made by Aristotle, who thought that genius in the arts and sciences must have something to do with the Saturnian, ambivalent humor known as "melancholy." "All extraordinary men distinguished in philosophy, politics, poetry and the arts," Aristotle maintained, "are evidently melancholic." Fifteenth-century philosopher Marsilio Ficino argued that what Aristotle meant by melancholy and what Plato meant by the divine *mania* must be one and the same: melancholy as a special kind of enthusiasm which Keats in "Ode on Melancholy" called the "wakeful anguish of the soul." Keats clearly understood melancholy as a state very different from depression or other pathology. He depicted wakeful anguish as detached longing derived from contemplation of the transience of life. In that sense, ancient melancholy is very like what is meant by omnivalence: a state of 'more'ness and living on the knife's edge. It's possible to confuse that state with pathology, though clearly the state is not in the least pathological.

Q: Creators also want to share their perspective, the perception of omnivalence, with others, because they believe it's something that as human beings we all *do* share. What about the psychotic?

S: The psychotic wants you to collude with him to support his delusion. But at the same time he also doesn't really want to let you into it because that would threaten the delusion.

Q: That's not the same as wanting to share your perspective.

S: Not the same thing at all.

■

Still, one might ask if the difference between pathology and creativity is really so clear, why do so many creators appear to be mentally disturbed?

Rothenberg says: "First there's the fact that in our society creative people are thought of as somewhat crazy, and we often don't give them the recognition and decent livelihood we give people in other professions. This is particularly true for artists. That has an effect on the creator's mental health. Also, creative thought processes themselves are fraught with anxiety."

So sometimes the creative and pathological become entwined. The recent, highly publicized studies of writers indicating a link between manic depression and creativity did not include creative scientists, who are presumably no less creative than writers. Scientists in our modern society generally receive better acceptance for doing creative work than do artists, and they apply their creative efforts to less personal material. Perhaps those are reasons why previous studies have found creative scientists are less prone than artists to suffer from various kinds of mental illness.

Rothenberg and Shainberg agree that, as with ambivalence, the mental disturbances of artists or scientists may supply material that can be mined for insight or turned to creative advantage. Unconscious processes which are ordinarily acted out (and can be debilitating) are consciously used by the creator in creative activity. Mental disturbances like manic depression may, as some believe, "supply intense energy as well as a way of seeing that, filtered through a creative mind and a discerning intellect, can be highly conducive" to creative productivity. However, this does not imply that pathology is in any way a requirement for creativity. It's more likely a manifestation of the way creative activity can turn a deficit into a talent.

Is creativity a therapy for a mentally disturbed creator? Probably not in any lasting sense, Rothenberg believes. At the deepest level creators' personal problems don't get worked through or resolved by being creative, though as Woolf and Tesla illustrate, creating can provide a remarkable outlet, taking the pressure off pathology. Both were able to transmute mental disturbances into useful creative talents. Woolf sometimes experienced spontaneous hallucinations but cultivated this pathology into a controlled and conscious capacity to form nonverbal images and scenes as part of her prewriting process.

It didn't, however, save her from hearing voices when she wasn't writing. Tesla transformed his hallucinatory sensitivity into the ability to visualize his inventions. Emily Dickinson was able to use her psychotic episodes to glimpse a host of insights that fit her vision. For some creators, creating becomes their reason to stay sane or at least stay in touch with sanity. It may even become their reason to stay alive. The open, ordering, sharing, life-giving properties of creative activity could be a major explanation for why so many injured people are drawn to create. Not because creativity requires pathology, but because the confusion, conflict and suffering these individuals experience can be given order and meaning by the creative act.

Can creating be a hazard to creators, make their personality disorders worse? Probably. Hemingway exploited his ambivalence and psychological uncertainty in his fiction, but the creative milieu (e.g., the pressures of being a famous writer) apparently aggravated his characterological ego problems. It's even possible his sense of omnivalence magnified his psychological uncertainty to the point where he began to cope with it by developing paranoias and alcoholism.

Creative insights and processes lie on the margin of our habitual reality and strike at it because they're a contact with the "unusual" and "dangerous" hidden realities of omnivalence and nuance. Creators work at the margins of our social and cultural categories and may experience severe psychological stress from seeing the arbitrariness of those categories. So holding the mirror of creative vision up to nature does not mean the visionary must suffer the mirror-maker's madness— but it sometimes happens.

In other words, while it's true that creators have sometimes found a way to use creativity to transmute a deep personal stress or turn a psychological deficit into a talent, others have lived fully creative lives without any trace of psychopathology. I'd like to emphasize that the effort to make a form for nuance may seem crazy when viewed from the outside. It may look like the same kind of departure from consensual reality that happens when people are mentally disturbed. But, as we've seen (I hope) there's an immense difference. Creators are trying to make a form for nuance that will communicate it to others living in consensual reality while at the same time highlighting its subtle departure from that reality. That is not the motive or effort of someone in the grip of a psychopathology.

But our assumption that there are strong links between creative behavior and crazy behavior is so strong that it probably clouds researchers' data in all kinds of subtle ways. For example, the excited and quiescent states that are a normal part of creative process may be misidentified as manic-depressive. Or the strangeness of paintings and poetry produced by manic depressives may be misidentified as "creative." Madness and creativity seem to have become interidentified in our minds out of stereotype and habit and because of a confusion brought on by our ancient aversion to things that look different. There may be another reason, too.

Could it be that by supporting the myth of the mad creator we have found a way to absolve ourselves of the uncertainty and omnivalence creators face? Asserting our desire to remain sane, we justify our timidity to engage in the long, arduous, and unusual process which creativity involves and from which genius sometimes springs.

INTER: What process is that?

MUSING: The alchemists had a name for it.

PART 3

THE GREAT WORK

Where I was born and where and how I have lived is unimportant. It is what I have done with where I have been that should be of interest.

—GEORGIA O'KEEFFE

I sit there before the typewriter for three hours every day and if anything comes I am there waiting to receive it. . . . If I waited for inspiration, I'd still be waiting. . . . I write every day. But often nothing comes of my efforts. They don't lead anywhere. I rewrite, edit, throw away. It's slow and searching. I'm not sure until it is down on paper. . . .

—FLANNERY O'CONNOR

She looked at the steps; they were empty; she looked at her canvas; it was blurred. With a sudden intensity, as if she saw it clear for a second, she drew a line there, in the center. It was done; it was finished. Yes, she thought, laying down her brush in extreme fatigue, I have had my vision.

—VIRGINIA WOOLF, *To the Lighthouse*

I do not really know how I became a writer. I can give certain dates and certain facts about my career. But the process itself remains mysterious.

—V. S. NAIPAUL

Question: How do you arrive at those ingredients [in your work]?
Louise Nevelson: Darling, how do you eat a pear?

249

OVERVIEW

The alchemical term *magnum opus* has several meanings: "The Great Work" is the whole of the process of alchemical distillation; it is the philosopher's stone, the projections of gold or other precious substances that may be made from the stone, and it is the distilled and purified alchemist himself. The Great Work is, in essence, the fire in the crucible.

For the individual who will eventually be dubbed a genius, making the *magnum opus* requires assiduously applying the distilling agents—the mercury and sulphur of talent and absorption, insight and history—to the raw material of vision. A first result of this chemistry is an increasing concentration of distilling agents themselves and a movement of the raw material toward the purified vision or *prima materia*. This process continues until at some point a critical boundary is passed, a spark is released and The Great Work materializes as both the creator and the product. The process is cyclical and paradoxical. Howard Gruber expresses it forcefully:

"Through being creative we become creative. Through struggle we become capable of struggle. Why does the first sound like a tautology, the second not? They are the same!"

And MIT systems theorist Peter Senge, an expert at analyzing feedback structures, says, "A powerful reinforcing process develops for the highly creative person: as he becomes more internally aligned, the results he creates in his life become more consistent with his personal purpose; this leads to deeper understanding of that purpose, clearer vision, and more commitment to his vision; and in turn, deeper alignment and creative capacity."

In the next four chapters we'll try to espy, though only cursorily, the actual movement of the process that takes place as The Great Work in all its senses evolves for creators. This movement puts us deep inside the creativity fractal. But at what scale? It will be impossible to tell because in every direction we explore, we'll find this fractal life around us.

The theme of these next five chapters will be "unfolding." In chapter 13 we'll observe how creators themselves unfold into their work and chapters 14, 15 and 16 will track the process by which particular creative works have unfolded. In these last three chapters we'll peer into the secrets of what Henry James called "the germ." Germs are nexus points of vision and talent. We'll find out how creators harness the power of these germs, and we'll see how by unfolding and nourishing a germ the creator liberates and gives a concrete form to nuance.

13

Constructing
the Egg

CRYSTALLIZING

There are certain key moments in creators' lives when they attune themselves to their creative destiny.

Such a moment came to the early nineteenth-century mathematician Evariste Galois when he was quite young. Galois was what educators today might call an "emotionally disadvantaged child" who, because of his failures, was removed from public school by his mother. One day, fortuitously, young Galois came across a geometry textbook written by the creative mathematician, Legendre. Galois was so excited by the work that "a single reading sufficed to reveal the whole structure of elementary geometry with a crystal clarity." The boy mastered the subject matter immediately, and the book initiated his entry into his creative career.

Pierre-Auguste Renoir was an accomplished apprentice porcelain decorator by the time he was twelve. But he showed little interest in or sensitivity to "art." Even though he made regular trips to the Louvre to sketch masterworks, they had little effect on him. He saw them only in terms of his intention to design porcelain. Then one day he noticed the sixteenth-century Fontaine des Innocents. "I stopped spellbound," he said afterward. A biographer reported, "He gave up the idea of lunch in a restaurant, and instead bought sausage at a nearby shop and returned to the fountain. He walked round and round it slowly, studying the group of statues from every

253

angle. From that moment he felt a particular affinity with the sculptor Jean Goujon; his work possessed everything he [Renoir] loved: grace, solidity, and elegance, with the feeling of living flesh." Renoir evidently now realized these qualities as vital to his own work as a painter.

Howard Gardner and Joseph Walters, taking inspiration from a paper by Feldman, have called such transforming moments in a creator's development "crystallizing experiences." They say that the "dramatic nature" of these moments "focuses the attention of the individual on a specific kind of material, experience, or problem," and the creator later, sometimes repeatedly, revisits these moments "to reshape his self-concept." Or as Gardner put it somewhat more succinctly in my interview with him, "These are moments when the creator says 'God, this is more me than anything I've done before.' "

Gardner views the crystallizing moments as events that activate or bring into play one of a creator's intelligences: Galois's mathematical talent was sparked by the aesthetic beauty of the well-written geometry textbook; the Indian boy Srinivasa Ramanujan's mathematical talent was launched by reading a synopsis of six thousand theorems so sketchy it required his logical-mathematical intelligence to fill in the gaps.

But equally important—and perhaps simultaneous with the sudden triggering of talent—is the meaning these moments have for the creator's vision. Renoir seems to have had awakened in him by Goujon's sculpture subtle omnivalent vibrations of Renoir's own very particular sense of the human form. The result was that Renoir became attracted to the possibility of expressing those omnivalent vibrations, such nuances, in art.

Gardner and Walters distinguish two types of crystallizing moments, "initial" ones, which start a creator toward a particular creative career and "refining" moments, which open up a vital new perspective for a career already in progress.

Initial crystallizing experiences often seem oracular to the creator. Her art teachers in grade school praised Louise Nevelson for her drawings. One day the town librarian asked her what she wanted to be in life.

There was a big plaster of Joan of Arc in the center of the library, and I looked at it. Sometimes I would be frightened of things I said because they seemed so automatic. The librarian asked me what I was going to be, and of course I said, "I'm going to be an artist." "No" I added, "I want to be a sculptor, I don't want color to help me." I got so frightened, I ran home crying. How did I know that when I never thought of it before in my life?

Joseph Conrad claimed he never imagined himself as an author until that day ashore when he began the novel *Almayer's Folly* out of idleness. "I cannot even point to boredom as a rational stimulus for taking up a pen," he said. "The necessity which impelled me was a hidden, obscure necessity, a completely masked and unaccountable phenomenon. . . . I cannot trace it back to any mental or psychological cause which one could point out and hold to." Conrad's experience of his crystallizing event was entirely consistent with his vision, which viewed humanity as immersed in and compelled by mysterious forces.

Conrad was thirty-one when he crystallized into his creative career. Nevelson was nine. The American dancer and choreographer José Limón was also quite young when his initial crystallization took place. As a boy he had been as fascinated as any child by dance and had seen Spanish dancers, Mexican dancers, tap and ballet dancers, but "then pure accident brought me to a performance by [the modern dancer] Harald Kreutzberg. I saw the dance as a vision of ineffable power. A man could, with dignity and a towering majesty, dance."

The initial realization that some creative field or activity holds the potential for expressing omnivalence and formulating an individual-universal equation can strike any age, though a field may impose restrictions on the individual's ability to act on the realization. Obviously if Limón had been in his forties when he saw Kreutzberg dance, he would have been past the age when it is physically possible to train for a career as a dancer. That's not to say other avenues might not have been open to him for acting on this excitation of vision— becoming a dance commentator or teacher, for example, or translating his feeling for dance into some other art form.

Anything can crystallize a creator's motivation to enter a creative career. It can come with the encouragement of a teacher or a new experience. Darwin, for example, was not considered particularly bright and didn't have the slightest idea that he possessed a talent for science until he was a young man at Cambridge University and received powerful crystallizing encouragement from his professor of botany, John Henslow. Henslow successfully supported him as the candidate scientist for the voyage on the *Beagle,* a voyage which Darwin likened to a rebirth. And Langston Hughes drew crystallizing inspiration from a visit as a boy to Kansas City where he heard an orchestra of blind musicians play the blues. His biographer says, "The music seemed to cry, but the words somehow laughed. The effect on him was one of piercing sadness, as if his deepest loneliness had been harmonized. . . . Between the church and the blues singers, the world of black feeling and art opened before Langston."

Whatever the crystallizing inspiration is, it reveals to creators that there is a direction to go in which they can express their deep sense of *truth* about life, a direction that feels more like them than anything they have previously done.

Phyllis Greenacre is convinced that genius is "polymorphous," capable of expressing itself in many forms. Is it an accident of crystallizing that caused Faulkner, for example, to be a writer rather than a painter, or Einstein a physicist rather than a concert violinist? There may well be several routes open to some creators for the expression of their omnivalence and truth. But the key is finding a creative field conducive to the raw material of an individual's vision and to the potential talent or combination of talents. Some geniuses may be polymorphous. Others may be quite narrowly focused. In either case, finding an intersection of talents, vision and field entails a long process with several "refining" crystallizations.

Musicians interviewed by Gardner and Walters recalled that their early crystallizing attraction to music had been followed by a crystallizing attraction to a particular instrument. "There has to be some orientation toward the actual physical process of playing around *that* particular instrument," said one violinist. He had tried the flute and piano but when he took up the violin suddenly he *"knew* the violin was . . . me."

Refining crystallizations occur at relatively mature stages as well. As a young adult, Pierre Boulez discovered the music of Olivier Messiaen and this music crystallized a great change in his approach to his work. "Here was the music of our time, a language with unlimited possibilities. With it music moved out of the world of Newton and into the world of Einstein."

Georgia O'Keeffe was already an accomplished artist when she underwent a crisis and a refining crystallization. One day she went into her studio, shut the door and locked it. She hung her most recent efforts on the wall, noting that what she had painted was largely imitation or directed to the taste of other people. None of it was her, she felt. It then occurred to her that there were abstract shapes in her mind unlike anything she had been taught. "This thing that is your own," she later explained, "is so close to you, often you never realize it's there." Although she wasn't sure yet how she would paint this "thing" that was her, her task suddenly seemed simple. That was the direction she must go.

O'Keeffe was inspired to become an artist by her early sensitivity to such nuances as the feeling of bright sunlight on a patterned quilt and by an initial crystallizing experience that took place when, as an eighth grader, she found a drawing in one of her mother's books that she thought so beautiful she wanted to make something like it. The refining crystallization that occurred during her later "crisis" drew her closer to her vision, and the crisis story is a good example of the circular paradox of vision and talent: O'Keeffe's early inchoate vision had led her to explore her talent for painting. This had taken her to a crisis that required further a refining or distilling of her vision; that distillation, in turn, further extended the maps of her talent.

It's not unusual for the refining crystallizations to have a long incubation. René Descartes had rejected most of what he learned in school as a confused mass of knowledge that contained no method for organizing or making sense of it. At age twenty, he set himself the task of finding a true method of knowledge. After two years in seclusion thinking about the problem, he returned to society uncertain that his thoughts were in the right direction. Then one night while serving on military duty, he had a series of dreams. The dreams crystallized for him that he was indeed on the right track and revealed to him that it would be his destiny to unify the sciences, reform knowledge and search for truth. The dreams were a sign that his vision had crystallized. They were part of the circular paradox that in defining his vision he was also refining it.

Descartes's experience also emphasizes that crystallizations are not just isolated flashes in a creative career but part of a continuous process.

THE UNFOLDING CONTEXT

One of William Faulkner's biographers, David Mintner, remarks that at least once Faulkner "was moved to wonder if he 'had invented the world' of his fiction 'or if it had invented me.'"

The apprenticeship that led to that double invention was tortuous.

A sensitive boy, small for his age, Faulkner did poorly in school but was a great reader. The people in his hometown of Oxford, Mississippi, began to think him "quair" because of the way he "sat or stood motionless, quiet, as though held still by some inner scene or some inner sense of himself." At about age ten he started writing poetry, partly in sympathetic identification with the gigantic image of Col. W. C. Falkner, his great-grandfather, who had fought in the Civil War and was a writer. Faulkner later said his early poetry writing was his "youthful gesture" of "being different." Mintner thinks it was a way of overcoming his small stature and his father's alcoholism. Perhaps the poetry he read and tried to write also touched some omnivalent chord, resonated with some nuance of the way the world felt for this young observer looking upon passing life from within his "stillness."

As he progressed through adolescence, Faulkner took on

the airs of an aesthete and dandy, and townspeople started calling him "Count" as well as "quair." Mintner says that in the dandy pose young Faulkner "found ways of expressing his sense of himself as observer, thinker, poet, and, by implication his sense of his world, perhaps especially of his large, hapless father, as *other*." Mintner depicts Faulkner's growing omnivalence about the world. In poetry, Faulkner found elements of his developing vision such as truth and the possibility of the individual-universal equation. "In the poetry he was reading, particularly that of Swinburne, he discovered . . . a word-oriented world that promised purity, holiness . . . its thrilled effect depended on words. . . ."

At the same time that he longed for ethereal purity, Faulkner strove to be a man of action in everyday reality. He threw himself into hunting, baseball, football. During the First World War he enlisted in the Royal Canadian Air Force. But his pilot training was cut short when the war ended.

Between the pure, imagined world of art and the world of action and reality, Faulkner began to cultivate what Mintner calls a sense of "doubleness." On one side of the doubleness was his attraction to a real world requiring action and courage, which eventually made him suspicious of the rarefied imagined world of art. On the other side was the purity of art, which left him discontented with reality.

At an early stage in the development of this doubleness, Faulkner came under the crystallizing tutelage of a college-educated young man, Phil Stone. Stone encouraged Faulkner's poetry writing and introduced him to the French symbolists, Verlaine, Valéry and Baudelaire. The works of these poets are characterized by intense longing and a perception that the physical world is symbolic of something more than itself. The symbolists also preached that everything in that world is intimately connected to everything else. The symbolist poets must have resonated deeply with Faulkner's incipient vision because he spent several years imitating them slavishly and using them as models for his identity as a poet.

It was an identity he would never quite give up. Years later after he had received international recognition as a novelist, he continued to refer to himself wistfully as a "failed poet." In fact he was a perfectly bad poet. His particular combination of talents and vision wasn't suited to poetry and it is safe to say that had he continued in that genre he would have remained unknown. But it wasn't until he was almost thirty that he recognized this fact.

Faulkner's refining crystallization into fiction writing didn't occur immediately, even after he had written his first two novels, *Soldier's Pay* and *Mosquitoes;* he continued to consider himself a poet. Neither novel is particularly outstanding or promising. However, the long search to distill his true talents and vision finally came to fruition suddenly with *Flags in the Dust* (published originally under the title *Sartoris*) when he turned for his fictional material to the stories he had heard about his great-grandfather Colonel Falkner and others of his clan. In writing that novel, he discovered his "postage stamp" universe and major image of wide scope, Yoknapatawpha County. Faulkner realized that through Yoknapatawpha County he could bring forth the hidden reality of his vision. In the style, structure and orientation of *Flags in the Dust,* the poetry and realism that were contradictory strains in Faulkner's doubleness coalesced. With this novel he said he felt his characters "stand up on their hind legs and cast a shadow." The writers who had strongly attracted him in the past like Balzac, Conrad, Joyce and T. S. Eliot suddenly settled into their proper place in his vision by informing his technical approach to the novel. In fact, everything had fallen into place, everything that just a few months before had been merely contradictory and conflicting elements in his career. Several of Faulkner's greatest works like *The Sound and the Fury* and *As I Lay Dying* followed quickly.

Mintner says that Faulkner "had undergone an evolution in his soul resulting from his creative activity and discoveries about his own life." In his life he discovered that his childhood sweetheart whom he was finally about to marry "meant more to him as his first love than as his fiancée. In his art he had discovered Caddy Compson [from *The Sound and the Fury*] and in her 'man's history of his impossible desire.' " His life and art thus each acquired a double nature and the doubleness of one mirrored the doubleness of the other.

Says Mintner: "The doubleness Faulkner had discovered and made his own meant that he would never be wholly satisfied with living in the world he imagined and so created; but it also meant that he would never really belong to the world around him or to the creatures of it." He had created for himself a permanent state of omnivalence, the hunger of 'more,' which both art and life now would feed. He had evolved to the point where he "thrived on division. In his need to go in and out, up and down, from engagement to detachment, immersion to flight, and in his imaginative dependence on mutually supportive oppositions (Yoknapatawpha and Lafayette, Jefferson and Oxford, imaginary kingdom and actual land) we locate his dependence on contraries." The 'more'ness of revealing and concealing (truth) stirred in these contraries. No wonder Faulkner couldn't be sure whether he invented his creative world or it invented him.

■

The story of Faulkner's development illustrates, among other things, that the initial motivation to engage in creative activity may be mixed. In his case, it was part compensation for his size, part attraction to the nuance and "truth" he found in literary works. But whatever its inception, the motivation evolves toward an expression of the individual-universal equation. Faulkner's story also shows that despite the occasional dramatic crystallization, a creator's development occurs in thousands of small acts, adjustments, insights and shiftings of perspective. It is like a pearl which may be started by something trivial, but accretes over time into a treasure.

Gruber calls this pearl-making "constructing a point of view." He says elegantly, that it's "the slow process by which the thinker constructs the mental circumstances of his own insights." In his book *Darwin on Man,* Gruber depicts a several-year evolution of Darwin's point of view which was quite different from the evolution just described for Faulkner.

That difference is precisely Gruber's message. Each creator's development, he believes, is unique and unpredictable.

Darwin started out on the *Beagle* voyage as a naturalist interested in Lyell's theory of geological change. After five years of reading, observation and thought during the trip— five years during which he was presumably guided by his themata—Darwin moved toward becoming an evolutionist. Actual formulation of his evolutionary theory would take years more. During those years, Darwin shifted the evidence around and viewed it from various angles, tried out hypotheses and developed his tree of life image. This image gave him an important lever on the hidden reality he was trying to expose and permitted him to shift the evidence in yet new directions. Though he was quite familiar with Malthus's argument on population, one day while reading the actual text, the decisive shift in perspective occurred in Darwin's mind and the still somewhat cloudy vistas of a theory of evolution by natural selection lay stretched out before him.

"We don't think in order to solve problems," Gruber says, "we solve problems in order to help us construct the point of view we're moving toward." There's also the complement of this: "The person evolves a special point of view within which to look at a problem."

Gruber beautifully documents the glacial movement of Darwin's point of view as it unfolded in the notebooks containing lists of thoughts, theories, questions, images, dreams, sketches, arguments, theories abandoned and revisited, comments on arguments, leads to follow up, and Darwin's reminders to himself. In the process insights were anticipated, apparently forgotten and later rediscovered in new contexts. Gruber reports, "The underlying order is something to be constructed, not observed." The effort was monumental.

Building a point of view means creating a context that unites the creator's amorphous inner vision with the outward requirements of the creative field and its audience.

Van Gogh, aware that he had failed to communicate his inner vision through evangelism, struggled for an alternative means. He keenly understood the metamorphosis that would occur if he could find that means. "A man who has seemed good for nothing and incapable of any employment, any function, ends in finding one and becoming active and capable of acting," he wrote his brother Theo. He explained that at the moment he seemed idle, but that was only because he lacked a way to convey to others what was in him. He lacked a context. His first step in creating such context so that others could see what was in him (and so that he himself could truly see it) was to crystallize his energies toward a career as a painter.

Doris Wallace reports that British novelist Dorothy Richardson was advised by H. G. Wells to write like "a feminine George Eliot" and to try her hand at short stories instead of novels. Richardson took the advice but each of her attempts at short fiction "foundered on 'an idea,'" she said later in some unpublished notes. "Somehow too easy, utterly distasteful and boring when thought of as being written with the idea close clasped in the hand. . . . Became aware of the mass lying unexpressed behind any way of presenting I had met. . . . Novels to date exclude the essential: firsthand life." Such novels, she continued, "assume life." A hidden reality, an omnivalent nuance, had been left out. Richardson was undergoing a crisis and crystallization similar to Georgia O'Keeffe's.

Attraction to the field because of its openness to the nuances and talents which the creator-in-the-making possesses is eventually counterbalanced by the discovery that the field does not, in its most important details, accommodate the creator's specific nuances and talents. This discovery requires building a new context in the field so that the specific inner perspective will make sense to others. During the apprenticeship period, Richardson found—as many creators have—that her vision wasn't identical with what she had admired in the visions of others. Richardson admired Tolstoy and Flaubert but quickly realized their "masculine realism" was too far removed from her own vision. Henry James was closer and "really shocked her," according to Wallace, because James told a whole story from inside one point of view. But even James hadn't captured the particular omnivalence she sought.

V. S. Naipaul said, "Every serious writer . . . knows that

however much he might have been educated and stimulated by the writers he has read or reads, the forms matched the experience of those writers, and do not strictly suit his own.''

Generally a long time is required before the creator's context shifts enough for the *magnum opus* to emerge. Gruber estimates that a hardworking genius can expect at best one or two insights per day, maybe five hundred per year. To achieve this the creator must expend an apprenticeship in constant motion, developing insight strategies and learning to separate insight from opinion; finding and developing talents, turning deficits into talents; appropriating pathology to the creative task; making maps of maps in the brain to enrich synesthesia; composing and decomposing to learn the schema of the creative field (for example, young Richard Feynman decomposing radios to find out how circuits work); learning from mentors and models; getting a handle on personal creative working routines; developing the capacity for absorption; evolving images of wide scope and networks of enterprise. Cultivating the ability to think oppositionally would allow the creator to transform contexts quickly, breaking the currently operating mindset repeatedly to plumb the material from new angles, keeping open a negative capability. During the apprenticeship period, the different nuance themes (themata) link up and creators recognize the nuances of other works in the creative field as having both relevance and irrelevance to the personal creative purpose. Most importantly, throughout apprenticeship, creators develop what Einstein called the capacity for "self-criticism.''

Thomas Kuhn believes that in science an "essential tension" always exists between the traditional forms, dogmas and paradigms embodied in the great works of the past and the new view being proposed by a creator. That tension also exists in the creator. After all, it is the great works and forms of tradition which attracted the creator to the field in the first place. These exemplars instill in the creator a conservatism which monitors the wild flights of the grand attempt to re-create reality. Niels Bohr once expressed the essential tension by explaining that he regularly spent three days a week trying to imagine all the wild theories he could and another three days trying to disprove them. (Presumably on the seventh day, he rested.)

This essential tension involves playfulness; but it also involves pain. LaViolette says. "When you get an idea there's often this thrill of satisfaction and you tend to charge that very highly. It's easy to get trapped into thinking that that's the way things are. You have to be able to criticize your idea. That involves pain." Probably not by coincidence, the sensation of pain circulates in the same loop as the feeling tones.

Of course, that other, deeper factor also contributes to the capacity for self-criticism—the desire for truth which is a primary ingredient in any great creator's vision. As painter Robert Motherwell says, creators are always struggling against self-deception. "It's not that the creative act and the critical act are simultaneous. It's more like you blurt something out and then analyze it. After each brush stroke, you're analyzing it. Is this stroke an authentic expression or not?" Here "authentic" means consistent with vision. If vision is to be expressed, the expression will have to be the truth, though it's going to be a different truth from the one traditionally accepted.

Altogether the creator's constant motion to build a new point of view, to construct a new context, amounts to the formation of what Conrad called the "inward voice that decides."

The whole movement to evolve that inward voice entails linking feedback loops which join talent and vision, with the problem or material the creator is focusing on, with insight strategies, and with the tradition of the creative field. These interlocking loops, at a certain point (indicated in some creators by a "crystallizing" moment) interact to form what systems theorists call a "self-organizing structure."

Scientists have found that such structures—which exist all through nature, from chemical reactions, to cyclones, to animal societies, to our planetary ecology—are characterized by several basic feedback forms. One of the feedback forms is regulatory; like a thermostat it keeps other system loops in balance and check. Another type, called autocatalytic feedback, produces more of itself. A third type, through its continuous cycling, turns very small changes into very large ones. This amplifying feedback is largely responsible for a system's evolution. Because they are composed of interlocking feedback loops, self-organizing structures can adjust to shocks and shifts and not be destroyed. They can also amplify well-placed small effects very quickly and so dramatically transform themselves.

The creative self-organizing structure can be viewed in terms of these feedback principles. For example, an instance of regulatory feedback in creativity is self-criticism; talent and absorption are autocatalytic, producing more of themselves; and the feedback loops which constitute a sensitivity to nuance turn small changes into large ones. Once formed, the creative self-organizing structure can withstand the shocks and shifts of continued immersion in uncertainty, of infertile periods, of the inability to find the answer to a problem, of poverty, mistakes, lack of recognition, and injuries of all kinds, including the physical loss of some elements of talent. (One thinks of Beethoven adjusting to deafness, for example; ballerina Alicia Alonso dancing flawlessly when almost blind, and physicist Stephen Hawking unable to communicate except by computer yet creating even as his body withdraws him from the world.)

The evolution of the creative self-organizing structure occurs through amplification of the subtleties of the vision's themata, nuance and omnivalence. Feynman describes creative self-organization as a state in which "anything can happen, in spite of what you're pretty sure should happen." At any minute a thought or stray piece of information may cause the system to transform into a new organization, a new context. The transformation can happen at different scales in the creative process. At the broadest scale, it happens when the whole vision coalesces for the first time, as it did for Faulkner writing *Flags in the Dust,* for Darwin when he was reading Malthus, for O'Keeffe realizing that she must paint to her mind's own abstract patterns. And it can happen at a day-to-day scale in the solution to a particular creative problem in a particular creative work—finding the right phrase or the right brush stroke.

The mathematician Karl Friedrich Gauss described such a sudden reorganization: "Finally, two days ago, I succeeded not on account of my painful efforts, but by the grace of God. Like a sudden flash of lightning, the riddle happened to be solved. I myself cannot say what was the conducting thread which connected what I previously knew with what made my success possible."

Maurice Wilkins points out that the creator is always "observing carefully, selecting and rejecting facts, choosing and rejecting directions to follow, and all the time keeping an open and enquiring state of mind. As a result, observations and ideas are woven together to form somewhat new relationships. These may dissolve away, but, at a critical stage, they may reach a point where they suddenly click together to a much greater degree than before." That's why Gauss couldn't find the "conducting thread" between the new state and the old. There was no thread; there was a whole movement of the system which had rolled over into a new perspective.

Gruber explains this movement by troping upon the familiar metaphor Gauss used comparing the creative moment to a bolt of lightning. A bolt of lightning is not a single moment of flash but includes a period of preparation when the electrical charge is built up between the thundercloud and the ground. The buildup involves a positive feedback mechanism in which a myriad of low-intensity collisions of ice or water droplets produce the charge that will be released at high intensity later on. In one type of lightning the flash isn't a single stroke but multiple strokes proceeding by branching steps. Lightning's aftermath, thunder, involves still different processes and lasts much longer. Gruber says, "Not only is the individual lightning stroke complex; it is part of a more complex system, the thunderstorm as a whole. And each storm is a part of a still wider worldwide system of storms. . . ." Similarly, the apparent flash of creative insight must be seen as a dynamical aspect of a much larger self-organizing process.

But let's switch metaphors for a different view.

It is claimed that alchemy was exceptionally slow because alchemists were required to repeat their experimental operations hundreds of times in the knowledge that no two trials, even if done the same way, could ever be exactly identical. Relentlessly, the hierophant recapitulated his experiments until something vital changed, some transmutation took place. The alchemist could never tell what had caused the transmutation because *all* that he had done had caused it. Everything was part of the distillation, including those times when nothing seemed to change.

In the light of this metaphor we might glimpse how nuance is responsible for these apparent sudden insights in creative process—the so-called nonlinear aspect of creativity. The creator's attention to nuances causes subtle contextual shifts—until at some point these small shifts nudge the mind across a critical threshold where an entirely new context comes in view.

The creative self-organizing structure, of course, doesn't end with the solution to a particular problem, a particular insight or even the congealing of vision in a *magnum opus.* Vision evolves, the creator evolves, the *magnum opus* leads to a new *magnum opus*—otherwise the creative life dies. The completion of a work, the acceptance of a work by its intended audience, changes in the creator's personal life, historical changes—all have an effect on the further development of the creative enterprise. There's no fixed beginning to such an enterprise, and no predicting it's direction. A strategy or technique rejected in the early part of a career may be embraced later on because the vision unfolds to include it or to require it. Anything may happen. The vision may be as different in its early stages from its later stages as the style of *Romeo and Juliet* is different from that of *King Lear.* Yet it will also be self-consistent in its evolution. Think of the earth's ecosystem from the pre-Cambrian ooze to the present day. The earth's environment has radically changed and yet it also has a continuous identity, unique in the universe.

THE DAILY OBSESSIONS

But now let's reverse the tape a bit because we've passed too quickly by some important scenes in the creator's development. These scenes include the nitty-gritty, the nuts and bolts of creative process.

In order for contexts to shift and a new context to unfold, day-to-day work must be done. I want to look here at some of the ways creators accomplish that daily work. But I also want to stress and underline and place in capital letters the fact that there are as many such ways of working as there are creators.

INTER (in shadows except for a pair of pale feet propped up on a table): There's something else you passed by, too.

MUSING: What's that?

INTER: You called this chapter "Constructing the Egg." Don't you think you should tell your readers what this bloody egg is?

MUSING: Sorry. Of course, the egg is the crucible, the alembic in which the distillation of mercury, sulphur and the raw material takes place. The egg is also the alchemist, so the distillation, in effect, constructs the egg in which the distillation occurs. It is out of the egg that the philosopher's stone will hatch.

Idiosyncratic Tactics of Thought

A successful distillation and egg construction requires creators to develop an unusually acute working knowledge of the idiosyncrasies of their own minds. Gardner says, "Individuals whose stock and trade is to do things which are novel, are people who've got to have a pretty good command of how they work."

In his humorous memoir Richard Feynman repeatedly emphasizes his need to work scientific problems through for himself and not take anybody's word for whether the answer is true. He's aware that for him this means translating the most abstract problem into a physical item he can see in his mind; it also means having to reinvent the argument if he's going to understand it. He remembers attending a scientific conference and listening to an important paper which he didn't understand. He told his sister, "It's all so complicated."

His sister replied, "What you mean is *not* that you can't understand it, but that you didn't *invent* it. You didn't figure it out your *own* way, from hearing the clue." Feynman took the paper upstairs and reinvented it. Then he understood it perfectly.

Descartes said, "As a young man, when I heard about ingenious inventions, I tried to invent them myself, even without reading the author."

Darwin admitted that he had a foggy memory and was an awkward and poor thinker without the gift of quick grasp or the ability to abstract very well. This self-assessment—perhaps self-knowledge—caused him to be very careful about collecting data, keeping notes and working through problems. It was just the kind of painstaking way of thinking that turned out to be well-suited to solving the evolutionary riddle.

During their apprenticeship period, creators learn what kinds of thinking tactics work best for them. Divergent thinking, for example, might be a useful tactic for some creators at some stages, allowing them to generate a large number of different ideas or images around a problem they're working on. Other creators might find it useful to doodle or play at certain points in the creating process. Clustering related images and ideas is another tactic. A frequent approach among creators is to overload the brain with information about the problem until confusion sets in, then step away to a fresh environment. That's what Henri Poincaré did when he was working on the problem of Fuchsian functions. His brain confounded, Poincaré went on an excursion and forgot his mathematical work. Then as he was stepping onto an omnibus, the answer came. Poincaré employed this "principle of forgetting" frequently when working on problems. It was a good tactic for him, but might not be for everybody.

Psychologist David Perkins notes a great many mental tactics in his book *The Mind's Best Work.* Among them, "directed remembering," "problem finding," "critical reasons," "search by scanning," working from the concrete to the abstract or abstracting new ideas from particulars.

Creators often use tactics uniquely their own on a regular

basis: Woolf's prewriting activity in which she formed nonverbal images; Nevelson's careful selection of pieces of scrap wood to prepare herself mentally for later work. Edison's habit of announcing he'd invented a device before he actually had should probably also be included here as a tactic because he evidently used it to stimulate his mental absorption in the problem.

One creative tactic employed quite frequently by creators might be called "the shortcut." While working on the DNA problem, James Watson found it necessary to know about crystallography and several other scientific specialties in order to evaluate the data he needed to find the structure of DNA. While most scientists would have despaired or plunged into a lengthy postdoctoral fellowship, Watson simply gleaned from a textbook just those pieces of information required for his problem, and ignored all the rest of crystallographic theory. He also learned how to ask questions from experts in different fields in order to elicit the requisite information and insights. This shortcut tactic is the direct outgrowth of creative absorption and the focus of creative vision. The same tactic allowed Edison to become an inventor in the field of chemistry long before he should have been able to learn the field.

Creators are perhaps more aware of the subtle mechanisms of their own thought processes than most people are because it's only by taking maximum advantage of those subtleties that they can do their highly subtle, nuance-filled jobs.

Some creators, like Darwin, are aware that they must work slowly in order to accommodate the way their minds produce insight. Other creators feel their creative energies are best tapped by doing certain parts of their creative work quickly—Mozart, for example, or van Gogh. According to Richard Brower, van Gogh could execute a painting in two or three hours and his creative mind was fully activated by "working quickly and spontaneously." But van Gogh also "believed it required long, hard work to develop the skills to do this. . . . He was fond of quoting Whistler who'd said something like, 'it took me two hours to do the painting but forty years to learn how to do it in two hours.'"

Van Gogh's sensitivity to his own creative process suggests we should put under the heading of idiosyncratic mental tactics the keen awareness individual creators have about how a piece generally unfolds for them.

Composer Walter Piston apparently plans out the overall structure of a piece in his mind before he selects the notes for it.

According to a contemporary observer, Balzac put "the first draft down with great gaps between the single paragraphs and the enormously wide margins are filled in gradually, until the entire sheet, with its upward and downward radii, its tangential lines, etc. resembles the picture of a firework. . . . On every sheet, he uses only 8–10 lines, because he lacks sureness of expression and is unable to find at once the definitive formulation. Whereas at first he has only the skeleton of a novel ready, the details are invented by and by. Half his remuneration is spent on the correction of proofs." Dostoyevsky went over a piece of writing an average of ten times.

Thomas Mann, on the other hand, didn't secrete his work in layers but wrote laboriously, not going on to the next page until he had perfected the one he had before him.

In the next two chapters I'll have more to say about how creative works themselves come into being; the point here is that each creator must find out how (s)he works best, for no two creators will work best in the same way.

Routines and Conditions

Understanding the idiosyncratic nature of one's creative thinking process goes hand in hand with finding the right time of day, the right environment to work in. And just as mental tactics may be added to or dropped from the creator's repertoire, routines and conditions required by the creator aren't static and may change over a lifetime.

At the outset of his career Hemingway wrote sitting in cafés during the early morning hours. Later he wrote standing up. He composed his first drafts in notebooks. He said he started work by rereading and editing what he had written before and always stopped writing when he was still "going good" so he'd have something to begin with the next day. Each day he would tally his production, which was usually about five hundred words. After his morning's work, he would refuse to think about writing any further and would read, drink or go deep-sea fishing.

Louise Nevelson works sometimes in two- or three-day spurts without sleeping and eating nothing more than "a can of sardines and a cup of tea and a piece of stale bread." On ordinary working stints she wears cotton clothes so she can sleep in them and go to work immediately without changing when she gets up. While she's sculpting, she doesn't "want anyone to come and park themselves."

Many creators, like Nevelson, feel that solitude is a necessary condition of their creative process. Goethe said: "Nothing will change the fact that I cannot produce the least thing without absolute loneliness." Others, like Picasso, prefer to work in company. Some creators work in silence, others surrounded by noise.

Tolstoy, Wagner and Ibsen were their most productive in sunny spring weather. Many painters have traveled far in search of a special light which they thought was a necessary condition for their art. Goethe walked in order to get ideas. Rousseau did his best thinking on trips he made alone and on foot. Duke Ellington composed many of his pieces on trains, evidently taking advantage of the rhythmic clacking and motion of the cars. Nietzsche listened to a musical performance in the evening and awoke full of "resolute insights and inspirations." He preferred to write when the sky was clear. The American poet Hart Crane wrote his poetry to records of jazz music.

A great number of creators, like Gauss, Darwin, Hemingway and Nevelson have preferred to create in the early morning immediately upon wakening. Descartes worked in bed as did Jean Toomer, who said the sight of his writer-uncle "in bed surrounded by the materials of a literary man" was one of the things that inspired him to take up writing. When in the throes of a project, Edison slept in his laboratory, sometimes on a table, so that he could start right up when he awoke. Possibly sleep gives distance on a problem and allows it to be seen from a fresh angle, but the reason most often given for the morning work schedule was expressed by Balzac who said he wanted to take advantage of the fact that "my brain works while I sleep."

A number of major discoveries have been actually reported as born from the brow of sleep itself, in the form of dreams. Dreams reputedly brought Descartes his new method of knowledge, Coleridge "Kubla Khan" and Kekule his discovery of the structure of the benzine rings (although Kekule's may have been more of a doze than a dream). Willis Harmon and Howard Rheingold argue in their book *Higher Creativity* that dreams put the creator in touch with a broader archetypal consciousness.

Certainly thoughts in close proximity to hypnagogic states might be looser, freer. That may be true on the nether end of sleep, as well. Emily Dickinson worked at night in the dark when others in the house were in bed. Presumably these conditions allowed her to get closer to the subtle nuances in her vision.

Whatever the conditions and routines (s)he feels (s)he requires, a creator is likely to be acutely aware of them because (s)he has learned they are the doorway to absorption.

Sustained Effort—Sketchbooks, Journals and Notes

The ongoing absorption in the creative process also includes mechanisms creators develop and use regularly to organize different lines of creative inquiry, to provide a flow of germ material for creative rumination, and to keep themselves continually in the game of creating options and insights.

Virtually every visual artist has a sketchbook where visual germs and technical variations are tried out. Scientists, writers, even dancers and musicians keep notebooks. Darwin kept voluminous notebooks in which he carefully recorded the movement of his thought processes on the issues of evolution. As his thought branched and separated, he started new notebooks under new headings.

Presumably, writing something down when you're thinking about it, even if you don't review what you've written again, is a way of giving weight to the thought process. At the same time, the unfinished, informal nature of a notebook keeps the thoughts flowing. Nothing is committed yet. Anything goes.

For Virginia Woolf, diary-keeping was one ongoing project in her network of enterprises. She wrote in her diary daily after tea. The diaries were a place for her to write "observations," distinct from "the soul" she tried to capture in her fiction. Her biographer says, "She castigated herself if she did not catch every drop [of daily life] in the bowl of the diary. . . . Her diary spurts all the time, bathing her with scenes. . . . She enjoyed the rush and indiscretion [of writing in the diary]. . . . And all the while, the diary threw up seeds of books that lay yet far off in the future."

Beethoven wrote in his Sketchbooks obsessively. He told a friend, "I always carry about a notebook like this, and if an idea comes to me I make a note of it at once. I even get up in the night when something occurs to me, for otherwise I might forget the idea." Beethoven used his Sketchbooks to log inspirations so he could work on them at a later time, as a preliminary draft stage where he could try out variations, and as a place where the free act of reflection could turn up new inspirations.

Not all creators employ notebooks, sketchbooks, journals or diaries, but a great many do, and the variety of ways they keep them and use them is large. Other creators accomplish a similar freestyle absorption with their work through such devices as writing letters (as Conrad did) or regularly meeting and discussing their creative activity with colleagues.

Attitude toward Chance, Mistakes and Failure

Louis Pasteur averred that "*le hazard ne favorise que les esprits préparés,*" usually translated as, "Chance favors the prepared mind" but perhaps more accurately, "Chance *only* favors the prepared mental spirit."

Creators generally take a very positive attitude toward accidents, often considering them an essential element in the creative process.

Stravinsky said, "In the course of my labors I suddenly stumble upon something unexpected. This unexpected element strikes me. I make a note of it. At the proper time I put it to profitable use. . . . One does not contrive an accident: one observes it to draw inspiration therefrom. An accident is perhaps the only thing that really inspires us."

Photographer Cartier-Bresson made an illustrious career out of being ready for the chance facial expression or gesture that would make a great picture. The shutter needed to click at "the decisive moment," he said. Robert Capa's famous photo of a Republican soldier being shot during a charge in the Spanish Civil War is an example of a creator's readiness for chance. Or is it chance? Bresson and Capa photographed hundreds of great pictures which just happened to catch things right. They also, of course, photographed thousands where things weren't right.

The best known instance of chance in modern science is the discovery by Alexander Fleming of penicillin. Gwyn Macfarlane, author of a recent biography of Fleming, charges the discovery resulted from an "incredible series of chance events."

The penicillin mold, it's now believed, didn't blow in through Fleming's window but came from the laboratory of a mycologist on the floor below. The mycologist just happened to have isolated a particularly powerful strain of the penicillin mold and had inadequate equipment so that the atmosphere became loaded with spores. The temperatures while Fleming was away on a vacation were unusual for that time of year. A cold spell favored the growth of an accidental mold spore on Fleming's forgotten petri dish and at the same time retarded the growth of bacteria. Then the temperature rose and the cocci grew everywhere except near the mold. Fleming's dish should have been destroyed but wasn't due to a housekeeping error. Then the return from vacation by his student caused Fleming to look again at the dish he had previously discarded.

One investigator concludes, "All these events, acting in concert, brought to Fleming's notice a phenomenon that cannot, even now, be reproduced unless the conditions in which the experiment is carried out are exactly right. Had only one link in this chain been broken, Fleming would have missed his opportunity."

Of course Fleming himself was a link in this chain. He had been on the lookout for an antibacterial substance and had made a related discovery earlier. So he was the right person to take advantage of the chance sequence of events. He was a highly developed selective encoder who was both disorganized in just the right degree and methodical enough to have created the circumstances that allowed events to fall his way.

On the other hand, Fleming never assiduously followed up his finding and became discouraged after learning that penicillin loses its potency quickly—a problem later overcome by other scientists. It would take ten years before a team of researchers would turn Fleming's exotic finding (which he had by then forgotten about) into the "wonder drug."

On these grounds Macfarlane rejects the Fleming myth and argues that he was far from the genius he is credited with being by history and the popular press. Chance made Fleming. But isn't chance, like history, at least a part of genius?

In his well-known book *Chase, Chance and Creativity,* medical researcher James Austin proposes that there are four kinds of chance that figure into creative activity: 1) blind luck that doesn't depend on any personal characteristics by the recipient; 2) the good luck that comes from "persistence, willingness to experiment and explore"; 3) chance that occurs as a faint clue overlooked by everyone except the creator who, because of his training and experience, is prepared to notice it and grasp its significance (Fleming was the recipient of this brand of chance); and 4) chance that comes to people like Darwin reading Malthus or Archimedes discovering the principle of displacement. This type of chance occurs in the context of the creator's unique approach to life.

The first type of chance, blind luck, almost never (or perhaps never) leads to a shift in worldview we associate with great creations. The remaining three types of chance repeat in varying degrees the historical dilemma posed in chapter 11.

Creativity demands chance. Archimedes' whole creative life prepared him to take advantage of a chance observation when stepping into his bath. Question: Was it in fact a chance observation or a likely one given Archimedes' immersion in the problem? If Darwin hadn't read Malthus wouldn't some other "chance" event have given him the piece he needed for the evolution problem? But what about Fleming? Here we could say the creator's vision, or at least his absorption, was weak and the context of chance events great. That only underscores the fact that chance, like history, is a Möbius strip.

Creators actively court chance. They're always ready to notice and amplify into insight some accident of their environment virtually everybody else thinks is trivial or fails to notice. This capacity is, in a deep sense, what makes creators creative.

▪

Creators make mistakes all the time, even when they're intuitively sure they're right. Poincaré said: "When a sudden illumination seizes upon the mind of the mathematician, it usually happens that it does not deceive him, but it also sometimes happens, that it does not stand the test of verification; well, we also notice that this false idea, had it been true, would have gratified our natural feeling for mathematical elegance."

In other words, creators' visions can mislead them at times, but the vision's desire for truth eventually corrects the error.

Creators, Rothenberg says, "feel free to range far and wide, take chances and think thoughts that invariably lead to some error."

Creators also actively court mistakes as part of their creative process. They learn that a drip of paint on the canvas, a wrong chip in the marble, even a mistake in an otherwise well-planned experiment can lead to a major breakthrough. The mind makes ruts very quickly and even more so when it stalls and spins its wheels. When a mistake shows up, most people despair, give up or back down the rutly path again. But the creator seizes the mistake as a way to break out. A mistake may suddenly create a space between thoughts sunken into each other because the creator got mired in the details of some perception. Seizing upon the mistake, the mind suddenly bursts into the open and takes a new route toward vision.

This approach to mistakes is very different from the one taken by our educational system which punishes mistakes, marks them wrong. This may well be one reason why creators as a group don't do well in school.

▪

Failure also has a different meaning in the creative process. An example is Edison's failure to simulate the resistance in the Atlantic telegraph cable.

In 1873 Edison was investigating improvements for oceanic telegraphy and decided to make a table top model of the Atlantic cable. He used carbon in order to simulate in a small space the total resistance on the ocean cable. The experiment failed because the slightest bumping of the lab table or loud noise changed the pressure of the connecting wires on the graphite and altered its resistance.

Three years later Alexander Graham Bell announced the invention of the telephone. The Bell phone had a weak voice transmitter, however, and Edison conducted a number of experiments to try to improve on it. Eventually he realized that he had learned something valuable from his earlier failure. He incorporated the pressure sensitivity of graphite into a carbon-rubber button for the phone's speaker.

In the self-organizing system of creativity, the results of a failure may be just what is needed to shift a context enough so that a chance event can lead to a new perspective. Cézanne coined a wonderful phrase that captures the whole paradoxical process of mixing chance and intentional tactics. He called the creator's creative activity "making a find."

INTER: Well, perhaps it's a nice phrase. But if you ask me, this *magnum opus* business sounds like a lot of work.

MUSING: It is. And we haven't yet gotten to one of the most important ingredients required to make a particular *magnum opus*.

14

Germinations
from Salt

NaCl → THE FINAL REAGENT

In alchemic texts, there is a third distilling agent cited as key
to the transformation of the *prima materia* into the stone. This
reagent is salt. In its common form salt is said to symbolize the
original raw material and to bring the distilling process full
circle. Adding salt to the raw material in the presence of
mercury and sulphur makes the transformation complete.
From the salt grain grows the philosopher's stone.

From a creator's germ grows a work of genius.

■

The kaleidoscopic shifts that take place as a particular great
work emerges from its inception into its finished shape, of
course, constitute such an incalculably subtle event that there
is no really good way to describe it. In this chapter we'll simply
try to suggest the event by concentrating on one genre of
creation, literature, and by following some vivid clues left by
authorial creators as to how their work unfolds.

■

E. L. Doctorow, author of the modern literary best-seller
Ragtime, has said, "I've discovered that you cannot start a book
with an intention, a calculation. You start writing before you
know what you want to write or what it is you're doing."

Doctorow's novel *Loon Lake* started when he was driving in the Adirondacks and noticed the title words on a road sign. What starts a piece, Doctorow said, "can be a phrase, an image, a sense of rhythm, the most intangible thing. Something just moves you, evokes feelings you don't even understand."

Sherwood Anderson's experience, like that of many authors, accords with Doctorow's observation:

I was walking in the street or sitting in a train and overheard a remark dropped from the lips of some man or woman. Out of a thousand such remarks, heard almost every day, one stayed in my head. I could not shake it out. And then people constantly told me tales and in the telling of them there was a sentence used that intoxicated. "I was lying on my back on the porch and the street lamp shone on my mother's face. What was the use? I could not say to her what was in my mind. She would not have understood. There was a man lived next door who kept going past the house and smiling at me. I got it into my head that he knew all that I could not tell mother."

A few such sentences in the midst of a conversation overheard or dropped into a tale someone told. These were the seeds of stories. How could one make them grow?

Virginia Woolf, too, regularly had pieces begin in this way. Example: Depressed and exhausted after completing the first draft of *To the Lighthouse,* she was one day struck by a feeling as though a gigantic, desolate wave had swelled, crashed and spread over her. It was "interesting" she wrote later, "but acutely unpleasant." In the midst of a "waste of water" she imagined "a fin passing far out. . . . I hazard the guess that it may be the impulse behind another book." The book was *The Waves.*

Launching pad images and powerful but nebulous sensations like these are the alchemic grains of salt that Henry James called "germs." Unable to resist a pun, James defined germs both as an infection that sends the hapless author into a literary fever and as a seed-cell ready to germinate into a full-blown literary life-form.

It is clear from the description of them by authors that germs are not "ideas" in any usual sense of that word. Presumably if you have a good idea for a story, you could tell it to someone and (s)he would think it was a good idea, too. But most germs are notably vague or even nonsensical. Joseph Conrad called them "indistinct ideas." Fundamentally they are nuances crystallized in some way that feels immediate and tangible to the author. Despite being "indistinct" the germ seems to jump out at the author as shockingly as a diamond in a coal mine.

But why should that be? Why should Loon Lake launch one author into a novel where for another it might mean nothing more than a place to stop for gas? The obvious answer is that a germ is in some way a fractal chip of vision. It is to the author like the chance discovery of a lens that holds promise of bringing the vision into focus in a concrete form. The germ contains an omnivalent nuance, a 'more'ness, a gleam of truth, a sense of wholeness. The wholeness of a germ is one of its most important characteristics.

THE WHOLE OF THE VIRUS

James reported that a chance comment at a dinner party about a mother and son fighting over an inheritance was the seed that stimulated him to *The Spoils of Poynton*. That idle phrase, James said, made him instantly aware of "the *whole* of the virus" (emphasis added) that would spread to be his story. As James's statement suggests, a germ's wholeness also feels highly physiological or sensory. Possibly it is synesthetically sensory. James called it a "vital particle." Poet Denise Levertov describes the sensory element vividly. "You can smell the poem before you can see it. Like some animal . . . the smell of a bear; you know, you might begin to hear it kind of going . . . pad . . . pad . . . around the house."

In the simplest terms, the process of creating a literary work is the process of finding and unfolding such germs.

Levertov says she waits until the germ feeling unfolds itself "into some phrases, some words, a rhythm, because if I try to push that into being by will before the intuition is really at work, then it's going to be a very bad beginning, and perhaps I'm going to lose the poem altogether." The author can "smell" and "hear" the germ but obviously its omnivalence and nuance make it an elusive animal.

So Levertov waits, but her waiting is undoubtedly not passive. The chances are she's busy monitoring her ongoing thoughts or probing different materials—constantly on the lookout for anything that will help the seed grow.

One might compare the germ to a bell sounding a note which at first only the creator can hear. Because of the variations in the metal, in the shape and in the turning or casting process, even bells manufactured to ring exactly the same pitch have a distinctly individual sound. This is because each bell vibrates its own complex of overtones. Like tuning forks, if a bell of A at some octave is rung in the vicinity of a cluster of other bells at different octaves, the A bells of that octave and all the octaves above it will resonate in sympathy. But depending on the overtones of the particular bell, bells of some other pitches will also vibrate, and vibrations will even occur in the materials of nearby objects. Analogously, the author uses the vibration of his or her germ to scan different material, alert for whatever resonates in sympathy. But unlike real bells, the vibratory nature of the authorial bell is actually changed by this process. It is a feedback loop: Each piece of material which is found to vibrate with the germ adds to the germ's complex overtones, affecting what will vibrate next.

The activity of finding resonance with the germ involves the author in a constant shifting in the mind or on the page of words, images, dialogue—changing a phrase or point of view, trying to get the material to "work," that is, to resonate with the germ. Sternberg's insight strategies, selective encoding, selective combination and selective comparison, Rothenberg's janusian thinking, and the guiding power of the visionary images of wide scope—all come into play in this activity of tuning disparate material to the ring of the germ. It's a remarkable process.

Rothenberg reports how one metaphor was tuned to the germ's vibration by Pulitzer prize-winning poet James Merrill. Though Rothenberg doesn't identify Merrill by name as his research subject, the poem whose revisions he followed is that poet's "18 West 11th Street."

Merrill's childhood home on 11th Street in New York City was accidentally blown up many years after he'd left it by members of the Weather Underground, a group of revolutionaries active in the 1960s. The poem's seed was clearly the poet's sense (a sort of crystallized nuance) that his feelings about his childhood and the activities of the saboteurs must be synonymous in some mysterious way. In the poem, Merrill manages to merge the two worlds through a metaphor about a mirror that was in the house. In the final version of the poem he calls the mirror "a mastermind" that "kept track above the mantel."

Rothenberg reports that Merrill wrote at least thirty-three versions of this metaphor over a two-year period before arriving at the final formulation. At first there was no mantel in his poem at all, only a "jamb and lintel." Lintel led to mantel and remained for fifteen versions until mantel led to the idea of the mirror as "a mental world" above the mantel. Rothenberg cites the poet as saying that for a time he became stuck in the temptation to rhyme "mantel" with "mental," but he knew the image wasn't quite right for the germ and kept working. Finally, the word "mastermind" occurred to him and was recognized as having the proper vibration.

How does the writer decide when an image with just the right vibration has been found? The answer is far from simple. The whole context of the poem determines what fits and what doesn't. But the determiner of the whole context of the poem is the creator's vision acting through the germ. Joseph Conrad affectingly described the process: "Scores of notions present themselves—expressions suggest themselves by the dozen, but the inward voice that decides:—this is well—this is right—is not heard sometimes for days together." The "inward voice" Conrad was waiting for was the voice of his vision focused through the germ.

The process of tuning into the seed idea ends when the writer has gotten everything to vibrate together and there seems nowhere else to go. However, with a process made of omnivalence, often the end is not definite. There is always the feeling that 'more' could be done. Valéry said that a creative work is never finished, only abandoned.

DIFFERENT GERM EXPERIENCES

Creators have many varieties of experiences finding and unfolding their seed ideas.

Locating the germlike vibration of material can be as much a matter of taking away as it is of adding or changing. Hemingway said he edited ruthlessly in order to get down to the germ. "All you have to do," he said, "is write one true sentence. Write the truest sentence that you know. So finally I would write one true sentence, and then go on from there. It was easy then because there was always one true sentence that I knew or had seen or had heard someone say. If I started to write elaborately, or like someone introducing or presenting something, I found that I could cut that scrollwork or ornament out and throw it away and start with the first true simple declarative sentence I had written." His "one true sentence" became the germ.

Consistent with this paring approach, Hemingway believed that what an author left out of a story was more important than what (s)he put in because the taking away created what he called the "fourth dimension" (that is the omnivalence) of the story. Hemingway worked to scale down his description so that it was almost as cryptic and pregnant for the reader as the germ itself was for the writer. Hemingway said that he had tried several times to write his story "The Killers" but didn't get it right until one afternoon he saw what he had to leave out in order for the right omnivalent space to open up. "I guess I left as much out of the 'The Killers' as any story I ever wrote. Left the whole city of Chicago." Of "A Clean, Well-Lighted Place" he said, "I left everything out of that one." So germs and germ vibrations are what writers both expand from and try to boil their way down to.

But whether it involves adding, changing, or editing down to the seedlike material, the unfolding process is generally painstaking. Valéry pointed out that a work may take months or years, only to pass through a reader's mind as a momentary shock. He said, "One may (very roughly, of course) compare this effect to the fall, in a few seconds, of a mass which has been carried up, piece by piece, to the top of a tower without regard to the time or the number of trips."

Not surprising that writers sometimes come to feel that the germ-unfolding effort which infected them and spread through their work was as potent as a literal virus. Conrad wrote to his editor, *"Nostromo* is finished, a fact upon which my friends may congratulate me as upon a recovery from a dangerous illness."

Of course, occasionally writers like Coleridge have claimed that they experienced full-blown inspirations which catapulted them from germ to finished product without any of these nourishing drops of sweat and pain in between. Perkins and many other creativity scholars question these claims, however. The evidence shows that behind even apparently spontaneous inspirations lies a great deal of drafting and mental work.

The situation with these seeming instant creations is perhaps analogous to that of the Zen artists, who could sit for months before an empty canvas and then execute a painting and the accompanying poem in a few seconds. Evidently, for months they had unfolded the germ in their minds and then splashed the result on the rice paper.

Pulitzer prize-winning poet Richard Wilbur has a slow-motion version of this approach. In an interview several years ago Wilbur said his seed ideas are first anchored to his consciousness as "suggestive or wispy notes" he jots in a "little blank book" or on scraps of paper and envelopes. When he sets out to actually write the poem associated with one of these seeds, he is forced by idiosyncratic tactics of his own creative personality to wait until he's sure the resonance of the line is right in his mind before he puts the words down. He knows it will be almost impossible for him to revise what he's written if it isn't right. "I don't dare set things down, for fear I'll leave them there." Sometimes weeks or months go by between lines. Then a line seems to appear without drafting, but the drafting has been done mentally.

Novelist V. S. Naipaul has quite a different way of unfolding germs. In the early part of his career, he says,

I felt it as artificial, that sitting down to write a book. And that is a feeling that is with me still, all these years later, at the start of a book—I am speaking of an imaginative work. There is no precise theme or story that is with me. Many things are with me; I write the artificial self-conscious beginnings of many books; until finally some true impulse—the one I have been working toward—possesses me, and I sail away on my year's labor, And that is mysterious still—that out of artifice one should touch and stir up what is deepest in one's soul, one's heart, one's memory.

A writer need not always start with a germ or even any particular material in which (s)he suspects a germ might be lurking. Instead, as an idiosyncratic tactic (s)he might engage in some regular germ-finding activity. Some poets routinely "play" with language, rhythms, images, listening for a "vital particle" which James had also called a "grain of gold." Many writers use their diaries and journals as germ-finding playgrounds. In a sense, germ finding or germ seeking is a constant activity for the writer. (S)he is always on the alert for anything that resembles a chip from the hidden reality of vision, a grain of the *prima materia.*

Sometimes a piece will evolve, in effect, out of a number of different incomplete germs, coming together like beads of mercury. William Faulkner said *The Sound and the Fury* began when he started thinking about the characters of a little girl and her brothers he had just used in a short story, "That Evening Sun." He then remembered some scenes from his own childhood—the funeral of his grandmother and splashing games he had played in a local stream. These germ fragments coalesced into an image of Caddy Compson in muddy drawers climbing a tree to peer into a window at the wake of her grandmother while her brothers looked on. Faulkner said that when he began to write about the events and characters he felt would be connected with this image, he had no plan. Nevertheless, the entire tale "seemed to explode on the paper before me."

Goethe described a similar experience where the germ for his *The Sorrows of Young Werther* brought together bits of images and ideas that had strong, long-standing nuances and ambivalence attached to them, including his feelings about a broken love affair from the past. The event that precipitated the novel was the suicide of a young man by the name of Jerusalem who had shot himself after a rebuff by a married woman. Goethe said:

I was collecting elements that had been floating within me for a number of years. I endeavored to retain a vivid picture of the cases that had been most urgent and most frightening to me. Yet nothing would take shape. What was lacking was an occasion in which they [these elements] could be embodied. All of a sudden, I hear the news of Jerusalem's death, and immediately after the general rumor the most precise circumstantial description . . . [and my idea took shape] like water in a vessel, which, on the freezing point, turns into ice at the slightest shock.

Germs contain for the creator the qualities of wholeness, nuance, ambiguity, open-endedness and also concrete specificity. Borges seemed to sum up all this with his sentence, "The aesthetic act is the imminence of a revelation never fulfilled."

Probably what is appealing to a writer about the germ in the first place is that imminence. Then, in unfolding the germ, (s)he tries not to fulfill the revelation but to re-create the imminence (or 'more'ness) of it on a scale both broad and focused enough so that the reader can experience it, too. This is evident in Merrill's "mastermind above the mantel" image which is clearly more "imminent" and omnivalently evocative (and also more specific) than the "mental world" image which he rejected.

Now let's change the scale of the fractal a little for one more look at germs and germ unfolding in literature.

TWO EXAMPLES

Worksheets, drafts and journals provide an invaluable perspective into a creator's thought process. Here's an example.

London	London
I wander thro each dirty street	I wander thro' each charter'd street,
Near where the dirty Thames does flow	Near where the charter'd Thames does
mark	flow
And see in every face I meet	And mark in every face I meet
Marks of weakness marks of woe	Marks of weakness marks of woe.
In every cry of every man	In every cry of every Man.
every infants cry of fear	In every Infants cry of fear.
In every voice of every child	In every voice; in every ban
In every voice in every ban	The mind-forg'd manacles I hear.
mind d manacles I hear	
The german forg— links I hear	
ed	
How	How the Chimney sweepers cry
But most the chimney sweepers cry	Every blackning Church appalls,
Every blackning Church appalls	And the hapless Soldiers sigh
Blackens oer the churches walls	Runs in blood down Palace walls
And the hapless soldiers sign	
Runs in blood down palace walls	

But most the midnight harlots curse
From every dismal street I hear
Weaves around the marriage hearse
<u>And blasts the new born infants tear</u>

But most thro' midnight streets I hear
How the youthful Harlots curse
Blasts the new born Infants tear
And blights with plagues the Marriage
   hearse.

     thro wintry
But most ~~from every~~ streets I hear
How the midnight harlots curse
Blasts the new born infants tear
   smites
And ~~hangs~~ with plagues the marriage
  hearse

But most the shrieks of youth
         I hear
But most thro midnight &c
How the youthful

    This is a poem by William Blake, with its draft on the left. We'll start our look at it with a few explicit assumptions. The most important one is that the germ of this poem lies in the title, "London." I suspect Blake began his piece not with an idea or a message he wanted to sell but with an imminent, omnivalent sensation of the city he lived in and its universal meaning. Perhaps he'd just come home from walking around the seamier neighborhoods and was experiencing the kind of sorrow Dickens later felt at the human misery created in the urban environment. Or he hadn't been out at all but was just reflecting on the various impressions he had that the city harbored a kind of hidden reality which he wanted (or needed) to express.

    Our second explicit assumption is that Blake wrote the lines in order down the page. The deletions and additions we leave an open question; we don't know in what order they were made.

    It is clear from the worksheet that at some point in the process, Blake executed a significant revision in the first two lines of his poem. He changed the word "dirty" to "charter'd." Why?

    There's no record of Blake's precise thinking on this or any of the other changes but we can hazard a guess based on the differences in the effect of the two versions. The word "dirty" in both lines sounds like a complaint, a banal opinion, or a piece of weak description. By contrast, "charter'd" (which means both "mapped" and "made official by law") becomes a rather mysterious and "imminent" word in its context. "Charter'd" conjures up the mind of man mapping and structuring the city and the universe to his own frame. Since there are no actual deletions of "dirty" in the first draft, Blake could have made this change quite late in the poem's evolution.

In the third line Blake changes "see" to "mark," probably after writing line four. "Mark" is a much more omnivalent word than "see" because it cuts at least two ways. The speaker is marking in the sense of seeing, but he's also marking in the sense of putting a mark on the faces in the street. One implication is that the marks of weakness and woe are also being stamped there by the speaker, who is a part of the misery he is talking about. "Mark" also reflects "charter'd" in that mapping is an act of making marks, and laws and charters are markers and boundaries.

In the second stanza, Blake starts his changes by deleting the weak "In every voice of every child" and replacing it with the more specific and dramatic "In every infants cry of fear." He is benefiting again from the effects of repetition. The repetition of a word twice in the first two lines of the poem is varied in the second two, which repeat the word "mark" three times. In the second stanza "cry" is repeated twice. The mind quickly sets up expectations about patterns—i.e., the number of times a word will be repeated—and variations such as Blake created here keep the mind off balance and prevent it from getting a definitive fix on the poem. They help keep the poem imminent, in other words.

The last line in the second stanza is a minor miracle. Blake's first version of the line is banal, almost laughable, "The german forged links I hear." Evidently he needed to write the line down in order to appreciate its banality and give birth to its famous descendant, "The mind-forg'd manacles I hear." At this point, context is surely exerting its effect on his effort to tune his material to the germ. Context is establishing connections between "mark," "ban," and "mind-forg'd manacles"—all having to do with how the city's unhappiness is a product of human thought dividing things up and binding things together by categories, "mark"ing them, that is. The "charter'd" change seems inevitable in this context and perhaps Blake didn't bother to "mark" it down on the first draft because he already knew he was going to make it in the final.

In the third stanza, changing the chimney sweepers' cry from "Blackens oer the churches walls" to "Every blackning church appalls" creates more omnivalence. Is the church appalled by the cry? If so, why? Because the church wants to do something about the cry or because it is offended to hear such cries in its sanctified environs? Is the blackening being done by the cry or is it the church that is blackening things? That suggests another possibility: that the cry is the sound of the sweepers themselves being appalled at the blackening churches. Omnivalence galore.

The "blackening cry" is also another form of the continual marking going on in the poem.

Speaking of marking, something especially interesting happens next. In lines three and four of the third stanza Blake writes, "And the hapless soldiers sign / Runs in blood down palace walls." In the revision "sign" is changed to "sigh." Why? After all, wouldn't "sign" be better as another image of marking? I think it's precisely for that reason Blake *doesn't* use the word. With "sign" he's in danger of falling into a brain-dulling pattern turning his series of "mark" images into a message. Messages don't have omnivalence or imminence. He opts to gently enrich the line and open up more space between. Why do soldiers sigh, we wonder. And the mark aspect remains implicit, running in blood down the palace walls. Interesting to speculate whether Blake stumbled on sigh because the word looks like sign. Chance favors the prepared mind.

I'll stop here. The last stanza is fascinating but I think our point is clear. I should note, however, that in the last stanza's "curse" and "blights," the mark imagery carries right through to the end of the poem.

One of the insights this worksheet offers is that in the activity of following out the omnivalence of the germ and applying the germ's vibration to the material, the creator derives a holistic or fractal result. In the end, one part of the piece ("charter'd," say) reflects other parts ("mark," "blackning," "blood" and "blights"). One might call this deep creative patterning "reflectaphoric."

In a traditional metaphor two logically dissimilar terms are compared in such a way that omnivalence is created in the space between them. In literary works, reflectaphors include metaphor, irony, symbolism, pun, image, varying word repetition—any technique which has the effect of simultaneously comparing and contrasting one element in the work with others and creating that omnivalent space, that sense of imminence not revealed.

In the poem "London" the images just mentioned are all similar in their relation to "mark"ing but also quite different (for example, blood running down palace walls is logically quite dissimilar from a "charter'd" street). Together the images create a reflectaphoric structure, a network of omnivalent relationships, each one reflecting the others (as the "mark" elements reflect each other) and the imminence of the whole.

Reflectaphoric structure seems a natural one to evolve out of a process in which the creator is seeking material that vibrates at the same frequency as the germ. The germ's complex overtones become echoed in each part of the work. These echoes or reflections give the work its underlying wholeness. The reflected overtones are also the seismic signatures of the creator's hidden reality. So a piece which begins with a sense that a germ is an implicit wholeness (a whole story, a whole poem) ends by embodying that wholeness in a reflectaphoric form. The effect is possibly why Thomas Mann once suggested that great artists do their work with mirrors.

Reflectaphors are also a natural structure for creating the individual-universal equation. For example, Blake's use of the reflectaphoric "mark"ed images turned the individual city of London where he lived into a universal symbol of the human condition.

■

On September 30, 1926, Virginia Woolf stirred from a visionary reverie and wrote that she saw "a fin passing far out." The journal entry marks the beginning of a subtle three-year process during which Woolf ripened this seed to the point where she could actually begin to compose what by some lights is the most radical and outstanding novel of the twentieth century.

There is no way to synopsize *The Waves*. It follows the perceptual thought processes of six friends as they pass from childhood to middle age and concludes with a long section narrated by one of them in old age. There is no plot and virtually no conventional development of character. The narrators' thoughts pulse through the book like waves crashing on a seashore.

According to one critic, the germ described as the "fin far out" was an especially powerful one for Woolf. It provided "a constant goal and measure of the entire creative process involved in writing" her novel, a sort of gyroscope guiding her on a difficult intuitional journey.

Two months after the journal entry, while she was typing *To the Lighthouse* Woolf put down some further thoughts on the germ. Now she said she had a sense of being "haunted by some semi-mystic very profound life of a woman." She mulled over the possibility of concentrating this woman's story, obliterating time and compressing the life so that one incident "say the fall of a flower might contain it." Her thoughts, still quite vague at this point, had more to do with the problems of writing a novel that contained the amorphous *qualities* of the germ than they did with developing a particular character, image or idea.

Her next entry about the new novel was on February 21, 1927, and included the thought that the book should be "away from facts; free; yet concentrated; prose yet poetry; a novel and a play."

By March 1927, her insight that the germ required a new kind of novel became mingled with initial plans for another book, *Orlando.* Nevertheless, that summer she gave a name to the "fin far out" novel. She called it *The Moths:*

Now the Moths will I think fill out the skeleton which I dashed in here; the play-poem idea: the idea of some continuous stream, not solely of human thought, but of the ship, the night, etc. all flowing together: intersected by the arrival of the bright moths. A man and a woman are to be sitting at table talking. Or shall they remain silent? It is to be a love story; she is finally to let the last great moth in. The contrasts might be something of this sort; she might talk, or think, about the age of the earth; the death of humanity; then the moths keep on coming. Perhaps the man could be left absolutely dim. France: hear the sea: at night; a garden under the window. But it needs ripening.

Woolf had come to the point where she was beginning to think openly of the germ in terms of tensions and contraries.

In late spring 1927 she worked on the first of three literary essays she would write during the germ-ripening period. It appears she shifted to this project in her network of enterprises partly as a way to explore from a critical perspective the possibility that the only way to satisfy her germ would be to invent a new kind of novel. In this first of the essays she speculated about the future of the novel. "The psychological novelist has been too prone to limit psychology to the psychology of personal intercourse. . . . We long for some more impersonal relationship. We long for ideas, for dreams, for imaginations, for poetry." In the second essay, she conjectures that the future feminine novel will not be a "dumping-ground for the personal emotions," a curious statement that amply applies to the autobiographical novel she had just finished, *To the Lighthouse,* as well as to the works of other women novelists. Woolf seems to be shaking herself free of the last book which had meant so much to her. She evidently needs to do that if she is to take on a book requiring a totally different state of mind. It is part of the process of shifting the context so that she can see the new book clearly.

In October 1927 Woolf was seized by the compulsion to write *Orlando,* the novel she had begun to plan in March. It was a much lighter novel than *To the Lighthouse* and was apparently another way to shift context. All the while she felt *The Moths* hovering "somewhere at the back of my brain" but she resolved not to think about it until it had "grown heavy in my mind like a ripe pear."

Scholars think that sometime in the summer of 1928 Woolf attempted a first sketch of *The Waves.* Very little of the detail in the sketch ultimately found its way into the novel itself, but in it she began to engage in the image-forming process that usually preceded her work on a piece.

In November 1928 she decided to "attack this angular shape in my mind. I think *The Moths* (if that is what I shall call it) will be very sharply cornered."

However, it wasn't until May 1929 that she moved in on the "angular shape."

I am not trying to tell a story. Yet perhaps it might be done in that way. A mind thinking. They might be islands of light—islands in the stream that I am trying to convey; life itself going on. The current of the moths flying strongly this way. A lamp and a flower pot in the centre. The flower can always be changing. But there must be more unity between each scene than I can find at present. Autobiography it might be called. How am I to make one lap, or act, between the coming of the moths, more intense than another; if there are only scenes? One must get the sense that this is the beginning; this the middle: that the climax—when she opens the window and the moth comes in. I shall have the two different currents—the moths flying along; the flower upright in the centre; a perpetual crumbling and renewing of the plant. In its leaves she might see things happen. But who is she? I am very anxious that she should have no name. I don't want a Lavinia or a Penelope: I want "she." But that becomes arty. Liberty greenery yallery somehow: symbolic in loose robes. Of course I can make her think backwards and forwards; I can tell stories. But that's not it. Also I shall do away with exact place and time. Anything might be out of the window—a ship—a desert—London.

She is hunting for resonances for her germ. A single character, nameless; images of moths; flowers "crumbling and
renewing."

By June 1929 Woolf recognized that the images she had
developed so far for the germ were static. They created no
narrative progression. She also rejected the moths idea because moths don't fly in daylight, a fact which vitiated her
sense of the image. She thought now about writing an opening
sequence on childhood and then went on to remark, "Could
one not get the waves to be heard all through?"

Woolf's realization of the way in which waves, her long-
standing image of wide scope, might apply to this new novel
proved revolutionary. The germ and the strong vision-bind-
ing nuance from her own childhood had found their resonance. A few days later she began the first draft of *The Waves.*

The book went through two handwritten drafts and two
typewritten ones. Her progress was swift and direct, considering the incredible subtlety and complexity of the project.
Though her diary indicates she was troubled about her progress on the piece, the drafts show a greater compositional
assurance than was the case with her other novels. Having
resisted the impulse to begin actual writing on this book,
having allowed the germ so long a time to ripen and having
remained so long in its imminence and omnivalence and nuance, Woolf apparently found that it now implied structure,
characters, images, tensions—everything she needed. All of
these sprang into place almost as soon as she set pen to page.
Because all these elements unfolded in resonance with the
germ, the novel is immensely reflectaphoric. Woolf's germ of
the "fin far out" had been polished during those three years
into a highly focused lens for her vision. Now, through this
lens the rays from her hidden reality imprinted their shapes on
the manuscript page.

When she had finished the first draft of *The Waves* on February 7, 1931, Woolf wrote with the exuberance of someone
who has passed through a germ-inspired fever, "I have netted
that fin."

15

More Salt Grains to Stone

NaCl → TURNING OVER A FEW GERMS

INTER (hunched over a table, playing a game of solitaire with tarot cards): Now tell me, does this germ thing apply to other creators, musicians, artists, scientists?

MUSING: Not in the same way, but similarly. Suppose we look at a few quickly: activities glimpsed by lightning.

First, *germ finding.* Some flashes:
Isadora Duncan "spent long days and nights in the studio" standing "quite still, my two hands folded between my breasts, covering the solar plexus," waiting for the germ. "I was seeking and finally discovered the central spring of all movement, . . . the unity from which all diversities of movements are born, the mirror of vision for the creation of the dance." Her goal was "a first movement from which would be born a series of movements without my volition."

John-Steiner reports that film director Federico Fellini's starting point is "not a cameo in a single frame, but a landscape of faces." Fellini says:

The richest part of a preparation for a movie is the choice of faces, heads, that is the human landscape. During this period I am capable of seeing five or six thousand faces that suggest the comportment of my characters to me, their personalities, and even the narrative cadence of the film.

298

Duke Ellington regularly meditated on the personal styles of the musicians in his band as inspirations for his pieces, zeroing in on those styles to find a germ. Choreographer George Balanchine also used his dancers' particular skills and body types as pathways to the germ.

Many artists find germs for pieces in other works of art, for instance Eisenstein, who was frequently inspired by paintings. A work of art, of course, has truth and omnivalence built in so it's a natural source for the germ sensation. Some coloration of the original piece's omnivalence touches a creator's vision and demands a new piece expressing that coloration. The new piece will generally end up unrecognizably different from the one that inspired it.

▪

A few lightning streaks of *germ unfolding:*

Louise Nevelson explained what germ unfolding is like for her: "It's like if you have a tiny jewel, say a pin. And then you get a dress for it and do your hair for it. And you make a whole picture because you want to enhance that one thing."

Giacometti once advised Picasso that a sculpture must be finished "in accordance with its generating force."

Auguste Rodin also saw the sculptor's task as keeping resonance with the germ, which he called a "global idea." "Till the end of his task," Rodin said, "it is necessary for him to maintain energetically, in the full light of consciousness, his global idea so as to reconduct unceasingly to it and closely connect with it the smallest details of his work. And this cannot be done without a very severe strain of thought."

Borrowing Rodin's image, mathematician Jacques Hadamard described his mind as focused on "the global image" when thinking through a difficult mathematical problem.

Igor Stravinsky saw his work as proceeding from a germ which he called "the foretaste of discovery." Germ and process of unfolding are inseparable, Stravinsky felt:

This foretaste of the creative act accompanies the intuitive grasp of an unknown entity already possessed but not yet intelligible, an entity that will not take definite shape except by the action of a constantly vigilant technique. . . . This premonition of an obligation, this foretaste of a pleasure, this conditioned reflex, as a modern physiologist would say, shows clearly that it is the idea of discovery and hard work that attracts me.

Stravinsky went on to say that the germs or foretastes occurred mostly by accident, "and the true creator may be recognized by his ability always to find about him, in the commonest and humblest thing, items worthy of note."

Van Gogh, according to Brower, moved from germ to completed expression by the following stages. He "painted a work in one session, perhaps in two or three hours. He didn't work from sketches. He most often had a conceptualization for a work [germ] and he would evolve a series of paintings for a particular subject, trying to get closer and closer" to approximate his germ.

Chopin's struggles to unfold his germs are reminiscent of Conrad's. George Sand left an account:

His creation was spontaneous, miraculous. He found it without seeking or foreseeing it. It came to his piano, sudden, complete, sublime, or it sang itself in his head during a walk, and he urged himself to remember it until he got it down on the piano. But then began the most nerve-wracking labor that I have ever witnessed. It was a series of efforts, irresolutions, impatiences, to recapture certain thematic details as he had heard them in his head. He analyzed too much that which he had first grasped as a whole, in trying to write it down. . . . He shut himself in his room for entire days, weeping, walking, breaking his pens. . . . He would spend six weeks on a page. . . .

THE BIRTH OF A PAINTING

There are numerous accounts of Picasso's germ-unfolding process. Picasso was interested in helping researchers develop generalizations and insights into creativity, and so permitted others to scrutinize his working methods. His own thoughts on the way his paintings evolved seemed paradoxical. "Basically," he once said, "a picture doesn't change. . . . The first 'vision' [germ] remains almost intact, in spite of appearances." A moment later he appeared to have changed his mind, "A picture is not thought out and settled beforehand," he now insisted. "While it is being done it changes as one's thoughts change."

In a famous film made of Picasso at work, there is a clue to the meaning of this apparent contradiction. The viewer is left with a distinct impression Picasso was always looking for something quite specific as he worked. In one sequence of the film, for example, he draws a horse's head, subjecting it to numerous styles—romantic, realistic, cubist—and numerous complexities in each style. What he finally settles on retains some elements of all the styles and complexities. In another sequence the reverse happens. A picture grows complex and then he strips away the complexity and simplifies it. But why did Picasso feel his final versions were "better" than the others? He confides to the filmmaker that what he wants to show is "the surprising truth at the bottom of the well." The true painting, he seems to indicate, can only occur after a *process* uncovers what he is certain is there.

In her biography of Picasso, Françoise Gilot describes the evolution of a portrait he painted of her.

According to Gilot, Picasso's absorption in his work was intense. "While I work I leave my body outside the door, the way Moslems take off their shoes before entering the mosque," he told her. He could stand in front of the canvas three or four hours at a stretch. When daylight faded, he would switch on two spotlights that left everything but his canvas in darkness. The painter, he said, must become hypnotized "as though he were in a trance. He must stay as close as possible to his own inner world. . . ."

Because Gilot wasn't sitting for the portrait, she was able to watch as it developed. Picasso explained that he had taken as his germ for the piece his inchoate sense of the "rhythm of your nature." He wanted to capture rhythm on the canvas.

Picasso first tried to do that in a realistic portrait but said, "It's just not your style. A realistic portrait wouldn't represent you at all." Next he tried changing the furniture the Gilot figure was sitting on and realized that she was "not at all the passive type. I can only see you standing." Evidently, Picasso both *knew* the rhythm of Gilot's nature and was *discovering* that rhythm in the process of painting her.

At this point he remembered that his friend Matisse had once proposed painting Gilot with green hair and this idea shifted the master's context dramatically. He now painted the hair of the woman in the portrait as a leaf and by stages transformed her into a flower. When he had done with the portrait, now called *La Femme Fleur,* he said to Gilot, "You're like a growing plant and I'd been wondering how I could get across the idea that you belong to the vegetable kingdom rather than the animal. I've never felt impelled to portray anyone this way. It's strange, isn't it? I think it's just right, though. It represents *you.* "

The portrait Picasso created both individualized his subject and universalized her—and his perception of her—to create the individual-universal equation. In the process he also created a canvas filled with visual reflectaphors, omnivalent mirrors (for example, in the painting her face and breasts are reflections of each other and also reflect parts of a flower). Picasso's work on *La Femme Fleur* demonstrates that for him germ finding and germ unfolding were a circular paradox, for they were the same thing. This can be seen even more clearly in *Guernica.*

Picasso's famous painting began with his horror of the Fascist atrocities in the Spanish Civil War, in particular the bombing of a Basque village, Guernica. This feeling crystallized into a germ which deposited itself as a rough sketch on a small piece of blue paper. Perhaps Picasso was following da Vinci's advice to artists to do an untidy sketch because it suggests new possibilities.

Rudolph Arnheim in his classic study of the evolution of *Guernica* notes:

Picasso's first sketch for *Guernica* contains much of the final basic form. . . . We discern the bull on the left, in his final location.

Figure 6 Finished *Guernica*. Reproduced by permission of the Museo Nationale del Prado and the Artists' Rights Society of New York.

Not only the head but the entire body is turned away from the scene—as though this turning away was the basic thought, later refined when the bull was made to face the event but with his head averted. The bird sits on the bull, at the exact spot where it will later hover on the table. The horse seems to lie dead on its back, thereby representing the extreme effect of the murderous assault—a function later transferred to the dead child. The horse's raised hindlegs are significant as the early establishment of a central rising vertical, which later caused much experimentation. The woman is pushing the lamp through the window; she, too, is in her final place. The horizontal base of prostrate bodies underlies the entire principal scene, more radically and simply than the warrior will finally do it.

Obviously there is much that is different from the final form, too. There is a huge amount of detail to be worked out.

Unfolding the sketchy germ image plunged Picasso into weeks of work testing the details of the figures and their relation to each other. Within the context established by the original germ sketch, one idea would give birth to another, each change refining and altering that context. The figure of the bull—one of Picasso's important images of wide scope—received considerable revision.

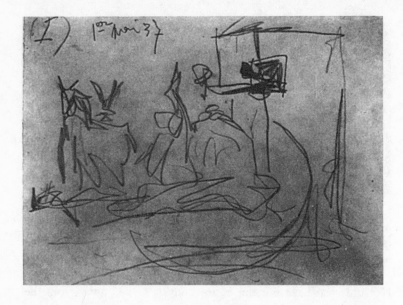

Figure 7 *Guernica* germ. Reproduced by permission of the Museo Nationale del Prado and the Artists' Rights Society of New York.

Many of the studies he did of the figures for the painting were complex and detailed. An example is *Mother with dead children.* Finding the appropriate level of detail in the figures was an important part of the germ-unfolding process. Evidently Picasso wanted to get many elements into the painting and eventually saw that each one would have to be relatively simple if the overall piece wasn't to disintegrate into visual confusion. But by probing each separate figure, he could come to a deeper grasp of the figure's visual potential and meaning and could scale it back. Detailing the figures was probably also instrumental in learning about the "tone" or appropriate level of complexity for the piece *as a whole.* This tone was implicit in the germ sketch but would not have been clear until Picasso actually tried out the figures. Scaling back detail in the figures

Figure 8 *Mother with dead children, Guernica*. Reproduced by permission of the Museo Nationale del Prado and the Artists' Rights Society of New York.

was undoubtedly guided by the central need to create omnivalence, a multilevel elusive richness. This could be accomplished by having the figures exist with a visual "tension" (as Picasso called it) between their similarities and their differences, that is, by making reflectaphors.

One of the easier visual reflectaphors to see in *Guernica* is the cries and expressions of the figures. Note how in individual and very different ways they mirror each other. Subtler reflectaphors exist in the way lines which form part of one figure also form parts of other figures, so the "same" line is also a "different" line.

The process of *Guernica* demonstrates quite clearly that Picasso was not stating a contradiction but plain fact when he said that a picture "remains almost intact" from its first inspiration and yet "is not thought out and settled beforehand." He was indicating that the creative process is a holistic one, like the process of the birth and development of a living thing. In nature the final form of an oak tree or human being is given from the seed at the outset, and yet it is not given, too, because the form is also shaped as it grows. Arnheim remarked: "Picasso did not simply deposit in *Guernica* what he had thought about the world; rather did he further his understanding of the world through *Guernica.*" Out of his individual horror had grown a universal perception. Using the germ which, remember, was a lens of his overall vision, Picasso found and focused into being the shapes of a hidden reality— and distilled a philosopher's stone of his genius.

TALES OF TWO COMPOSERS

The two composers most frequently compared in the literature on creativity are certainly Mozart and Beethoven. Both musical giants, they represent—or seem to—stark contrasts in creative process and thus the differences between them have generated some confusion about the definition of genius.

In the play *Amadeus,* Mozart's rival Salieri is horrified to discover that the prodigy who comports himself so vulgarly is possessed of a divine gift. Aghast, the plodding Salieri learns that Mozart makes no drafts of his beautiful compositions. They simply "come" to him and he copies them down. The play supports the popular notion that Mozart's kind of effortless inspiration must be what genius really is.

The reality of Mozart's compositional process is quite different from this image, however. In fact, his process is perfectly consistent with the way other creators work.

In a famous letter, Mozart said that his musical germs came to him most often when he was alone, in a good mood, traveling in a carriage, walking, after dinner or late at night. Apparently, in these loose moments various bits of musical notions floated through his mind and some he recognized as having a germlike resonance, an omnivalence or nuance. Those, he said, "I retain in memory, and am accustomed to hum them to myself." As he hummed, the "peculiarities of the various instruments," "the rules of counterpoint" and other elements began to accumulate around the germ fragment and "provided I am not disturbed, my subject enlarges itself, becomes methodized and defined." These early stages which ripened the germ and started it unfolding apparently took some time. During that time Mozart would work sporadically on several different germs he kept in his mind. When the germ reached a critical mass and he had gotten major elements of the composition to resonate together with the germ and form a context, he wrote the piece down.

The transition stage from mind to page has caused many creativity theorists to romanticize Mozart's process. In his letter, Mozart claimed that at some point the whole piece

though it be long, stands almost complete and finished in my mind; so that I can survey it, like a fine picture or a beautiful statue, at a glance. Nor do I hear in my imagination the parts *successively,* but I hear them, as it were, all at once. . . . When I proceed to write down my ideas, I take out of the bag of my memory, if I may use that phrase, what has been previously collected into it in the way I have mentioned. For this reason the committing to paper is done quickly enough, for everything is, as I said before, already finished; and it rarely differs on paper from what it was in my imagination.

As alluded to in chapter 8, Howard Gardner has argued that Mozart was a "top-down" composer, meaning that he started with the large structure—its shape and thrust, its basic dynamics—and then filled in the moment-by-moment details later. He could apparently hold this dynamic outline in his mind and adjust it, perhaps something like the way Tesla did with the mental image of his inventions. It wasn't that Mozart literally heard the piece all at once with all its details; instead he heard and mentally saw its general structure.

Consequently, Mozart's statement about committing the piece to paper is a little misleading.

Researchers who have looked at Mozart's unfinished manuscripts have found clues to his working methods. He would begin work in a full score with prepared staves for the individual instruments and voices. In the first few measures he might write out all the parts but would quickly abandon this procedure and follow the main melodic line, distributing it among the various instruments. In some of his unfinished manuscripts, the melodic bits are strewn all over the otherwise blank score. In places where a polyphonic passage required the scoring of other parts, he would stop and work them out. Once having fixed the overall structure, Mozart would go back and work out the details of the missing parts. Sometimes this secondary creative activity would turn up a new musical dimension to the piece which he would excitedly move to integrate into the whole composition.

Mozart, as one critic has put it, was no musical revolutionary. "He spoke the musical language of his time. He made liberal use of musical ideas of others, the urge for originality being as alien to him as to any composer of his time." Put another way, Mozart's vision of musical structure, like his prodigious talent, made a good fit or co-incidence with the musical idioms of his day. Certainly there were differences between his vision and the musical reality of his times but Mozart's hidden reality lay mostly in subtleties and details of musical form and execution, not in broad disjunctions. Chances are the high co-incidence between his vision of musical structure and conventional structure facilitated his mental tactic of doing much of the germ unfolding in his head. The reason is simple. The current musical schemas, the variation schemas he had developed in his own previous compositions, and his musical images of wide scope such as his "law of growing animation"—all would have been so familiar to Mozart he would not have needed to agonize over them very much. Since in most cases a new piece was unlikely to stray very far from previous schemas, he had only to determine how far and in what way in order to have at his command most of the information he needed to "see" how the piece would develop. Significantly, whenever Mozart attempted a new musical genre, or when later in his career he attempted more complex transformations of the inner parts of his works, the master's creative method shows signs of struggle. There is evidence of laborious sketches, erasures and corrections— enough to make poor Salieri's plodding heart warm.

Mozart liked to let as much of his germ as possible gather resonance in his head—until he could spill it out like magic on the score. In contrast, Beethoven left a fearful trail of his efforts scattered across the pages of his Sketchbooks. One wonders, however, if this contrast is so great as it seems.

Certainly as far as the origins of the germs themselves, the two composers had something in common.

Beethoven wrote:

You will ask where I get my ideas from. I cannot say for certain. They come uncalled, sometimes independently, sometimes in association with other things. It seems to me that I could wrest them from Nature herself with my own hands as I go walking in the woods. They come to me in the silence of the night or in the early morning, stirred into being by moods which the poet would translate into words, but which I put into sounds; and these go through my head ringing and singing and storming until at last I have them before me as notes.

Reportedly the E-major adagio in quartet op. 59 owed its beginning to Beethoven's contemplation of a starry night.

Beethoven recorded his germ inspirations in his Sketchbooks. When a subject like Bonaparte or Lenore or Coriolanus presented itself to him, he would search the Sketchbooks to see if it resonated with one of the musical-emotional germs (snatches of melodies, phrases and musical ideas containing omnivalent nuances) he had recorded there. Bringing these together would give birth to a piece.

The Sketchbooks also recorded his effort to work through the dynamics of his pieces, both in notes and in thoughts. For example, one section reads:

Perhaps the dissonances throughout the whole opera might not be quite resolved, or else in some totally different manner, for our civilized music cannot be concerned in such weird and desolate times.

The Sketchbooks show that Beethoven developed his musical seeds by crisscross routes, shifting and juggling context. Like Mozart, he was usually working on several pieces or parts of a piece simultaneously, or alternately. But unlike Mozart, he left a record of his mental process. Sometimes the pages of the Sketchbook which he left free for one composition or movement would get used up and the different composition or movement became intermingled (a converging network of enterprise), contributing to what one critic calls "the unity of his works, whether considered singly or in groups." Even when he reached the scoring stage, the revision continued and he would score many times, crossing out and rejecting passages in a messy hand. But through all this activity, the germ remained central.

I alter a great deal, discard it and try again until I am satisfied. And then inside my head I begin to work it out, broadening it here, restricting it there, deepening it and heightening it; and since I am conscious of what I am trying to do, I never lose sight of the fundamental idea [germ]. It rises up higher and higher, and grows before my eyes until I hear and see the image of it, molded and complete, standing there before my mental vision.

Unlike Mozart, Beethoven invented a new kind of music, what has been called the "heroic" style. His vision and talent did not fit as neatly into the schema he inherited as Mozart's had. It would be silly to talk about either composer being the greater genius. Each in his own way mastered the rigors of tuning into his vision, capturing germs and unfolding them into reflectaphoric form by means of what Stravinsky called "a harmony of varieties," that is, by making "dissonances," as Schönberg put it, "the remote of consonances." Mozart's and Beethoven's similarities allow us to value the wonderful differences in their creative personalities and the corollary differences in the ways they used reflectaphors to bring out hidden realities.

WHERE WAS THE GERM FOR RELATIVITY?

With the theory of general relativity, Albert Einstein restructured the meaning of Newton's laws of gravity and transformed the way we look at the cosmos. Question: What was the germ for this discovery?

Lightning flash:

A small boy marvels at the compass he sees in his father's hand. Its needle is held in an invisible field and the sight of this mystery excites in the five-year-old an emotional commitment to the theme of continuum, invariance and their associated nuances—and launches him toward a career in science. Was the germ here?

Lightning flash:

An adolescent who has failed his entrance exam to the polytechnic enrolls in a progressive school where his unusual mind is given free play so that the young man further crystallizes into a future in science. One day the adolescent dreams up a thought experiment—imagining himself astride a light ray, an image of wide scope. Was the germ here?

Lightning flash:

It is 1905 and an obscure twenty-six-year-old patent technician has just proposed the theory of special relativity which says that events in the continuum of space are relative. Was the germ of general relativity here?

Lightning flash:

Two years later, the now well-known inventor of special relativity is working on a journal article trying to extend his theory to cover gravity. He has an additional stimulus which puts his special relativity theory in a new context. He wonders why the scientific explanation for the electricity that is produced when a magnet moves relative to a conductor is different from the explanation of what occurs when a conductor moves relative to a magnet. Was this selective comparison (bisociation) the germ?

Lightning flash:

Einstein has had his "happiest thought," imagining that a person falling from the roof of a house would be both in motion and at rest. This janusian insight leads directly to his formulation of general relativity. Surely *this* was the germ.

INTER (flicking on the lights): Okay, I give up, which is it?

MUSING: You see my point.

INTER: No.

MUSING: "Germ" is only a relative (sorry) term. In a creative life there are points when vision coalesces and takes a specific form. But this action is like a vortex forming in a stream. The vortex or germ is inseparable from the overall flow. That's true not only for scientists like Darwin and Einstein who may work on a single problem for years. It's true of artists whose books or musical compositions are all interconnected. In fact, the real germ of any individual scientific discovery or artwork can never be precisely specified, only proximate germs. Proximate germs are lenses focusing the creator's vision at that moment. In art the germ-lenses lead to reflectaphoric structures. In science, the creator's discovery itself may not produce a reflectaphoric form, but as our lightning-traced sketch of Einstein's progress suggests, there can be something distinctly reflectaphoric in the pattern by which scientific creators make their discoveries. Perhaps that's because germs themselves reflect, like jeweled microcosms, the whole creative process.

For example, consider the similarity between germs and crystallizations and images of wide scope. In all three cases, the creator experiences an intimate and concrete insight into the vision, more: a momentary encapsulation of it. But germs, crystallizations and images of wide scope also have quite different roles to play in the creative activity. In crystallizations creators see a general direction for their career; in images of wide scope they discover a tool for use in many creative circumstances; in germs they see the incipient forms of particular projects. But more than other facets of creativity, germs have a special meaning for creators. Perhaps this is because a germ not only encapsulates the *prima materia* of vision, it highlights creativity's magic. A germ is as seemingly invisible and inconsequential as a grain of salt, yet it holds the secret power to unfold into an enduring artifact, a philosopher's stone, of truth. There are few things in the world as powerful and magical as that.

16

Companions in Quest

THE MYTH OF THE LONE CREATOR

Carefully mixing the volatile salt with mercury and sulphur, scrupulous in his quest of his philosopher's stone, the alchemist worked alone. Yet even in legend, no alchemist was truly alone. Surrounded by the texts of his predecessors, he began his work as their apprentice. Moreover, the legend is wrong. Alchemists collaborated all the time.

The Count of Cagliostro collaborated with the infamous hierophant Joseph Balsamo and a Greek named Altotas on alchemical researches that reaped no gold but discovered a process for mimicking silk from flax. Nicholas Flamel, a fugitive of the fourteenth century, reputedly succeeded in deciphering the book of the mystical Bath-Kôl and produced from its instructions the philosopher's gold—with the aid of his constant companion and wife, Perrenelle. Two centuries later Johann Valentin Andreae started the "invisible college" or Rosicrucians, organized to collect and share information among alchemists and occultists in much the same way the modern scientific community is organized.

But group alchemic quest has an even more venerable history. According to some texts, the search for the Holy Grail was an alchemic metaphor and the knights of the round table banded together harmoniously under Arthur to seek the cup which was in truth the philosopher's stone.

■

Like the legend of the lone alchemist, the legend of the lone creator is also wrong. In recent years, investigators have begun to appreciate that creators collaborate in all sorts of ways in order to do their work. In fact collaboration is one of the best kept secrets in creativity.

INDIRECT AND DOMESTIC COLLABORATIONS

A creator's first collaborations are usually during the apprenticeship period and take what could be called a "direct" or "indirect" form. The direct form finds the creators-to-be working with their more experienced mentors on actual creative projects. It's a form of collaboration common in the apprenticeships of scientists. For example, one study ascertained that as of 1968 two-thirds of the fifty-five American Nobel laureates in science had started out their careers working in the laboratories of previous Nobel laureates.

In indirect collaboration, the young creator is influenced by the attention and tutelage of an older colleague. Hemingway and Faulkner, for instance, collaborated indirectly with Sherwood Anderson, who gave both important inspiration and help toward literary careers. They quickly turned on him and did satires of his work, however, as if to rid themselves of his influence.

Most creators engage in some variety of a "domestic collaboration." This is where one partner in the collaboration doesn't participate very much directly or indirectly in the creative work but provides a support environment so the work can take place. Historically women have played this role. But not always.

We've already mentioned the support given to Virginia Woolf by her husband, Leonard, and to Georgia O'Keeffe by her husband, Alfred Stieglitz. As a writer himself and an editor, Leonard Woolf commented on his wife's writing and suggested changes. He wasn't in any sense her mentor or co-creator, however. His collaborative role was complex and interpretations of the psychodynamics of the Woolfs' marriage vary, but according to one reading, Leonard worked to keep his wife on an even keel and helped her through her mental crises.

Several years older than O'Keeffe, Stieglitz took the young painter under his wing because he admired her work. "What would you like to do?" he asked her shortly after she showed up at his studio in New York. "I'd like to go on painting." Stieglitz said, "I will make that possible." He did.

Theo van Gogh wasn't an artist of any kind, but he made his brother Vincent's creativity possible. Psychiatrist Gedo conjectures that Theo made a pact with Vincent, asking his brother to take up painting seriously in order to forestall Vincent's suicide. "Apparently, on his own, Vincent had been unable to accept his artistic vocation as a personal goal," Gedo says, but in collaboration with his brother it was possible. The pact was that Theo would support Vincent financially and psychologically, and in return Vincent would give Theo his paintings and would not take his own life. Shortly after he learned that Theo was fatally ill, Vincent carried out his deferred suicide.

The usual form of domestic collaboration is less dramatically symbiotic. Jesse Conrad's management of a household conducive to her husband's difficult temperament is typical. The domestic partner collaborates with the creator to create the conditions and foster the habits that make absorption and negative capability possible.

DIRECT COLLABORATIONS

In the history of creative genius there are a number of famous direct co-equal collaborations between mature creators. Picasso and Braque worked side by side to develop cubism. They criticized each other's paintings, exchanged theoretical ideas and each tried to make his pieces indistinguishable in style from the other's. Both men learned a great deal from the collaboration and later applied what they learned to their own evolving styles and visions. The list of Picasso's other direct collaborators is quite long and includes the creators Apollinaire and Jean Cocteau. There were also several women who became Picasso's domestic collaborators.

Werner Heisenberg was in something of an apprentice position to the older Niels Bohr, but they collaborated directly. Bohr stimulated Heisenberg to solve the problem that led to quantum mechanics and Heisenberg's solution stimulated Bohr to the idea of complementarity. Together the two hammered out the basis for modern quantum theory. But progress together wasn't always congenial. Heisenberg reported that Bohr reduced him to tears in one argument over the proper interpretation of Heisenberg's "uncertainty principle." Bohr collaborated regularly with many scientists.

A rather subtle direct, though seemingly indirect, collaboration is suggested by the tale of Darwin and Wallace. As Gruber has pointed out, the younger Wallace was stimulated in his thinking about evolution by reading Darwin's reports of his *Beagle* discoveries. Meanwhile, Darwin had developed the main points of his theory but delayed putting it all together. Partly he delayed because of his grave and justified fear that the theory would be violently attacked by Victorian society. Partly he delayed because of his obsessive desire to make sure the theory was absolutely correct before he released it. Despite having worked through the main issues, Darwin probably remained somewhat vague about the overall coherence of his ideas. It's a rule of creation that until you attempt to put something down in a finished form, you don't really know whether the whole thing works or not. Gruber has said Darwin tended to forget insights and then rediscover them. This propensity adds weight to the possibility that though Darwin had his complete theory, it was also significantly not complete in his mind. In 1856 Darwin finally set to work on a big book about his theory, but, according to Gruber "it would have been monstrous and would never have commanded the attention the *Origin* got."

Then in June 1858 Darwin received a package from the Malayan jungles which contained a bombshell. In a few pages, a penniless young naturalist whose existence Darwin had only recently become aware of summed up evolutionary theory with an elegance still admired by evolutionary biologists. The long-distance collaboration was complete. In July Darwin's scientific friends presented to the Linnaean Society Wallace's paper and evidence that Darwin had conceived the same theory some years before. A few weeks after the society's meeting Darwin began *On the Origin of Species,* a relatively concise and focused form of his ideas which he completed in under a year. One can't help but think that seeing Wallace's clear formulation of the theory had something to do with catalyzing and clarifying Darwin's thinking as well as giving him impetus to formally set down his ideas.

Sometimes direct collaboration between high-level creators produces very indirect beneficial results.

Ford Maddox Ford and Joseph Conrad wrote three novels together, none of them of note. Nevertheless, it is clear from the testimony of both men that real value was received from the effort. Conrad was subject to fits of exhaustion and despair about his writing which Ford helped him weather. When one of Conrad's manuscripts was accidentally burned up in the middle of a magazine serialization, Ford helped his friend reconstruct it. The two could spend hours discussing the connotations of some word Conrad was considering for one of his stories. Ford prodded his colleague for memories of his life at sea and took down what was said so that Conrad could later revise it; Ford also provided "a good deal of knowledge of the practical sides of English life that Conrad naturally ignored;" he corrected proofs of Conrad's stories; and he suggested subjects for stories because "I had a knack of getting hold of subjects that appealed to him." On the other side, Ford admitted that "I at least learned the greater part of what I know of the technical side of writing during the process" of collaboration.

The biographies of Conrad, Picasso, van Gogh, Bohr and

many other geniuses indicate that these creators were involved in a wide variety of collaborative relationships. For example, van Gogh collaborated domestically with his brother and indirectly with other artists—sharing self-portraits, paintings, and aesthetic ideas, maintaining what Brower calls "a complex network of correspondence with significant collaborators during his tenure of living alone." Van Gogh attempted a remarkable direct collaboration with Gauguin at Arles. For several weeks the two painters lived and worked together, visited museums and fell into heated discussions about art. Though short-lived and poorly ended, the experiment nonetheless helped van Gogh crystallize his vision.

Is there something about creativity that *demands* collaboration of one form or another?

When he returned from the *Beagle* voyage, Darwin made use of a number of scientific collaborators from the British Museum, experts in geology and zoology, to help him process into publication the volumes of data and specimens he brought back with him. Sternberg says, "In collaboration, you look for the other person to supply strengths you don't have." From his British Museum collaborators, Darwin needed technical help. However, it was unnecessary for these collaborators to share his creative vision or his intention to develop an evolutionary theory.

James Watson, however, needed another kind of collaborator. In physicist Francis Crick and X-ray crystallographer Maurice Wilkins, the microbiologist Watson found not only companions with the skills he needed to break the genetic code, but creators who were as passionate as he was about finding the secret of life. Each collaborator had his own vision (his own themata and nuances, sense of omnivalence), but these visions overlapped. Constant heated discussions kept their creative absorption at a peak. When one of the three would express an insight, it would be seized upon by the others, criticized or elaborated—given an importance it might not have had in an individual mind. Each scientist would judge the new insight in the light of his own themata to see if it resonated. It's evident from Watson's book that the dissonance among the visions and the differences in style, knowledge and talents allowed the team to propose and dispose of a great many possibilities, constantly shifting the elements of the context their data formed—until the whole fell into proper place.

In fact, some fields require direct collaboration as a condition for engaging in the creative activity. More and more this is becoming the case with science. Watson, Crick and Wilkins are one example. The atomic bomb project under the direction of Robert Oppenheimer is another. It is not unheard of these days for scientific papers to have more than a hundred authors. The vision directing large-team scientific research like the supercolliding experiments conducted at CERN in Switzerland is a collective one. A thousand people contributed to the CERN work that won Carlo Rubbia and Simon van der Meer their Nobel prizes in 1985. The collaborators presumably all agreed on the themata implicit in the grand unification theory which the experiments were designed to extend. However, the nuances the various researchers felt for these themata, the drive to formulate an individual-universal equation through their work and any sense of omnivalence and negative capability must have been unique for each individual.

Large-team collaborations usually have a driving force like Oppenheimer or Rubbia—someone whose individual vision and absorption is so powerful that it provides a focal point for the creative project.

In filmmaking the director, or sometimes the producer, takes this role. When the talented radio and theater director Orson Welles came to Hollywood in 1940 he was a rank amateur in film. He needed to learn quickly in order to produce his classic *Citizen Kane.* Welles started by talking to a host of film technicians—art directors, sound specialists, cinematographers—to see which ones he liked best. At night he would watch movies with them, discussing technique. He encouraged radical ideas from any source. His openness and ability to synthesize what others suggested into his own vision made *Kane* a remarkable creative enterprise. Below is Robert Carringer's description of how Welles worked with his director of cinematography, Gregg Toland:

Welles not only encouraged Toland to experiment and tinker, he positively insisted on it. . . . From the first days of shooting, they approached the film together in a spirit of revolutionary fervor. This atmosphere continued to characterize their relationship throughout the production. Those involved say there was a kind of running game between the two, with Welles coming up with one farfetched idea after another and challenging Toland to produce it and Toland delivering and then challenging Welles to ask for something he could not produce. Some of the devices Toland came up with he had already used in other films, but others were new or used in significantly new ways in *Citizen Kane.* One example is the distorted image of the nurse who enters Kane's death room. For this shot, Welles wanted a surreal effect, as if the camera were actually seeing through one of the broken pieces of glass. To accomplish this, Toland fitted the camera with one of his gadgets. . . . The result is a forerunner of the extreme wide-angle fish-eye lens that came into general use in the 1960s.

Gruber says, "Creative people must use their skills to devise environments that foster their work. They invent new peer groups appropriate to their projects. Being creative means striking out in new directions and not accepting ready-made relationships. . . ." Each creator therefore invents new forms of collaboration. Welles's collaboration with his technicians was different from that of Eisenstein, who had in place a disciplined platoon of people to work on films with him. Edison was one of the first scientists to use a team approach to invention; his team supplied him with special skills he didn't have and with dedicated comradeship; the vision, the projects and the images of wide scope were mostly his. Duke Ellington collaborated, as we have noted, by focusing on the musical identities of his players. According to one commentator, "As a piece was developing, it would frequently be up to the men in the sections to work out the harmonics, usually from chords

Duke would supply." Ellington "knew that each musician in the band had to make the music his own. He might do so by being left deliberately without instructions, discovering on his own what Ellington had intended him to." Einstein worked alone most of the time but was in constant contact with colleagues, sharing insights, asking questions.

▪

Growing realization of the extent to which creators collaborate is balanced by a growing realization of how difficult collaboration is.

Gruber has demonstrated this in an experiment. He and his colleagues invented a box which allows two people to peer into it and see the shadow cast by what is to them an unknown object. Because of the angle, each viewer sees a different shape to the shadow. Their task is to share the information about what they see in order to identify the object casting the shadow. For instance, if a cone is placed in the box, one viewer sees a circle, the other a triangle.

Gruber says that when he began the experiments he thought the collaboration would take place "like two astronomers taking a fix on the heavens from different positions, and they see the world in slightly different ways. They don't fight it out and they don't yield to each other. They take respectful advantage of the fact that one sees it from here and the other from there, and they put together a richer, more soundly based idea of what is really out there than either one could reach alone."

But that wasn't what happened. "Well, the first thing that happened—even though the situation had been carefully explained—is the *you're crazy phenomenon:* 'How can you see a triangle? I see a circle!' This was true with intelligent, highly educated adults."

Even with a simple object, like a cone, the viewers found it difficult to collaborate. "Observers have to develop a way of talking about it, free themselves of their preconceptions. Cognitive and communication problems exacerbate each other. The first 20 minutes often go badly. Over time the pair develop skills of communication and interpretation, and improve their work."

Creating a cooperative synthesis, Gruber and his colleagues discovered, is a surprisingly difficult thing to do.

But Gruber believes creative collaboration is a process we must come to understand. "The way that people retain their individuality while combining their efforts and talents in something that transcends them both—understanding that is vital to the survival of humanity." At the moment we know very little about this dimension of creative process.

DANCE TO THE GRAIL

When I told David Feldman that I was going to interview one of the founders of the Pilobolus Dance Theatre he jumped a little in his seat.

"My wife and I love them. But they're an anomaly. Virtually all my theories of creative development would say that what the people of Pilobolus did is impossible."

According to the story, Pilobolus grew out of a dance class attended in 1971 by two Dartmouth undergraduates, Moses Pendleton and Jonathan Wolken. At the time they took the class with a young teacher, Alison Chase, neither Pendleton or Wolken had ever studied dance before. Chase's teaching style for the non-dancers was free-form. Rather than imposing exercises or choreography, she let them explore balance and movement. Pendleton said of the class, "Since we couldn't stand on our own two feet, we stood on each others'." Wolken describes their early activity as making "collective shapes" and finding out "which of them would stand up and which would fall over."

Soon others joined the movement group and, Pilobolus was founded. By 1974 they were deeply immersed in their unique form of collective choreography and in a few years had soared to an important place in the dance world.

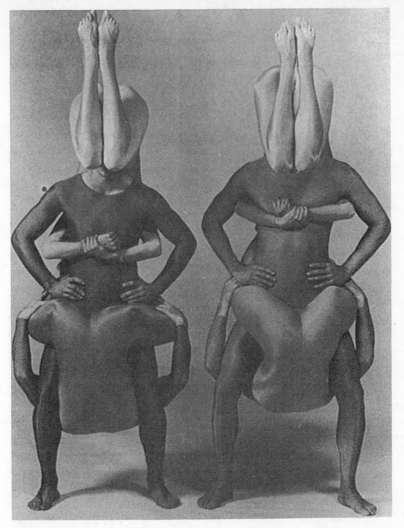

Figure 9 Shapes from the Pilobolus Dance Theatre.

Journalists and critics delight in describing the troupe's dances. A 1978 article in *Time* magazine proclaimed:

They slip with disconcerting ease from dance patterns in which they are sexually distinct figures, to movements in which they are asexual hominoids, and then further, to strange massings in which we see not

Figure 10 Shapes from the Pilobolus Dance Theatre.

figures but a wholly unfamiliar tree of elbows and buttocks, then a viscous fluidity of flesh that breaks like a wave, then a great, undifferentiated lump that slams itself about on the sculptor's table, startling us with its momentary resemblances to beasts remembered from dreams. . . . They glory, women and men, in chunks of muscle and spasms of energy, and their grace, like their abundant humor, is the careless result of motion. A body hurtles headfirst through the air, strikes another body—clay thrown at clay—and somehow sticks there, funny and graceful.

They have been described frequently as blobs of protoplasm or other biological creatures seen through a microscope. Arlene Croce, *New Yorker* critic, called their dance "a double-edged" frame of mind, where things are not as they seem, and every image carries more than one possible interpretation. They revolutionized the concept of dance.

"It should not have happened that they were able to do what they were able to do with as little background and training," Feldman said. "You're not supposed to be able to do dance without years of training. How could it have happened?" I promised to try to get an answer to his question when I interviewed Wolken.

A few weeks later in the spring of 1986 my wife, Joanna, and I drove down to Washington, Connecticut, where Pilobolus is headquartered, for the interview which took place on the tree-shaded back patio of an old house. In my initial letter to him I told Wolken I was interested in learning how the company's pieces evolve and in probing his own relationship to the collaborative creative process. On the phone, he had suggested we enroll in a workshop he was giving in Hadley, Massachusetts, near our home, in order to get a firsthand perspective on the process. I objected that though Joanna was a dancer, I was the furthest thing from it. "Nonsense! You're healthy, aren't you?" Consequently, several months after the interview I found myself in a dance loft with Wolken, Joanna, a few dancers and a few nondancer fans of Pilobolus I had inveigled into joining us. From what Wolken had told me in the interview about how his company works, I had a vague idea what to expect.

Virtually all the company's pieces are choreographed ensemble. According to Wolken, a piece usually emerges out of the hours troupe members spend together in free-form experiments with movement. The troupe meets in the early morning and during the generative phase, works in silence, pushing and pulling each other, tilting angles, pressures, stacking themselves, rolling. "We go in and simply start moving."

One member of the troupe may have a specific idea for a movement or some experience to share and the group explores it. "When I come into the studio I'm full of stories, ideas. I feed everybody a little something of that experience and it changes what we're working on. That's why I don't feel left out when somebody in the company goes off to do a project. I look forward to their coming back and sharing some of that. We borrow freely from everything, but that's okay.

After we're done with it, it won't look the same." He says he has the distinct feeling that "the collaboration is stronger than the individual." He relies on the energy of the other members of the company; they all keep each other going. "One of the nice things about group process, you appreciate people's differences. You learn to trust each other's differences." Each day is also different. The process "reacts to air pressure, whether you ate well." In the push and pull of the day's activities, the troupe is looking for something.

▪

Certainly I felt self-conscious standing in a line with Silvio, Cindy and Ila, facing the other students. Wolken wanted us to get a sense of what it meant to move coherently as a group. He told us to stand there and just fold and unfold our arms. "But make something happen," he said. Isolated individuals in a row, we folded and unfolded for several minutes. The effect was dreadful. Among the four of us there was no rhythm, no sense of order to when we moved; we were not together in any sense. "It's the 'restaurant effect,' " Wolken explained. "A lot of clatter. You can't read the movement." He stopped a moment and talked about "transparency," how the audience can see right into the truth, the authenticity (or inauthenticity) of your movements. Certainly I felt transparent standing there—and mighty inauthentic.

"Look. You want to work at the extremes," Wolken suggested. "Pattern, the edge of the room, clumping, randomness, synchronized movement. Those are extremes. Movement at the extremes the audience can read. Now I want to try something different." He ordered the four of us to wait with our arms folded and to all unfold them at exactly the same time. The task seemed impossible. If one of us started to unfold, it would be too late; we would not be coordinated. For what seemed an interminable time we stood there. Then by some single impulse all our arms went down. "Comments?" Wolken asked our audience. One woman said, "God, the tension waiting to see if they could do it was terrific." "That's it," Wolken said, "That's important."

▪

Wolken says that during one of their eight-hour days choreographing in the studio the members of Pilobolus are "watching thousands of movements." What they're looking for is a movement that's on the edge, a movement that's evocative, omnivalent. "It has to be evocative." The troupe as a whole decides. From time to time "a kind of group consciousness takes place" when they all agree that a particular movement has the evocative quality. "When you all agree on something, it's a punctuation. It's nailed down." The piece will be built on those agreed-on omnivalent moves. "These are germ cells that develop over time." From his description it's apparent that the germ moves are like crystals relating themselves to one another once a first crystal has been introduced. The germ moves become the core of the piece.

Gathering these core moves isn't easy in the group setting. Sometimes all but one member may feel a move is evocative. "Someone is imperious and you have to live with it and go on."

Some of the string of germ movements appear by "accident" in the push and pull of the daily studio activity. Others emerge from going over and over an "interesting" movement, focusing it. "The difference between a successful movement and an unsuccessful one is timing. Searching for something evocative you can go past it. Often you can work fruitlessly trying to get it right. No matter what you do, it doesn't shine." The company members also draw on "a closet full of movement" which they can introduce in the effort to tune new movements into resonance with the germs. From years of working together, they have a shorthand which allows them to evolve relatively quickly through the process of trying out moves and tuning them.

After about two weeks of this activity, the troupe has developed "a large balloon of germ moves. We write them down, group them in a rudimentary skeleton so we can identify the gaps and holes."

▪

Wolken wanted Philip, Schellie and Silvio to walk back and forth across the room. "See what happens." Nothing much for a while, and then Philip started pacing quickly and mechanically, swinging his

328 ■ John Briggs

*arms. Schellie watched him for a time as she walked back and forth
and then her rhythm seemed to become infected by his. Silvio strolled,
humped over a little, dejected. Soon Schellie and Philip were traveling
in sync, like lateral pistons, trying to entice Silvio into their rhythm.
He resisted and resisted, and we wondered if the omnivalence they were
creating would hold.*

*The three seemed a little amazed at what had happened once the
spontaneous piece was over. "You see, don't give in. You want to stay
on the edge of the tension."*

■

Once the core moves are grouped together into a loose
shape, the troupe associates certain of the moves with images
or a story. "You begin to find the piece's identity." The group
then starts to "knead" the images they see in the germ moves,
draw them out and find transitional moves to fill in the gaps.
"Movement comes first; motion and then emotion." At this
point they begin to think of the piece in terms of an imagery
"that does not explain itself fully," evocative imagery, imminent imagery, omnivalent imagery, the imagery of nuance.

The process of making transitions between the core moves,
developing the imagery or story, and adding the emotion to
the motion is "like tuning an engine." Wolken explains later
that he used to be a race-car driver and that he thinks of dance
as working on the edge like a racer driving "at the edge of the
envelope."

During the tuning "you average things out. What works on
one day might not on another. It's a long process. Even after
we've performed it, the piece continues to mature and we
might take it back and break it down to redo a section."

■

*Four of us were struggling with our afternoon's composition. Some
of it we liked, the rest was "restaurant effect." Wolken came over to
help us. "Use people's strengths rather than weaknesses," he advised.
"If you can stand on your head, use that." Then after whirling
around to demonstrate a move, his form resembling a concentrated*

halfback more than a dancer, he said, "Work it out, solve it. Find your own technique." Unlike dancers who stress the necessity for learning technique first, Wolken believes technique is only useful when you need to solve a particular problem, get a particular effect; then you learn or invent the technique you need. I suspect a good many creators would agree with him.

A little later, Wolken was helping Wendy, Mike and Ila tune their piece. "Don't put the hand up, slow down, let the gaps open up," he prodded somewhat impatiently. "Wait a beat. Let the audience expect something. A thousand things are going through their minds in that second. Then—now—you give them something. String the piece together with these coherent phrases, those tensions."

▪

I wouldn't presume to say what Wolken's creative vision is but it is certainly implicit in Pilobolus. He said that when he and Pendleton and Chase started they "had outrageous self-confidence." They felt sure that the shapes they discovered together in Chase's class were "right" somehow; they had uncovered a hidden reality that an audience would want to see. For Wolken the hidden reality seems to emerge from somewhere between two sides of a contrary. It's a contrary containing themata of continuity and discontinuity, and he repeatedly expresses it: "We have rules. You make the rules as you go. You see what rules work, then you figure out whether they're appropriate next time. This is definitely what I like in Pilobolus. Somebody says 'I'm bored' and boom, you're off into another direction." This paradoxical position also shows up in his habit of explaining a point very meticulously and then capping it with the phrase, "It doesn't matter" as if to ironically undercut and reestablish himself in the unknown.

The paradox is perhaps implicit in Wolken's background. Wolken's father is an biophysicist and Wolken himself spent time in his father's lab. The name of the troupe comes from biology. Pilobolus is an exploding, photosensitive mushroom. At Dartmouth Wolken was a philosophy major. Though the philosophical and scientific aspects of his vision are clearly evident in the analytical way he talks, when I asked him about philosophy and science he turned skeptical. "Their effort isn't put into questioning but into proving things." Again the paradox: down-to-earth precision and up-in-the-air questioning, at the same time.

But it isn't a paradox either, for the thrust of Wolken's creative work is clearly the grasping of some truth—not a scientific or philosophical truth—but a truth of movement. "First motion, then emotion," he says, stressing the sensory aspect of this truth. And "What I like is moving and being right there on the edge of what you do." It's a truth saturated with nuance—"evocative" he calls it—and with uncertainty. When Pilobolus first started, he said, their goal was a kind of "brinkmanship": making dance forms that appeared on the edge of toppling. Now the goal is evocation. He agreed that these are two shades of the same thing: two forms of omnivalence.

I asked him if he thought he could have developed a Pilobolus career, even a dance career, on his own. "We definitely couldn't have done this alone. We goaded each other on." The vision of Pilobolus is a collective one, reflected differently in each member.

So the simple answer to Feldman's question—How could the members of Pilobolus have developed so quickly into dancers?—is this: Creators ultimately don't care about genres or techniques or discipline except as these things can be used as instruments of vision. In most cases, extended apprenticeship may be necessary to unfold the vision. In other cases, not. In 1971, as they moved around Alison Chase's classroom studio, the future members of Pilobolus suddenly glimpsed on a neglected edge of the field of creative dance a hidden reality, like a glimpse of the fabulous castle which legend says housed the grail. They saw that by pooling their talents and their individual perspectives they had already come in sight of this reality. And they believed that if they continued to work together, then others might see it, too.

EPILOGUE

So ends this "construal" of the data about creative genius. A way of thinking about the subject which may be useful. You could consider what you've read as a kind of status report. In a hundred years much if not all of the speculation and science in books such as this may appear as quaint, as whimsical as the pre-Pasteur theory of spontaneous generation. Even so, I suspect the puzzle of creativity will not be solved. In fact, it seems just as likely that the puzzle will grow.

INTER (opening the door to a computer room): Ha. But what about this artificial intelligence? Maybe that will solve the problem.

MUSING: It might. "Artificial creativity" it's sometimes called. However, our construal suggests this is not likely to come to pass. Wholeness, nuance, omnivalence, truth, the drive for an individual-universal equation, these seem to me qualities difficult to program into a computer. Vision itself is a qualitative phenomenon. The profound alterations in worldviews that occur as a result of a creative genius in science and art are also qualitative. Could a computer be programmed to make such qualitative shifts? Ambivalence and nuance in the human mind exist as evidence of the limitations of our categories. Computers operate by categories. Could we construct categories that create nuance and omnivalence without engaging the computer in the old science fiction paradox of telling a machine to disprove its own logic?

David Peat, in examining "expert systems"—the current form of the quest for an artificial intelligence—concludes:

Society tends to praise those who have trained their minds to engage in hard intellectual work. But the lesson of the expert computer system may be that this intellectual labor is not that impressive after all. In fact "thinking," which has such a high premium in our society, may not be as significant as other activities of the mind. . . . Taken in this sense it may indeed be true that computers will soon be in a position to simulate much of what we take as thinking

331

but that does not necessarily mean that these computers will be particularly intelligent, creative, and capable of deep insight.

Some theorists have proposed different approaches from expert systems, where interacting feedback loops would allow creativity to *emerge* out of complexity. The hope is that a self-organizing structure of loops will form. Can something mechanical give birth to something nonmechanical? Or is it necessarily the reverse. But this is an old quandary and it would probably be rash to foreclose it. Anything is possible when it comes to creativity.

INTER: Another quandary or two, please. First, you've tried pretty hard to convince us that this creativity and genius thing doesn't depend on any one contingency such as having a particular talent. But you do claim it depends on the creator making what you call nuance and omnivalence central to their lives. Why do some people do that and others don't?

MUSING: As I've said, I believe we all experience these perceptions. An uncanny vibration in the patch of light on the wall, the reminiscent sound of a child's shout on a playground, the feel of a breeze on a sunny day—the sense of nuance, of "more" there than we have words or concepts for, the sense of being instantaneously in touch with the mystery and truth of existence. Everyone has such moments when they are outside of the categories of consensual reality and into a rich, hidden realm. Why do a few people devote their lives to explaining such perceptions while most let them go and anchor themselves in the consensual world? The fact is, I don't know. Probably there are as many reasons for giving supreme value to perceptions of a hidden reality as there are creative people who devote their lives to creativity. One creator may have come under the influence of a teacher or read a book that sparked off the drive; another may have exercised a talent which led to nuance or omnivalence; another may have had these perceptions (and the concommitant desire to express them) nurtured by homelife or experience. Perhaps it seems frustrating not to be able to pin down a specific cause why one person would self-organize around nuance and another would not. On the other hand, this means that creativity is basically a freedom. It means that at any time anybody may self-organize, self-create themselves into creativity, possibly even into genius.

However, this self-creation of creativity and genius is not a matter of will. A successful editor heard I was writing a book about creativity and pulled me aside one day to tell me that as a young man he had given all his energies to a dream of becoming a great writer—and he had failed. He challenged me to prove creativity and genius aren't something you're born with.

Perhaps this man wasn't as driven by the need to discover and express the truth of a hidden reality as he was driven by his image of becoming a literary genius. He spent six years—which is a long time—but he didn't spend his whole life. Later, he concluded he must have lacked the right genes, a special talent for language, the right personality type, or some other essential ingredient of creativity. But I believe he had all the ingredients for creativity. He just didn't distill them.

INTER: *Ergo* my second quandary. What is creativity?

MUSING: Ah, you've caught me out. So far I've been reluctant to neatly define it. The reason is that the most mechanical acts have some creativity in them. To speak any ordinary sentence is creative; to move about the world is creative; making a casserole from what you happen to find in the refrigerator is creative.

But I think now we can see that as common as creativity is, the total commitment of a life to the expression of creative truth is extremely rare. This is because high-level creativity and genius is not a particular trait or flash here and there but a sustained way of life, a self-organizing structure. Though I'm convinced that everybody possesses what creative genius is based on, a unique perspective and moments of omnivalence, great creators are rare because most of us don't allow a creative self-organizing structure to form. Instead, we permit our omnivalence to fade and our unique perspective to become homogenized into the general cultural perspective. Our ideas, opinions, beliefs, ambitions become important to us. They become more important than our fleeting perceptions of something "more," our unique but unformed vision which may at first seem only a subtle difference, a nuance, but can be a door into an immense, ultimately sharable, even universal way of seeing. Perhaps the secret of genius is simple. Like the alchemist's work to discover the right proportions of ingredients needed to make the fire in the crucible, it is simply the creator's analogous effort to step through that door.

Notes

PROLOGUE

Page 1 The Michael Polanyi epigraph is from *Personal Knowledge: Towards a Post-Critical Philosophy.* New York: Harper & Row, 1962, p. 124.

The Doris Wallace epigraph is from "Giftedness and the Construction of a Creative Life," in *The Gifted and Talented: Developmental Perspectives,* eds. Frances Degen and Marion O'Brien. Washington, D.C.: American Psychological Association, 1986, pp. 361–85.

INTRODUCTION: SMOKE FROM THE FIRE

Page 4 An account of Newton's alchemical inspiration for gravity can be found in Morris Berman, *The Reenchantment of the World.* Ithaca: Cornell University Press, 1981.

Page 5 What little I know about alchemy comes from portions of C. G. Jung's *Alchemical Studies,* Bollingen series 20, vol. 13. Princeton: Princeton University Press, 1967; from the Encyclopedia Britannica, 1958 ed., s.v. "Alchemy"; and three popular sources: Louis Pauwells and Jacques Bergier, *The Morning of the Magicians,* trans. Rollo Myers. New York: Avon Books, 1963; Richard Cavendish, *The Black Arts.* New York: Capricorn, 1967; and Arthur Edward Waite, *Alchemists Through the Ages.* New York: Rudolf Steiner, 1970. These sources give varying levels of credence to the claims of alchemy. The most enthusiastic—the Pauwells and Bergier book—goes so far as to associate ancient alchemy with certain processes in modern chemistry and nuclear physics.

Page 7 The anecdote about Gauss can be found in Gordon Rattray Taylor, *The Natural History of the Mind.* New York: Dutton, 1979, p. 257.

Ellington's late start: from E.J. Hobsbawm, "Slyest of Foxes." *The New York Review of Books* 34, no. 18 (19 Nov. 1987): 3.

Part of this list of geniuses who were youthful duffers comes from Taylor, and Alfred Hock, M.D., *Reason and Genius.* New York: Philosophical Library, 1960.

Tiepolo's feat is also reported in Hock, p. 65.

Page 8 Tesla's germ phobia is recounted in Margaret Cheney, *Tesla: Man Out of Time.* New York: Dell, 1981, p. 1.

Page 9 Genius and IQ: Two examples of the growing literature questioning IQ-type measures are Stephen Jay Gould, *The Mismeasure of Man.* New York: W.W. Norton, 1981; and Richard S. Mansfield and Thomas V. Busse, *The Psychology of Creativity and Discovery.* Chicago: Nelson-Hall, 1981. The problem-solving

334

idea of creativity is an old one. One recent theorist advocating this idea asserts that the same mental processes he went through when he came up with the spur-of-the-moment idea of using a quarter to make an emergency repair on his car's master cylinder are, at some greater increment, the creative processes used by an Einstein or Newton; genius as a matter of degree. The theorist is Robert Weisberg, *Creativity, Genius and Other Myths.* New York: W.H. Freeman, 1986, p. 5. Freud made perhaps the most famous attempt to paint a psychological profile for genius. He saw high creativity as a sublimation of sexual energy, a "special disposition" in which "The libido evades the fate of repression by being sublimated from the very beginning into curiosity" by some such childhood circumstances as befell Leonardo da Vinci. This analysis of creativity appears in Freud's "Leonardo da Vinci and a memory of His Childhood" in *The Complete Psychological Works of Sigmund Freud,* vol. 11, London: Hogarth Press, 1968, pp. 79–80. Many have argued for a link between creativity and madness. For a discussion of this see chapter 12 here. A psychiatrist who makes a case for the right-brain theory of creativity is Jan Ehrenwald, *The Anatomy of Genius: Split Brains and Global Minds.* New York: Human Sciences, 1984.

Included among those who have pointed out problems with maintaining a reductionist position are theoretical physicist David Bohm; theoretical chemist and Nobel laureate Ilya Prigogine; Alfred North Whitehead; systems theorist Ludwig Von Bertalanffy; and philosopher Henri Bergson. There are many others. The list is long and distinguished, though at the moment reductionism holds sway in science.

Conrad's statement about his "inward voice" is quoted in Frederick R. Karl, *Joseph Conrad: The Three Lives.* New York: Farrar, Straus and Giroux, 1979, p. 454.

Keller on mysticism in science: Evelyn Fox Keller, *A Feeling for the Organism.* New York: W.H. Freeman, 1983, p. 201.

Page 10 Hemingway on "mystery that does not dis-sect out": from Ernest Hemingway, *Selected Letters,* ed. Carlos Baker. New York: Charles Scribner's Sons, 1981, p. 770.

Page 11 On the work of the persons I interviewed: The reader should also be advised that I have not attempted to convey any of the serious academic debates about creativity circulating among these researchers. They do not always agree among themselves and they certainly don't agree with a great many other students of creativity. Rather than present these academic debates, my effort here has been directed toward creating a composite picture of the current research as it may be applied to the question of what vision is and how creators develop their expressions of it. A very many other interesting points about creativity I leave to my interviewees' own capable writings.

As far as the statements about creativity made by geniuses themselves go, there is the following problem: The reliability of creators' portrayals of their own creative experience has been questioned by a number of researchers. Some have even suggested that what creators say about how they work should be excluded from any scientific formulation of creativity. Researchers have pointed out, for example, that creators tend to have culturally influenced theories about how creativity works and that they express their experience in terms of those theories. However, one could counter that the theories creators hold about creativity must derive at least in part from their experience of creative process. It seems reasonable to say that creators are pretty perceptive people and are probably pretty attentive to what happens to them when they create. Such attention is an important part of the job of creating. Personally I suspect creators are as likely to be as honest and free of assumptions as any creativity researcher. Consequently, I have taken what creators have had to say about how they work very seriously. But it is true there are pitfalls. Sorting out the cultural cliches and self-serving statements of creators from the statements that offer real glimpses into creative process is not always easy. Crosschecking statements from different cultural, temporal and professional contexts helps.

It should be noted that crosschecking biographies against themselves also doesn't insure an objective reading. There are many famous instances where a mistake or myth from an early biographer becomes perpetuated unquestioningly by the generations of biographers who follow. In this case, all the biographies would agree and all would be wrong. There is also, of course, the problem of methodological assumptions that arise in intellectual history. For example, it would be difficult if not impossible for any modern biographer to avoid entirely the psychological assumptions about childhood and mental development that have grown up since Freud. Such assumptions undoubtedly strongly influence what "facts" turn up in a biography and the meaning given to those facts.

On my "broad-scale" approach of using as examples geniuses from many different fields and time periods: I would argue that with this approach it's possible to build a picture of genius that is not dependent on any particular biographical facts or interpretations. The object is to see what shape emerges when many facts and interpretations about and by geniuses of varying fields and epochs are all taken together. Such a rough and ready method doesn't by any stretch eliminate one's assumptions about creativity, but it at least subjects the assumptions to occasional scrutiny. When compiling this book, if I detected that some concern or experience showed up in a number of geniuses but not in one particular case, I was forced to ask why the particular case didn't fit. Was it because I didn't have enough information? Was it because of the presumptions of a biographer or of the genius himself about the creative process? Or was it because what I was looking at was not in fact common to genius? Some of my favorite ideas about genius were ruled out in this way.

Page 13 On the question of "moral giftedness" I am referred by David Feldman to a study currently being done on this subject by Ann Colby of Clark University and Bill Damon of Radcliffe under a grant by the Institute of Noetic Sciences in Sausalito, California. I regret not being able to include a discussion of this fascinating subject here.

I also regret that I have not been able to include significant material on creativity from non-Western cultures, though chapter 6 touches on this issue in a small way. What little I do know about non-Western creativity, suggests that the process described in *Fire in the Crucible* has many universal qualities. However, the concept of a "genius"—the individual historically important creator—is probably a Western invention.

PART 1: VISION AND THE *PRIMA MATERIA* OVERVIEW

Page 15 Nevelson's epigraph is from *Louise Nevelson in Process,* a film by Susan Fanshell and Jill Godmillow, prod. Perry Miller Adato (Corporation for Public Broadcasting, 1977).

Dickinson's lines are from the poem "There's A Certain Slant of Light," in *Final Harvest: Emily Dickinson's Poems,* ed., Thomas H. Johnson. Boston: Little Brown 1961, p. 36.

Conrad on "a moment of vision": from Joseph Conrad, *Typhoon and Other Tales.* New York: New American Library, 1925, p. 22.

Page 16 Octavio Paz on vision: Octavio Paz, *The Monkey Grammarian,* trans. Helen R. Lane. New York: Grove Press, 1981, p. 126.

Jung on the *prima materia* is from *Alchemical Studies* (5), p. 147.

Page 17 Gorden on painting is quoted in Marion Milner, *On Not Being Able to Paint.* New York: International Universities Press, p. *xii.*

Von Hartmann is quoted in Hock, *Reason and Genius* (7).

Page 18 Polanyi discusses vision in Michael Polanyi, "The Creative Imagination," in *The Concept of Creativity in Science,* eds. Dennis Dutton and Michael Kraus. Boston: Nijhoff, 1981, p. 93.

Virginia Woolf on a hidden reality. The passage is quoted and wonderfully discussed in Mark Hussey, *The Singing of the Real World: The Philosophy of Virginia Woolf's Fiction.* Columbus: Ohio State Press, 1986, p. 35.

Page 19 Gardner's statement about vision appears in Howard Gardner, *Art, Mind, and Brain: A Cognitive Approach to Creativity.* New York: Basic Books, 1982, p. 90.

Page 20 Polanyi on the hidden reality: Polyani, "The Creative Imagination," (18) p. 23.

CHAPTER 1: QUALITIES OF MIND

Page 21 Einstein on his lack of "mind muscles": I ran across this quote in an article by Joel Greenberg, "Einstein: The Gourmet of Creativity." *Science News* 115 (March 31, 1979): 216.

Page 22 Einstein's remarks about how the impact of the compass "never left me" are reported in Gerald Holton, "On Trying to Understand Scientific Genius." *The American Scholar,* 41 (Winter 1971–72): 98–99.

Einstein's remarks about the compass on his 74th birthday are quoted in Ronald W. Clark, *Einstein: The Life and Times.* New York: Avon Books, 1971, p. 29.

Einstein on the compass as containing something "deeply hidden," from Holton, "On Trying to Understand Scientific Genius": (22).

Page 23 The story of Einstein and the light ray is told in Gerald Holton, *Thematic Origins of Scientific Thought: Kepler to Einstein.* Cambridge: Harvard University, 1973, p. 358.

Pages 23–24 Einstein's enthusiastic reaction to the Schrödinger equation can be found in the selection of his letters from Karl Przibram, ed., *Letters on Wave Mechanics,* trans. Martin J. Klein. New York: Philosophical Library, 1967.

Page 24 Heisenberg's disgust over Schrödinger's theory and his effort to persuade Einstein of quantum mechanics is reported in Holton, *Thematic Origins* (23), p. 26.

Einstein's castigation of the "tranquilizing philosophy"" of quantum mechanics is from Przibram, *Letters,* (23–24).

Page 25 Einstein's comment that "I may have started it" is quoted in Holton, "On Trying to Understand Scientific Genius," (22): 99.

Page 26 On the notion that the themata are qualities: Historically the scientific method has been based on measuring quantities and a tradition has grown up that only the quantifiable is real. There is a current shift away from this tradition, which is synonymous with a shift from scientific reductionism to what might be called an emerging science of wholeness. For a discussion of the qualitative vs. quantitative world view see John Briggs and F. David Peat, *Turbulent Mirror.* New York: Harper & Row, 1989. One of the more relevant aspects of this discussion lies in the possibility that the qualities of the physical universe *precede* the quantifiable things we can measure—that there was symmetry, for example, before there were any measurable "things" to be symmetrical.

Holton's comments about a possibly early focus for themata come from one of my interviews with him.

Einstein's "feeling of direction": Holton, "On Trying to Understand Scientific Genius" (22): 103.

Page 28 The "merely personal" statement by Einstein is quoted in Holton, *Thematic Origins* (23), p. 110.

Einstein on "one of the strongest motives that lead persons to art and science": is quoted in Gerald Holton, *The Scientific Imagination: Case Studies.* London: Cambridge University Press, 1978, pp. 231–32.

Holton's observation of Einstein's childhood paradise comes from Holton, *Thematic Origins* (23), p. 111.

The claim of Einstein's dyslexia is reported and dismissed by Clark, *Einstein: The Life and Times,* p. 27. The idea that music acted as a "psychological safety valve" is also from this source, p. 29.

The "songs to God" information comes from one of my interviews with Holton.

Page 29 On chunking: David Perkins and Howard Gardner, among other researchers, have questioned the reliability of creators' memories of their early experiences. It is well to be aware of this problem. See also note for (11–12).

Pages 30–31 Holton's comment about the thema of discreteness and Heisenberg's proposal of the thema of symmetry are both from Gerald Holton, *The Scientific Imagination* (28), p. 19. The Einstein quote about "adhering to the continuum" is also from this source, p. 24.

Holton's idea that at any given moment in scientific history scientists in a field share common thematic perceptions bears some resemblence to Thomas Kuhn's notion that scientists of a period share a "paradigm." The paradigm revolutionary—like Einstein—would be the scientist who sees things differently, the one who dwells, in Holton's terms, on different themata from those implied in the approach to nature being taken by the majority of the scientist's colleagues.

Page 32 Holton's suggestion about the effect of switching fields came up in one of my interviews with him.

Page 33 Hovey's work on Franklin and Keegan's on Darwin are both cited in Howard Gruber and Sara N. Davis, "Inching Our Way Up Mount Olympus: The Evolving Systems Approach to Creative Thinking" in *The Nature of Creativity,* ed. Robert J. Sternberg. Cambridge: Cambridge University Press, 1988. The work by both Hovey and Keegan was doctoral work done under the direction of Gruber.

Page 34 On themata as a "basic toolbox of primitive perceptions": Howard Gardner said in my interview with him that he thinks there might be a link between Holton's themata and very early childhood patterns of apprehending the world. Gardner speculates about these childhood perceptual patterns in Howard Gardner, *Arts and Human Development: A Psychological Study of the Artistic Process.* New York: Wiley, 1973.

On themata in the arts: Holton says that he borrowed the idea of themata from anthropologists and folklorists. However, folklore themes such as the descent into the underworld seem not of the same order as Holton's themata in science. I suspect that there is a more direct connection, such as the one I try to describe in my reply to Interrogator.

Page 35 Conrad on "solidarity": from Conrad, *Typhoon* (15), p. 20.

CHAPTER 2: SUBTLE VIBRATIONS

Page 36 Woolf's St. Ives memory is from Virginia Woolf, "A Sketch of the Past" in *Moments of Being.* London: Granada, 1976, p. 75.

Gordon's comment on the rhythm of the waves permeating Woolf's fiction is from Lyndall Gordon, *Virginia Woolf: A Writer's Life.* New York: W.W. Norton, 1984, p. 43.

Page 37 Love on Woolf's "early memories": Jean O. Love, *Virginia Woolf: Sources of Madness and Art.* Berkeley: University of California, 1977, p. 9.

Virginia Woolf, *The Waves.* New York: Harcourt, Brace, Jovanovich, 1931, p. 9.

Page 38 Virginia Woolf, *Mrs Dalloway.* New York: Harcourt, Brace & World, 1953, pp. 3, 11.

Virginia Woolf, *Jacob's Room.* New York: Harcourt, Brace & World, 1959, p. 7.

Page 39 That St. Ives was only one of many nuances is indicated clearly in Woolf, "A Sketch of the Past" (36), p. 78.

340 ■ John Briggs

Some other nuances are mentioned in Gordon, *Virginia Woolf* (36), p. 7.

Woolf's comment that all her life was "built on that" is quoted in Love, *Virginia Woolf: Sources* (37), p. 226.

Woolf on "what is meant by 'reality' ": from Virginia Woolf, *A Room of One's Own.* London: Hogarth Press, 1927, reprinted 1977, pp. 165–66.

Page 40 Keats on the passage from Shakespeare quoted in Aileen Ward, *John Keats: The Making of a Poet.* New York: Viking Press, 1963, p. 273.

Ansel Adams on Edward Weston's rock: from Ansel Adams, *Camera and Lens: The Creative Approach.* Dobbs Ferry, N.Y.: Morgan & Morgan, 1970, p. 24.

Beethoven on where his ideas came from: Paul Mies, *Beethoven's Sketches: An Analysis of His Style Based on a Study of His Sketch Books,* trans. Doris L. MacKinnon. New York: Dover, 1974, p. 159.

Pages 40–41 Georgia O'Keeffe's memory is from *Georgia O'Keeffe.* New York: Viking Press, 1976, p. 1.

Page 41 Louise Nevelson's memory of the trip from Russia is from Louise Nevelson, *Dawns & Dusks: Taped Conversations with Diana MacKown.* New York: Charles Scribner's Sons, 1976, p. 6. The memory of the running horse is also from this source, p. 15.

Page 43 Manuel on Newton: Frank E. Manuel, *A Portrait of Isaac Newton.* Cambridge: Harvard University, 1968, p. 84.

Page 44 Gruber reports on the wildness nuance in Howard Gruber, "Darwin's 'Tree of Nature' and Other Images of Wide Scope," in *On Aesthetics in Science,* ed. Judith Wechster. Cambridge: MIT Press, 1978, pp. 122–39. Other information about this nuance is from my interview with Gruber.

Some of the Tesla information here comes from Cheney, *Tesla: Man Out of Time* (8). Other Tesla information comes from David Peat and Andrew Michrowski in letters and personal interviews.

Page 45 The story of Tesla's pump episode is told in Cheney, *Tesla: Man Out of Time* (8), p. 8

Peat's quote about resonance is from his book about Tesla: David Peat, *In Search of Nikola Tesla.* Bath: Ashgrove, 1963, pp. 27–29.

Page 46 The story of Curie's attraction to nuance is told in Robert Reid, *Marie Curie.* New York: Saturday Review Press, 1974.

Page 47 A further note here about nuance: In a letter to me Howard Gruber suggested that the way I was using the term nuance seemed to include several ideas which could be segregated from one another: nuance as shades of meaning, nuance as a recombination of meanings, and nuance as the result and cause of nonlinear shifts that take place in creative process. These are the three he mentions. Probably there are also other dimensions or subclasses of nuance that could be discriminated. However, I decline to discriminate them. The fact is I have intentionally resisted drawing too fine a definition for the term nuance because I believe that in too fine a definition the concept would lose its meaning altogether. The concept of nuance is itself a nuance, in other words. Holton's concept of themata, in my view, is in a similarly delicate position. For example, from one perspective, the thema of continuum is distinct from the thema of invariance. But from another perspective they shade into each other. This is even true for opposing themata like continuum and discreteness. By nuance I mean to describe just those areas where our categorical discriminations shade into each other. It is in those areas, I believe, that creativity finds nourishment.

CHAPTER 3: THE OPEN BRAIN

Page 48 Gray's account of how the feeling tone idea came to him is in William Gray, "Understanding Creative Thought Processes: An Early Formulation of the Emotional-Cognitive Structure Theory." in *Man Environment Systems* 9, no. 3 (January 1979): 3.

Report of research indicating that recalling facts you learned is facilitated by being in the same mood you learned them in: from "Post-Learning Shock Induces State-Bound Recall." *Brain/Mind Bulletin* 11, no. 15 (September 29, 1980).

Page 49 The quote beginning "the emotional coding of cognitions" is from Gray, "Understanding Creative Thought" (48), p. 2.

Page 50 LaViolette's observations here are from my interview with him.

LaViolette points out that Maclean's theory is not directly related to the emotional cycle theory. In fact, he says the emotional cycle hypothesis "suggests that the three brains operate together." The LaViolette theory, he notes, "uses the triune theory's divisions of the brain in its explanations but is quite different in its general thrust." Accordingly, it is the divisions that I'm focusing on here, so as to clarify how the emotional cycle process is said to work.

Page 52 A report of the Hubel and Weisel experiments can be found in David H. Hubel and Torsten N. Weisel, "Brain Mechanisms of Vision" in *The Brain.* San Francisco: W.H. Freeman, 1979, pp. 84–93.

Daniel N. Stern, *The Interpersonal World of the Infant.* New York: Basic Books, 1985.

Woolf's observation about the fusion of senses in her early memories is reported in Love, *Virginia Woolf: Sources* (37), p. 224. Woolf's memory of her mother's dressing gown is from Woolf, "A Sketch of the Past" (36), p. 76.

Page 53 The quotation from Gray about "wondering" is from Paul A. LaViolette, "Thoughts about Thoughts About Thoughts," *Man-Environment Systems* 9, no. 1 (January 1979), p. 20.

Page 54 Woolf's memory of the trip from London to the St. Ives nursery reported in Woolf, "A Sketch of the Past" (36), p. 76.

LaViolette's description of the PCDT loop is from Paul LaViolette, "Thermodynamics of the 'Aha' Experience." Paper presented at 24th Annual North American Meeting of the Society for General Systems Research, Symposium on Psychotherapy, Mind and Brain, San Francisco, California, Jan. 10, 1980, p. 6.

Pages 54–55 The quote fragment beginning "to the point where it would massively transform" is from LaViolette, "Thoughts about Thoughts" (53). He was speaking generally here, not specifically about Woolf's experience, but the statement fits, so I adopted it.

342 ■ John Briggs

Page 56 The idea that creators have an inborn sensitivity to nuance: Phyllis Greenacre, *The Quest for the Father.* New York: International University Press, 1963, p. 15. The difficulty, of course, is to determine just what is meant by a sensitivity being inborn.

Woolf on the past "as an avenue lying behind": Woolf, "A Sketch of the Past" (36), p. 78.

LaViolette's statement about tuning into feelings is from my interview with him.

Page 57 What happens when you look at a tree is part of a wonderful discussion of creativity in Erich Fromm, "The Creative Attitude" in *Creativity and Its Cultivation.* New York: Harper & Row, 1959, pp. 54–56.

Woolf on "lying in a grape": from Virginia Woolf, "A Sketch of the Past" (36), p. 76.

Woolf's difficulty with language is reported in Love, *Virginia Woolf: Sources* (37), p. 218. Love's comment about the "protoplasmic accident" is also here, on pp. 226–27.

Page 58 De Beauvoir's memory of her difficulties with language is quoted in Simone de Beauvoir, *Memoirs of a Dutiful Daughter.* Cleveland: World, 1959, pp. 19–20.

Page 59 Einstein's explanation of why he was the one to develop relativity is reported in Clark, *Einstein: The Life and Times* (22), pp. 27–28. The curious relationship between deficit and discovery suggested by this statement is discussed in chapter 8.

LaViolette comments on "priming" and how Woolf kept the St. Ives memory alive are from my interview with him.

Page 60 Newton's famous statement on keeping the problem before him is quoted in Manuel, *A Portrait of Isaac Newton* (43), p. 86.

Pages 60–61 The LaViolette exchange here is from my interview with him.

Page 61 Some relevant publications by Bergström are "An Entropy Model of the Developing Brain," *Developmental Psychobiology* 2, no. 3 (3 July 1969): 139–52; "Neural macrostates: An Analysis of the Function of the Information-Carrying Systems of the Brain," *Synthese* 17 (1967): 425–443; and "Quantitative Aspects of Neural Macrostates," *Cybernetic Medicine* 1 (1973): 9–17.

Pages 62–63 Bergström's descriptions of the nonspecific state, including the "possibility cloud," come from his discussion of his ideas during a "Conference on Meaning" held at The Isle of Thorns, Sussex, Great Britain, 1986.

On the concept of "synaptic space": from Bergström, "Creativity, Brain and Language." I have this paper in manuscript. I don't know where it was published. Bergström informs me in a letter that he is pleased to see that his phrase describing this struggle for synaptic space as "neuro-Darwinism" is catching on.

The effect of alcohol on the brain is discussed in a paper called "Alcohol, Creativity and the Brain," which I also have only in manuscript.

Pages 63–64 Faraday's description of light and shade is quoted in L. Pearce Williams, *Michael Faraday: A Biography.* New York: Basic Books, 1965, p. 82.

Page 64 Edelman's theory is described in numerous publications including Gerald M. Edelman and Vernon B. Montcastle, *The Mindful Brain: Cortical Organization and the Group-Selective Theory of Higher Brain Function.* Cambridge: MIT Press, 1982; and Israel Rosenfield, "Neural Darwinism: A New Approach to Memory and Perception" *The New York Review of Books* 33, no. 15 (9 October 1986): 21–27. Rosenfield's article is an excellent and lucid review of the development of Edelman's theory.

Research which has found the large number of neuronal connections in children's brains was reported in Sandra Blakeslee, "Rapid Changes Seen in Young Brain." *The New York Times,* 24 June 1986, p. C1.

Page 65 Sessions' statement on "those primitive movements" is quoted in Brewster Gheslin, *The Creative Process.* New York: New American Library, 1952, p. 46.

Page 66 Jenkins on Edison's game: This material comes from my interview with Jenkins.

CHAPTER 4: AS ABOVE, SO BELOW

Page 67 Quotation about adepts' attempts to copy the seven days of creation is from Cavendish, *The Black Arts* (5), p. 152.

Page 68 Woolf trying to compose "the perfect whole" of her experience: from Love, *Virginia Woolf: Sources* (37), p. 6.

Holton lists wholeness as one of his one hundred or so themata. It appears, however, to be a theme common to all creators in one form or another.

Dickinson's statement, "my country is truth," appears in Richard B. Sewall, *The Life of Emily Dickinson.* New York: Farrar, Straus and Giroux, p. 10.

Page 69 Dictionary definition of truth: Henry Cecil Syld, ed. *The Universal English Dictionary.* London: Routledge & Kegan Paul, s.v. "truth."

Page 70 Kandinsky on truth: Wassily Kandinsky, "Reminiscences," in *Modern Artists on Art,* ed. Robert L. Herbert. Englewood: Prentice-Hall, 1964, p. 39.

Page 71 Heidegger on truth: from Martin Heidegger, *Existence and Being.* Chicago: Henry Regnery Co., 1949, pp. 292–324.

The Emily Dickinson quote on "slant truth" is from Johnson, *Final Harvest* (15), p. 248. One might take Dickinson even farther and argue that in fact the only way to tell the truth is to tell it slant because it is in its essence a slanted or perpetually tangential phenomenon, a matter of nuance.

Faulkner on truth: from Michael Milgate, *The Achievement of William Faulkner.* New York: Random House, 1966, p. 152.

Page 71 All quotes from Conrad that follow here are from Conrad, *Typhoon* (15).

Page 72 On "visualizing": from Adams, *Camera and Lens* (39), p. 15.

On Dickinson's audience: A creator's motivation to create using public language is not only a motivation to share their vision with others but also to understand and to discover the vision through the public language.

Artist's "love affair with the world": Phyllis Greenacre, "The Childhood of the Artist: Libidinal Phase Development and Giftedness" (1957), reprinted in *Emotional Growth: Psychoanalytic Studies of the Gifted and a Great Variety of Other Individuals.* New York: International Universities Press, 1971, p. 490.

344 ■ John Briggs

Page 73 The Conrad quote here is from Conrad, *Typhoon* (15), p. 21.

Duncan on "my art" is from Isadora Duncan, *Isadora: The Autobiography of Isadora Duncan.* New York: Award Books, 1968, p. 9.

Page 75 Kuhn's discovery about science and truth is contained in Thomas S. Kuhn, *The Structure of Scientific Revolutions.* Chicago: University of Chicago Press, 1970, and *The Essential Tension: Selected Studies in Scientific Tradition.* Chicago: University of Chicago Press, 1977. See especially p. 103 of the former and p. 289 of the latter.

Max Black on metaphors and models: Max Black, *Models and Metaphors: Studies in Language and Philosophy.* Ithaca: Cornell University Press, 1962.

Jenkins' comments on technology came up in my interviews with him.

Page 76 McClintock on "everything is one": Keller, *A Feeling For* (9), p. 204.

Einstein on the universe as a "significant whole": Albert Einstein, *Ideas and Opinions.* New York: Dell, 1973, p. 48.

Page 77 Darwin quotes here: The first is from Hock, *Reason and Genius* (7), p. 86. The second is from Howard Gruber, "The Self Construction of the Extraordinary" in *Conceptions of Giftedness,* eds. Robert J. Sternberg and Janet E. Davidson. Cambridge: Cambridge University Press, 1986, p. 260.

Nevelson on the purpose for "being here": Nevelson, *Dawns & Dusks* (41), p. 24.

Wordsworth seeing into the life of things: from "Lines Composed a few Miles Above Tintern Abby, on Revisiting the Banks of the Wye, During a Tour July 13, 1798." See William Wordsworth, *The Poems,* vol. 1, ed. John O. Hayden. Harmondsworth: Penguin Books, 1977.

Information about Bohr's sense of chosenness comes from one of my Holton interviews.

Pages 77–78 Woolf's ambition is spelled out in Gordon, *Virginia Woolf* (37), p. 92.

Page 78 Watson's ambition is eloquently revealed in James D. Watson, *The Double Helix.* New York: Atheneum, 1968.

Klee's on humility: from Paul Klee, "On Modern Art" in *Modern Artists on Art* (70), p. 77.

Faulkner's idea that "someone else would have written me" is from Jean Stein, "William Faulkner: An Interview" in *William Faulkner: Three Decades of Criticism,* eds. Frederick J. Hoffman and Olga W. Vickery. New York: Harcourt, Brace & World, 1960, p. 67.

Page 79 Proust is quoted in an excellent article by V.S. Naipaul, "On Being a Writer," *The New York Review of Books* 34, no. 7 (23 April 1987): 7.

The facts here about Dickinson and her poems are from Sewall, *The Life of Emily Dickinson* (68), p. 6.

Page 80 The concepts of "self-asserting" and "self-transcending" are discussed in Arthur Koestler, *The Act of Creation.* New York, Macmillan, 1964.

Keat's statement about "Men of Genius" is quoted in Aileen Ward, *John Keats: The Making of a Poet.* New York: Viking Press, 1963, pp. 138–39.

Fromm on creator becoming one with the world: from Fromm, "The Creative Attitude" (57), p. 51.

Hollander's memory of his first contact with the keyboard comes out in "Child's Play: Prodigies and Possibilities," *Nova* (Boston: WGBH, 1985).

Sartre on writing as existing: from Jean Paul Sartre, *The Words: The Autobiography of Jean-Paul Sartre*. New York: George Braziller, 1964, p. 153. Before leaving the list of creators exhibiting the humility-conceit paradox, I would like to add Picasso. There is a story that before a show at the Louvre Picasso was allowed to hang his paintings in the galleries next to the old masters. He delighted in the comparison and felt that he was their equal: conceit. But it is also well known that in his later years the master said that he had always felt he wasn't really an artist but an entertainer, a fraud: humility. I suspect the humility-conceit paradox has something to do with the creator's negative capability, as discussed in chapter 5. For example, there is a curious amalgam of humility and conceit implied in Leonardo's advice that the painter who doesn't doubt will accomplish little.

Tesla's belief that his work was a matter of life and death is reported in Nikola Tesla, *My Inventions*. Zagreb: Skolska Knjiga, 1977, p. 44.

Page 81 Van Gogh's feeling about his work is explored in John E. Gedo, M.D., *Portraits of the Artist: Psychoanalysis of Creativity and Its Vicissitudes*. New York: The Guilford Press, 1983, p. 113.

Beethoven's depression is reported in Maynard Solomon, *Beethoven*. London: Granada, 1980, p. 171.

Holton's comment on the creator's work as a life and death issue is from one of my interviews with him.

Page 82 Faulkner on his work as a "keystone of the universe": from Joseph Blotner, *Faulkner: A Biography*, vol. 2. New York: Random House, 1974, p. 1576.

The observation of Faulkner's literary biographer about Yoknapatawpha as an inexhaustible kingdom: from David Mintner, *William Faulkner: His Life and Work*. Baltimore: Johns Hopkins University, p. 80.

Welty's report of her sense of characters whose lives "already existed" is from Eudora Welty, *One Writer's Beginnings*. New York: Warner, 1984, p. 108.

Mozart's famous description of his process quoted in Gheslin, *The Creative Process*, p. 45.

Descartes' holistic endeavor to find "the universal principle" is described in Jack R. Vrooman, *René Descartes: A Biography*. New York: G.P. Putnam, 1970, p. 78.

On the question of the creator seeking an underlying unity through the "network of enterprises": Gruber has written me to caution that sometimes a creator gets into a project that is *not* related to the central purposes. (S)he has, in Gruber's words, "some project that is just a flyer."

Page 83 The difference between creative work and "work in the marketplace": from Vera John-Steiner, *Notebooks of the Mind: Explorations of Thinking*. Albuquerque: University of New Mexico Press, 1985, p. 221.

Turgenev's comment on need for an integral self is quoted in Radoslav A. Tsanoff, *The Ways of Genius*. New York: Harper & Row, 1949, p. 38.

LaViolette on the importance of a creator's interest in the nature of reality is from my interview with him.

Page 84 Nevelson on the dowel: from Nevelson, *Dawns & Dusks* (41), p. 81.

Koestler on the intersection of "trivial" and "absolute" planes from Koestler, *The Act of Creation* (80), p. 365.

Mondrian's equation from Piet Mondrian, "Plastic Art and Pure Plastic Art" in *Modern Artists on Art* (70), p. 116.

Page 85 Description of Mona Lisa is from H. W. Janson and Dora Jane Janson, *The Picture History of Painting: From Cave Painting to Modern Times.* New York: Washington Square Press, 1957, p. 88.

Page 86 The article on computer analysis of Mona Lisa is by Lillian Schwartz, "Leonardo's Mona Lisa" *Art & Antiques* (January 1987): 50–54.

Page 87 The interpretation of Van Gogh's painting as self-portrait: from Albert Lubin, *Stranger on the Earth.* New York: Holt, Rinehart & Winston, 1972.

Page 88 Stravinsky on the "harmony of varieties": from Igor Stravinsky, *Poetics of Music in the Form of Six Lessons.* Cambridge: Harvard, 1970. Bernstein's point about musical metaphor is made in Leonard Bernstein, *The Unanswered Question: Six Talks at Harvard.* Cambridge: Harvard University Press, 1976. Schoenberg's idea of music as "reshaping of a basic shape" is quoted in Howard Gardner, *Frames of Mind: The Theory of Multiple Intelligences.* New York: Basic Books, 1983, p. 102. The idea that "dissonances are the remote of consonances" is from Arnold Schoenberg, *Style and Idea.* New York: Philosophical Library, 1950, p. 105.

A discussion of how the structure of artworks is made up of reflections can be found in John Briggs, "Reflectaphors: The (Implicate) Universe as a Work of Art" in *Quantum Implications,* eds. David Peat and Basil Hiley. London: Routledge & Kegan Paul, 1987, pp. 414–36. Hemingway on parts representing the whole: from Ernest Hemingway, *Death in the Afternoon.* New York: Charles Scribner's Sons, 1960, p. 278.

Leonardo's description of visual reality is quoted in Antonina Valletin, *Leonardo da Vinci: The Tragic Pursuit of Perfection,* trans. E.W. Dickes. New York: Viking Press, 1938, pp. 151–52. The second da Vinci quote here is from p. 111 of this source.

CHAPTER 5: CONTRARIES

Page 90 Description of polarities in Woolf's personality: Love, *Virginia Woolf: Sources* (37), p. 4.

Portrait of Mead's opposition: from Jane Howard, *Margaret Mead: A Life.* New York: Facwett Crest, 1984, p. *xiv.*

Chaplin's polarities: from David Robinson, *Chaplin: His Life and Art.* New York: McGraw-Hill, 1987.

Welles's shy confidence reported in Barbara Lemming, "Orson Welles: The Unfulfilled Promise." *New York Times Magazine,* 14 July 1985.

Edison's polarities reported in Robert Conot, *Thomas A. Edison: A Streak of Luck.* New York: DaCapo, 1979, p. 20.

Faulkner's "conflicting urges": from Mintner, *William Faulkner* (82), p. *x.*

Page 91 Studies of the androgynous characteristic of creative personality: from Frank Barron et al., *New Directions in Psychology II.* New York: Holt, Rinehart and Winston, 1965, pp. 40, 90.

Studies of the manic-depressive tendency of artists: from Constance Holden, "Creativity and the Troubled Mind," *Psychology Today* (April 1987): 9–10. See also Holden's book *Manic-Depressive Illness.* London: Oxford University Press, 1987. A discussion of some of the difficulties with these studies and with the equation of pathology and creativity appears in chapter 12 and in the notes for that chapter.

Holton's essay about creative polarities has already been referred to here: Holton, "On Trying to Understand Scientific Genius" (22).

Page 92 Bohm's argument on the Einstein's notion of "signal" as a discrete element of the continuum is drawn out in David Bohm, *Wholeness and the Implicate Order.* London: Routledge & Kegan Paul, 1980 and is discussed in John P. Briggs and F. David Peat, *Looking Glass Universe.* New York: Simon and Schuster, 1984.

Darwin's wildness and simplicity themata are discussed (though the term themata is not used) in Howard E. Gruber, "Darwin's 'Tree of Nature' and Other Images of Wide Scope," *On Aesthetics in Science* (44), pp. 120–40.

Page 93 The quoted phrase about the *prima materia* comes from Cavendish, *The Black Arts* (5), p. 147.

Page 94 Rothenberg's comment here about the "high level of ambivalence" in creators is from one of my interviews with him.

Da Vinci pulled "to and fro" from Vallentin, *Leonardo da Vinci* (88), p. 25. The description of Leonardo as "full of distress" and "self-accusation" is from p. 533 of this source.

Page 95 The description of Leonardo's relationship with Salai is from Ehrenwald, *Anatomy of Genius* (8), p. 63.

Page 96 The bird incident reported in Vallentin, *Leonardo da Vinci* (88), p. 1. Freud thought the incident with the bird was a fellatio fantasy indicating young Leonardo's confusion between the penis and his mother's nipples. See citation (94) here.

Da Vinci's assertion that "that painter who has no doubts will achieve little" is reported in Vallentin's biography (88), p. 236.

The principal biography of Beethoven I am working with here is Solomon, *Beethoven* (81).

Page 98 Solomon identifies the "immortal beloved" as Antonie Brentano, an acquaintance of Beethoven in Vienna. The author's argument sounds plausible but I'm not familiar with the scholarship of the controversy. The quote which begins, "Your love makes me" is from p. 263 of Solomon's biography.

Beethoven's complaint, "Thou mayst no longer be a man" is from p. 265 of Solomon's biography. The observation about *Fidelio* as "a seething compound" is on p. 278, and about Beethoven's "striving to free" on p. 201.

Page 99 Mary Gedo's assessment of Picasso's ambivalence toward women is from Mary Mathews Gedo, *Art as Autobiography.* Chicago: University of Chicago Press, 1980, p. 79.

Getting Picasso up in the morning is described in Françoise Gilot and Carton

348 ▪ John Briggs

Lake, *Life with Picasso.* New York: McGraw-Hill, 1964, p. 157. Picasso on how he paints is from p. 59 of this source.

Page 100 The story of Newton's miraculous survival is reported in Manuel, *A Portrait of Isaac Newton* (43), pp. 23–24. This is also the source of all the following quotes on Newton. The "Kindred" and "Titles" list is from pp. 27–28 of this source.

Page 101 O'Keeffe's first memory is reported in Laurie Lislie, *Portrait of an Artist: A Biography of Georgia O'Keeffe.* New York: Seaview, 1980, pp. 3, 4.

Hemingway's early suicidal tendencies are reported in Peter Griffin, *Along with Youth: Hemingway, The Early Years.* New York: Oxford University Press, 1985, p. 195.

Young Hemingway's boast, " 'Fraid of nothing" is reported in Carlos Baker, *Ernest Hemingway: A Life Story.* New York: Charles Scribner's Sons, 1969. Much of the information anyone has about Hemingway's life comes from this official biography.

Hemingway's appreciation of doubt and uncertainty appears in many forms in his fiction and pronouncements. After he was wounded in Italy, for example, he became friends with a Count Greppi. Griffin (see note above) says, "Ernest liked the count because he said that after passing through years of certitude he was again unsure of many things." Hemingway portrayed the count in *A Farewell to Arms.*

Page 102 Hemingway's ambivalence toward his sexual identity and androgyny discussed by Kenneth S. Lynn, *Hemingway.* New York: Simon & Schuster, 1987.

Genius avoiding conflicts to do the best work is an idea expressed in Bernard C. Meyer, M.D., *Joseph Conrad: A Psychoanalytic Biography.* Princeton: Princeton University Press, 1967. Rothenberg also takes this position.

Page 103 Hughes' ambivalence is reported in Arnold Rampersad, *I, Too, Sing America: The Life of Langston Hughes,* vol. 1902–1941. New York: Oxford University Press, pp. 3, 4.

Rothenberg's statement on ambivalence as the human condition is from one of my interviews with him.

Bleuler's definition of ambivalence is quoted and discussed in Alex Holder, "Theoretical and Clinical Aspects of Ambivalence," in *Psychoanalytic Study of the Child,* vol. 30. New Haven: Yale University Press, 1975, pp. 197–200.

Page 104 Experiment on alertness in conflict reported in Daniel E. Berlyne, "Conflict and Arousal," *Scientific American* 215 (August 1966): 82–87.

The idea that tolerated ambivalence can provide "an enrichment" is from Desy Safán-Gerard, "Chaos and Control in the Creative Process," *Journal of the American Academy of Psychoanalysis* 15, no. 1 (1985): 129–38.

Negative capability is defined in Frederick Page, ed., *Letters of John Keats.* London: Oxford University Press, 1965, p. 53.

Bernard is quoted in Jacques Hadamard, *The Psychology of Invention in the Mathematical Field.* New York: Dover, 1945, p. 48.

Mead on doubt: from Howard, *Margaret Mead* (90), p. 43.

Arp on "the fire of balance": quoted in Rudolf Arnheim, *Entropy and Art: An Essay on Disorder and Order.* Berkeley: University of California Press, 1971, pp. 53–54.

Page 105 LaViolette's observation on pain and amplification of nuances is from my interview with him.

Observations of a "condition for creativeness": from Fromm, "The Creative Attitude" (57).

O'Keeffe on the "knife's edge": from *Georgia O'Keeffe,* produced and directed by Perry Miller Adato. New York: WNET/THIRTEEN, 1977.

The connection between scientist's ability to stay with problem and negative capability came up during my interview with Holton.

Creative tolerance for ambiguity was investigated and discussed by Else Frenkel-Brunswik, "Intolerance of Ambiguity as an Emotional and Perceptual Variable" in *Perception and Personality: A Symposium,* eds. J.S. Bruner and D. Kerch. Durham: Duke University Press, 1949.

Page 106 Bohm's book is David Bohm and David Peat, *Science, Order and Creativity.* New York: Bantam, 1987. His comments about opposites come from one of my interviews with him. Bohm proposes that scientists conduct their activity artistically in the sense that they might simultaneously pursue opposing ideas instead of choosing among them.

Page 107 Bohr and the "two sorts of truths": from Albert Rothenberg, M.D., "Janusian Process and Scientific Creativity: The Case of Niels Bohr," *Contemporary Psychoanalysis* 19, no. 1 (1983): 100–119.

Page 108 Reference to the book *Tale of a Danish Student:* from Ruth Moore, *Niels Bohr: The Man, His Science, and the World They Changed.* Cambridge: MIT Press, 1985, p. 15. Bohr's joy over paradox is from p. 140 of this source.

On complementarity: Bohr also wanted to apply his idea to resolving conflicts between people. He apparently thought that if persons holding irreconcilable points of view could only see them as complementary, prejudices could be overcome and a new kind of mutual tolerance would be discovered. Maurice Wilkins writes about this aspect of Bohr's thinking in Maurice H. F. Wilkins "Complementarity and the Union of Opposites" in *Quantum Implications* (88), pp. 338–61.

CHAPTER 6: OMNIVALENCE

Page 110 Woolf before the Bloomsbury group: from Woolf, *Moments of Being* (36), p. 212.

Page 111 "In Another Country" is from Ernest Hemingway, *The Short Stories of Ernest Hemingway.* New York: Charles Scribner's Sons, 1953, pp. 267–73.

Hemingway's hunger: Ernest Hemingway, *A Moveable Feast.* New York: Charles Scribner's Sons, 1964, p. 57.

Page 112 Russell's observation about Conrad is quoted in Keith Simonton, *Genius, Creativity and Leadership: Historiometric Inquiries.* Cambridge: Harvard University Press, p. 56.

Borges on "imminence": from "Jorges Luis Borges: A Conversation with Roberto Alifano," trans. Nicomedes Suárez Aváuz and Willis Barnstone, *The American Poetry Review,* November–December 1983.

The story of Russell and Frege is told in Michael Guillen, *Bridges to Infinity.* Boston: Jeremy P. Tarcher, 1983, p. 20.

Page 113 Lorca on *"duende"* from Federico García Lorca, "Theory and Function of the *Duende"* in *The Poetics of the New American Poetry,* eds Donald Allen and Warren Tallman. New York: Grove Press, 1973, pp. 91, 100.

The oppositions in Mona Lisa's smile are discussed in Albert Rothenberg, *The Emerging Goddess: The Creative Process in Art, Science and Other Fields.* Chicago: University of Chicago Press, 1979, p. 170.

Woolf on art as symmetry and discord: Love, *Virginia Woolf: Sources* (37), p. 276. Stravinsky on music as a "harmony of varieties": from Stravinsky, *Poetics of Music* (87), p. 32.

Page 114 Bohm's comments on the "space between" are from one of my interviews with him.

Langer on the ironical structure of human feeling: from Susanne K. Langer, *Feeling and Form.* New York: Charles Scribner's Sons, 1953, p. 252.

For discussions of humor which suggest that it has a category-breaking structure similar to irony and metaphor, see Koestler, *The Act of Creation* (80), and Henri Bergson, *Laughter: An Essay on the Meaning of the Comic,* trans. Cloudesley Breton and Fred Rothwell. New York: Macmillan, 1911.

Page 115 Bohm's observation about what happens "if you hold these opposites together" comes from one of my interviews with him.

Shainberg's comment on consciousness is from my interview with him.

Page 116 Darwin's statement about "the delight one experiences . . ." is from Charles Darwin, *Darwin's Diary of the Voyage of H.M.S. Beagle,* ed. Nora Barlow. Cambridge: Cambridge University Press, 1934.

Page 117 Eisenstein's childhood memory is from Jay Leyda and Zina Voynow, *Eisenstein at Work.* New York: Pantheon, 1982, p. *ix.*

Page 118 Shainberg on the creator's willingness to be aware of what exists beyond the creative form is from one of my interviews with him.

Beethoven on his experience of omnivalence and the universal-individual equation: from Mies, *Beethoven's Sketches* (40), pp. 160–61

Newton on the "ocean of truth" is quoted in Howard Gardner, *Frames of Mind: The Theory of Multiple Intelligences.* New York: Basic Books, 1983, p. 147.

Page 119 O'Connor on the essential mystery: from Margaret Meaders, "Flannery O'Connor: Literary Witch," *Colorado Quarterly* (Spring 1962).

The University of Chicago study of creators' feelings about improving their work is reported in Weisberg, *Creativity, Genius and Other Myths* (8), p. 126. The improved level of the creativity in the work of the experimental subjects was judged by a team of professional creators who ranked the subjects' productions. This is a standard method of evaluation for many pieces of creativity research. The method is obviously vulnerable to vagaries in the tastes of the individual creators asked to make the judgments.

Koestler's list of scientists displaying "oceanic wonder" is in Koestler, *The Act of Creation* (80), p. 683.

Page 120 Isadora's suspenseful state of performing is reported in Gheslin, *The Creative Process* (65), pp. 14, 15, and Duncan, *Isadora* (73), pp. 72, 73.

Descartes' attempt to unify all the sciences and mathematics: Of course, not a few people have complained that Descartes' methodological doubt and his project to reveal the mind of God led him to close down what I'm calling omnivalence and fall into a rigid system of abstraction.

Van Gogh's desire to be a prophet: Vincent van Gogh, *The Complete Letters of Vincent van Gogh,* 2nd ed., vol. 1. Greenwich, Conn.: N.Y. Graphic Society, pp. 197–198.

Emily Dickinson's rewriting the Bible in her own poems from Sewell, *The Life of Emily Dickinson* (68), p. 677.

Cézanne's substitute religious experience discussed in Kurt Badt, *The Art of Cézanne,* trans. Sheila Ann Ogilvie. New York: Hacker Art Books, 1985, p. 147.

Einstein on his "cosmic religious feeling": from Albert Einstein, *Ideas and Opinions* (76), p. 48.

Page 122 Edison's mystical interests reported in Conot, *Thomas A. Edison* (90), p. 427.

Schrodinger's comment about the need to transfuse Western science with Eastern thought is quoted in Keller, *A Feeling for* (9), p. 204. The picture of McClintock's mysticism is also from this source.

Pages 122–123 Woolf's "yearning toward the numinous" is reported in Hussey, *The Singing of* (18), pp. 137, 141.

Page 123 Lévi-Strauss's charge that creativity is an illusion is reported in Gardner, *Art, Mind and Brain* (19), p. 35. Gardner's observation about the dangers of making something new in a tribal culture comes from my interview with him.

Faulkner on truth which touches the heart: from William Faulkner, "The Bear" in *Go Down, Moses.* New York: Modern Library, 1942, pp. 260–61, 296–97.

Page 124 "Transpersonal experience" is discussed in John Briggs, "The Magic of Masks," *Science Digest* (November 1985): 70. Halpin's comments on West Coast masks are also from this source.

Page 125 Laughlin's comment on entrainment of brain is from my interview with him.

The masking tradition in Bali is described in Roy Jenkins, "Two-Way Mirrors," *Parabola* 6, no. 3 (Summer 1981): 17–21.

Page 126 Bohm's comments about the way scientists treat mathematics as "pure spirit" comes from Renée Weber, *Scientists and Sages.* London: Routledge & Kegan Paul, 1987, p. 146.

"Sacred space" and "sacred time": See Mircea Eliade, *The Sacred and the Profane.* New York: Harcourt, Brace & World, 1959; and *Patterns in Comparative Religion.* New York: World, 1958.

On the matter of originality and nuance: Laughlin tells me that he and his wife recently visited Japan and spoke to a Noh mask maker and the actor for whom the mask was intended. The Laughlins learned that the maker's mask contained apparently subtle variations from the traditional form which the actor talked about at great length. He said these subtleties opened him to the uniqueness of his own acting performance. Evidently, even in a traditional masking art, there may be "originality" based on a nuance which the mask wearer sees—a personal hidden reality which becomes part of his expression of the mythical or hidden reality of the mask.

Pages 126–127 An explanation of Bohm's idea on the implicate order can be found in Bohm, *Wholeness and the Implicate Order* (92), and Briggs and Peat, *Looking Glass Universe* (92). Bohm's idea that new theories make "the ambiguity subtler" was expressed to me in an interview.

Theories as masks: See Edward Harrison, *Masks of the Universe.* New York: Macmillan, 1985.

Page 127 Wilkins on his extension of "complementarity": from Wilkins, "Complementarity and the Union of Opposites" (88), p. 345.

Page 129 Woolf on the need to constantly remake vision: from Virginia Woolf, *To the Lighthouse.* New York: Harcourt, Brace & World, 1955, p. 270.

PART 2: THE DISTILLING AGENTS
OVERVIEW

Pages 131–132 Mann epigraph on infant prodigies: Thomas Mann, "The Infant Prodigy" in *Stories of Three Decades.* New York: Alfred A. Knopf, 1936, pp. 173–81.

Nevelson epigraph: Nevelson, *Dawns & Dusks* (41), p. 23.

Amiel epigraph: *The Inner Life: Selections from the Journal of Henri-Frédéric Amiel,* trans. Oscar Kuhns. New York: Eaton and Mains, 1914.

Jackson epigraph: quoted in Philip P. Weiner, ed., *Dictionary of the History of Ideas: Studies of Selected Pivotal Ideas,* vol. 2. New York: Charles Scribner's Sons, 1973, p. 305.

Aristotle epigraph: Aristotle, *The Basic Works of Aristotle,* ed. Richard McKeon. New York: Random House, 1941, p. 1479.

Edison epigraph: Corot, *Thomas A. Edison* (90), p. 468.

O'Keeffe epigraph: quoted in *Georgia O'Keeffe* (40–41).

Seneca epigraph: Rudoslav A. Tsanoff, *The Ways of Genius* (83).

Page 133 Descriptions of Mandelbrot's work and ideas may be found in several citations: H. O. Peitgen and P. H. Richter, *The Beauty of Fractals.* Berlin: Springer Verlag, 1986; Benoit Mandelbrot, *The Fractal Geometry of Nature.* New York: W.H. Freeman, 1982; Briggs and Peat, *Turbulent Mirror* (26).

Page 134 Mandelbrot's deficit is described in James Gleick, "The Man Who Reshaped Geometry," *The New York Times Magazine,* 8 Dec. 1985.

CHAPTER 7: QUICKSILVER

Page 136 Galton's viewpoint on heredity and genius was perhaps influenced by the fact that he was himself the scion of an eminent scientifical father and grandfather, was cousin on his mother's side to Charles Darwin of the distinguished

Darwins and was a prodigy. For a review of Galton's work see Roy Herbert, "Hereditary Genius," *New Scientist* (15 March 1984): 35–37.

Page 137 The point that "genes do not make specific bits" is from Gould, *The Mismeasure of Man* (8), p. 156. The Binet question is from p. 182 of this source.

Page 138 Poincaré's showing on the IQ test is reported in Simonton, *Genius, Creativity and Leadership* (112).

The study that followed IQ "geniuses" for sixty years is reviewed in Daniel Goleman, "1,528 Little Geniuses and How They Grew," *Psychology Today* (February 1980): 28–43.

Perkins on IQ: from David Perkins, *The Mind's Best Work.* Cambridge: Harvard University Press, 1981, p. 253. See also Bruce Bower, "IQ's Generation Gap," *Science News* 132 (Aug. 15 1986): 108.

Page 139 Gardner on what IQ doesn't test: from my interview with him.

Sternberg's comment on creativity tests comes from my interview with him.

Feldman's observation on the failure of creativity tests is from David Henry Feldman, ed., *Developmental Approaches to Giftedness and Creativity.* San Francisco: Jossey-Bass, 1982, p. 32.

Page 140 Howard Gardner, *Frames of Mind* (88), p. 119 contains a good review of the subtleties of locating brain function anatomically. In addition, see Daniel Goleman, "Left vs. Right: Brain Function Tied to Hormone in the Womb," *The New York Times,* 24 Sept. 1985, p. C1, and Gordon G. Globus, Grover Maxwell and Irwin Savodnik, eds., *Consciousness and the Brain: A Scientific Philosophical Inquiry.* New York: Plenum Press, 1976.

Diamond's work reported in "Einstein's Brain May Hold Clues to Nature of Genius," *Brain/Mind Bulletin* 10, no. 6 (4 March 1985): 1.

Pages 140–141 Harnad's comment on Diamond research was reported in "Getting into Einstein's Brain," *Science News* 127 (25 May 1985): 330.

Page 141 Geshwind's work appeared in Norman Geschwind, M.D. and Albert M. Galaburda, M.D., "Cerebral Lateralization: Biological Mechanisms, Association and Pathology: II. A Hypothesis and a Program for Research," *Archives of Neurology* 42 (June 1985): 521.

Research showing left-handers have a larger corpus callosum was reported in "Right-handers reduced brain connection," *Science News* 128 (17 August 1985): 102.

Page 142 Startling claims made for the Infant of Lubec appear in "Child's Play" (80).

Daisy Ashford's story is reported in Roderick MacLeish, "Gifted by Nature, Prodigies Are Still Mysteries to Man," *Smithsonian* (March 1984): 72.

Page 143 Sidis's story is told at great length in Amy Wallace, *The Prodigy: A Biography of James Sidis, America's Greatest Child Prodigy.* New York: E.P. Dutton, 1986.

Nadia's story is told in Gardner, *Art, Mind and Brain* (19), pp. 184–91.

The story of Fuller is told in Steven B. Smith, *The Great Mental Calculators: The Psychology, Methods and Lives of Calculating Prodigies.* New York: Columbia University Press, p. 178.

Page 144 The teacher's comment to Ruth Lawrence appears in David Henry Feldman with Lynn Goldsmith, *Nature's Gambit: Child Prodigies and the Development of Human Potential.* New York: Basic Books, 1986, p. 15.

354 ■ John Briggs

The notion that Mozart didn't produce works of genius until he'd been in the field a while comes from John Hayes, *The Complete Problem Solver.* Philadelphia: Franklin Institute Press, 1981.

Prodigies are not genius. This idea and much of what follows here that comes from Feldman and can be found in his book *Nature's Gambit* (143).

Page 145 Prodigies as the result of reincarnation: I was curious enough about this idea to investigate it by asking Ian Stevenson of the University of Virginia what he thought about it. Stevenson is one of the few orthodox scientists who has done methodical investigation of reincarnation claims. He has conducted careful studies of "cases" of reincarnation where the so-called "memories" of previous lives could be checked by independent sources. He believes there is a great deal to the reincarnation hypothesis. Nevertheless, Stevenson indicated that his work has uncovered no connection between reincarnation and prodigious abilities. On the other hand, Feldman reported several incidents among his prodigies where they had experiences that could be labeled past-life memory. There may be other explanations, Feldman believes, but they might not be the kinds of explanations scientists are used to. I leave it to interested readers to consult *Nature's Gambit* on these phenomena and draw their own conclusions. Also of interest might be Ian Stevenson, *Cases of the Reincarnation Type,* vol. 1. Charlottesville: University Press of Virginia, 1975.

Page 146 The game of "mo" is described in Mihaly Csikszentmihalyi and Rich E. Robinson, "Culture, Time, and the Development of Talent" in *Conceptions of Giftedness* (77), p. 269. Almost everyone who has read about this game thinks it would be a dandy one to play, or at least watch.

Page 147 Certain recent revisions to the Leslie Lemke story were reported to me by Lynn Goldsmith. They are included in the text here.

Page 148 Sidis doesn't want to talk about math with Fadiman: from Wallace, *The Prodigy* (143).

Page 149 The assertion that "there are no prodigies" in literature is from V. S. Naipaul, "On Being a Writer" (79).

Feldman's observation about chess players is from "Child's Play" (79).

Page 150 On flow: Mihaly Csikszentmihalyi, *Beyond Boredom and Anxiety.* San Francisco: Jossey-Bass, 1975.

The link between flow and hypnosis: Daniel Goleman, "Concentration Likened to Euphoric States of Mind," *The New York Times,* 5 March 1986, p. C1.

The link between flow and genetics has shown up in Daniel Goleman, "Major Personality Study Finds that Traits are Mostly Inherited," *The New York Times,* 2 Dec. 1986, p. C1. See also citations for chapter 10 under absorption.

The idea that what prodigies are doing is "all of life" comes from one of my interviews with Feldman. His comment on the specificity of prodigious talent is also from an interview.

Page 151 Bamberger's research is reported in Jeanne Bamberger, "Cognitive Issues in the Development of Musically Gifted Children," in *Conceptions of Giftedness* (77), pp. 417–37; and "Growing Up Prodigies—The Midlife Crisis," in *Developmental Approaches* (139), pp. 61–77.

Page 152 Quote and material on calendar twins is from Oliver Sacks, "The Twins" 32, no. 21 *The New York Review of Books* (28 February 1985): 16–20.

The idea of "pure talent" comes from my interview with Feldman.

Page 153 Stories of calculating prodigies: Smith, *The Great Mental Calculators* (143), p. 14.

Prodigy midlife crisis: from Bamberger, "Growing Up Prodigies," in *Developmental Approaches* (139).

Page 154 The idea that talent isn't "a stable characteristic": Csikszentmihalyi and Robinson, "Culture, Time and the Development of Talent" in *Conceptions of Giftedness* (77), p. 271.

Loss of twin's calculating power: Sacks, "The Twins" (152), p. 20.

Page 155 Feldman on fit between talent and prodigy: from one of my interviews with him.

CHAPTER 8: MERCURIAL MAPS

Page 157 Gardner's theory is contained in Gardner, *Frames of Mind* (88).

Page 158 Feldman on Gardner's motives for proposing seven intelligences: from my interview with him.

Page 159 Edelman's work on the immune system: See Gerald Edelman, ed. *Cellular Selection and Regulation in the Immune Response,* vol. 29. Society of General Physiologists Series. New York: Raven Press, 1974; Gerald Edelman, "Expression of Cell Adhesion Molecules During Embryogenesis and Regeneration," *Experimental Cell Research* 161 (1984): 1–16; Lief H. Finkel and Gerald Edelman, "Interaction of Synaptic Modification Rules Within Populations of Neurons," *Proceedings of the National Academy of Science,* vol. 82 (Feb. 1985): 1291–95.

Page 161 The experiments on monkey hands is reported in Jeffrey L. Fox, "The Brain's Dynamic Way of Keeping in Touch," *Science* 225 (August 1984): 820–21.

Page 162 On feedback: See citation (266).

Mozart's family background is described in Marcia Davenport, *Mozart.* New York: Charles Scribner's Sons, 1960, p. 4.

Page 163 Developmental rates of intelligences reported in Gardner, *Frames of Mind* (88).

The picture of young Mozart is from Davenport, *Mozart* (162), p. 7.

Page 164 Gardner's insight into Mozart's fabled memory is found in Gardner, *Art, Mind and Brain* (19), p. 67.

Page 165 The idea that creator must "maintain her or his talent over the life-span" is from Csikszentmihalyi and Robinson, "Culture, Time, and the Development of Talent" in *Conceptions of Giftedness* (77), p. 283.

356 ▪ John Briggs

Page 166 Early developmental profile for mathematicians: Karl Friedrich Gauss was a mathematics prodigy at six. Pascal had laid the foundations for conic sections before he was sixteen; Evariste Galois proved himself a genius in the theory of equations well before he was killed in a duel at twenty-one; Clerk Maxwell had his first mathematical paper read before the Royal Society at fifteen.

Mathematician Hardy on aging: from G. H. Hardy, *A Mathematician's Apology.* Cambridge: Cambridge University Press, 1967, p. 63.

Report on statistical examination of mathematical creators is in Gruber, "The Self-Construction" from *Conceptions of Giftedness* (77), p. 255.

On the ability of some mathematical creators to work past the usual prime: Lynn Goldsmith wondered in her marginalia on this part of my manuscript "whether certain subspecialties are more amenable to longer careers." [Corollary: do certain kinds of (mathematical) thinking 'map' best onto young minds while others require—or at least tolerate—older (wiser? More measured? more/less focused??) minds?]. Gruber thinks the whole notion that mathematicians peak early is simply wrong. Gardner, on the other hand, suggests that the problem is mathematicians become too hide-bound as they get older; they become caught up in the politics of their profession and fall victim to their early success—lose mental flexibility.

Page 167 Woolf's synesthesia: from Love, *Virginia Woolf: Sources* (37), p. 224.

Einstein's tingling at the end of the fingers: from one of my interviews with Holton.

Page 168 Tesla's famous self-starting motor story is reported in Cheney, *Tesla: Man Out of Time* (8), pp. 23–60 *passim* and Roger N. Shepard, "Spontaneous Geometric Images May be the Key to Creativity," *Psychology Today* (June 1983): 63–68. Herschel's statement about "visual impressions" is from this last source.

Page 168 Watson's use of model is described in Watson, *The Double Helix* (78).

Further note on the scientist's ability to visualize: According to Holton, the ability to project how an object will look when rotated in space has been found to be one of the very few even remotely reliable indicators of a talent for physics. Arthur I. Miller points out in his book *Imagery in Scientific Thought.* Cambridge: MIT Press, 1986 that historically there has been a tenacious synesthetic connection between the spatial and logical-mathematical talents in physicists. For example, scientists in the 1920s discovered that the atom isn't like a tiny solar system with electrons orbiting a nucleus but is a complex of matter and energy which is describable mathematically and impossible to visualize. Miller says that the great quantum physicists like Heisenberg and Richard Feynman overcame this restriction on visualization by drawing diagrams of atomic interactions. They insisted the drawings were not to be taken as images of what the atomic domain looks like but as pictures of abstract relationships. Miller concludes that the physicists seemed to find it impossible to practice their profession without having at least some kind of picture, even if they believed it was a purely imaginary one.

Page 169 Feynman on visualization: from Richard P. Feynman as told to Ralph Leighton, *Surely You're Joking, Mr. Feynman: Adventures of a Curious Character.* New York: W.W. Norton, 1985, pp. 85–86.

Hadamard visualizes a formula as a ribbon: from Hadamard, *The Psychology of Invention* (104), p. 78. Mandelbrot feels geometry as sensual: from Gleick, "The Man Who Reshaped Geometry" (134).

John-Steiner on authors relying on music: from John-Steiner (83), p. 33.

Dickinson wrote poems to hymns: from Sewell, *The Life of Emily Dickinson* (68), pp. 408, 713–14.

Page 170 Duncan on music and bodily kinesthetic mapping: from Duncan, *Isadora* (73), p. 199.

Wright on his synesthestic experience: from Walter Sorrell, *The Duality of Vision: Genius and Versatility in the Arts.* London: Thames and Hudson, 1970, p. 28.

Page 171 The quotes from Rodin and Moore here are cited in a different context in Gardner, *Frames of Mind* (88), p. 188.

Woolf's comment about what makes her a writer is from Woolf, *Moments of Being* (36), pp. 69–70.

Page 172 Stephen Spender on his sense memory: from Gheslin, *The Creative Process* (65), pp. 120–21.

On modern science and interpersonal talent: It's also true that a creative scientist like Bohr can transform a field through his interpersonal talent. Bohr's way of working collaboratively with other scientists (see chapter 16) did much to stimulate science toward collective undertakings.

Page 173 Beethoven and Bellini discussion is from Stravinsky, *Poetics of Music* (88), p. 40. I should note that Stravinsky was also conscious of his own deficit. He said in Igor Stravinsky and Robert Craft, *Expositions and Developments.* Garden City: Doubleday, 1962, pp. 50–51, "I could not have made a career as a pianist however—ability apart—because of the lack of what I call 'the performer's memory.' " He did have a composer's memory, he said; such a memory is of a different order: ". . . . a composer's first memory impression is already a composition." It is a memory for what starts particular pieces, "germs" (see chapters 14 and 15 for a discussion of germs).

Creators "conscious of special skills": This comment is from my interview with Gardner.

Perkins's comment about creators capitalizing on their talents is from my interview with him.

Page 174 Lévi Strauss's inability to compose music is discussed in Gardner, *Art, Mind and Brain* (19), p. 36. The information about Lévi-Stauss seeing schematic pictures when working through a problem is from Hadamard, *The Psychology of Invention* (104), p. 90.

Creators as wounded: This idea is portrayed brilliantly in Edmund Wilson, *The Wound and the Bow: Seven Studies in Literature.* London: W.H. Allen, 1952.

Holton on Einstein's late use of language: from Holton, "On Trying to Understand Scientific Geniuses" (22), p. 102. Phyllis Greenacre's alternative proposal, "sensitivity" is from Phyllis Greenacre, M.D., "The Childhood of the Artist: Libidinal Phase Development and Giftedness," in *The Psychoanalytic Study of the Child*, vol. 12. New York: International Universities Press, 1957, p. 54.

Page 175 Yeats' dyslexia is discussed in Eileen Simpson, *Reversals.* Boston: Houghton Mifflin, 1979, p. 47.

Dsylexia and the brain, research reported in "Dyslexia's Cause Reported Found," *The New York Times,* 20 Jan. 1987, p. C1. and Gardner, *Art, Mind and Brain* (19), p. 305.

Flaubert's dyslexia is discussed in Simpson, *Reversals* (175), p. 48.

Sternberg's comment on dyslexia is from my interview with him.

Page 176 Tesla's hallucinations turned to talent follows from Cheney, *Tesla: Man Out of Time* (8), p. 11.

Page 177 Gruber on Darwin: Gruber, "Darwin's 'Tree of Nature' " in *On Aesthetics in Science* (44), p. 249.

On van Gogh's lack of promise: *In A Brilliant Light: Van Gogh in Arles,* directed and photographed by Gene Searchinger, New York: Equinox Film Productions, Metropolitan Museum of Art, 1984.

The woman who suddenly learned to paint, reported in Tom Valero, "A Glimpse of How Mind Produces Art," *Boston Globe,* 16 Jan. 1989, p. 45.

CHAPTER 9: INSIGHT ARCHITECTURE

Page 179 Rothenberg's definition of janusian thinking is from personal correspondence.

Page 180 The opposites experiment is reported in Rothenberg, *The Emerging Goddess* (113), pp. 196–206.

Texas A & M opposites test was reported on in "Newsline," *Psychology Today* (March 1980): 19.

Page 181 Rothenberg's story of iceman is from John Briggs, "Artists Under a Microscope," *The Hartford Courant Magazine,* 7 October 1979.

Page 182 Einstein's janusian moment is told in Albert Rothenberg, "Einstein's Creative Thinking and the General Theory of Relativity: A Documented Report," *American Journal of Psychiatry* 136, no. 1 (Jan. 1979).

The Mona Lisa's smile and other examples of janusian thinking are from Rothenberg, *The Emerging Goddess* (113). Bohr's janusian thinking is described in Rothenberg, "Janusian Process and Scientific Creativity" (107).

Page 183 Nevelson's janusian orientation is from Nevelson, *Dawns & Dusks* (41), pp. 197, 138, 153. Edisons's is described in Belvin B. Ellis, "Pattern for Creativity: Mental Fun with *Fun*damentals," manuscript.

Bulloch's janusian thinking is described in John Briggs, "The Genius Mind," *Science Digest* (December 1984): 103.

Page 184 Eli Siegel's aesthetic realism with its notion that "the resolutions of conflict in self is like the making one of opposites in art" is an example of oppositional aesthetics that don't quite make sense. Siegel's statement seems pithy but in the end it is difficult to have any good idea what it means in terms of actual creative process.

Simultaneous opposition is not synthesis: Art as synthesis is the contention of Silvano Arieti, *The Magic Synthesis.* New York: Basic Books, 1976.

Rothenberg has a good discussion of difference between his idea and synthesis in Rothenberg, *The Emerging Goddess* (113), p. 256.

Page 185 The story of Edison and the janusian light bulb circuits is told in Conot, *Thomas A. Edison* (90), p. 314, and the janusian aspect of it was explained to me by Belvin Ellis in personal correspondence.

The three insight strategies here are described in Robert J. Sternberg and Janet E. Davidson, "The Mind of the Puzzler," *Psychology Today* (June 1982): 37–42 and Janet E. Davidson and Robert J. Sternberg, "The Role of Insight in Intellectual Giftedness," *Gifted Child Quarterly* 28, no. 2 (Spring 1984): 59.

Page 187 The story of Archimedes: from Koestler, *The Act of Creation* (180), p. 106.

Page 188 Ellington's selective comparison: from Derek Jewell, *Duke: A Portrait of Duke Ellington.* New York: W.W. Norton, 1977, p. 82.

The idea that "everyone uses all" of the strategies is from my interview with Sternberg.

Page 189 On metaphor: One example of the different ways in which theorists use metaphor is Rothenberg's placement of metaphor into a new category of creative thinking he calls "homospatial thinking." As he defines it in *The Emerging Goddess* (p. 69), homospatial thinking is "actively conceiving of two or more discrete entities occupying the same space, a conception leading to the articulation of new identities. Concrete objects such as rivers, houses, and human faces, discrete sensations such as wet, rough, bright, and cold, and also sound patterns and written words are superimposed, fused, or otherwise brought together in the mind and totally fill its space. Although the process is often visual, it may involve any of the sensory modalities: auditory, tactile, olfactory, gustatory, or kinesthetic." Rothenberg's definition works well for metaphors which juxtapose two concrete terms as indicated by his examples of metaphor, "black holes in space" and "iron curtain." (pp. 131–32). It is less clear (at least to me) how the homospatial definition works for the most frequent type of poetic metaphor which juxtaposes a concrete term with a highly abstract one, for example "Bring me my arrows of desire" (Blake) or "Time's Winged Chariot" (Marvell). In the latter metaphors, desire or time may be made to seem palpable by the metaphoric juxtaposition but the abstract terms are not discrete entities in space—they are not entities at all. My own opinion is that Rothenberg's homospatial thinking captures something about what happens in creative metaphor but his notion of janusian thinking also could be applied to what happens in creative metaphor and perhaps comes closer to describing metaphors of the concrete/abstract type. I know that he does not agree with me on this point.

Page 190 Darwin's notebook entries are from Gruber, *Darwin on Man: A Psychological Study of Scientific Creativity.* New York: Dutton, 1974, p. 422.

Page 193 How Darwin used tree of life is in Gruber, "Darwin's 'Tree of Life,' " from on *Aesthetics in Science* (44), pp. 127, 135, 134, 136. Gruber's speculation about the number of images is also from this source, p. 137.

Page 195 Osowski quote is from Richard Eder, "Metaphor's Role at Core of Thought," *The New York Times,* 15 April 1980, p. C1. Other information about his findings is from Gruber and Davis, "Inching Our Way" (33).

Gruber also reports here on investigations by graduate students and colleagues on the images of wide scope in John Lock and Dorothy Richardson.

Eisenstein's image of wide scope: Material here is from Leyda and Voynow, *Eisenstein at Work* (117), p. *x*.

The idea of Mozart's "law of growing animation" is reported in Edward E. Lowinsky, "On Mozart's Rhythm" in Paul Henry Lang, ed., *The Creative World of Mozart.* New York: W.W. Norton, 1963, p. 55.

Page 196 Bohm told me about his image of wide scope in one of my interviews with him.

Edison's images of wide scope are described in Reese Jenkins, "Elements of Style in Edison's Thinking," in *From Bridge to the Future: A Centennial Celebration of the Brooklyn Bridge,* ed. M. Lattimer et al., *Annals of the New York Academy of Sciences,* vol. 24 (1984), pp. 151–53.

Page 198 Filling in the gaps: Jenkins points out that others of Edison's day had also used this image. However, as Gruber insists, what makes an image of wide scope powerful for a creator is the "intensity of the emotion which has been invested in it, that is its *value* to the person." It seems a fair conjecture that Edison's early successes in overcoming his hearing impairment would have given the fill-in-the-gaps metaphor a particularly strong emotional value for the inventor. For that reason he would have given the idea a wide scope.

CHAPTER 10: THE ABSORBING FLAME

Page 200 May on absorption: from Rollo May, *The Courage to Create.* New York: Random House, 1975.

Hogarth's comment on genius may be found in the early pages of Sorrell, *The Duality of Vision* (170).

Bach on his secret: from Tsanoff, *The Ways of Genius* (83), p. 74.

Wells on Conrad: quoted in Louis Menand, "Inspired by Despair," *The New York Times Book Review,* 25 January, 1987, p. 16.

Page 201 Nevelson on absorption: from Nevelson, *Dawns & Dusks* (41), p. 42.

Gruber on absorption: from "Child's Play" (80).

Study of chess masters: from Adrianus Dingeman deGroot, *Thought and Choice in Chess.* The Hague: Mouton, 1965.

Flaubert on Emma Bovary's poisoning: from Miriam Allott, ed. *Novelists on the Novel.* New York: Columbia University Press, 1959, pp. 155–56. See also Mario Vargas Llosa, *The Perpetual Orgy: Flaubert and Madame Bovary,* trans. Helen Lane. New York: Farrar, Straus and Giroux, 1986 for an intimate account of Flaubert's compositional process.

Picasso on use of his "energy potential": from Gilot and Lake, *Life with Picasso* (99), p. 348.

Page 202 Darwin on marrying: the two quotes here are cited in Doris Wallace, "Giftedness and the Construction of a Creative Life" (1), p. 371.

Page 203 Faulkner to his publisher on idleness: from Mintner, *William Faulkner* (82), p. 89.

Conrad on his laziness: from Karl, *Joseph Conrad: The Three Lives* (9), p. 19.

Page 204 Auden on major poets writing bad poems and the information about the high productivity of great creators: from Simonton, *Genius, Creativity and Leadership* (112), p. 78.

Conditions for creative work: Faulkner once commented that he thought the best job for a novelist would be as the night manager in a brothel: "The place is quiet during the morning hours, which is the best time of the day to work. There's enough social life in the evening, if he wishes to participate, to keep him from being bored; it gives him a certain standing in his society . . ." From Stein, "William Faulkner: An Interview" in *Three Decades* (78), pp. 68–69. He wrote *As I Lay Dying* while working as the night supervisor in the Oxford power plant.

Page 205 Wallace on women novelists: from Doris Wallace, "Giftedness and the Construction of a Creative Life" *The Gifted and Talented* (1), p. 370.

McClintock's absorption: Keller, *A Feeling for* (9), pp. 34, 35, 31.

Ulam on mathematicians being "disconnected from external affairs": from Stanislaw Ulam, *Adventures of a Mathematician.* New York: Charles Scribner's Sons, p. 447.

Page 206 Kornberg's comment on focus and restlessness is from my interview with him.

Darwin's notebooks are reprinted and discussed in Gruber, *Darwin on Man* (190). Gruber's concept of the creator's network of enterprises is also discussed there.

Page 207 Absorption a special trait: See P. Qualls and P. Sheehan, "Imagery Encouragement, Absorption Capacity and Relaxation During Electromyograph Biofeedback," *Journal of Personality and Social Psychology* 4, no. 2 (1981): 370–77; R.R. Pagano and S. Warrenburg, "Meditation: In Search of a Unique Effect" in *Consciousness and Self Regulation,* vol. 3, eds. R. J. Davidson, G. E. Schwartz and D. Shapiro. New York: Plenum, 1983; and A. Tellegan and G. Atkinson, "Opening to Absorbing and Self-Altering Experiences ('Absorption'), a Trait Related to Hypnotic Susceptibility," *Journal of Abnormal Psychology* 83 (1974): 268–77.

Absorption as genetic, one researcher's reservation: from Goleman, "Major Personality Study." See previous discussion on page (137) of the text.

Page 208 Laughlin on the neurophysiology of absorption: Charles D. Laughlin, "The Prefrontal Sensorial Polarity Principle: Toward a Neurophenomenological Theory of Intentionality," manuscript, p. 14.

Page 210 Amabile on the effect of reward on creativity, *passim:* Teresa M. Amabile, Beth Ann Hennessey and Barbara S. Grossman, "Social Influences on Creativity: The Effects of Contracted-for-Reward," *Journal of Personality and Social Psychology* 50, no. 1 (1986): 14–23; and "The Social Psychology of Creativity: A Componential Conceptualization," *Journal of Personality and Social Psychology* 45, no. 2 (1983): 357–76.

A curious note on the a connection between absorption and creativity: Children diagnosed as suffering from manic-depressive mood swings have been shown to experience the intense focus of absorption when doing creative things. The absorption quiets the mood swings, researchers speculate. One possibility is that creative activity spawns absorption that allows these children to integrate the polar psychological states that otherwise afflict them.

Page 211 Primate absorption is reported in Desmond Morris, *The Biology of Art: A Study of the Picture-Making Behavior of the Great Apes and Its Relationship to Human Art.* New York: Alfred A. Knopf, 1962.

The data here in the corrolation of birth order to genius is from Simonton, *Genius, Creativity and Leadership* (112), pp. 26–27.

Page 212 The data corrolating genius with the loss of a parent is from J. Marvin Eisenstadt, "Parental Loss and Genius," *American Psychologist* 33, no. 3 (March 1978): 211–32.

Graham Bell's family theme: Monica McGoldrick and Randy Gerson, *Genograms in Family Assessment.* New York: W.W. Norton, 1985, p. 121.

Page 213 Hughes' innocence: Arnold Rampersand, *I, Too, Sing* (103), p. 239.

McClintock's innocence: Keller, *A Feeling for* (9), p. 70.

Dickinson loves to be a child: Sewall, *The Life of Emily Dickinson,* (68) pp. 331–32.

Page 214 On the child watching a ball roll: Fromm, "The Creative Attitude" (57), p. 45.

Play in "potential space": D. P. Winnicott, *Playing and Reality.* New York: Basic Books, 1971, p. 54.

De Maupassant and Flaubert: Allott, *Novelists on the Novel* (201), p. 130.

Nevelson on creating with the "whole consciousness and unconsciousness": Nevelson, *Dawns & Dusks* (41), p. 119.

Page 215 Faulkner's remark about admiring Gide is quoted in Mintner, *William Faulkner* (82), p. 225. His comment on grandmothers and the "Ode on a Grecian Urn" was from Stein, "William Faulkner: An Interview" (78), p. 68.

Pages 215–216 McClintock "had to go in that direction": from Keller, *A Feeling for* (9), p. 28.

Page 217 Conrad's complaint about feeling his brain while writing is quoted in Karl, *The Three Lives* (9), p. 424.

Welty on courage: Welty, *One Writer's Beginnings* (82), p. 114.

On Edison's absorption: Jenkins pointed out to me that Edison's absorption in his creative work was so great that he continually sank the money he made from his inventions into new labs and equipment to make new inventions. "If where you put your money is where you put your value, then what Edison valued most was the process of inventing," Jenkins says.

CHAPTER 11: TO BURN WITH ONE'S TIME

Page 218 The need to study the "person-world" connection: Howard E. Gruber, "Giftedness and Moral Responsibility: Creative Thinking and Human Survival," in Horowitz and O'Brien, *The Gifted and Talented* (1), p. 302.

Page 219 Hegel and Carlyle paradox brought out in Simonton, *Genius, Creativity and Leadership* (112), pp. 134, 135.

Stein on interaction of creator and history: "Composition as Explanation" in *Writings and Lectures 1909–1945,* ed. Patricia Meyerowitz. Baltimore: Penguin Books, 1971, reprint 1974, p. 21.

Pierre Menard's fictional attempt to rewrite *Don Quixote:* from Jorges Luis Borges' story "Pierre Menard, Author of the *Quixote*" in *Labyrinths: Selected Stories and Other Writings,* eds. Donald A. Yates and James E. Irby. New York: New Directions, 1964.

Page 220 Skills of one period may not be required in another: Gardner, *Frames of Mind* (88), pp. 165–66.

Page 221 Carver's story is told in Linda O. McMurry, *George Washington Carver: Scientist and Symbol.* New York: Oxford University Press, 1981, p. 311 and *passim.*

Pages 222–223 Women and history and genius: See Virginia Woolf, "Shakespeare's Sister" in *A Room of One's Own* (39), and Germaine Greer, *The Obstacle Race: The Fortunes of Women Painters and their Work.* New York: Farrar, Straus and Giroux, 1979.

Page 223 Gardner on dissonance between creative person and domain: from my interview with him. Feldman agrees with this position.

Rothenberg's statement about how scientific knowledge becomes polarized comes from my interview with him.

Page 225 Jean Toomer material here is from Nellie Y. McKay, *Jean Toomer, Artist: A Study of His Literary Life and Work, 1894–1936.* Chapel Hill: University of North Carolina Press, 1984, pp. 20, 21, 56, 26, 29, 46, 47, 243, 6.

Page 227 Toomer's dilemma: All this is not to say that Toomer wasn't perfectly correct when he insisted that we should live without labels. But in the period when Toomer wrote—and today—we do not live without them. In his life, Toomer felt compelled to resist this fact.

Page 230 Brackman on Darwin: Arnold Brackman, *A Delicate Arrangement: The Strange Case of Charles Darwin and Alfred Russell Wallace.* New York: Times Books, 1980.

Wallace's image of wide scope: George P. Richardson, "The Feedback Concept in American Social Science With Implications for System Dynamics." Ph.D. diss., Sloan School of Management, MIT, p. 13.

Page 231 Bohm's proposal to further explore the creative vision of scientists comes from my interview with him. See also note for page (106).

Page 232 Is Darwin's theory wrong? For a discussion of this see Robert Augros and George Stanciu, *The New Biology.* Boston: Shambhala, 1987. Discovery of oxygen is told in Kuhn, *The Essential Tension* (75), p. 171.

Page 233 The story of the discovery of calculus is similar to that of oxygen. Hadamard in *The Psychology of Invention* (104), pp. 144–45 traces the origins of the idea of calculus from Heraclitus to Kepler. "Then in Fermat's hands, the principle received mathematical expression. . . . The operation performed by Fermat is precisely what we now call differentiation. Does this mean, as many are inclined to think, that he invented the Differential Calculus? In one sense we must answer 'yes,' for we see him applying his method to various problems, and even pointing out that the method could be applied to similar ones. But in another sense we must say 'no,' for the method he used appeared to nobody in his time, not even to himself, as a general rule for solving a whole class of problems, or as a new conception the properties of which deserved further investigation. Adapting an expression of Poincaré, we can say that things are more or less discovered, *not* discovered outright from complete obscurity to complete revelation." Newton and Leibniz, of course, got the credit for discovering calculus.

William James on individual and community: quoted in Chet Raymo, "A Legacy of Genius on Scraps of Paper/Science Musings," *The Boston Globe,* 9 March 1987, p. 42.

The fact that half Nobel laureates invented their fields I owe to Gardner from our interview.

Page 234 "Kafka and his Precursors": from Jorges Luis Borges, *Other Inquisitions, 1937–1952,* trans. Ruth L.C. Simms. New York: Washington Square Press, 1965, p. 113.

CHAPTER 12: MADNESS AND THE MIRROR-MAKER'S NIGHTMARE

Page 236 Story of Hemingway in Mississippi is told in John Updike, *Hugging the Shore: Essays and Criticism.* New York: Alfred A. Knopf, 1983, p. 166.
　　Tesla's phobia: Cheney, *Tesla: Man Out of Time* (8), pp. 9, 10.

Page 237 Woolf's voices: from Gordon, *Virginia Woolf* (37), p. 273.
　　No genius without madness: This statement is usually misunderstood. By "madness" Seneca was evidently referring to the Platonic force of divine inspiration, not insanity and we moderns understand it.
　　Genius as sanity: The idea of the touch of madness in creativity has historical luminaries like Seneca, Aristotle and Dryden to plead its case. Sanity has Charles Lamb who maintained in his essay, "The Sanity of Genius" (1826) that genius "manifests itself in the admirable balance of all the faculties."

Page 238 The study of psychosis among poets is reported in Simonton, *Genius, Creativity and Leadership* (112), p. 35.
　　The newspaper article on manic-depressive illness and creativity is from "What if There Were No Manics?" *The Boston Globe,* 2 March 1987, p. 41. The conclusion that creative episodes are "indistinguishable from hypomania" is from Holden, "Creativity and the Troubled Mind" (91). A strong caveat on research linking manic-depressive behavior with creativity should be stressed. I think that the psychiatric profession consistently misreads the attitudes of creative people as manic depression because manic depression fits the ancient stereotype of the

creative personality. This stereotype is so embedded in our conceptions of creativity that it has been difficult for researchers to avoid.

Page 239 On the sociology and politics of madness and sanity: See, R.D. Laing, *The Politics of Experience.* New York: Ballantine Books, 1967; David Shainberg, *The Transforming Self: New Directions in Psychoanalytic Process.* New York: Intercontinental Medical Books, 1973; Sander L. Gilman, *Seeing the Insane.* New York: John Wiley & Sons, 1982; and Elaine Showalter, *The Female Malady: Women and Madness and English Culture.* New York: Pantheon, 1985.

Conrad on the aversion to the unusual—described in his short story "Outpost of Progress": from Conrad, *Typhoon* (15), p. 185.

Pages 239–240 The quote here on the artist's "inner torment" is from Samuel G. Freedman, "How Inner Torment Feeds the Creative Spirit," *The New York Times,* 17 Nov. 1985.

Page 240 Rothenberg doesn't agree: from one of my interviews with him.

Rothenberg's distinction between pathology and creativity is spelled out in Rothenberg, *The Emerging Goddess* (113), and many of his papers.

Rothenberg's statement beginning, "Even if creativity and illness" and the report of his opposites experiment is from Albert Rothenberg, "Psychopathology and Creative Cognition," *Archives of General Psychiatry* 40 (Sept. 1983): 937–42. Shainberg's statements in this section are from my interview with him.

Page 243 The story of Millikan was told by Holton in my interview with him.

Page 244 Aristotle and Marsilio Ficino: reported in Weiner *Dictionary of the History of Ideas* (131–132), p. 309.

Page 246 Emily Dickinson's psychosis is discussed in John Cody, *After Great Pain: The Inner Life of Emily Dickinson.* Cambridge: Harvard University Press, 1971.

PART 3: THE GREAT WORK
OVERVIEW

Page 249 O'Keeffe epigraph: from *Georgia O'Keeffe* (40–41), p. 1.

O'Connor epigraph is from *Recent Southern Fiction: A Panel Discussion, Bulletin of Wesleyan College,* January 1961; and Frank Daniel, "Flannery O'Connor Shapes Own Capital," *Atlanta Journal and Atlanta Constitution,* 22 July 1962.

Woolf epigraph is from Woolf, *To the Lighthouse* (129), p. 310.

Naipaul epigraph is from Naipaul, "On Being a Writer" (79), 118.

Nevelson's epigraph is from *Nevelson in Process* (15).

Page 251 Gruber says "through being creative we become creative": from Gruber, "The Self-Construction" (76), 114, p. 252.

Senge on creative feedback: from Rachel Gaffney, "Systems Thinking in Business: Philosophy and Practice, An Interview with Peter Senge," *Revision* 7, no. 2 (Winter 1984/Spring 1985): 60.

366 • John Briggs

CHAPTER 13: CONSTRUCTING THE EGG

Page 253 Seven Stories of attuning moments for Galois and Renoir are told in Joseph Walters and Howard Gardner, "The Crystallizing Experience: Discovering an Intellectual Gift" *EDRS* (data base), 30 March 1984, pp. 1–3.

Page 254 Walters and Gardner investigated the crystallizing experience by conducting interviews with teachers and highly talented students in the visual arts, mathematics and music. They also conducted a biographical review of twenty-five geniuses in these areas.

On the mathematical wonder-boy Ramanujan: See James R. Newman, Srinivasa Ramanujan, *Scientific American* 178 (June 1948): 54–7, and James Gleick, "An Isolated Genius is Given His Due," *The New York Times,* 14 July 1987, p. C1.

Page 255 Nevelson's crystallizing moment: Nevelson, *Dawns & Dusks* (41), p. 14.

Conrad's crystallization: from Leo Gerko, *The Two Lives of Joseph Conrad.* New York: Thomas Cromwell Co., 1965, p. 69.

Limón's crystallization: He is quoted in Selma J. Cohen ed., *The Modern Dance: Seven Statements on Belief.* Middletown, Conn.: Wesleyan University Press, 1965, p. 91.

Page 256 Darwin's help from Henslow is reported in Greenacre, *The Quest for the Father* (56), p. 61.

Langston Hughes's crystallization: from Hughes, *I, Too, Sing* (103), p. 16.

Polymorphous genius: from Greenacre, "The Childhood of the Artist" (72), p. 61.

Page 257 The quote from the violinist and from Boulez appear in Walters and Gardner, "The Crystallizing Experience" (253), pp. 30, 15.

O'Keeffe's refining crystallization: from Lisle, *Portrait of An Artist* (101), p. 66.

Pages 257–258 Descartes' crystallizing dreams: Vrooman, *René Descartes* and Jacques Maritain, *The Dream of Descartes,* trans. Mabelle L. Andison. New York: Philosophical Library, 1944. Descartes' dream is a good example of a creative germ (discussed in chapters 14 and 15). To anybody else such a dream might have been meaningless but to Descartes it had tremendous significance. Descartes first dreamed that strong winds were blowing him away from a church toward people who weren't being blown by the wind. He awoke and fell asleep again, dreaming that a bolt of lightning had struck his room. This was followed by a third dream in which Descartes saw himself holding a dictionary which contained the words "What path shall I follow in life?" and then *"Est et Non."* Still in a dream state, Descartes then interpreted his previous dreams, concluding that the dictionary represented "all the sciences grouped together" and *"Est et Non"* indicated "Truth and Falsity in human attainment and in secular sciences." Overall, he took the dream to mean that he was the one to reform knowledge. If one considers the helplessness and terror of the first dream, and the self-assurance of the interpretation dream, Descartes crystallizing experience illustrates the activity of the humility-conceit paradox—or, to put it another way, a possible curious relationship between doubt, terror, fear, awe and creative ambition.

Page 258 Material that follows here is from Mintner, *William Faulkner* (82), pp. 103, 14, 19, 116, 239.

Page 261 The statement that "the thinker constructs the mental circumstances of his own insights" is from Gruber, "Darwin's 'Tree of Nature' " (44), p. 131.

Page 262 Gruber notes in *Darwin on Man* (294), p. 117 that "In his *Autobiography,* written thirty years later, Darwin describes himself as having the fundamental insight about the nature of evolutionary divergence sometime *after* 1844—yet this was an insight achieved much earlier, in 1837. One plausible conclusion is that Darwin had the same insight *at least twice.* " Evidently, in order to have felt the shock of the insight twice, the context that the insight illuminates would have to have been different each time. Perhaps the first time Darwin realized the mechanism of evolutionary divergence, the context still contained older, less germaine ideas. Other elements needed for the grasping the whole evolutionary package were not yet in place. The second time Darwin had the insight, the context contained new elements which the first occurrence of the insight had probably helped bring to the fore. The whole movement emphasizes Gruber's point that creative process is a feedback process, not a linear progression or accumulation of insights leading by steps to a new point of view.

Page 263 Van Gogh on context shift: Van Gogh, *The Complete Letters* (120), p. 198.
    Dorothy Richardson's crystallization: quoted in a personal communication from Doris Wallace.

Page 264 The statement which begins "every serious writer" is from Naipaul, "On Being a Writer" (79).

Page 265 Kuhn on the conservatism of creators: from *The Essential Tension* (75), pp. 225–39.
    LaViolette on pain: this statement is from my interview with him.
    Motherwell on "the creative act and the critical act": from Freedman, "How Inner Torment Feeds" (239–240), p. 22.

Page 266 Self-organizing structures as they apply to creativity are discussed in Briggs and Peat, *Turbulent Mirror* (26). See also Erich Jantsch, *The Self-Organizing Universe.* Oxford: Pergamon, 1980; Ludwig von Bertalanffy, *General Systems Theory: Foundations, Development, Applications.* New York: George Braziller, 1968, and the now classic article which defines the role of positive feedback: Margoroch Maruyama, "The Second Cybernetics: Deviation-Amplifying Mutual Causal Processes," *American Scientist* (June 1963): 164–79, 250–56. This article is much admired by Gruber as a containing a clue to creative process. In my own view, the cybernetic concept of feedback is not quite as relevant to creativity as the notion of evolving feedback systems described in Jantsch, Bertananffy and the systems dynamics researchers like Peter Senge at MIT. A more complete discussion of feedback and creativity can be found in the final section of *Turbulent Mirror.*
    Feynman on how "anything can happen": from Feynman, *Surely You're Joking* (169), p. 83.
    Gauss's flash: from Hadamard, *The Psychology of Invention* (104), p. 15.

Page 267 Wilkins on things clicking together: from Wilkins, "Complementarity and the Union of Opposites" from *Quantum Implications* (88), p. 22.

The lightning metaphor extension comes from Gruber and Davis, "Inching Our Way" in *The Nature of Creativity* (33). Philosopher John Dewey makes a similar extension of this metaphor.

Page 269 Gardner on what creators know about themselves: from my interview with him.

Feynman working through problems: from Feynam, *Surely You're Joking* (169), p. 249.

Page 270 Descartes on inventing inventions: from George Polya, *How to Solve It*. New York: Anchor Books, 1957, p. 93.

Darwin's feeling about his foggy memory is reported in Hock, *Reason and Genius* (7), p. 70.

Perkins' list of mental tactics is in David Perkins, *The Mind's Best Work* (138), *passim.*

Page 271 Van Gogh's working method was described to me by Brower in a personal communication.

Page 272 Walter Piston's working method is described in Gardner, *Art, Mind and Brain* (19), p. 360.

Balzac's working method is described in Hock, *Reason and Genius* (7), p. 85.

Page 273 Hemingway's writing habits are described by him in Ernest Hemingway, *By-Line Ernest Hemingway,* ed. William White. New York: Charles Scribner's Sons, 1967, pp. 216–17.

Nevelson's work habits: from Nevelson, *Dawns & Dusks* (41), p. 121.

Goethe on the need for loneliness: quoted in Hock, *Reason and Genius* (7), p. 108. Nietzsche full of "resolute insights" is also from this source.

Toomer seeing his uncle writing in bed: from Darwin T. Turner, introduction *Cane* by Jean Toomer. New York: Liveright, 1975, p. *xii.*

Page 274 Balzac's brain works while he sleeps: from Hock, *Reason and Genius* (7), p. 95.

Kekule's dream: See "The Great Kékulé Debate: Do Scientists Dream?" *Brain/Mind Bulletin* 2, no. 13 (28 July 1986): 1–2, and Willis Harmon and Howard Rheingold, *Higher Creativity.* Los Angeles: Jeremy P. Tarcher, 1984.

On dreams, a note: Dreams, as everyone knows, are a very curious phenomenon. On the one hand they often seem to contain a code of some sort, the mind's message to itself. The form of the code may depend on the culture. In twentieth century Western society the code seems to involve such symbols as are discussed by modern psychiatry and psychology—i.e., symbols of repressed desires and fears. If dreams do harbor codes, then dreams are ultimately denotative phenomena, another way the brain has of categorizing its experience. On the other hand, dreams appear creative, irreducible and connotative—filled with nuance. I have tried to explain why I think this is such a curious and perplexing issue in John Briggs, "This Other-ness and Dreams," in Montague Ullman and Claire Limmer, eds. *The Variety of Dream Experience.* New York: Continuum, 1987, pp. 105–17. Jonathan Winson of Rockefeller University believes that dreams are the mechanism which converts short-term to long-term memory. In his book *Brain and Psyche*. Garden City: Anchor Doubleday, 1985, Winson argues that a basic set of "survival strategies" are laid down in our minds during an imprinting period in the first two years of life. These strategies are our first abstractions, our first categories, as it were. Winson thinks that in the hippocampus region of the brain the stories of and images of dreams are constructed from a combination of these primitive categories and our daily experiences. The short-term memory of daily experiences is thus converted into long-term "storage" via these primitive categories. In short, Winson sees the dream as a nuance converter, a device for translating the data-drenched day input of experience into a more simplified form. Winson's approach might explain the paradox of how the dream can be both associated with creativity, full of nuance, and yet interpretable as largely denotative code or set of emotional categories.

Page 275 Woolf's use of her diary: Gordon, *Virginia Woolf* (36), p. 178.
Beethoven's use of his sketchbook: Mies, *Beethoven's Sketches* (40), p. 148.
Pasteur on chance: from James H. Austin, *Chase, Chance and Creativity*. New York: Columbia University Press, 1978, p. 72.

Page 276 Stravinsky on accident: Stravinsky, *Poetics of Music* (87), p. 53.
Fleming's story is told in "The Rise of a Wonder Drug," *Nova*. Boston: WGBH, 1986.

Pages 276–277 The investigator who concluded that Fleming's coincidence of events was extraordinary is Ronald Hare, *The Birth of Penicillin*. London: George Allen & Unwin, 1970.

Page 277 Austin's book is cited above.

Page 278 Poincaré on mistakes: quoted in Koestler, *The Act of Creation* (80), p. 212.
Rothenberg on mistakes: from Briggs, "Artists Under a Microscope" (181), p. 55.

Page 279 Edison's failure leading to success is described in Reese V. Jenkins and Keith A. Neir, "A Record of Invention: Thomas Edison and His Papers" in *IEEE Transactions on Education,* vol. E-27, no. 4 (Nov. 1984).
Cézanne's phrase "making a find" is reported in Kurt Badt, *The Art of Cézanne* (120).

CHAPTER 14: GERMINATIONS FROM SALT

Page 281 Story of the title of *Loon Lake* is told in Bruce Weber, "The Myth Maker," *The New York Times Magazine,* 20 October 1985, p. 75.
Sherwood Anderson's description of how stories start for him is from Eugen Current-García and Walter H. Patrick, *What Is the Short Story.* Glenview, Il: Scott, Foresman, 1974, p. 70.
Woolf's fin from Virginia Woolf, *The Waves: The Two Holograph Drafts,* transcribed and edited by J.W. Graham. London: Hogarth Press, 1976, p. 16.

Page 282 James on germs: Henry James, *The Art of the Novel.* New York: Charles Scribner's Sons, 1934, pp. 119–39.

Conrad's letter citing germs as "indistinct ideas" is quoted in Karl, *The Three Lives* (9), p. 19.

Levertov's bear is from William Packard, ed. *The Craft of Poetry.* Garden City: Doubleday, 1974, p. 87.

Page 284 The Story of the evolution of Merrill's poem is told in Albert Rothenberg, M.D., "Creativity, Articulation, and Psychotherapy," *Journal of the American Academy of Psychoanalysis* 2, no. 1 (1934): 55–85.

Conrad on the "scores of notions" which present themselves to his "inward voice": from Karl, *The Three Lives* (9), p. 454.

Valéry on abandoning a work rather than finishing it: Auden refers to this statement in Packard, *The Craft of Poetry* (282), p. 3.

Page 285 Hemingway's "one true sentence": from Ernest Hemingway, *The Moveable Feast* (111), p. 12.

Pages 285–286 What Hemingway left out is told in A. E. Hotchner, *Papa Hemingway.* New York: Random House, 1966, p. 164.

Page 286 Valéry on painstaking creative process: quoted in Hadamard, *The Psychology of Invention* (104), p. 17.

Conrad on completing *Nostromo:* quoted in Roger Tennant, *Joseph Conrad: A Biography.* New York: Atheneum, 1981, p. 160.

Questions about claims of spontaneous productions are examined in Perkins, *The Mind's Best Work* (138). See also: Elisabeth Schneider, *Coleridge, Opium and Kubla Khan.* Chicago: University of Chicago Press, 1953; and John Livingston Lowes, *The Road to Xanadu.* Boston: Houghton Mifflin, 1927.

Emily Dickinson found many germs in other writers' poems. In fact other artworks are a frequent source of germs for creators. Poems and other artworks convey omnivalence but each person who experiences the artwork does so in a unique way. Dickinson would try to recapture the particular shade of omnivalence she felt in the original poem in her own version. The poems of the bible were a frequent germ source of inspiration for her.

Page 287 Wilbur on setting down lines: from Packard, *The Craft of Poetry* (282), p. 177.

Naipaul on the artificiality of sitting down to write: from Naipaul, "On Being a Writer" (79).

Page 288 The germ for *The Sound and Fury* is reported in Blotner, *Faulkner* (82), pp. 566, 633–34.

Goethe on the germ for *The Sorrows of Young Werther:* quoted in Hock, *Reason and Genius* (7), pp. 90–91.

Borges on the aesthetic act as "the imminence of a revelation": from Aváuz and Barnstone, "Jorge Luis Borges' Poetry: A Conversation" (112).

Page 289 The worksheets of "London" appear in David V. Erdman, ed., *Notebook of William Blake.* Oxford: Clarendon Press, 1973.

On Blake's motivation to express the "imminent": We could also make the opposite assumption, that Blake started off with a fairly banal opinion about the squalor of London and that the process of revision led him to the kind of omnivalence expressed in the line "the sweepers cry/every blackning church appalls." In either case, the vision (where vision equals a sense that omnivalence is important, that it is an experience which requires expression and exploration) guides the unfolding of the germ.

Page 293 On reflectaphors and reflectaphoric structure: The creator need not consciously set out to create this sort of structure. It is a by-product of the quest for omnivalence. See John Briggs, "Reflectaphors" in *Quantum Implications* (88).

Page 294 The germ as a "gyroscope": I'm borrowing this image from Gruber, though he uses it in quite a different way.

Discussion which follows about the development of *The Waves* germ comes from Woolf, *The Waves: The Two Holograph Drafts* (281), pp. 1–26, with citations at 18, 19, 21, 23, 26 respectively.

Page 297 Woolf's statement that she had "netted that fin" comes from Gordon, *Virginia Woolf* (36), pp. 203–4.

CHAPTER 15: MORE SALT GRAINS TO STONE

Page 298 Duncan on germ finding: from Duncan, *Isadora* (73), pp. 72–73.
Fellini on germ finding: quoted in John-Steiner, *Notebooks* (83), p. 24.

Page 299 Ellington's germ finding strategy: see Jewell, *Duke* (188), pp. 21–25.
Nevelson on germ unfolding: from Nevelson, *Dawns & Dusks* (41), p. 25.
Giacometti on germ unfolding: from Gilot and Lake, *Life with Picasso* (99), p. 206.
Rodin and Hadamard on the "global idea" and "global image": from Hadamard, *The Psychology of Invention* (104), p. 65.

Pages 299–300 Stravinsky on germ unfolding: Stravinsky, *Poetics of Music* (88), p. 51.

Page 300 About van Gogh's process of germ unfolding: from Brower, a personal communication.
George Sand's account of Chopin is quoted in Tsanoff, *The Ways of Genius* (83), p. 75.

Page 301 The statement which begins, "a picture doesn't change" is from Rudolf Arnheim, *The Genesis of a Painting.* Berkeley: University of California Press, 1962, p. *iii*.
The film of Picasso is *Le Mystère Picasso* by George Clouzot (1956), recently released in video cassette as *The Mystery of Picasso* (1982).

Page 302 Gilot's account of Femme Fleur is in Gilot and Lake, *Life with Picasso* (99), pp. 116–21.

Page 303 On Picasso's first sketch of *Guernica:* Arnheim, *The Genesis* (301), pp. 33–31. The statement that "Picasso did not simply deposit *Guernica*" is also from this source, p. 10.

Page 307 Mozart's famous letter about his method of composition is quoted in Gheslin, *The Creative Process* (65), pp. 44–45.

   Gardner's argument for Mozart as "top down composer" appears in Gardner, *Art, Mind and Brain* (19), p. 365.

Page 308 Evidence of Mozart's worksheets discussed in Erich Hertzmann, "Mozart's Creative Process" in *The Creative World of Mozart* (195), p. 22. Mozart wrote pieces like *The Magic Flute* at breakneck speed. He struggled with the *Requiem*, however.

   The statement which begins "he spoke the musical languages" is from the Hertzmann chapter, p. 29.

Page 309 Beethoven on where he gets his ideas and the series of quotes of Beethoven: from Mies, *Beethoven's Sketches* (40), pp. 159, 146, 151. The statement about the "unity of his works" is from p. 148 of this source.

CHAPTER 16: COMPANIONS IN QUEST

Page 314 Study of Nobel laureates' apprenticeships in the laboratories of previous laureates: from A. Carl Leopold, "The Act of Creation: Creative Processes in Science," *Bioscience* 28, no. 7 (July 1978): 436–40.

Page 315 Gedo on van Gogh's domestic collaboration: from Gedo, *Portraits of the Artist* (81), p. 115.

Page 316 Bohr and his brother: from Moore, *Niels Bohr* (108), p. 17.

   Gruber on the book about evolution Darwin first started: from personal communication.

   Brackman in *A Delicate Arrangement* (230) argues that Darwin didn't discover the principle of divergence *until* he saw it in Wallace's paper. However the tree of life diagram *is* the principle of divergence. It seems to me plausible that for Darwin the problem of evolution was so wrapped up in the detail of the long process and many facts he had used in thinking about it, that the big picture was somewhat submerged. It was this which Wallace helped him bring into relief. Perhaps when he saw Wallace's paper, he said to himself, "Yes that's what I've been thinking all the time." Brackman is undoubtedly right—it must have been a horrible and thrilling moment. See also previous discussion of Darwin discovering the insight more than once.

Page 317 Information on the Ford-Conrad collaboration comes from two sources: Ford Madox Ford, "Working with Conrad," *The Yale Review* (Fall 1985): 13–28, and Ford Madox Ford, *Joseph Conrad: A Personal Remembrance.* Boston: Little Brown, 1924. The quote about what Ford and Conrad provided each other is from the first source.

Page 318 Brower on van Gogh's collaboration: from Richard Brower, "Vincent Van Gogh: The Creative Encounter Between Van Gogh and Gauguin." Ph.D. diss., Rutgers University, 1986, p. 46.

Page 319 Watson's collaboration: see Watson, *The Double Helix* (78).

Page 320 Welles' collaborative method: See Robert L. Carringer, *The Making of Citizen Kane.* Berkeley: University of California Press, 1985, p. 81.

The quote which begins "creative people must use their skills" is from "Breakaway Minds: Howard Gruber Interviewed by Howard Gardner," *Psychology Today* (July 1981): 70.

Pages 320–321 How Ellington collaborated: James Lincon Collier, *Duke Ellington.* London: Oxford University Press, 1987. The quote beginning "knew that each musician" is from Hobsbawm, "Slyest of the Foxes" (7), p. 6.

Page 321 Gruber's shadow box experiment is reported in Howard E. Gruber, "From Epistemic Subject to Unique Creative Person at Work," *Archives de Psychologie* (1985): 180. His comment about "the first thing that happened" is from my interview with him. His statement that "the way that people retain their individuality" is from "Breakaway Minds" (320), p. 73.

Moses Pendleton's rememberance of the origins of Pilobolus is from a newspaper clipping I was given. Unfortunately, I don't have a record of which newspaper it was. But the date was December 3, 1978.

Page 325 Wolken's memory of the origins is from my interview with him.

The description of Pilobolus is from *Time* (20 November 1978): 113–14.

All the quotations in the remaining section about Pilobolus are from my interview with Wolkin and the class I took with him.

EPILOGUE

Pages 331–332 On expert systems: The long quote beginning "society tends to praise" is from F. David Peat, *Artificial Intelligence: How Machines Think.* New York: Baen Books, 1985, p. 333. Other discussions of this subject: Marvin Minsky, "Why People Think Computers Can't," *Technology Review* (November/December 1983): 65–81, and Douglas Hofstadter, *Gödel, Esher, Bach: The Eternal Golden Braid.* New York: Vintage, 1979.

INDEX